ESSENTIALS OF MARKETING

Fourth Edition

JIM BLYTHE
University of Plymouth

FINANCIAL TIMES

An imprint of **Pearson Education**

Harlow, England • London • New York • Boston • San Francisco • Toronto • Sydney • Singapore • Hong Kong
Tokyo • Seoul • Taipei • New Delhi • Cape Town • Madrid • Mexico City • Amsterdam • Munich • Paris • Milan

Pearson Education Limited

Edinburgh Gate
Harlow
Essex CM20 2JE
England

and Associated Companies throughout the world

Visit us on the World Wide Web at:
www.pearsoned.com

———————————————

First published under the Financial Times Pitman Publishing imprint 1998
Second edition published 2001
Third editon published 2005
Fourth edition published 2008

© Financial Times Professional Limited 1998
© Pearson Education Limited 2001, 2008

ISBN: 978-0-273-71736-2

British Library Cataloguing-in-Publication Data
A catalogue record for this book is available from the British Library.

Library of Congress Cataloging-in-Publication Data
Blythe, Jim.
   Esssentials of marketing / Jim Blythe. -- 4th ed.
         p. cm.
   Includes bibliographical references and index.
   ISBN 978-0-273-71736-2
1. Marketing. I. Title.
   HF5415.B485 2008
   658--dc22
                                        2008026073

10 9 8 7 6 5 4 3 2
11 10 09

Typeset in 10/14pt Palatino by 30
Printed and bound in Italy by Rotolito Lombarda

The publisher's policy is to use paper manufactured from sustainable forests.

ESSENTIALS OF MARKETING

Essentials of Marketing, 4th edition, Companion Website at **www.pearsoned.co.uk/blythe** to find valuable **student** learning material including:

- Video Case Studies that accompany every chapter which demonstrate how top marketing managers refer to marketing theory in the working environment.
- Self-assessment questions designed to test your knowledge of each chapter

We work with leading authors to develop the strongest
educational materials in marketing, bringing cutting-edge
thinking and best learning practice to a global market.

Under a range of well-known imprints, including
Financial Times Prentice Hall, we craft high quality
print and electronic publications which help readers
to understand and apply their content, whether
studying or at work.

To find out more about the complete range of our
publishing, please visit us on the World Wide Web at:
www.pearsoned.co.uk

Brief contents

Contents

List of tables

List of figures

Preface

Essentials of Marketing has been around for nearly twelve years, and much has changed in that time. Marketing itself has moved on – for example, in 1996, when I was writing the first edition, the Internet was virtually non-existent. Environmentalism was still in its infancy as a movement, and mobile telephones were the possessions of the wealthy. The book has moved on and developed as well during that time – much is still the same, of course, but comparison of the first edition with this edition shows a lot of changes. For this edition, the biggest change is the removal of a dedicated chapter on international marketing, and a new chapter on services marketing. The global marketplace is too ubiquitous to be put into a silo of its own, so international issues are now raised in each chapter, where relevant. Equally, services marketing is now so important that it deserves special treatment.

My aim has been to provide an overview of marketing thought and practice for students new to marketing, for students on short introductory marketing courses, for overseas students who need a plain-English guide, and to anyone who needs a quick grasp of the subject. I have tried to keep the language straightforward and avoid too much jargon, and I have also tried to include examples from all parts of the world, rather than be too UK-centred.

Specific features of this edition are:

- Relevant and up-to-date case studies, all of which are new for this edition.
- Up-to-date and full referencing for the more academic student.
- Recommended further reading for each chapter.
- Extended coverage of global marketing theory in each chapter.
- A new chapter on services marketing.

Overall, the book is intended to offer an insight into what marketing is all about: it is written by an enthusiast, a believer in the marketing ethos. Marketing is about facilitating exchange. It is about allowing people the choices to be able to live the kind of lives they would wish for themselves and their families, and it delivers a standard of living. But above all, marketing is about ensuring that business meets the needs of its customers.

No book is the work of one person, and I would like to acknowledge the people who have helped me write this one. First of all, my wife Sue, who has provided many of the examples I have used, and who knows not to disturb me when I am 'on a roll'. Second, my colleagues in the academic world who have provided me with answers, provided me with questions, and who have been amazingly generous with their time and good wishes. Third, my students past and present, who have asked me difficult questions and made me look up the answers or rethink my position. Fourth, everyone at Pearson: Jane Powell, who worked with me on the first edition, David Cox who has worked with me on this edition, and the production people who have turned my words into a book. Finally, my former colleagues in industry, who showed me that the marketing concept is not obvious to everyone, and that marketers also need to understand the viewpoint of other professionals.

Any errors and omissions are, of course, mine.

Jim Blythe
July 2008

Supporting resources
Visit **www.pearsoned.co.uk/blythe** to find valuable online resources:

Companion Website for students
- Online Video Case Studies that illustrate the examples used in each chapter.
- Accompanying self-assessment questions that help you test your knowledge.

For instructors
- An extensive Instructors Manual that includes extra teaching material relating to each chapter, essay questions, and extra Case Studies.
- PowerPoint slides for each chapter which provide useful definitions of key terms and figures.

Also: The Companion Website provides the following features:

- Search tool to help locate specific items of content.
- E-mail results and profile tools to send results of quizzes to instructors.
- Online help and support to assist with website usage and troubleshooting.

For more information please contact your local Pearson Education sales representative or visit **www.pearsoned.co.uk/blythe**.

Guided tour

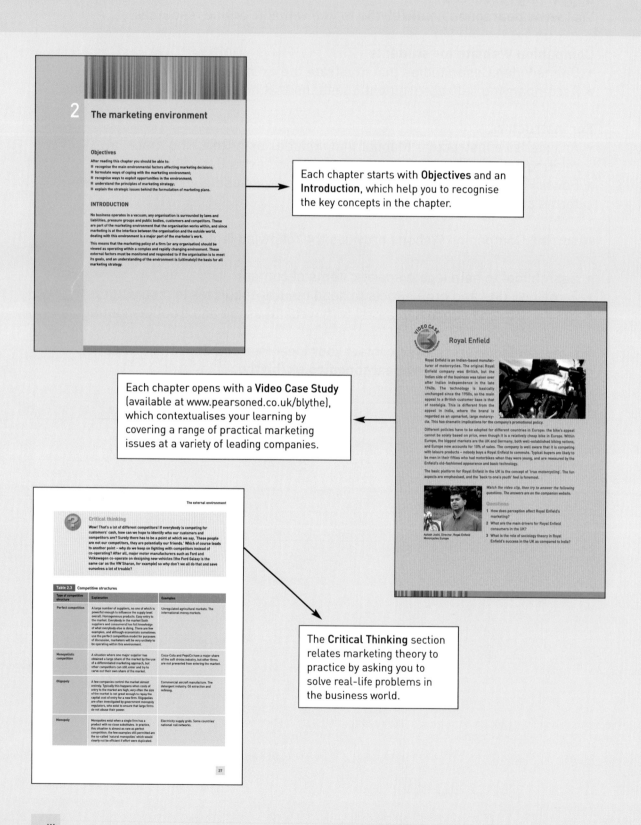

Each chapter starts with **Objectives** and an **Introduction**, which help you to recognise the key concepts in the chapter.

Each chapter opens with a **Video Case Study** (available at www.pearsoned.co.uk/blythe), which contextualises your learning by covering a range of practical marketing issues at a variety of leading companies.

The **Critical Thinking** section relates marketing theory to practice by asking you to solve real-life problems in the business world.

The **Summary** helps you bring together and synthesise the main themes in each chapter.

References are included for each chapter to help you to take your independent studies further.

The **Questions** that conclude the Case Study help you to check and reflect on your own understanding of the chapter.

The **Case Study** shows how the topics and issues of the chapter relate to the real world.

Acknowledgements

We are grateful to the following for permission to reproduce copyright material:

Figure 1.2 and Table 10.2 from Kotler, P. Marketing Management, 11th edn, © 2003. Reproduced by permission of Pearson Education, Inc., Upper Saddle River, New Jersey; Figure 6.12, Table 7.6 and Figure 8.1 from S. Dibb, L. Simkin, W. Pride and O. C. Ferrell, *Marketing: Concepts and Strategies*, 3rd European edn, copyright © 1997 by Houghton Mifflin Company, reprinted by permission of Houghton Mifflin Harcourt Publishing Company; Figure 11.4 from A. Parasuraman, V. A. Zeithamland and L. L. Berry. (1985) 'A conceptual model of service quality and its implications for future research', *Journal of Marketing*, 49 (Fall), reproduced by permission of the American Marketing Association.

Electrolux

Electrolux is a long-established Swedish electrical goods manufacturer. The company prides itself on producing innovative products based on finding solutions for consumers. Often the company finds itself producing items that people were not aware they needed, but it does not seek to innovate for innovation's sake.

Understanding customers is therefore paramount for Electrolux. Aware that customers are the driving force of everything the company does, Electrolux know that they will only succeed in a cluttered market if they are able to offer real advantages that other manufacturers cannot match. Company representatives observe how people relate to their appliances, and are aware of macro-trends in the market – for example, the move towards open-plan kitchen and dining areas, so that appliances are on show for guests and family.

Monitoring what competitors are doing is also important. The company watches what all the main competitors are doing, not for the purpose of copying them, but in order to find gaps in the market – areas where competitors are not meeting customer need.

Hans Stråberg, President of the Electrolux Group

Watch the video clip, then try to answer the following questions. The answers are on the companion website.

Questions

1 How does Electrolux manage exchange?

2 What is the role of customer need in the Electrolux strategy?

3 How would a brand manager for Electrolux try to go about his or her job?

1

What do marketers do?

Objectives

After reading this chapter you should be able to:

- describe the main roles marketers have;
- explain the responsibilities of various types of marketing manager;
- explain the core concepts of marketing;
- explain how marketing activities fit in with other business disciplines;
- describe the development of the marketing concept.

INTRODUCTION

This chapter is an introduction to the basic concepts of marketing, seen in terms of the roles that marketers carry out in their day-to-day jobs. Although marketers have many different job titles, what they have in common is the same orientation towards running the organisation; marketing is concerned with ensuring the closest possible fit between what the organisation does and what its customers need and want.

ABOUT MARKETING

Marketing is the term given to those activities which occur at the interface between the organisation and its customers. It comes from the original concept of a marketplace, where buyers and sellers would come together to conduct transactions (or exchanges) for their mutual benefit. The aim of marketing as a discipline is to ensure that customers will conduct exchanges with the marketer's organisation, rather than with the other 'stallholders'. To do this effectively, marketers must provide those customers with what they want to buy, at prices which represent value for money.

This basic concept of managing exchange leads us on to the most important concept in marketing, that of customer centrality. Marketing, above all else, uses the customer (who is often also the consumer) and his or her needs as the starting-point for all decisions. Of all the building-blocks of marketing, in both theory and practice, this is far and away the most important: it is also often difficult to do because it involves thinking like someone else.

The two most widely used definitions of marketing are these:

Marketing is the management process which identifies, anticipates, and supplies customer requirements efficiently and profitably. (UK Chartered Institute of Marketing)

Marketing is the process of planning and executing the conception, pricing, promotion and distribution of ideas, goods and services to create exchange and satisfy individual and organisational objectives. (American Marketing Association 2004)

Both of these definitions have been criticised. The Chartered Institute of Marketing (CIM) definition has been criticised because it takes profit as being the only outcome of marketing, whereas marketing approaches and techniques are widely used by organisations such as charities and government departments which do not have profit as their goal. The American Marketing Association (AMA) definition has also been criticised for failing to take account of the increasing role of marketing in a broader social context, and for appearing to regard consumers as being passive in the process. The same criticism could equally be applied to the CIM definition. Interestingly, neither definition includes the word 'consumer'. This may be because there are many customers who buy the product, but do not themselves consume it (for example, a grocery supermarket buyer might buy thousands of cans of beans, but dislike beans himself). Equally, someone can be a consumer without actually making the buying decision – an example would be a child whose parents make most of the decisions about food, clothing, entertainment and so forth on behalf of the child.

To the non-marketer, marketing often carries negative connotations; there is a popular view that marketing is about persuading people to buy things they do not want, or about cheating people. In fact, marketing practitioners have the responsibility for ensuring that the customer has to come first in the firm's thinking, whereas other professionals might be more concerned with getting the balance sheet to look right or getting the production line running smoothly. Marketers are well aware that the average customer will not keep coming back to a firm that does not provide good products at an acceptable price, and without customers there is no business.

Competition in many markets is fierce. If there is room for four companies in a given market, there will be five companies in there, each trying to maximise their market share; the customer is king in that situation, and the firms that ignore the customer's needs will go out of business. Marketers therefore focus their attention entirely on the customer, and put the customer at the centre of the business.

THE DEVELOPMENT OF THE MARKETING CONCEPT

The marketing concept is a fairly recent one, and has been preceded by other business philosophies. These philosophies have not necessarily come about in the linear manner implied by the following section: although at different times there may have been a general way in which business was conducted, there have certainly been considerable overlaps between the different paradigms, and many firms which have not been part of the general trend.

Production orientation

During the nineteenth century it was often thought that people would buy anything, provided it was cheap enough. This belief had some truth in it, since the invention of the steam engine allowed very much cheaper mass-produced items to be made. If an item was on sale at around one-tenth the price of the hand-made equivalent, most customers were prepared to accept poorer quality or an article that didn't exactly fit their needs. The prevailing attitude among manufacturers was that getting production right was all that mattered; this is called **production orientation**. This paradigm usually prevails in market conditions under which demand greatly exceeds supply, and is therefore somewhat rare in the twenty-first century.

With rising affluence people are not prepared to accept standardised products, and global markets allow manufacturers to reap the benefits of mass production despite providing more specialised products: therefore the extra cost of having something that fits one's needs more exactly is not high enough to make much difference.

Product orientation

Because different people have different needs some manufacturers thought that an ideal product could be made, one that all (or most) customers would want. Engineers and designers developed comprehensively equipped products, with more and 'better' features, in an attempt to please everybody. This philosophy is known as **product orientation**.

Product orientation tends to lead to ever more complex products at ever-increasing prices; customers are being asked to pay for features which they may not need, or which may even be regarded as drawbacks.

Sales orientation

As manufacturing capacity increases, supply will tend to outstrip demand. In this scenario, some manufacturers take the view that a 'born salesman' can sell anything to anybody and therefore enough salesmen could get rid of the surplus products. This is called **sales orientation**, and relies on the premise that the customer can be fooled, the customer will not mind being fooled and will let you do it again later, and that if there are problems with the product these can be glossed over by a fast-talking sales representative. Up until the early 1950s, therefore, personal selling and advertising were regarded as the most important (often the only) marketing activities.

Sales orientation takes the view that customers will not ordinarily buy enough of the firm's products to meet the firm's needs, and therefore they will need to be persuaded to buy more. Sales orientation is therefore concerned with the needs of the seller, not with the needs of the buyer (Levitt 1960). Essentially, what these businesses try to do is to produce a product with given characteristics, then change the consumers to fit it. This is, of course, extremely difficult to do in practice.

It should be noted that selling orientation and the practice of selling are two different things – modern salespeople are usually concerned to establish long-term relationships with customers who will come back and buy more.

Consumer orientation

Modern marketers take the view that the customers are intelligent enough to know what they need, can recognise value for money when they see it, and will not buy again from the firm if they do not get value for money. This is the basis of the *marketing concept*.

Putting the customer at the centre of all the organisation's activities is easier said than done. The marketing concept affects all areas of the business, from production (where the engineers and designers have to produce items that meet customers' needs) through to after-sales services (where customer complaints need to be taken seriously). The marketing concept is hard to implement because, unlike the sales orientation approach which seeks to change the mass of customers to fit the organisation's aims, the marketing concept seeks to change the organisation's aims to fit one or more specific groups of customers who have similar needs. This means that marketers often meet resistance from within their own organisations.

At this point, it may be useful to remind ourselves of the distinction between customers and consumers. Customers are the people who buy the product; consumers are those who consume it. Customers could therefore be professional buyers who are purchasing supplies for a company, or possibly a parent buying toys for a child. The consumer might also be the customer, of course, but could equally be the recipient of a gift or the user of a service which is paid for by others.

Critical thinking

Many companies say that they are customer (or consumer) orientated, but how true is this? Do companies seriously expect us to believe that the customers come first, when they reserve the best parking space for the managing director? Or that the customer comes first when they raise their prices? Or that the customer comes first when the offices close at weekends?

In fact, would it be fairer to say that we always consider the customer's needs, since this is the best way of getting their money off them?

Societal marketing

Societal marketing holds that marketers should take some responsibility for the needs of society at large, and for the sustainability of their production activities. This orientation moves the focus away from the immediate exchanges between an organisation and its customers, and even away from the relationship between the organisation and its consumers, and towards the long-term effects on society at large. This need not conflict with the immediate needs of the organisation's consumers: for example, Body Shop operates a highly successful consumer-orientated business while still promising (and delivering) low environmental impact.

Kotler *et al.* (2001) say that products can be classified according to their immediate satisfaction and their long-run consumer benefits. Figure 1.1 illustrates this. In the diagram, a product which has high long-term benefits and is also highly satisfying is classified as a desirable product. For example, a natural fruit juice which is high in vitamins and also tastes good might fit this category. A product which has long-term benefits but which is not immediately satisfying, for example a household smoke alarm, is a salutary product. Products which are bad for consumers in the long run, but which are immediately satisfying (such as alcohol, cigarettes and confectionery) are called pleasing products: research shows that people believe that 'unhealthy' foods taste better (Raghunathan *et al.* 2006). Finally, products which are neither good for consumers nor satisfying are called deficient products: examples might include ineffective slimming products, or exercise equipment which is poorly designed and causes injury. In theory, firms should aim to produce desirable products – but consumers often choose the pleasing products instead, for example eating unhealthy foods when they feel unhappy (Garg *et al.* 2006).

Source: Kotler, P., Armstrong, G., Saunders, J. and Wong, V., 2001, *Principles of Marketing*. Pearson Education Limited © 2001.

The societal marketing concept includes the marketing concept in that it recognises the needs of individual consumers, but it goes further in that it aims to improve the well-being of the wider society in which the firm operates. This means that the organisation takes on responsibility for good citizenship, rather than expecting consumers to understand or take account of the wider implications of their consumption behaviour. The problem is that firms need to balance three factors: customer needs, company profits (or other objectives) and the needs of society as a whole. Since competing companies may not be so concerned about society at large, it is not clear how societal marketing will contribute to creating competitive advantage; it is very clear how customer orientation helps firms to compete, however.

Ultimately, consumer orientation and societal marketing both seek to ensure that the organisation (whether a business or a non-profit organization) should be looking to create greater value for customers, and thus meet the competition better (or even create competition in new markets.

Relationship marketing

During the 1990s, marketing thinking moved towards the *relationship marketing* concept. Traditional marketing has tended to concentrate on the single transaction with a short-term focus. Relationship marketing focuses on the 'lifetime' value of the customer. For example, a motor manufacturer might have one model aimed at young drivers, another aimed at families with children, and another aimed at middle-aged motorists. Each segment might be treated as a separate and unique entity. Under a relationship marketing paradigm, the organisation recognises that the young motorist will pass through each lifestyle stage in turn, and is then a customer for a different model each time. Relationship marketing aims to determine who will be (or could be) the most loyal customer throughout his or her life: marketers are responsible for establishing and maintaining these relationships.

In practice, relationship marketing has met with its greatest success in the business-to-business world. Companies which sell to other companies have generally been most proactive in establishing long-term co-operative relationships: for example, aircraft engine manufacturers such as Rolls-Royce and Pratt & Whitney need to establish close relationships with aircraft manufacturers such as Airbus Industrie and Boeing, since the designs of airframes and engines need to be co-ordinated. The ability to adapt the designs to meet the needs of the other company has obvious advantages in terms of cost savings and (eventually) greater profits, but it also has an advantage from the supplier's viewpoint in that close co-operation makes it harder for competitors to enter the market. Customers that have committed to a shared design process are unlikely to want to start the process all over again with another supplier. Creating this kind of loyalty has a significant effect on future revenues (Andreassen 1995).

The key elements in relationship marketing are the creation of customer loyalty (Ravald and Gronroos 1996), the establishment of a mutually rewarding connection, and a willingness to adapt behaviour in order to maintain the relationship (Takala and Uusitalo 1996).

Critical thinking

Do we really want to have a relationship with the companies which supply our needs? Of course politeness is one thing – but we aren't going to go on a long walking holiday with our bank, are we? Maybe the relationship is a bit one-sided: the company wants to lock us in to a long-term deal, and offers us all kinds of incentives to do so, whereas actually we would rather be free to choose between firms. We soon learn that threatening to leave means we get freebies, so the more they try to hang on to us, the more we take advantage!

Hardly the basis for a long-term relationship, is it?

There is more on relationship marketing throughout the book: it has become, like the Internet, central to marketing practice in recent years.

MARKETING AND OTHER BUSINESS DISCIPLINES

As the marketing concept has evolved from production orientation through to customer orientation, the role marketing occupies relative to other business functions has also evolved. Under a production-orientated regime marketing usually occupies a departmental role; the marketing role is contained within a marketing department which carries out the communications functions of the firm.

Figure 1.2 shows the evolution of marketing's role within the organisation.

Figure 1.2	Evolution of marketing's role

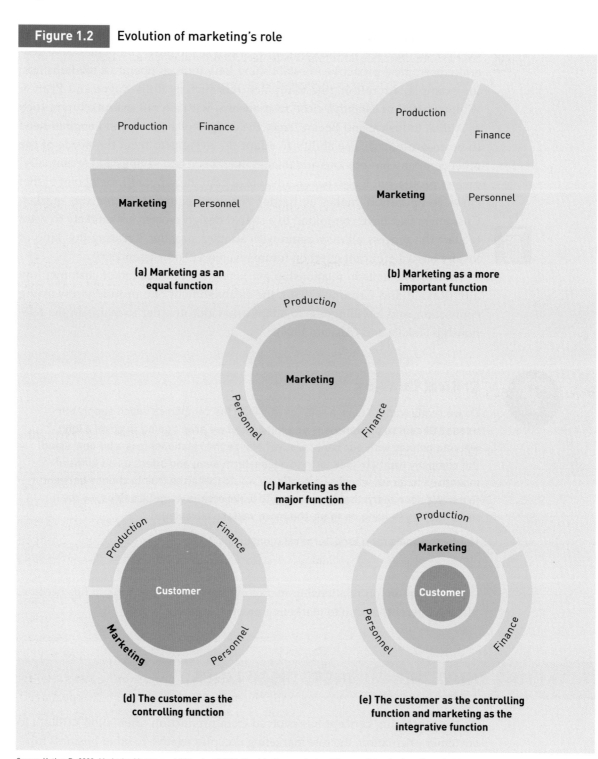

(a) Marketing as an equal function

(b) Marketing as a more important function

(c) Marketing as the major function

(d) The customer as the controlling function

(e) The customer as the controlling function and marketing as the integrative function

Source: Kotler, P., 2003, *Marketing Management*, 11th edn, © 2003. Reprinted by permission of Pearson Education Inc., Upper Saddle River, NJ.

If customers are central to the organisation's thinking, marketers act as the moderating group. Marketing can be seen in several ways, as follows:

- As a moderating force in the exchange process.
- As the driving philosophy of the business. Looked at in this way, everyone in the organisation becomes concerned primarily with adding value for the customer.
- A managerial function. This aspect of marketing means that marketers manage resources to obtain the most positive responses from customers.
- A dynamic operation, requiring analysis, planning and action. Because customers' needs, tastes and requirements change rapidly, marketing needs to change also. A product-orientated firm does not have this difficulty, since it seeks to change its customer base (either by persuading customers to buy, or by seeking out new customers) rather than change the product or the overall offer.
- A catalyst for change. Market-orientated firms need to change to meet customer need: marketers are at the forefront of these changes because they represent the customer.

MARKETING ON A DAY-TO-DAY BASIS

Marketers deal with the **marketing mix**, which was described by McCarthy (1960) as the four Ps of marketing. These are:

- *Product*. The product should fit the task the target consumers want it for, it should work, and it should be what the consumers expected to get.
- *Place*. The product should be available from wherever the firm's target group of customers find it easiest to shop. This may be a high street shop, it may be mail order through a catalogue or from a magazine coupon, or it may even be doorstep delivery.
- *Promotion*. Advertising, public relations, sales promotion, personal selling and all the other communications tools should put across the organisation's message in a way that fits what the particular group of consumers and customers would like to hear, whether it be informative or appealing to the emotions.
- *Price*. The product should always be seen as representing good value for money. This does not necessarily mean that it should be the cheapest available; one of the main tenets of the marketing concept is that customers are usually prepared to pay a little more for something that really works well for them.

The 4-P model has been useful when applied to the manufacture and marketing of physical products, but with the increase in services provision the model does not provide a full enough picture. In 1981 Booms and Bitner proposed a 7-P framework to include the following additional factors:

■ *People*. Virtually all services are reliant on people to perform them, very often dealing directly with the consumer: for example, the demeanour of waiters in restaurants forms a crucial part of the total experience for the consumers. In a sense, the waiter is part of the product the consumer is buying.

■ *Process*. Since services are usually carried out with the consumer present, the process by which the service is delivered is, again, part of what the consumer is paying for. For example, there is a great deal of difference between a silver-service meal in an upmarket restaurant, and a hamburger bought from a fast-food outlet. A consumer seeking a fast process will prefer the fast-food place, whereas a consumer seeking an evening out might prefer the slower process of the restaurant.

■ *Physical evidence*. Almost all services contain some physical elements: for example, a restaurant meal is a physical thing, even if the bulk of the bill goes towards providing the intangible elements of the service (the decor, the atmosphere, the waiters, even the dishwashers). Likewise a hairdressing salon provides a completed hairdo, and even an insurance company provides glossy documentation for the policies it issues.

Each of the above elements of the marketing mix will be dealt with in greater detail throughout the book, but it is important to recognise that the elements need to be combined as a mix. Like a recipe, one ingredient of the mix will not substitute for another, and each ingredient must be added in the right quantities at the right time if the mix is to prove successful in achieving consumer satisfaction. Each organisation will tend to have its own approach to the mix, and therefore no two firms will follow exactly the same marketing approach. This is one of the features that distinguishes marketing from the other business disciplines such as accountancy or company law. The marketing mix concept is also useful as a way of thinking about marketing, but in practice many marketing activities do not fall neatly within the boxes: there is considerable overlap. For example, a money-off special offer overlaps between pricing and sales promotion.

To illustrate how the marketing concept is implemented in practice, the next section looks at some of the jobs marketers have.

MARKETING JOBS

In a sense, everybody in the organisation is responsible to some extent for ensuring that the consumers' needs are met. Clearly, though, some individuals will have greater responsibility than others for this; some of the job titles which marketers hold are shown in Table 1.1.

In market-orientated companies it is the customer who has the major say in what happens, and it is the marketing team that works within the company to ensure that everything is geared to the customer's (and consumer's) needs. Not

Table 1.1 Marketing job titles and descriptions

Job title	Job description
Brand manager	Responsible for all the decisions concerning a particular brand. This concept was originally introduced at Mars; brand managers compete with each other as well as with other firms for market share in the chocolate bar market, even though they are all working for the same firm. This tends to result in greater efforts and greater corporate share all round.
Product manager	Responsible for all the decisions around a group of similar products within a firm. For example, a biscuit manufacturer might have one product manager in charge of chocolate-covered snack biscuits, and another in charge of savoury biscuits for cheese.
Sales manager	Responsible for controlling, training and motivating the salesforce and the sales back-up team. Sales managers often also have a role in credit control, since they are in the best position to know the individual customers and can give an opinion on the customer's creditworthiness or (as a last resort) on the least damaging way to get the customer to pay up.
Salesperson	Finds out what each customer needs, and tries to arrange for it to be delivered. Salespeople do this by selecting from the range of products which the company has on offer, and explaining those products in terms of how they will meet the client's needs.
Advertising manager	Controls media purchases, deals with advertising agencies, generally handles the flow of information to the company's customers and consumers.
Public relations manager	Monitors the company's public image and applies corrective measures if the company is acquiring a bad reputation. Organises events and activities that will put the company in a good light, and tries to ensure that the company behaves responsibly towards its wider publics.
Market research manager	Collects evidence about what it is that consumers really need, and what they would really like to buy. Sometimes this also includes monitoring competitors' activity so that the company can take action early to counteract it.

all companies are market-orientated in the sense of putting customer satisfaction at the core of everything the business does; even some marketing managers see marketing as being purely a departmental responsibility rather than an organisational one (Hooley *et al.* 1990). In fact everyone within the firm has some responsibility for ensuring customer satisfaction; those who have contact directly with the firm's customers have a particular role to play (for example secretaries, delivery drivers, receptionists, telephonists and credit controllers).

 The **marketing orientation** is adopted because it works better than any other orientation; customers are more likely to spend money on goods and services that meet their needs than on those that do not. In other words, looking after customers is good for business, and organisations which adopt a customer orientation are more likely to meet their objectives than those which do not.

KEY CONCEPTS IN MARKETING

Apart from customer centrality, there are several more key concepts which are the running themes of any marketing course or career. These will be dealt with in more detail later in the book, but they are as follows:

■ *Managing exchange*. This goes further than promoting exchange through clever advertising and sales techniques: it also means ensuring that goods are where they should be, when they should be, and ensuring that the products themselves are worthy of exchange.

■ *Segmentation and targeting*. This is the idea that people can be grouped according to their needs (i.e. there are groups of potential customers who are looking for the same type of product) and that we can, and should, devote our limited resources to meeting the needs of a few groups rather than trying to please everybody.

■ *Positioning*. As marketers, we often seek to create an appropriate attitude towards our brands, and the firms we work for. This perception needs to be accurate, at least for our target customers, otherwise they will be disappointed and will not do business with us again. The position our brand occupies in the minds of the target group is therefore critical, and in this context the brand is the focusing device for all our planning – it is the lens through which our customers see us.

DEFINITIONS OF SOME MARKETING TERMS

Customers are the people or firms who buy products; *consumers* actually use the product, or consume it. Frequently customers are also consumers, so the terms might be used interchangeably, but often the person who buys a product is not the one who ultimately consumes it.

A **need** is a perceived lack of something. This implies that the individual not only does not have a particular item, but also is aware of not having it. This definition has nothing to do with necessity; human beings are complex, and have needs which go far beyond mere survival. In wealthy Western countries, for example, most people eat for pleasure rather than from a fear that they might die without eating – the need for enjoyment comes long before there is a necessity for food.

A **want**, on the other hand, is a specific satisfier for a need. An individual might need food (hunger being awareness of the lack of food) and want a curry.

Wants become **demands** when the potential customer also has the means to pay for the product. Some marketers have made their fortunes from finding ways for people to pay for the products, rather than from merely producing the product. The demand for a given product is therefore a function of need, want, and ability to pay.

A **product** is a bundle of benefits. This is a consumer-orientated view, because consumers will buy a product only if they feel it will be of benefit. Diners in a restaurant are not merely buying a full stomach; they are buying a pleasant evening out. Customers in a bar are not buying fizzy water with alcohol and flavourings in it; they are buying a social life. Here a distinction should be made between *physical goods* and *services*. For marketers both of these are products, since they may well offer the same benefits to the consumer. An afternoon at a football match, or a case of beer, might serve the same morale-raising function for some men. Services and physical goods are difficult to distinguish between, because most services have a physical good attached to them, and most physical goods have a service element attached to them. The usual definition of services says that they are mainly intangible, that production usually happens at the same time as consumption, that they are highly perishable, and that services cannot be owned (in the sense that there is no second-hand market for them).

Publics are any organisations or individuals that have actual or potential influence on the marketing organisation. This is an important definition for public relations practitioners, because they have the task of monitoring and adjusting the firm's activities relative to all the firm's publics, which can include government departments, competitors, outside pressure groups, employees, the local community, and so forth.

Markets are all the actual and potential buyers of the firm's products. Few firms can capture 100% of the market for their products; marketers more commonly aim for whichever portions of the market the firm can best serve. The remainder of the customers would go to the competition, or just be people who never hear of the product and therefore do not buy it. Even giant firms such as Coca-Cola have less than half of the market for their product category. For this reason marketers usually break down the overall market into *segments* (groups of customers with similar needs and characteristics) or even *niches* (very specific need and product categories).

Price is the amount of money a product is sold for. *Value* is what the product is worth to the customer or consumer. The value is always higher than the price, or no business would result, but individual customers will make a judgement as to whether the product is good value or poor value. If the product is poor value, the customer will try to find alternatives; if the product is good value, the customer will remain loyal. The decision about value for money is, of course, subjective: what one customer considers a great bargain, another customer might see as a waste of good money.

MEETING MARKETING RESISTANCE

Most organisations still tend to see marketing as one function of the business, rather than seeing it as the whole purpose of the business. Marketing departments are frequently seen as vehicles for selling the company's products by whatever means present themselves, and marketers are often seen as wizards who can manipulate consumers into buying things they do not really want or need. This means that many marketers find that they meet resistance from within the firm when they try to introduce marketing thinking.

This is at least in part due to the fact that the practice of marketing is difficult. Adopting a marketing stance means trying to think like somebody else, and anticipate somebody else's needs. It means trying to find out what people really need, and develop products that they will actually want. It means bending all the company's activities towards the customer. Inevitably there will be people within the firm who would rather not have to deal with these issues, and would have a quieter life if it were not for customers.

Table 1.2 shows some typical arguments encountered within firms, together with responses the marketer could use.

Overcoming this type of resistance is not always easy, due to the following factors:

- Lack of a leadership which is committed to the marketing concept.
- Lack of a suitable organisational infrastructure. For example, information about customers and consumers is a great deal more difficult to communicate throughout the firm if the firm's information technology systems are inadequate.
- Autocratic leadership style from senior management. In companies where the top managers believe that only their own ideas are right, the idea of changing the corporate direction in order to meet customer need better is less likely to take root.
- Inherent mistrust of marketing by some individuals in positions of power.
- A preference for a production or sales focus (as seen in Table 1.2).
- A transactional approach to business, in which making each sale is seen as the appropriate focus rather than thinking in terms of getting customers to return.

In an ideal corporate situation, marketing would be seen as the co-ordinating function for every department. The marketing function would be supplying information about the customer base, there would be common control systems in place to ensure that each department contributes primarily to customer satisfaction, the business strategy would be based around customer need, and goals for the organisation would be realistic and aimed at customer satisfaction. In practice, most firms have some way to go in reaching this ideal.

QUOTATIONS ABOUT MARKETING

For companies to be successful, the management must put the customer first. Here are some quotations that illustrate this.

> Probably the most important management fundamental that is being ignored today is staying close to the customer to satisfy his needs and anticipate his wants. In too many companies the customer has become a bloody nuisance whose unpredictable behaviour damages carefully-made strategic plans, whose activities mess up computer operations, and who stubbornly insists that purchased products should work.
>
> (Lew Young, Editor-in-Chief of *Business Week*)

Table 1.2 Reasons not to adopt a marketing philosophy

Source	Argument	Response
Production people	This is what we make efficiently. It's a good, well-made product, and it's up to you to find people to sell it to.	You might like the product, but the customers may have other ideas. What we need to do is not just 'keep the punters happy' but *delight* our customers and ensure their loyalty in future.
Accountants and financial directors	The only sensible way to price is allocate all the costs, then add on our profit margin. That way we know for sure we can't lose money! Also, how about cutting out the middle man by selling direct to the retailers?	If you use cost-plus pricing, you will almost certainly either price the product lower than the consumers are prepared to pay, in which case you are giving away some of your profit, or you'll price it too high and nobody will buy the product. And that way you'll *really* lose some money! And cutting out the wholesalers means we'd have to deliver odd little amounts to every corner shop in the country, which would make our transport costs shoot up. Not to mention that the retailers won't take us seriously – we need the wholesalers' contacts!
Legal department	We have no legal obligation to do more than return people's money if things go wrong. Why go to the expense of sending somebody round to apologise?	With no customers, we have no business. We have all our eggs in one basket; we can't afford to upset any of them.
Board of Directors	Business is not so good, so everybody's budgets are being cut, including the marketing department. Sorry, you'll just have to manage with less.	If you cut the marketing budget, you cut the amount of business coming in. Our competition will seize the advantage, and we'll lose our customer base and market share – and we won't have the money coming in to get it back again, either.
Front-line staff	I'm paid to drive a truck, not chat up the customers. They're getting the stuff they've paid for, what more do they want?	Giving the customer good service means they're pleased to see you next time you call. It pays dividends directly to you because your job is pleasanter, but also it helps business and keeps you in a job.
Salesforce	You're paying me commission to get the sale, so getting the sale is all I'm interested in.	You can get sales once by deceit, but what happens when you go back? How much more could you sell if your customers know you're a good guy to do business with? And apart from all that, if you're doing your best for the customers, you can sleep at nights. Collaboration between sales and marketing is known to improve overall business performance (Le Meunier-Fitzhugh and Piercy 2007).

> Marketing is so basic that it cannot be considered a separate function ... It is the whole business seen from the point of view of its final result, that is, from the customer's point of view.
> (Peter F. Drucker, 1973)

> There is only one boss – the customer. And he can fire everybody in the company from the chairman on down, simply by spending his money somewhere else.
> (Sam Walton, American founder of Wal-Mart Stores,
> the largest retail chain in the world)

And finally, Tom Watson of IBM was once at a meeting where customer complaints were being discussed. The complaints were categorised as engineering complaints, delivery complaints, servicing complaints, etc., perhaps ten categories in all. Finally Watson went to the front of the room, swept all the paper into one heap, and said 'There aren't any categories of problem here. There's just one problem. Some of us aren't paying enough attention to our customers.' And with that he swept out, leaving the executives wondering whether they would still have jobs in the morning. IBM salespeople are told to act at all times as if they were on the customer's payroll – which of course they are.

Case study 1
Toshiba

In 1875, a new engineering company was founded in a newly industrialising Japan. The company, Tanaka Sheizo-sho, began by making telegraph equipment. Under the brand name of Shibaura Seisaku-sho the company became a manufacturer of heavy electrical equipment, eventually merging in 1939 with Tokyo Denki, Japan's largest manufacturer of domestic electrical products. The new company's official name, Tokyo Shibaura Denki, quickly became shortened to Toshiba, and the company adopted this as their official name in 1978.

During the Second World War, Toshiba was cut off from world markets and sources of raw materials: the company developed the first Japanese radar systems during this period, but it was not until after the war that they were able to begin expanding again. This time, in common with other Japanese companies, the shortage of raw materials became a spur to invention. Toshiba developed transistor technology from a laboratory novelty to a fully fledged set of techniques: they developed the first transistor TV set in Japan, the first microwave oven, and were involved in developing space communications equipment. In 1970, they unveiled the world's first video telephone, and in 1971 the world's first expanded integrated circuit TV.

Toshiba were not slow to see the possibilities of computer and communications technology, either. In 1978 they unveiled the first Japanese word processor, and launched a communications satellite; the following year saw them release the world's first optical-disk data storage system (the first CD, in other words). In 1985, Toshiba launched the world's first laptop, a combination of their engineering brilliance and their ongoing parsimony with raw materials.

During the 1990s a further stream of new devices appeared from the Toshiba labs: the world's smallest transistor, the first sub-notebook PC, the microfilter colour TV tube, the DVD, the flat TV screen, the DVD video player and recorder, and the first MPEG device.

The twenty-first century saw Toshiba developing high-definition TV and high-definition DVD recording devices, as well as NAND flash memories and broadband processors.

The company's basic commitment is stated in their corporate documentation:

We, the Toshiba Group companies, based on our total commitment to people and to the future, are determined to help create a higher quality of life for all people, and to do our part to help ensure that progress continues within the world community.

The company goes on to express its commitment to its customers, employees and shareholders. The company's brand tag line, 'Toshiba Leading Innovation' gives some idea of how the company sees itself carrying out its corporate mission, but the company is by no means entirely technology-driven: each year Toshiba conducts a customer satisfaction survey in which 6000 individual customers and 1200 corporate respondents from 230 client companies are asked for their views on how the company can improve what it does. Toshiba's customer satisfaction statement rests on five factors, as stated below:

1 We provide products, systems and services that are safe and reliable.
2 We respond to requests and enquiries from customers sincerely, rapidly and appropriately.
3 We value the voice of customers and endeavour to develop and improve products, systems and services to deliver customer satisfaction.
4 We provide appropriate information to customers.
5 We protect personal data provided by customers.

As a direct result of Toshiba's discussions with customers, changes are made in the design and function of products: for example, the following changes resulted from surveys conducted in recent years:

- Exposure to X-rays from Toshiba medical equipment was halved.
- Shock-resistant mobile PCs were developed following observation of how people handled the equipment.
- A more user-friendly washing-machine control panel was developed.

Recently, the company has started to use questionnaires sent to mobile telephones of customers. This has increased response rates dramatically – often several thousand responses come in from each questionnaire, giving the company some extremely rapid feedback on new products. As in its new product development, Toshiba want to be at the forefront of technology in its customer research. For the past 130 years, Toshiba has maintained engineering excellence without losing sight of customer needs.

Questions

1 How would you define Toshiba in terms of the development of the marketing concept?
2 Why is price not mentioned in Toshiba's customer care ethos?
3 How has research informed new product development?
4 How might the Second World War have affected Toshiba's development of new devices in the 1990s?
5 Why does the company aim for a global market?

SUMMARY

This chapter has been about the terms and concepts of marketing. Here are some key points from this chapter:

- Marketing is about understanding what the consumer needs and wants, and seeing that the company provides it.
- A need is a perceived lack; a want is a specific satisfier.
- Customers buy things; consumers use them.
- Price is what something costs; value is what it is worth.
- A product is a bundle of benefits; it is only worth what it will do for the consumer.
- Consumer (or customer) orientation is used because it is the most profitable in the long run.

CHAPTER QUESTIONS

1 In a situation where supply exceeds demand, which orientation would you expect most firms to have?
2 Why might a consumer feel that paying £150 for a pair of designer jeans represents good value for money?
3 What needs are met by buying fashionable clothes?
4 What needs might a mother meet by buying a child sweets?
5 Why should marketers always refer back to the consumer when making decisions?

Further reading

The Marketing Book **edited by Michael Baker** (London, Heinemann/Chartered Institute of Marketing, 1991) contains a very good chapter by Michael Baker himself on the history of the marketing concept.

Marketing: Concepts and Strategies, **4th edn by S. Dibb, L. Simkin, W. Pride and O.C. Ferrell** (London, Houghton Mifflin, 2000) contains a realistic and interesting Appendix on careers in marketing.

Principles of Marketing, **3rd edn by Frances Brassington and Stephen Pettitt** (Harlow, Financial Times Prentice Hall, 2002) has a good overview of marketing's relationship with other business disciplines in Chapter One.

References

Andreassen, T.W.: 'Small, high-cost countries' strategy for attracting MNCs' global investments', *International Journal of Public Sector Management*, **8** (3) (1995), pp. 110–18.

Booms, B.H. and Bitner, M.J.: 'Marketing strategies and organisation structures for service firms', in *Marketing of Services*, J. Donnelly and W.R. George, eds (Chicago, IL, American Marketing Association, 1981).

Drucker, P.F.: *Management: Tasks, Responsibilities, Practices* (New York, Harper & Row, 1973).

Garg, Nikita, Wansink, Brian and Inman, J. Jeffrey: 'The influence of incidental affect on consumers' food intake', *Journal of Marketing*, **71** (1) (2006), pp. 194–206.

Hooley, G.J. *et al.*: 'The marketing concept: putting theory into practice', *European Journal of Marketing*, **24** (9) (1990), pp. 7–23.

Kotler, P.: *Marketing Management, Analysis, Planning and Control*, 11th edn (Upper Saddle River, NJ, Prentice Hall, 2003).

Kotler, P., Armstrong, G., Saunders, J. and Wong, V.: *Principles of Marketing* (Harlow, Financial Times Prentice Hall, 2001).

Le Meunier-Fitzhugh, Ken, and Piercy, Nigel F. 'Exploring collaboration between sales and marketing', *European Journal of Marketing*, **41** (7/8) (2007), pp. 939–55.

Levitt, T.: 'Marketing myopia', *Harvard Business Review* (July–August 1960), pp. 45–56.

McCarthy, E.J.: *Basic Marketing: A Managerial Approach*, 9th edn (Homewood, IL, Irwin, 1987; 1st edition 1960).

Raghunathan, Rajagopal, Naylor, Rebecca Walker and Hoyer, Wayne D.: 'The unhealthy = tasty intuition and its effects on taste inference, food enjoyment, and choice of food products', *Journal of Marketing*, **70** (4) (2006), pp. 170–84.

Ravald, A. and Gronroos, C.: 'The value concept and relationship marketing', *European Journal of Marketing*, **30** (2) (1996), pp. 10–30.

Takala, T. and Uusitalo, O.: 'An alternative view of relationship marketing: a framework for ethical analysis', *European Journal of Marketing*, **30** (2) (1996), pp. 45–60.

St Paul's Cathedral

St Paul's Cathedral is an icon of London. Built just after the Great Fire of London, it is a major tourist attraction based at the heart of London's financial district. At the same time it is a working church, with a congregation and regular religious services. Around 700,000 visitors a year visit St Paul's, about 75% of whom come from overseas, but it still needs £5.5 million a year to keep its doors open.

St Paul's, as a religious monument, is a non-profit organisation. It is primarily a place of worship, and the Dean and Chapter welcome anybody to come in, but equally the church needs contributions, so entrance charges are levied for visiting some parts of the building. This is regarded as a compromise between free access for Christian worshippers and others, and the need for finance. No-one has to pay to come to a service, since this would conflict with the church's primary purpose, and some people object strongly to having to pay to go into a church.

Reconciling the needs of visitors and the needs of the church is only part of the problem – meeting the needs of people who may only be in London for a short visit, while at the same time remaining competitive with other major attractions in London (of which there are many, spread out over a large city). The fact that the cathedral has been there for nearly 350 years is, paradoxically, not helpful – people can always come back next year, or in another fifty years, and the cathedral will still be there.

Canon Precentor Lucy Winkett

Watch the video clip, then try to answer the following questions. The answers are on the companion website.

Questions

1 How can St Paul's reconcile the conflict between the internal and external environments?

2 What micro-environmental factors most impact on St Paul's?

3 What macro-environmental factors most affect St Paul's?

2

The marketing environment

Objectives

After reading this chapter you should be able to:

- recognise the main environmental factors affecting marketing decisions;
- formulate ways of coping with the marketing environment;
- recognise ways to exploit opportunities in the environment;
- understand the principles of marketing strategy;
- explain the strategic issues behind the formulation of marketing plans.

INTRODUCTION

No business operates in a vacuum; any organisation is surrounded by laws and liabilities, pressure groups and public bodies, customers and competitors. These are part of the marketing environment that the organisation works within, and since marketing is at the interface between the organisation and the outside world, dealing with this environment is a major part of the marketer's work.

This means that the marketing policy of a firm (or any organisation) should be viewed as operating within a complex and rapidly changing environment. These external factors must be monitored and responded to if the organisation is to meet its goals, and an understanding of the environment is (ultimately) the basis for all marketing strategy.

THE MARKETING ENVIRONMENT

The marketing environment represents a complex array of threats and opportunities for the organisation, and can sometimes seem difficult to categorise. Generally speaking, the marketing environment can be divided into two areas: the **external environment** and the **internal environment**. The external environment is concerned with everything that happens outside the organisation, and the internal environment is concerned with those marketing factors that happen within the organisation. Often organisations concentrate far more attention on the external environment than on the internal environment, but both are of great importance.

There are two basic approaches to dealing with environmental forces: reactive and proactive. The **reactive manager** regards environmental factors as being uncontrollable, and will therefore tend to adjust marketing plans to fit environmental changes. **Proactive managers** look for ways to change the organisation's environment in the belief that many, even most, environmental factors can be controlled, or at least influenced in some way (Kotler 1986).

THE EXTERNAL ENVIRONMENT

The external environment consists of two further divisions: factors close to the organisation (called the **micro-environment**), and those factors common to society as a whole (the **macro-environment**). Micro-environmental factors might include such things as the customer base, the location of the company's warehouses, or the existence of a local pressure group that is unsympathetic to the business. Some micro-environmental factors (for example, availability of skilled employees) overlap into the internal environment. The macro-environment might include such factors as government legislation, foreign competition, exchange rate fluctuations or even climatic changes.

The external environment is often not susceptible to direct control; the best that marketers can do is to influence some elements of it, and to react in the most appropriate ways to avoid the threats and exploit the opportunities it presents.

Situational analysis

Managers need to know where they are now if they are to be able to decide where they are going. This analysis will involve examining the internal state of health of the organisation, and the external environment within which the organisation operates.

At the simplest level, managers can use SWOT analysis to take stock of the firm's internal position: SWOT stands for Strengths, Weaknesses, Opportunities and Threats. Strengths and weaknesses are factors which are specific to the firm; opportunities and threats arise from the external environment. These factors can be broken down further, as shown in Table 2.1.

| Table 2.1 | SWOT analysis |

	Internal factors	External factors
Positive factors	*Strengths* What are we best at? What intellectual property do we own? What specific skills does the workforce have? What financial resources do we have? What connections and alliances do we have? What is our bargaining power with both suppliers and intermediaries?	*Opportunities* What changes in the external environment can we exploit? What weaknesses in our competitors can we attack? What new technology might become available to us? What new markets might be opening up to us?
Negative factors	*Weaknesses* What are we worst at doing? Is our intellectual property outdated? What training does our workforce lack? What is our financial position? What connections and alliances should we have, but don't?	*Threats* What might our competitors be able to do to hurt us? What new legislation might damage our interests? What social changes might threaten us? How will the economic (boom-and-bust) cycle affect us?

The list in Table 2.1 is not, of course, comprehensive. Equally, a threat might be turned into an opportunity: a competitor's new technological breakthrough might lead us to consider a takeover bid, for example, or new legislation might provide a loophole which we can exploit while our competitors have to abide by the new rules.

STEP (Socio-cultural, Technological, Economic and Political) analysis is a useful way of looking at the external environment (it is also sometimes written as PEST). Table 2.2 shows some of the main changes that are occurring under each of those headings.

STEP and SWOT analyses are simply different ways of looking at the environment and at the firm's place in it. The external marketing environment is itself subdivided into micro- and macro-environments, as shown in Figure 2.1.

Table 2.2	Current environmental changes

	Example	Implications
Socio-cultural	Lifestyle expectations	As people have become more wealthy, they have come to expect more. In twenty-first century Britain, few people would consider living without a telephone, television, refrigerator, car, bank account or credit cards. In 1960, all these products were examples of things owned by only a minority of the population.
	Post-industrial society (Bell 1974)	As automation of manufacturing increases, more people work in service industries. Traditional class divisions are disappearing, with new ones rising to take their place; the growth of lifestyle analysis affects the way marketers portray their target consumers.
	Demography	A report prepared for the European Union shows that, within the 15 states which were members in 2002, life expectancy has increased dramatically and the birthrate has fallen: because people spend longer in education, working lives are shorter. Without immigration from the new Eastern European member states, the working population would shrink dramatically and governments would be compelled to raise the retirement age (a move which is happening in the UK and France anyway) (Cruijsen *et al.* 2002).
Technological	Information technology	Few serious marketers would consider not having a corporate website, yet only ten years ago such websites were rare, and were often merely 'presence' sites which directed visitors to a telephone number or address.
	Space technology	Apart from the revolution in communications (both telephone and television) that satellites have brought, there are increasing possibilities for new manufacturing techniques to be used in space, and even space tourism. Also, the technology used for rocketry has resulted in spin-offs for terrestrial production of goods.
Economics	Boom-and-bust cycle	At approximately eight-year intervals most national economies go into recession. This means that the production of goods and services shrinks, jobs are lost and businesses become bankrupt. Purchase of major capital items such as new kitchens, houses, cars and washing machines slows down, and consumers become less willing to buy on credit as job security reduces.
	Micro-economics	Micro-economics is concerned with exchanges and competition. Competitive activities are very much the domain of the marketer.

Table 2.2	continued	
	Example	**Implications**
Politics	**Influence of political parties**	Governments usually have policies concerning trade and industry: in part this is to ensure a growing economy and increased prosperity, in part it is to increase the number of jobs. Changes of government will often cause shifts in emphasis which might lead to disruption for individual firms.
	Legislation	Laws arise in two ways: government legislation (laws created by politicians) and case law, which is the law as interpreted by judges. Politicians can be influenced by petitions and by reasoned argument; this is called lobbying. Case law can be appealed by the parties to it, but is harder to influence. International law can sometimes have powerful influences on businesses, depending on where the firm is located. For example, European (EU) law must be passed through the national governments of the member states; changes during the 1990s mean that EU law supersedes national law and can therefore virtually be imposed on the member states. This makes it difficult to influence or control.

Figure 2.1	Micro- and macro-environment forces

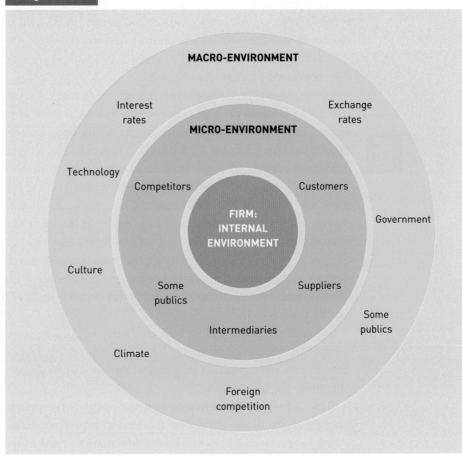

The micro-environment

The micro-environment is made up of those factors that impact closely on the organisation, and typically consists of the following elements:

■ competitors;

■ customers;

■ suppliers;

■ intermediaries;

■ micro-environment publics.

Competitors

Frequently firms fail to recognise who their *competitors* are. It is not at all unusual for firms to define competition too narrowly, simply because they define their business too narrowly. For instance, if a bus company defines itself solely as being in the bus business, the management might reasonably define the competitors as being other bus companies. If, on the other hand, the company defines itself as being in the transportation business, the management will recognise the competition from railways, taxis and even bicycles.

In the early days of the Internet, many retailers did not recognise that online retailing represents competition. Now, many bricks-and-mortar retailers have their own websites so that customers can order directly: although the Internet is, for various reasons, unlikely to replace bricks-and-mortar retailers entirely, it does represent a threat.

When assessing competitive threat, marketing managers need to decide which competitors offer the closest substitutes *in terms of meeting the consumers' needs*. Grouping consumers with similar needs and characteristics is called **segmentation** (see Chapter 4). Since each segment has different needs, the threat from competition will come from different sources in each case.

At the extreme, all businesses compete with all others for consumers' money; consumers have only a fixed amount to spend, and therefore a consumer who chooses to buy a more expensive house may at the same time be choosing not to have expensive holidays for the next two years. For most marketers this type of competition is not important, since there are usually far more immediate competitors to deal with. This would become an issue only if the company were in a monopolistic (or at least a dominant) position and could afford to encourage the overall market to increase.

Competitors can therefore be either firms supplying similar products or firms competing for the consumer's hard-earned money, but either way marketers need to provide a product that meets consumers' needs better than the products offered by the competition.

Table 2.3 shows the different types of competitive structure. In practice, most marketers are faced with monopolistic competition, where each company is trying to establish a big enough market share to control the market, but has no

Critical thinking

Wow! That's a lot of different competitors! If everybody is competing for customers' cash, how can we hope to identify who our customers and competitors are? Surely there has to be a point at which we say, 'These people are not our competitors, they are potentially our friends.' Which of course leads to another point – why do we keep on fighting with competitors instead of co-operating? After all, major motor manufacturers such as Ford and Volkswagen co-operate on designing new vehicles (the Ford Galaxy is the same car as the VW Sharan, for example) so why don't we all do that and save ourselves a lot of trouble?

Table 2.3 Competitive structures

Type of competitive structure	Explanation	Examples
Perfect competition	A large number of suppliers, no one of which is powerful enough to influence the supply level overall. Homogeneous products. Easy entry to the market. Everybody in the market (both suppliers and consumers) has full knowledge of what everybody else is doing. There are few examples, and although economists sometimes use the perfect competition model for purposes of discussion, marketers will be very unlikely to be operating within this environment.	Unregulated agricultural markets. The international money markets.
Monopolistic competition	A situation where one major supplier has obtained a large share of the market by the use of a differentiated marketing approach, but other competitors can still enter and try to carve out their own share of the market.	Coca-Cola and PepsiCo have a major share of the soft drinks industry, but other firms are not prevented from entering the market.
Oligopoly	A few companies control the market almost entirely. Typically this happens when costs of entry to the market are high; very often the size of the market is not great enough to repay the capital cost of entry for a new firm. Oligopolies are often investigated by government monopoly regulators, who exist to ensure that large firms do not abuse their power.	Commercial aircraft manufacture. The detergent industry. Oil extraction and refining.
Monopoly	Monopolies exist when a single firm has a product with no close substitutes. In practice, this situation is almost as rare as perfect competition; the few examples still permitted are the so-called 'natural monopolies' which would clearly not be efficient if effort were duplicated.	Electricity supply grids. Some countries' national rail networks.

real prospect of becoming the sole supplier for the product category. The largest firm in such a market may find it more worthwhile to seek to increase the total market for the product category than to try for a bigger share of the existing market. This approach has the added advantage that it will not attract the attention of the government monopoly regulators.

Michael Porter's Five Forces model offers a useful approach to competitor analysis (Porter 1990). The five forces are as follows:

1 *The bargaining power of suppliers*: the greater this is, the stronger the competitive pressures.

2 *The bargaining power of customers*: again, the stronger this is, the more competitive the environment.

3 *The threat of new entrants*: if it is easy to enter a market, or if there is a likelihood that the market is becoming attractive to new players, the market will become competitive.

4 *The threat of substitute products and services*: this threat is often not seen until it is too late. New products may come along which meet the same need as the existing product, but in a different way: it is sometimes difficult to see this threat until it is too late.

5 *The rivalry among current competitors*: in some markets, competitors are careful not to compete too strongly for fear of losing out in the long run – such markets are oligopolistic (see Table 2.3). In other markets, competition is fierce.

The main strength of Porter's model is that it broadens the concept of competition and enables marketers to look at the wider picture. Correct identification of competitors is essential; in simple terms, a firm's competitors are any firm that seeks to meet a similar need. This definition may be hard to apply in practice.

Customers

Customers may change their needs, or may even disappear altogether. Some years ago, the American company Johnson & Johnson became aware that much larger quantities of its baby shampoo and talcum powder were being sold than could possibly be accounted for by the number of babies in the country. Research discovered that many adults were using the products on themselves, so the company launched a promotion campaign based around the slogan, 'Are you still a Johnson's baby?' A new category of customer had become apparent, and the company was able to respond to this and capitalise on the changed environment. Clearly customers' needs are of paramount importance to marketers, and it is essential that new segments can be identified easily and accurately; however, it is also important to recognise that some segments may be disappearing, and to know when to switch the marketing effort to more lucrative segments.

Suppliers

Suppliers also form part of the micro-environment since they impact closely on the company. At first sight, suppliers would appear to be outside the scope of the marketing department, but in fact the firm relies heavily on the goodwill of its suppliers, and a good public relations exercise will always try to involve suppliers. A supplier can easily cause an adverse effect within a firm by supplying shoddy goods, or failing to meet delivery dates, and this will inevitably impact on the firm's customers. This is of greater importance for some firms than for others (retailers will be more concerned about suppliers than will government offices, for example) but most organisations need to monitor their suppliers and ensure that they are providing appropriate goods.

Current thinking in purchasing and supply is that the relationship between suppliers and their customers should be a close one, with frequent visits to each other's premises and a high level of information exchange. This is encompassed within the **logistics** approach to supply, in which the firm is seen as a link in a system for providing the right goods and services in the right place at the right time; the system as a whole takes raw materials and moves and transforms them into goods that consumers need. This philosophy relies on the supplier and purchaser integrating their activities and developing a mutual understanding of each other's problems. It is also (from the supplier's viewpoint) an example of good relationship marketing – establishing a close, long-term relationship is likely to prove more efficient in the long run than continually seeking new customers as existing customers go elsewhere for their supplies.

Intermediaries

Intermediaries are the retailers, wholesalers, agents and others who distribute the firm's goods. Relationships with these intermediaries need to be good if the firm is to succeed in getting its goods to the final consumer successfully (this is part of the logistics approach). Intermediaries may also include marketing services providers such as research agencies, advertising agencies, distribution companies providing transport and warehousing, and exhibition organisers – in fact, any individuals or organisations that stand between the company and the consumer and help in getting the goods out. These relationships are, of course, of great importance to marketers, but intermediaries have their own businesses to run and are working to their own agendas. As with suppliers, it pays dividends to establish good relationships with intermediaries, mainly by sharing information and by maintaining good communication links (see Chapter 8).

Micro-environment publics

Finally, some of the firm's publics form part of the micro-environment. 'Publics' is a generic term encompassing all the groups that have actual or potential impact on the company. The range of publics can include financial publics, local publics, governmental publics, media publics, citizen action publics and many others. The marketing activity concerned with these publics is called (not surprisingly) public relations; there is more on this in Chapter 9.

Financial publics might include the banks and shareholders who control the firm's finances, and who can pressure the firm to behave in particular ways. These pressures can be strong, and can even threaten the firm's existence; firms are often compelled by their financial publics to do things they would otherwise prefer not to. It is to address this problem that glossy company reports are produced for shareholders, and positive information about the company is issued to banks and others.

Local publics consist mainly of the firm's neighbours. These local organisations and individuals may well pressure the company to take local actions, for example clean up pollution or sponsor local charities. Obtaining the goodwill of the local public will, of course, make it much easier for the company to live harmoniously with its neighbours and will reduce short-term local difficulties. For example, Body Shop expects its franchisees to participate in projects that will help the local community, whether by supervising a play area or by raising funds for a local charity. Employees participate in these projects on company time; the activities improve the image of the company and generate positive feelings about the store among local residents. There is a spin-off for the firm's staff, who feel that they are working for a caring company; Body Shop employees tend to be very positive about their employer.

Each of the elements in the micro-environment is small enough that the organisation at the centre should have influence over most of them, and be able to react effectively to the remainder.

The macro-environment

The macro-environment includes the major forces that act not only on the firm itself, but also on its competitors and on elements in the micro-environment. The macro-environment tends to be harder to influence than does the micro-environment, but this does not mean that firms must simply remain passive; the inability to control does not imply an inability to influence. Often the macro-environment can be influenced by good public relations activities (see Chapter 9).

The main elements of the macro-environment are:

- demographic factors;
- economic factors;
- political factors;
- legal factors;
- socio-cultural factors;
- ecological and geographical factors;
- technological factors;
- macro-environment publics.

Demographic factors

Demographics is the study of population factors such as the proportion of the population who are of a given race, gender, location or occupation, and also of such general factors as population density, size of population and location. Demographic changes can have major effects on companies: the declining birth rate in most Western countries has an obvious effect on sales of baby products, but also means that, without immigration, the working population would be shrinking and consequently there would be a shortage of people to become employees (Cruijsen *et al.* 2002). Likewise, changes in the ethnic composition of cities, or in the population concentration (with few people living in the city centres of large cities) cause changes in the demand for local services and retailers, and (more subtly) changes in the type of goods and services demanded. There is more on this in Chapter 3.

Economic factors

Economic factors encompass such areas as the boom/bust cycle, and the growth in unemployment in some parts of the country as a result of the closing of traditional industries. Macro-economic factors deal with the management of demand in the economy; the main mechanisms governments use for this are interest rate controls, taxation policy and government expenditure. If the government increases expenditure (or reduces taxation), there will be more money in the economy and demand will rise; if taxation is increased (or expenditure cut), there will be less money for consumers to spend, so demand will shrink. Rises in interest rates tend to reduce demand, as home loans become more expensive and credit card charges rise.

Micro-economic factors are to do with the way people spend their incomes. As incomes have risen over the past 40 years or so, the average standard of living has risen, and spending patterns have altered drastically. The proportion of income spent on food and housing has fallen (Office for National Statistics 2003), whereas the proportion spent on entertainment and clothing has risen. Information on the economy is widely publicised, and marketers make use of this information to predict what is likely to happen to their customers and to demand for their products.

Political factors

Political factors often impact on business: recent examples are the worldwide movement towards privatisation of former government-owned utilities and businesses, and the shift away from protection of workers' rights. Firms need to be able to respond to the prevailing political climate, and adjust the marketing policy accordingly. For example, British Telecom, Deutsche Telekom and Telstra of Australia have all had to make major readjustments to their marketing approaches since being privatised, and in particular since seeing an upswing in competitive levels. Almost all the firms' activities have been affected, from cutting the lead time between ordering and obtaining a new telephone, through to price competition in response to competitors' cut-price long-distance and international calls.

Legal factors

Legal factors follow on from political factors, in that governments often pass laws which affect business. For example, Table 2.4 shows some of the legislation on marketing issues currently in force in various countries.

Sometimes judges decide cases in a way that re-interprets legislation, however, and this in itself can affect the business position. A further complication within Europe arises as a result of EU legislation, which takes precedence over national law, and which can seriously affect the way firms do business in Europe.

Case law and EU law are not dependent on the politics of the national governments, and are therefore less easy to predict. Clearly businesses must stay within the law, but it is increasingly difficult to be sure what the law says, and to know what changes in the law might be imminent.

For companies operating in global markets, legal issues can become a minefield: the fact that a product is legal in one country does not mean that it is, or even should be, in another. Product modifications required in different countries often mean that even a 'world' product has to be virtually re-invented each time it crosses borders, but the problem goes further for marketers, since some marketing techniques which are perfectly normal and acceptable in some cultures are regarded as unacceptable or manipulative in others. For example, a home improvement salesman calling at someone's home in the United States would be

Table 2.4 Example of legislation affecting marketing

Country	Legislation
France	TV advertising of films is illegal: the ban on advertising retail stores has been lifted now
UK	Consumers can opt out of receiving mailings and cold telephone calls: firms which contact people who have opted out can be fined.
Belgium	Recent rulings allow the British Office of Fair Trading to prosecute Belgian companies which send misleading mail shots to British companies or consumers.
Germany	Advertising for war toys and games of chance are forbidden (Chee and Harris 1988). Perhaps surprisingly, Germany was slow to implement the EU-wide ban on tobacco advertising.
Japan	All rooftop and flashing-light advertisements have been banned in Kyoto.

likely to bring a small gift such as flowers or a cake, as one would if calling to visit a friend. In the UK, this would be regarded with some suspicion, and the Office of Fair Trading have ruled that it is an unfair practice.

Socio-cultural factors

Socio-cultural factors are those areas that involve the shared beliefs and attitudes of the population. People learn to behave in particular ways as a result of feedback from the rest of society; behaviour and attitudes that are regarded as inappropriate or rude are quickly modified, and also people develop expectations about how other people should behave. In the marketing context, people come to believe (for example) that shop assistants should be polite and helpful, that fast-food restaurants should be brightly lit and clean, that shops should have advertised items in stock. These beliefs are not laws of nature, but merely a consensus view of what *should* happen. There have certainly been many times (and many countries) where these standards have not applied.

These prevailing beliefs and attitudes change over a period of time owing to changes in the world environment, changes in ethnic mix and changes in technology. These changes usually happen over fairly long periods of time. Since 1970 in most Western countries there has been a development towards a more diverse, individualistic society; a large increase in the number of couples living together without being married; and a marked increase in the acceptance (and frequency) of single-parent families (European Commission 2001).

Cultural changes over the same period include a major change in eating habits due to an increase in tourism, migration, and greater globalisation of food markets (Maucher 1993).

A very few cultural changes come about as the result of marketing activities: a recent example in the UK is the gradual replacement of Guy Fawkes night (at least as a family occasion) with Hallowe'en, an American import which has children dressing up in costumes and going from house to house 'trick or treat-ing'. Part of the thrust for this change has come about because Guy Fawkes celebrations involve letting off fireworks, which is a dangerous activity for amateurs, but much of the change has been driven by a desire by marketers to sell costumes, and by the influx of US-made films and TV programmes which show Hallowe'en celebrations.

Ecological and geographical factors

Ecological and geographical factors have come to the forefront of thinking in the past fifteen years or so. The increasing scarcity of raw materials, the problems of disposing of waste materials, and the difficulty of finding appropriate locations for industrial complexes (particularly those with a major environmental impact) are all factors that are seriously affecting the business decision-making framework (see Chapter 12). In a marketing context, firms are having to take account of public views on these issues and are often subjected to pressure from organised groups as well as individuals. Often the most effective way to deal with these issues is to begin by consulting the pressure groups concerned, so that disagreements can be resolved before the company has committed too many resources (see Chapter 9); firms adopting the societal marketing concept (see Chapter 1) would do this as a matter of course.

Technological factors

Technological advances in the past forty years have been rapid, and have affected almost all areas of life. Whole new industries have appeared: for example, satellite TV stations, cable networks, the Internet, CD recordings and virtual reality, and computer-aided design systems. All of these industries were unknown even twenty years ago. It seems likely that technological change will continue to increase, and that more new industries will appear in future. The corollary, of course, is that some old industries will disappear, or at the very least will face competition from entirely unexpected directions. Identifying these trends in advance is extremely difficult, but not impossible.

Clearly the Internet has had a tremendous impact on marketing. Nobody owns the Internet; it is a communications medium spread across thousands (even millions) of computers worldwide, which operates independently of the telephone companies that supply its cable connections, of the governments in whose countries it resides, and even of the computer owners in whose machines data are stored. The Internet therefore operates under its own rules; there is little or no international law to govern its use or abuse. From a marketing viewpoint, one major impact of the Internet is that it has placed market power even more firmly in the hands of consumers. People are able to compare prices and suppliers much more quickly, can comment to each other much more quickly about exceptionally good or exceptionally bad service, and can make themselves much better-informed about products than before.

The rapid growth in virtual shopping (accessing catalogues on the Internet) means that consumers can buy goods anywhere in the world and have them shipped – or, in the case of computer software, simply downloaded – which means that global competition will reach unprecedented levels. Virtual shoppers are able to access high-quality pictures of products, holiday destinations and even pictures of restaurant food before committing to a purchase. A recent development is the use of bots, which can be programmed to search the Internet on behalf of an individual and find products which might be of interest. A correctly programmed bot acts exactly like the individual, knowing what the person likes or dislikes, and developments in the pipeline would enable the bot to negotiate prices on behalf of the individual.

There is more on Internet marketing throughout the book, particularly Chapter 12.

Macro-environment publics

The macro-environment also contains the remainder of the organisation's publics.

- *Governmental publics* are the local, national and international agencies that restrict the company's activities by passing legislation, setting interest rates, and fixing exchange rates. Governmental publics can be influenced by lobbying and by trade associations.

- *Media publics*. Press, television and radio services carry news, features and advertising that can aid the firm's marketing, or conversely can damage a firm's reputation. Public relations departments go to great lengths to ensure that positive images of the firm are conveyed to (and by) the media publics. For example, a company might issue a press release to publicise its sponsorship of a major sporting event. This could generate positive responses from the public, and a positive image of the company when the sporting event is broadcast.

- *Citizen action publics* are the pressure groups such as Greenpeace or consumers' rights groups who lobby manufacturers and others in order to improve life for the public at large. Some pressure groups are informally organised; recent years have seen an upsurge in local pressure groups and protesters, and there has been a surge in the number of websites which protest about company or government activities. Most major companies' websites are shadowed by anonymous counter-culture sites: these carry derogatory stories about the companies. Such sites are difficult to stop, since the Internet is largely unregulated, and the people posting stories on the sites can remain anonymous.

Critical thinking

Why do we worry about citizen action publics? If people want to complain about us, why not let them? After all, nobody really pays much attention to a few soreheads complaining – they usually don't have much credibility, and they certainly don't have much of a budget.

In fact there may even be some advantages. If we look at the websites concerned, we might be able to gain some ideas for improving what we do, and meeting customer needs better – which, for marketers, is the name of the game. We could even go a step further, and invite such pressure groups to advise us in future, so that we can tailor what we do to meet their needs better.

THE INTERNATIONAL ENVIRONMENT

As business becomes increasingly global, marketers find themselves more and more in the position of doing business across cultural divides, and across national boundaries. International marketing differs from domestic marketing in the following ways:

- Cultural differences mean that communications tools will need to be adapted, and sometimes changed radically.
- Market segmentation issues are likely to be more geographically based.
- Remoteness of the markets makes monitoring and control more difficult.
- Both physical distribution (logistics) and place decisions will be affected by infrastructure differences in some overseas markets.

International marketing is important because of the economic theory of **comparative advantage**. This theory states that each country has natural advantages over others in the production of certain goods, and therefore specialisation and the trading of surpluses will benefit everybody. For example, although it is possible to grow tomatoes under glass in the Netherlands, they can be grown more easily and cheaply in Spain, so it makes economic sense for the Dutch to buy Spanish tomatoes and sell Spain chemical products that are produced more readily in the Netherlands.

Comparative advantage does not explain all of the thrust behind internationalisation; Japanese, US and UK multinationals have all made major impacts in overseas markets without having an apparent natural advantage over their overseas competitors. In some cases this can be explained by economies of scale; in others by the development of expertise within the firms; in others the reasons are historical.

WORLD TRADE INITIATIVES

Marketing to an international audience will usually bring **economies of scale** in manufacture, research and development, and marketing costs. Most governments encourage firms to market internationally because it brings in foreign exchange, which enables the country to buy-in essential imports (for example aluminium ore or oil), which are needed to support the national economy.

The downside of world trade is that it sometimes results in the export of cultural values as well as goods and services, so that traditional cultures become eroded. Evidence exists to show that Latin America and Africa have lost ground in terms of share of world markets owing to internationalisation (Preston 1993). Also firms have sometimes over-reached themselves and diseconomies of scale have resulted.

In general, though, the accepted view is that world trade results in greater wealth and higher standards of living for most of the world's population; trade is therefore regarded as beneficial in terms of its economic benefits, and governments worldwide try to encourage it, within the limits of getting the best deal for their own countries. Table 2.5 shows some of the major initiatives undertaken in recent years to encourage world trade.

| Table 2.5 | World trade initiatives |

Name	Description
World Trade Organization	An ongoing set of international negotiations to reduce customs duties which act as a barrier to trade. Approximately 116 nations are involved in the talks, which were initiated after the Second World War under the title The General Agreement on Tariffs and Trade. Tariffs among industrialised nations fell from an average 40% in 1947 to approximately 5% at present.
European Union	This is a trading group of 27 countries that have eliminated customs duties between the member states. This has caused some complications, and will continue to do so for some time, but border controls are minimal (and in some cases non-existent). Eventually the EU is likely to become a federal superstate as more of the economic decision-making is centralised.
North American Free Trade Agreement (NAFTA)	Creating a customs union between the USA, Canada and Mexico, this agreement seeks to cancel all tariffs (customs duties) between the member states by 2010.
Mercosur	A **customs union** between the nations of South America, this has already resulted in passportless travel throughout the continent (citizens need only carry identity cards) and in removal of tariff barriers on most items.
Cairns Agreement (IMF)	This is an agreement on world agricultural production and prices; compliance with it has been patchy, but the signatories to the Agreement continue to negotiate
Association of South-East Asian Nations (ASEAN)	A six-member group that has agreed to establish a free trade area in South-East Asia in the early part of the twenty-first century.
International Monetary Fund (IMF)	The IMF acts as a stabilising influence on the world economy by injecting funds into national economies, on a loan basis, subject to special conditions regarding government economic policies. The IMF exists to turn round ailing economies.
World Bank	The World Bank exists to fund projects which reduce poverty in the Third World. It is owned and funded by major economies: the United States has the biggest share, then Japan, then Germany, then the UK, then France.

The thrust behind much government thinking worldwide is to reduce tariffs and increase trade, while at the same time establishing trading blocs which can stand up to each other. The dominance of the United States of America has clarified the thinking of smaller countries, and there is little doubt that the European Union, Mercosur and the Asia-Pacific Economic Forum will make significant contributions to world competition.

Most governments are in favour of **exporting** their own manufacturers' goods but would prefer to restrict **importing** if possible: this is to protect the **balance of payments**. Having more foreign currency coming in than is going out (a positive balance of payments) allows the government to keep interest rates down and also helps keep inflation down (a fuller explanation of the mechanisms by which this happens is beyond the scope of this book; further reading is given at the end of the chapter). This means that negotiations about reducing tariff barriers tend to be long-drawn-out as each government seeks to open up markets abroad while keeping out foreign competition.

Developing countries frequently impose tariff barriers on importers in order to protect their fledgling industries; unfortunately, this often results in these industries becoming inefficient since they do not need to compete with more efficient overseas manufacturers (Preston 1993). For example, Venezuela adopted an import substitution strategy in 1983 which included multiple exchange rates: an official rate, a rate for debt payment, a rate for essential exports, and a free market rate. Importers had to wait several months for foreign currency, only obtaining the balance after the goods had arrived. This was hardly efficient, nor did it help business confidence, but it did protect Venezuelan manufacturers. Unfortunately the failure of Latin American and African countries to agree to reduce tariffs with other countries meant that their exports became priced out of the market; while other countries developed effective international trading systems, the Third World was left behind (Preston 1993).

Governments also influence or control **exchange rates**; this means that exporters lose some control over prices, as the government controls the rate at which one currency is exchanged for another. Having a low-value currency will encourage exports in the short run, but also raises the price of imports; this can result in increased costs, which raise the prices anyway. Having a strong currency, on the other hand, may make exporting difficult and will probably suck in imports as the imported goods become cheaper than home-produced ones.

Culture

Cultural differences encompass religion, language, institutions, beliefs and behaviours that are shared by the members of a society. It is as well for marketers to take the advice of natives of the countries in which they hope to do business, since other people's cultural differences are not always obvious.

Classic examples of errors arising from language differences abound. The General Motors Nova brand name translates as 'no go' in Spanish; Gerber means 'to throw up' in colloquial French, creating problems for the baby food manufacturer of the same name; and Irish Mist liqueur had to be re-named for the German market since 'mist' means 'excrement' in German. Many cultural problems are more subtle, and have to do with the way things are said rather than the actual words used. In Japanese, 'yes' can mean 'yes, I understand' but not necessarily 'yes, I agree'. Portuguese has a total of seven different words for 'you', depending on the status and number of people being addressed.

Body language is also not universal. The American sign for 'OK', with the thumb and forefinger making a circle, is a rude gesture in Brazil (equivalent to sticking up the index and middle finger in Britain, or the extended middle finger in the US and most of Europe). Showing the soles of the feet is considered insulting in Thailand, and while Americans are usually very happy to hear about an individual's personal wealth and success, Australians are less likely to take kindly to somebody acting like a 'tall poppy' in this way.

Sometimes local superstitions affect buying behaviour. American high-rise hotels do not have a thirteenth floor – the floor numbers go directly from twelve to fourteen. In China, consumers do not like to buy products where the price ends in a four, because four is a number associated with death: Chinese people prefer to buy products whose prices end in eight, which is considered lucky, and associated with financial prosperity (Simmons and Schindler 2003).

In general marketers need to be wary of **ethnocentrism**, which is the tendency to believe that one's own culture is the 'right' one and that everybody else's is at best a poor imitation (Shimp and Sharma 1987). This is not an easy task for managers: most managers tend to underestimate the differences between the overseas market and the home market (Pedersen and Petersen 2004). This can be due to the fact that we tend to judge other cultures from the perspective of our own culture – this is called self-referencing, and is clearly difficult to avoid.

It can be easier to aim for countries where there is some **psychological proximity**. These are countries with some cultural aspects in common. For example, English-speaking countries have psychological proximity with each other; Spain has psychological proximity with most of Latin America; and the former Communist countries of Eastern European are close. Within countries with large migrant populations there may be subcultures that give insights into overseas markets: Australia is well placed to take advantage of Far Eastern markets and Greek markets as well as other English-speaking markets, and Brazil has good links with Germany as well as with Portugal, Angola and Mozambique. In an interesting reversal, Ireland also has good contacts in many countries owing to the Irish diaspora of the past 200 years.

In most West African countries tribal loyalties cross national borders, so that people from the same tribe might inhabit different countries. In a sense, this is paralleled in the Basque country of France and Spain, and in the language divide in Belgium, where Flemish speakers feel closer to their Dutch neighbours than to their Walloon compatriots, and Walloons feel closer to the French than to their Flemish neighbours.

From a marketer's viewpoint, cultural differences are probably reducing as consumers become more globally minded: foreign travel, the widespread globalisation of the entertainment media, and existing availability of foreign products in most economies have all served to erode the world's cultural differences (Ohmae 1989). Increasingly, marketers are able to identify distinct subcultures that transcend national boundaries, for example the world youth culture fuelled by media such as MTV (Steen 1995).

Political factors

The *political environment* of the target country will also affect the entry decision. Table 2.6 shows some of the issues.

Table 2.6	Political factors in international marketing
Political factor	**Explanation and implications**
Level of protectionism	Some governments need to protect their own industries from foreign competition, either because the country is trying to industrialise and the fledgling companies cannot compete (as in some developing nations), or because lack of investment has resulted in a run-down of industry (as in much of Eastern Europe). Sometimes this can be overcome by offering inward investment (to create jobs) or by agreeing to limit exports to the country until the new industries have caught up.
Degree of instability	Some countries are less politically stable than others, and may be subject to military takeover or civil war. Usually the exporter's government diplomatic service can advise on the level of risk attached to doing business in a particular country.
Relationship between the marketer's government and the foreign government	Sometimes disputes between governments can result in trade embargoes or other restrictions. Obviously this is particularly prevalent in the arms trade, but trade restrictions can be applied across the board to unfriendly countries. For example, the USA still has a trade ban with Cuba for many items; Greece and Turkey have restrictions on travel and trade; and trade restrictions exist between Zimbabwe and Britain.

Economic influences

The *economic environment* of the target country is more than the issue of whether the residents can afford to buy our goods. In some cases the level of **wealth concentration** is such that, although the average **per capita income** of the country is low, there is a large number of millionaires: India is an example of this, as is Brazil. Economic issues also encompass the public prosperity of the country: is there a well-developed road system, for example? Are telecommunications facilities adequate? Is the population sufficiently well educated to be able to use the products effectively?

A crucial economic issue is that of foreign exchange availability. If the target country does not have a substantial export market for its own products, it will not be able to import foreign products because potential importers will not be able to pay for the goods in the appropriate currency. This has been a problem in some countries in the Third World and in some Communist countries, and there has as a result been a return to **barter** and **countertrading**. Countertrading is the export of goods on the condition that the firm will import an equal value of other goods from the same market, and in the international context can be complex: for example, a firm may export mining machinery to China, be paid in coal, and then need to sell the coal on the commodities market to obtain cash (a **buy-back** deal). These complex arrangements are becoming much rarer as the world moves towards freely exchangeable currencies: barter and countertrade are inherently inefficient.

The *demographic environment* includes such factors as family size, degree to which the country has a rural as opposed to an urban population, and the migration patterns that shape the population. Migration patterns can make marked changes to the structure of a country's consumption: consumption of Indonesian food in the Netherlands, of Thai food in Australia, of Indian food in the United Kingdom, and of Algerian food in France are all much greater than can be accounted for by the respective ethnic minorities in those countries (Paulson-Box 1994). Marketers have played a part in this culture-swapping process to the extent that segmentation by ethnicity is no longer possible (Jamal 2003).

THE INTERNAL ENVIRONMENT

Internal publics are the employees of the company. Although employees are part of the internal environment rather than the external environment, activities directed at the external environment will often impinge on employee attitudes; likewise employee attitudes frequently impinge on the external publics. Sometimes employees convey a negative image of the organisation they work for, and this is bound to have an effect on the perceptions of the wider public.

The organisation's internal environment is a microcosm of the external environment. All organisations have employees; they will develop a corporate culture with its own language, customs, traditions and hierarchy. Sub-groups and individuals within the firm will have political agendas; pressure groups form; and the organisation has its own laws and regulations.

From the viewpoint of a marketer, the internal environment is as important as the external one, since the organisational culture, rules, hierarchy and traditions will inevitably be a major component of the organisation's public face. The members of the organisation can give a positive or negative image of the firm after they leave work for the day and interact with their families and friends, and even while in work they will usually come into contact with some of the firm's external publics. Since the members of those external publics will regard such communications as being authoritative, the effect is likely to be stronger than anything the marketing department can produce in terms of paid communications. In other words, if the company's staff speak badly about the company to outsiders, the outsiders are far more likely to believe those comments than to believe the company's promotional campaigns.

The days are long gone when the loyalty of staff could be commanded, and giving orders was all that was necessary to ensure obedience. Employees expect to have a degree of autonomy in their daily tasks, and do not feel any particular obligation towards an employer simply by reason of being employed. The employees of the organisation therefore constitute a market in their own right; the firm needs their loyalty and commitment, in exchange for which the staff are offered pay and security. Internal marketing is the process of ensuring (as far as possible) that employees know and understand the firm's strategic policies, and should feel that putting these policies into practice will be in their own best interests.

As we saw in Chapter 1, marketing can be a unifying force within the firm, giving the lead to each separate organisational function and providing staff with a single direction. Equally, it can be seen as a manipulative force, seeking to persuade people to act in ways which do not come naturally.

There is more on handling internal relationships (together with some techniques for communicating with the internal environments) in Chapter 9.

Case study 2
Rio Tinto

Despite its Spanish name, Rio Tinto is a British company (the name literally means Coloured River). Originally formed in 1873 to exploit copper mines in Huelva Province, Spain, the company has parallel roots in Australia, where the Consolidated Zinc Corporation was formed in 1905 for the purpose of extracting zinc from mine waste at Broken Hill.

In 1962 the two companies merged to form the Rio Tinto Zinc Corporation, at that time (as now) one of the world's largest mining and metals corporations. At the same time, the Australian interests of both companies were merged to create the CRA (formerly Cozinc Rio Tinto of Australia Ltd). The two companies finally combined in 1995, under a single Board of Directors.

During the boom years of the 1960s, when the global economy was expanding at a rapid rate and demand for minerals was high, RTZ developed new mining interests worldwide: copper from South Africa, uranium from Namibia, iron ore in Australia, copper in Papua New Guinea, coal in Indonesia and bauxite in New Zealand.

During the 1970s and early 1980s the company diversified, but a downturn in the world metals market during the 1980s led RTZ to divest itself of many of its new acquisitions, and return to its core business of mining and metal-related industries such as aluminium smelting. Eventually this led to the acquisition of Canadian aluminium producer Alcan in 2007, a move which made RTZ the world's largest aluminium producer.

Rio Tinto has not passed through its commercial history without attracting controversy. It has been accused of exploiting workers, of damaging the environment, of colluding with oppressive regimes, and of crushing union opposition. The Richard West (1972) book, *River of Tears*, painted a harsh picture of RTZ's practices. These accusations do not seem to worry Rio Tinto, however: even a lawsuit brought by Bougainevilleans alleging that the civil war there was sponsored by Rio Tinto in order to regain its mine has not caused the company any major setbacks.

Any large company attracts controversy, and mining (by its very nature) is likely to cause environmental damage, to have high levels of injury among its workforce, and also create the high levels of investment and profit which make the company a target for lawsuits and criticism by left-wing organisations. Rio Tinto's strategy statement says that the company seeks to maximise returns to shareholders by finding, mining and processing mineral reserves in a sustainable, ethically and socially responsible manner. The corporate values are expressed as follows:

> We undertake Rio Tinto's business with integrity, honesty and fairness at all times, building from a foundation of compliance with relevant local laws and regulations and international standards.

> We support free and fair competition. We promote the rule of law and the Group's high standards wherever we are in the world. We have introduced a compliance programme that all Group businesses are required to put in place. This is based on a continuously developing system of training, monitoring and procedural checks and balances.

> Safe, efficient and innovative suppliers and contractors are strategically important to the success of the Rio Tinto business units. Rio Tinto expects to participate in a fair and competitive marketplace, and to provide a fair evaluation and selection process that is applied consistently to all prospective suppliers.

As we progress through the twenty-first century, Rio Tinto is likely to be faced with many more problems – increasing protests from environmentalists, labour groups, anti-globalisation lobbyists and opportunists with an eye to the company's cash reserves will continue to occur, and at the same time dwindling mineral resources will place pressure on the company to look even further afield for its basic living. Meanwhile, the company is of course reliant on the industrial health of the world economy to create markets for metals and ores – without these, there will be no customers.

Questions

1 What might Rio Tinto do to reduce the problems it has from various pressure groups?
2 To what extent is Rio Tinto a market-orientated company?
3 What business environment issues affect Rio Tinto's ability to plan ahead?
4 What environmental opportunities might there be for Rio Tinto?
5 How does Rio Tinto demonstrate its commitment to social responsibility?

SUMMARY

The environment within which the marketing department is operating consists of both internal and external factors. Internal factors are what happens within the organisation; external factors are those operating outside the firm, and consist of the micro-environment and the macro-environment. Macro-environmental factors are largely uncontrollable by individual firms; in fact, it is difficult for marketers to have any influence on them, except in the case of very large firms or powerful trade organisations.

While it may be possible for the largest firms to influence the macro-environment by lobbying Parliament, or even by affecting the national culture directly, small and medium-sized firms cannot alone hope to make sufficient impact on the external environment to make any major changes. Therefore these marketers need to learn to work with, or around, the macro-environmental factors they find, rather than seek to make changes.

Since the marketing environment has profound effects on the organisation, marketing strategy begins with two main activities: analysis of the environment (perhaps by

STEP analysis) to see what threats and opportunities exist, and analysis of the firm's position within that environment and within itself (perhaps by SWOT analysis).

Here are the key points from this chapter:

- Businesses and other organisations do not operate in a vacuum.
- The micro-environment is easier to influence than the macro-environment, but both are impossible to control.
- The business should be defined from the customer's viewpoint; this will help identify a broader range of competitors.
- Customers should be grouped into segments so that scarce resources can be targeted to the most profitable areas (see Chapter 4).
- Close relationships with suppliers and intermediaries will be helpful in influencing the environment.
- Public relations is about creating favourable impressions with all the company's publics.
- Case law and EU law can both affect businesses, and are harder to predict since they are independent of national government.
- The socio-cultural environment changes, but slowly.
- Technology changes rapidly and will continue to do so; this both creates and destroys industries.
- Internal publics need special attention, since they are the 'front line' of the company's relationships with its environment.

CHAPTER QUESTIONS

1 Why is the external environment impossible to control?

2 What can SWOT analysis tell a firm about its environment?

3 Given that businesses are made up of people, how is it that the same people are included as part of the firm's internal environment?

4 What are the most important factors making up the micro-environment?

5 What are the main problems faced when dealing with the macro-environment?

Further reading

This is a somewhat narrow area, with few books dedicated solely to the marketing environment. Most marketing strategy books will go into greater detail than is the case here, but the only text which is dedicated to discussion of the marketing environment is Adrian Palmer and Bob Hartley's book, *The Business and Marketing Environment* (Maidenhead: McGraw-Hill, 1999).

For an overview of the international business environment, try *International Marketing: Strategy, Planning, Market Entry and Implementation* by Roger Bennett and Jim Blythe (London, Kogan Page, 2002). This text covers the mechanics of international and global marketing, with comprehensive sections on exporting, documentation and international shipping principles and practice.

References

Bell, D.: *The Coming of Post-industrial Society: A Venture in Social Forecasting* (London, Heinemann, 1974).

Chee, H. and Harris, R.: *Global Marketing Strategy* (London, Financial Times Pitman, 1988).

Cruijsen, H., Eding, H. and Gjatelma, T.: 'Demographic Consequences of Enlargement of the European Union with the 12 Candidate Countries'. Statistics Netherlands, Division of Social and Spatial Statistics, Project Group European Demography, January 2002.

European Commission: *The Social Situation in the European Union 2001* (Luxembourg, Office for Official Publications of the European Communities, 2001), pp. 201–17.

Jamal, Ahmed: 'Marketing in a multicultural world: the interplay of marketing, ethnicity and consumption', *European Journal of Marketing*, **37** (11) (2003), pp. 1599–1620.

Kotler, P.: 'Megamarketing', *Harvard Business Review* (March–April 1986), pp. 117–24.

Maucher, H.O.: 'The impact of the single European market on regional product and price differentiation – the example of the European food industry', in C. Halliburton and R. Hunerberg (eds) *European Marketing; Readings and Cases* (Wokingham, Addison Wesley, 1993).

Office for National Statistics: *Household Expenditure Survey*, 2003.

Ohmae, K: 'Managing in a borderless world', *Harvard Business Review* (May–June 1989), pp. 152–61.

Paulson-Box, Elaine: 'Adoption of ethnic food: a dietary innovation in the UK', *Proceedings of the Marketing in Education Group Conference*, 1994, p. 792.

Pedersen, Torbin and Petersen, Bent: 'Learning about foreign markets: are entrant firms exposed to a "shock effect"?', *Journal of International Marketing*, **12** (1) (2004), pp. 103–23.

Porter, M.E.: 'How competitive forces shape strategy', *Harvard Business Review*, **57** (2) (1990), pp. 137–45.

Preston, Jill (ed.): *International Business: Text and Cases* (London, Pitman Publishing, 1993), p. 31.

Shimp, Terence and Sharma, Subhash: 'Consumer ethnocentrism; construction and validation of CETSCALE', *Journal of Marketing Research* (August 1987), pp. 280–9.

Simmons, C. Lee and Schindler, Robert M.: 'Cultural superstitions and the price endings used in Chinese advertising', *Journal of International Marketing*, **11** (2) (2003), pp. 101–11.

Steen, J.: 'Now they're using suicide to sell jeans', *Sunday Express* (26 March 1995).

West, Richard: *River of Tears* (London, Earth Island Publishers Ltd, 1972).

Royal Enfield

Royal Enfield is an Indian-based manufacturer of motorcycles. The original Royal Enfield company was British, but the Indian side of the business was taken over after Indian independence in the late 1940s. The technology is basically unchanged since the 1950s, so the main appeal to a British customer base is that of nostalgia. This is different from the appeal in India, where the brand is regarded as an upmarket, large motorcycle. This has dramatic implications for the company's promotional policy.

Different policies have to be adopted for different countries in Europe: the bike's appeal cannot be solely based on price, even though it is a relatively cheap bike in Europe. Within Europe, the biggest markets are the UK and Germany, both well-established biking nations, and Europe now accounts for 10% of sales. The company is well aware that it is competing with leisure products – nobody buys a Royal Enfield to commute. Typical buyers are likely to be men in their fifties who had motorbikes when they were young, and are reassured by the Enfield's old-fashioned appearance and basic technology.

The basic platform for Royal Enfield in the UK is the concept of 'true motorcycling'. The fun aspects are emphasised, and the 'back to one's youth' feel is foremost.

Ashish Joshi, Director, Royal Enfield Motorcycles Europe

Watch the video clip, then try to answer the following questions. The answers are on the companion website.

Questions

1 How does perception affect Royal Enfield's marketing?

2 What are the main drivers for Royal Enfield consumers in the UK?

3 What is the role of sociology theory in Royal Enfield's success in the UK as compared to India?

3

Consumer and buyer behaviour

Objectives

After reading this chapter you should be able to:

- explain how consumers make purchasing decisions;
- describe the differences between the ways in which professional buyers work and the ways consumers make decisions;
- explain how consumers develop a perceptual map of the product alternatives;
- develop ways of dealing with customer complaints.

INTRODUCTION

This chapter is about how buyers think and behave when making purchasing decisions. Buyers fall into two categories: *consumers*, who are buying for their own and for their family's consumption, and *industrial buyers*, who are buying for business use. In each case, the marketer is concerned with both the practical needs of the buyer or the buyer's organisation, and the emotional or personal needs of the individual.

CONSUMER BEHAVIOUR

The consumer decision-making process follows the stages shown in Figure 3.1.

Problem recognition

Problem recognition arises when the consumer realises that there is a need for some item. This can come about through **assortment depletion** (where the consumer's stock of goods has been used up or worn out) or **assortment extension** (which is where the consumer feels the need to add some new item to the assortment of possessions). At this point the consumer has only decided to seek a solution to a problem, perhaps by buying a category of product. The needs felt can be categorised as either **utilitarian** (concerned with the functional attributes of the product) or **hedonic** (concerned with the pleasurable or aesthetic aspects of the product) (Holbrook and Hirschmann 1982). The current view is that there is a balance between the two types of need in most decisions (Engel *et al*. 1995).

An internal stimulus, or **drive**, comes about because there is a gap between the **actual** and **desired states**. For example, becoming hungry leads to a drive to find food: the hungrier the individual becomes, the greater the drive becomes, but once the hunger has been satisfied the individual can move on to satisfying other needs. For marketers, the actual state of the individual is usually not susceptible to influence, so much marketing activity is directed at influencing the desired state (e.g. 'Don't you deserve a better car?'). Thus drives are generated by encouraging a revision of the desired state. The higher the drive level (i.e. the greater the gap between actual and desired states), the more open the individual is to considering new ways of satisfying the need: in simple terms, a starving man will try almost any kind of food.

Figure 3.1 Consumer decision-making

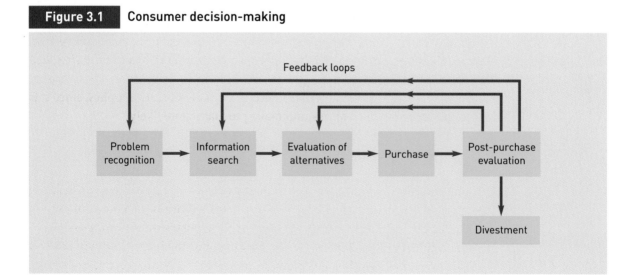

It is, of course, stimulating and enjoyable to allow gaps to develop between the desired and actual states: working up a thirst before going for a drink makes the experience more pleasurable, for example. Each individual has an **optimal stimulation level** (OSL), which is the point at which the drive is enjoyable and challenging, without being uncomfortable. OSL is subjective: research shows that those with high OSLs like novelty and risk-taking, whereas those with low OSLs prefer the tried and tested. Those with high OSLs also tend to be younger (Raju 1980).

Drives lead on to **motivation**, which is the reason why people take action. The level of motivation will depend on the desirability of the end goal, and the ease of achieving the end goal; motivations are subjective, so it is difficult to infer motivation from behaviour. Few actions take place as a result of a single motivation, and sometimes a motivation may not even be apparent to the individual experiencing it: in other words, some motivations operate below the conscious level.

Information search

Having become motivated to seek a solution to the need problem, consumers engage in two forms of information search.

- The **internal search** involves remembering previous experiences of the product category, and thinking about what he/she has heard about the product category.
- The **external search** involves shopping around, reading manufacturers' literature and advertisements, and perhaps talking to friends about the proposed purchase.

For most purchases, the internal search is probably sufficient. For example, a consumer who needs to buy biscuits will easily remember what his or her favourite brand tastes like, and will also remember where they are on the supermarket shelf. When buying a new hi-fi set, on the other hand, a fairly extensive information search might be carried out, reading manufacturers' brochures and looking around the hi-fi shops. The purpose of this exercise is to reduce risk; buying the wrong brand of biscuits involves very little risk, since the financial commitment is low, but buying the wrong hi-fi could prove to be an expensive mistake. For this reason many retailers offer a no-quibble return policy, since this helps to reduce the level of risk and make purchase more likely.

Evaluation of alternatives

Having found out about several competing brands, the consumer will *evaluate* the alternatives, based on the information collected or remembered. Too much choice leads to decision paralysis, in which the person finds it impossible to choose (Shankar *et al.* 2006), so in the first instance the individual will select a **consideration set**, which is the group of products that would most closely meet the need. Typically a consumer will use **cut-offs** to establish a consideration set: these are the minimum and maximum acceptable values for the product characteristics. For example, a consumer will typically have a clear idea of the acceptable price range for the product. (This price range might have a minimum as well as a maximum; the individual may not want something that is perceived as being cheap and nasty.) **Signals** are important when making choices; a particular price-tag, a brand name, even the retailer will have some effect on the consumer's perception of the product. Price is frequently used as an indicator of quality, for example, but this can be reduced in the presence of other signals. The purpose is to reduce confusion, which comes from three sources: similarity, information overload and ambiguity. Confusion and information overload leads to decision postponement, and also to loyalty behaviour – sticking with the tried and tested rather than risking a mistake with something new (Walsh *et al.* 2007; Wang 2006).

Occasionally the use of cut-offs eliminates all the possibilities from the consideration set, in which case the consumer will have to revise the rules. This can result in the creation of a hierarchy of rules. For marketers, the challenge is often to ensure that the product becomes a 'member' of the consideration set.

The decision-making process appears lengthy and complex as stated here, yet most of us make several purchasing decisions in a day without going through a lengthy decision-making process. This is because most of us use **heuristics**, or decision-making rules, for most purchases. These are simple 'if . . . then' rules that reduce risk by using previous experience as a guide. For example, an international traveller in a strange city might have a heuristic of eating only in restaurants that are full of local people, on the grounds that the inhabitants of the city would know which are the best restaurants. Heuristics divide into three categories:

- *search heuristics*, which are concerned with rules for finding out information;
- *evaluation heuristics*, which are about judging product offerings; and
- *choice heuristics*, which are about evaluation of alternatives.

The decision-making process may contain a number of **interrupts** – points at which the search is temporarily suspended. Interrupts come in four categories:

- **environmental stimuli**, which include in-store promotions (perhaps eye-catching posters for other products);
- **affective states**, which include physiological needs (the sudden need to go to the toilet or to have a coffee);
- *unexpected information*, for example a change of layout in the shop or some change in the product attributes; and
- *conflicts*, which occur when the consumer realises that the original decision-making plan cannot be followed, or an alternative plan appears that is not consistent with the original plan.

For example, an approach–approach conflict occurs when a second product is presented that would probably do the job just as well. This means that the consumer has to make a comparison, and the search pattern is temporarily suspended. An approach–avoidance conflict might arise when the consumer finds out the product is much more expensive than expected; an avoidance–avoidance conflict might arise when the two alternatives are equally distasteful (an example might be the reluctance to spend money on new shoes while at the same time not wanting to be embarrassed by wearing old ones).

The effect of the interrupt will depend on the consumer's interpretation of the event. Sometimes the interrupt activates a new end goal (for example, a long shopping trip might be transformed into a search for somewhere to sit down and have a coffee), or perhaps a new choice heuristic might be activated (for example, meeting a friend who recommends a brand). Sometimes the interrupt is serious enough for the search to be abandoned altogether; here the strength of the interrupt is important. Clearly a sudden desire for a cup of tea will not permanently interrupt a search process, but the news that one has lost one's job very well might.

In most cases, consumers will resume the interrupted problem-solving process once the stimulus has been absorbed and accepted or rejected.

Purchase

The actual *purchase* comes next; the consumer will locate the required brand, and perhaps choose a retailer he or she has faith in, and will also select an appropriate payment method.

Post-purchase evaluation

Post-purchase evaluation refers to the way the consumer decides whether the product purchase has been a success or not. This process usually involves a comparison between what the consumer was expecting to get, and what was actually purchased, although sometimes new information obtained after the purchase will also colour the consumer's thinking (Oliver 1980). Before the purchase, the consumer will have formed expectations of the product's capabilities in terms of

- **equitable performance** (what can be reasonably expected given the cost and effort of obtaining the product);
- **ideal performance** (what the consumer hopes the product will do); and
- **expected performance** (which is what the product probably will do).

Sometimes this evaluation leads to **post-purchase dissonance**, when the product has not lived up to expectations, and sometimes to **post-purchase consonance** when the product is as expected or better. In either event, the consumer will feed back this information into memory, to inform the internal search for next time.

One of the more interesting aspects of dissonance is that there is evidence to show that a small discrepancy between expectation and outcome may provoke a bigger change in attitude than a large discrepancy. This is because a small discrepancy may force the consumer to confront the purchase behaviour without offering a ready explanation for it: for example, a general feeling of being unhappy with a new car might crystallise around its poor acceleration (a major problem), and the consumer might simply shrug and accept this as part of the deal. On the other hand, if the only immediately identifiable problem is that the car's ashtray is poorly positioned, this may lead the owner to look for other faults with the car (and, of course, find them).

Consumers will usually act to reduce post-purchase dissonance. There are four general approaches to doing this:

1 Ignore the dissonant information and concentrate on the positive aspects of the product.

2 Distort the dissonant information (perhaps by telling oneself that the product was, after all, the cheap version).

3 Play down the importance of the issue.

4 Change one's behaviour.

From a marketing viewpoint, it is generally better to ensure that the consumer has accurate information about the product beforehand so as to avoid post-purchase dissonance, but if it occurs then marketers need to reduce it in some way. Research has shown that only one-third of consumers will complain or seek redress; the remainder will boycott the goods in future, or simply complain to others, either of which is a non-optimal outcome from the viewpoint of the marketer (Day *et al.* 1981). Consumers express dissatisfaction in one of three ways:

- **voice responses**, in which the customer comes back and complains.

- **private responses**, in which the consumer complains to friends. In some cultures this is more likely than voice responses (Ngai *et al.* 2007). The possibility of a repeated violation of trust appears to be more important in voice responses than the magnitude of the violation (Sijun and Huff 2007) which has implications for complaint-handling.

- **third-party responses**, which may include complaints to consumer organisations, trade associations and TV consumer programmes, or even legal action (Singh 1988).

The most effective way of reducing post-purchase dissonance is to provide a product that meets the customer's expectations. This is partly a function for the manufacturer, but is also a problem for the retailer to address since it should be possible to ensure that the consumer's needs are fully understood before a recommendation about a product is made. As a fall-back position, though, every effort should be made to encourage the consumer to complain if things do not come up to expectations. This is why waiters always ask if the meal is all right, and why shops frequently have no-quibble money-back guarantees. Ferry companies and airlines provide customer comment slips, and some marketers even make follow-up telephone calls to consumers to check that the product is meeting expectations. There is more on these techniques in Chapter 5.

Research shows that the perceptions of employees about the shared values of the firm, and especially their view of how fair the firm is in its dealings, are reflected in the way in which they deal with customer complaints. This in turn is reflected in the ways customers perceive the complaint-handling process (Maxham and Netemeyer 2003).

It is important that dissatisfied customers are allowed to voice their complaint fully, and that the appropriate compensation is negotiated in the light of:

- the strength of the complaint;
- the degree of blame attaching to the supplier, from the consumer's viewpoint;
- the legal and moral relationship between the supplier and the consumer.

A consistent failure to solve problems raised by post-purchase dissonance will, ultimately, lead to irreparable damage to the firm's reputation. The evidence from research carried out by the Coca-Cola Corporation is that consumers whose complaints are resolved satisfactorily tend to become more loyal than those consumers who did not have a complaint in the first place. In the last analysis, it is almost always cheaper to keep an existing customer than it is to attract a new one, and therefore it makes sense for suppliers to give customers every chance to express problems with the service or product provision. Customer retention is, according to one research exercise, associated with complaint-handling procedures – and nothing else (Ang and Buttle 2006).

Critical thinking

It sounds as if we are going back to the idea that the customer is always right. What about people who deliberately find fault with everything, in the hope of winning some concession from the company? What about simple misunderstandings, where someone has bought a product and then decided it wasn't what they wanted after all? And what about the people who buy a new item of clothing, wear it to go out for the evening, then bring it back the next day?

Surely we aren't expected to put up with fraud, lies and stupidity! Or is that a small price to pay for looking after the genuine cases – after all, the customers may not always be right, but they are always the customers!

Divestment

Finally, the **divestment** stage refers to the way the consumer disposes of the product after use. This could be as simple as throwing an empty food container into the bin, or it could be as complex as the trade-in of a second-hand car. This stage is of increasing importance to marketers, both in terms of green marketing (the environmental issues raised) and in terms of the possibility of making sales of new products (for example on trade-in deals). There is more on divestment in Chapter 12, in relation to the environmental impact of the disposal of packaging and used products.

This model of the decision-making process appears somewhat long and involved, but in practice most purchasing decisions are habitual, and the process is carried out quickly and virtually automatically. Table 3.1 shows a comparison of a non-habitual purchase and a habitual purchase, showing how each stage in the decision-making model is carried out.

Table 3.1   Habitual *v* non-habitual purchase behaviour

Stage in the process	New DVD player	Can of tuna
Problem recognition	The old DVD player doesn't have a facility for recording DVDs, and for some reason it suddenly skips to another part of the movie.	We used the last can yesterday, and we're going to the supermarket tonight.
Information search	Ask a few friends, see what they've got. Go online to a comparison site. Visit some local electronics stores (predominantly an external search).	Remember the brand that we like (predominantly an internal search).
Evaluation of alternatives	Discuss the options with one's husband or wife. Perhaps ask a knowledgeable friend for advice.	Find the right one on the shelves. Perhaps look at the Prince's brand, or even the store's own-brand.
Purchase	Return to the store or the website and make the purchase. Perhaps use a credit card to spread the cost.	Put the can in the basket and run it through the checkout with everything else. Possibly (if we're desperate for tuna) buy it from the corner shop.
Post-purchase evaluation	Try recording a movie from the TV. Judge the ease of use of the equipment, and the quality of recording and playback. Decide on aspects such as reliability as time goes on. File the information away, or pass it on to friends as necessary.	Eat the tuna. Was it up to the usual standard? If so, no further action. If not, perhaps go back to the shop and complain, or perhaps buy a different brand in future.
Divestment	When the DVD player becomes obsolete, sell it on eBay, give it to a friend, or simply throw it away.	Throw the empty can into the bin or take it for recycling.

PERCEPTION

Human senses constantly feed information into the brain; the amount of stimulation this involves would seriously overload the individual's system if the information were not filtered in some way. People therefore quickly learn to abstract information from the environment; the noise from a railway line near a friend's home might seem obvious to you, but your host is probably unaware of it. In effect, the brain is automatically selecting what is relevant and what is not, and for this reason the information being used by the brain does not provide a complete view of the world.

The gaps in the world-view thus created are filled in by the individual's imagination and experience. The cognitive map of the world is affected by the following factors:

- *Subjectivity*: the existing world-view of the individual.

- *Categorisation*: the pigeonholing of information. This usually happens through a 'chunking' process, whereby information is grouped into associated items. For example, a particular tune might make someone recall a special evening out from some years ago.

- *Selectivity*: the degree to which the individual's brain has selected from the environment. This is also a subjective phenomenon; some people are more selective than others.

- *Expectation*: the process of interpreting later information in a specific way. For example, look at this series of letters and numbers:

$$\mathcal{A\ B\ C\ D\ E\ F\ G\ H\ I}$$

$$10\ 11\ 12\ 13\ 14\ 15\ 16$$

In fact, the number 13 appears in both series, but would be interpreted as a B in the series of letters because that is what the brain is being led to expect.

- *Past experience*: this leads us to interpret information in the light of existing knowledge. This is also known as the **law of primacy**. The sound of sea birds might make us think of a day at the beach, but could in fact be part of an advertisement's soundtrack.

In practice, people develop a model of how the world works and make decisions based on the model. Since each individual's model differs slightly from every other individual's model, it is sometimes difficult for marketers to know how to approach a given person.

One of the problems for marketers is that the perception the consumers have of marketing communications may not be what was intended. For example, fast-paced advertisements on television attract people's attention involuntarily, but have little effect on people's voluntary attention, so the message is often lost.

Furthermore, a fast pace focuses attention on the style of the advertisement at the expense of its message (Bolls *et al.* 2003). Likewise, people often 'straighten up' gay imagery in TV shows or advertising if they find it embarrassing: in other words, they re-interpret the imagery to find a different explanation (Borgerson *et al.* 2006).

INFLUENCES ON THE BUYING DECISION

The main influences on the buying decision are of three types:

- *personal factors* are features of the consumer that affect the decision process;
- *psychological factors* are elements of the consumer's mental processes; and
- *social factors* are those influences from friends and family that influence decision-making.

Personal factors are shown in Table 3.2.

Involvement can be a major factor in consumer decision-making. Consumers often form emotional attachments to products, and most people would be familiar with the feeling of having fallen in love with a product – even when the product itself is hopelessly impractical. Involvement can also operate at a cognitive level, though; the outcome of the purchase may have important practical consequences for the consumer. For example, a rock climber may feel highly involved in the purchase of a climbing-rope, since the consequences of an error could be fatal. Whether this is a manifestation of a logical thought process regarding the risk to life and limb, or whether it is an emotional process regard-

Table 3.2 Personal factors in the buying decision

Personal factor	Explanation
Demographic factors	Individual characteristics such as age, gender, ethnic origin, income, family life cycle and occupation. These are often used as the bases for segmentation (see Chapter 4).
Situational factors	Changes in the consumer's circumstances. For example, a pay rise might lead the consumer to think about buying a new car; conversely, being made redundant might cause the consumer to cancel an order for a new kitchen.
Level of involvement	Involvement concerns the degree of importance the consumer attaches to the product and purchasing decision. For example, one consumer may feel that buying the right brand of coffee is absolutely essential to the success of a dinner-party, where another consumer might not feel that this matters at all. Involvement is about the emotional attachment the consumer has for the product.

ing a feeling of confidence about the product, would be hard to determine. People also become involved with companies and become champions for them (Bhattacharya and Sen 2003). Customers are often swayed by their relationship with the people who work for the firms they buy from: research shows that the relationship with the dealer is more important than the price when buying a new car (Oederkerken-Schroder *et al.* 2003).

Psychological factors in the decision-making process are as shown in Table 3.3. Consumers' attitudes to products can be complex. They vary according to:

- **valence** – whether the attitude is positive, negative or neutral;
- **extremity** – the strength of the attitude;
- **resistance** – the degree to which the attitude can be changed by outside influences;
- **persistence** – the degree to which the attitude erodes over time; and
- **confidence** – the level at which the consumer believes the attitude is correct.

People who are particularly knowledgable ('savvy' consumers) are usually competent in the use of technology, good at interpersonal networking both in person and online, they are marketing-literate, are empowered by their own consumer

256

Table 3.3   Psychological factors in the buying decision

Psychological factor	Explanation
Perception	This is the way people build up a view of the world. Essentially, this process of selection or analysis means that each person has an incomplete picture of the world; the brain therefore fills in the gaps by a process of synthesis using hearsay, previous experience, imagination, etc. Marketers are able to fill some of the gaps through the communication process, but will come up against the problem of breaking through the selection and analysis process.
Motives	The internal force that encourages the consumer towards a particular course of action. Motivation is a vector; it has both intensity and direction.
Ability and knowledge	A consumer who is, for example, a beginner at playing the violin is unlikely to spend thousands of pounds on a Stradivarius. Ability therefore affects some buying decisions. Likewise, pre-existing knowledge of a product category or brand will also affect the way the consumer approaches the decision. Pre-existing knowledge is difficult for a marketer to break down; it is much better to try to add to the consumer's knowledge wherever possible.
Attitude	Attitude has three components: **cognition**, which is to do with conscious thought processes; **affect**, which is about the consumer's emotional attachment to the product; and **conation**, which is about planned courses of behaviour. For example, 'I love my Volkswagen (affect) because it's never let me down (cognition). I'll definitely buy another (conation)'. Conations are only intended actions – they do not always lead to action, since other factors might interrupt the process.
Personality	The traits and behaviours that make each person unique. Personalities change very slowly, if at all, and can be regarded as constant for the purposes of marketing. Typically marketers aim for specific personality types, such as the gregarious, the competitive, the outgoing or the sporty.

effectiveness, and they know what to expect from firms (Macdonald and Uncles 2007). These personal characteristics make them efficient and effective at getting what they want from firms.

It should be noted that the conation component of attitude (see Table 3.3) is not necessarily consistent with subsequent behaviour; a consumer's intentions about future behaviour do not always materialise, if only because of the existence of interrupts. For example, an individual with a grievance against a bank may intend to move his/her account to a different bank, but find that the difficulties of switching the account would create too much paperwork to be worthwhile.

The traditional view of attitude is that affect towards an object is mediated by cognition; Zajonc and Markus (1985) challenged this view and asserted that affect can arise without prior cognition. In other words, it is possible to develop a 'gut feeling' about something without conscious evaluation.

Attitude contains elements of belief (knowledge of attributes) and opinion (statements about a product) but is neither. Belief is neutral, in that it does not imply attraction or repulsion, whereas attitude has direction; and unlike opinion, attitudes do not need to be stated.

From the marketer's viewpoint, attitudes are important since they often precede behaviour. Clearly a positive attitude towards a firm and its products is more likely to lead to purchase of the firm's products than a negative attitude. There is, however, some evidence to show that people often behave first, then form attitudes afterwards (Fishbein 1972) and therefore some car manufacturers find that it is worthwhile to give special deals to car rental companies and driving schools so that consumers can try the vehicles before forming their attitudes. Trial is considerably more powerful than advertising in forming attitudes (Smith and Swinyard 1983).

Social factors

Social factors influence consumers through:

- **normative compliance** – the pressure exerted on the individual to conform and comply;
- **value-expressive influence** – the need for psychological association with a particular group; and
- **informational influence** – the need to seek information from a group about the product category being considered.

Of the three, normative compliance is probably the most powerful, and works because the individual finds that acting in one way leads to the approval of friends or family, whereas acting in a different way leads to the disapproval of friends and family. This process favours a particular type of behaviour as a result. Good moral behaviour is probably the result of normative compliance.

Peer-group pressure is an example of normative compliance. The individual's peer group (a group of equals) will expect a particular type of behaviour, including (probably) some purchase behaviour. For example, most cigarette smokers began to smoke as a result of pressure from their friends when they were young teenagers. The desire to be a fully accepted member of the group is far stronger than any health warnings.

The main source of these pressures is **reference groups**. These are the groups of friends, colleagues, relatives and others whose opinions the individual values. Table 3.4 gives a list of types of reference group. The groups are not mutually exclusive; a formal group can also be a secondary group, and so forth.

Roles

The **roles** we play are also important in decision-making. Each of us plays many different roles in the course of our lives (in fact, in the course of a day) and will buy products to aid us accordingly (Goffman 1969). Somebody who is to be best

Table 3.4 Reference group influences

Reference group	Explanation
Primary groups	The people we see most often. Family, friends, close colleagues. A primary group is small enough to allow face-to-face contact on a regular, perhaps daily, basis. These groups have the strongest influence.
Secondary groups	People we see occasionally, and with whom we have a shared interest: for example, the members of a golf club or a trade association. These groups sometimes have formal rules that members must adhere to in their business dealings or hobbies, and may also have informal traditions (e.g. particular clothing or equipment) that influence buying decisions.
Aspirational groups	The groups to which we wish we belonged. These groups can be very powerful in influencing behaviour because the individual has a strong drive towards joining; this is the source of value-expressive influences. These groups can be particularly influential in fashion purchases.
Dissociative groups	The groups the individual does *not* want to be associated with. This makes the individual behave in ways opposite to those of the group: for example, somebody who does not wish to be thought of as a football hooligan might avoid going to football matches altogether.
Formal groups	Groups with a known, recorded membership list. Often these groups have fixed rules: a professional body will lay down a code of conduct, for example.
Informal groups	Less structured, and based on friendship. There are no formalities to joining; one merely has to fit in with the group's joint ideals.
Automatic groups	The groups we belong to by virtue of age, race, culture or education. These are groups that we do not join voluntarily, but they do influence our behaviour: for example, a woman of 45 will not choose clothes that make her look like 'mutton dressed as lamb'. Likewise, expatriates often find that they miss food from home, or seek out culture-specific goods of other types.

man at a wedding will choose a suitable suit, either to buy or to hire, to avoid looking ridiculous or otherwise spoiling the day. In terms of longer-lasting roles, the role of Father will dictate purchasing behaviour on behalf of children; the role of Lover may dictate buying flowers or wearing perfume; the role of Friend might mean buying a gift or a round of drinks; the role of Daughter might mean buying a Mother's Day present. In some immigrant families, parental roles involve negotiating cultural boundaries as well (Lindredge and Hogg 2006).

Family roles influence decision-making far beyond the normative compliance effects. Frequently different members of the family take over the role of buyer for specific product categories; the husband may make the main decisions about the car and its accessories and servicing, while the wife makes the main decisions about the decor of the home. Recent research shows that some convenience foods can empower mothers to take control of their 'caretaker' role within the family, provided marketers can remove the guilt feelings many women feel about using convenience foods (Carrigan and Szmigin 2006). Older children may decide on food, choosing the healthy or environmentally friendly alternatives, and often help their parents to learn about new products (Ekstrom 2007).

In terms of its functions as a reference group, the family differs from other groups in the following respects:

- *Face-to-face contact* on a daily basis.
- *Shared consumption* of such items as food, housing, car, TV sets, other household durables.
- *Subordination of individual needs* to the common welfare. There is never a solution that will suit everybody.
- *Purchasing agents* will be designated to carry out the purchasing of some items. As the number of working parents grows, pre-teens and young teens are taking an ever-increasing role in family shopping.

Conflict resolution within the family decision-making unit is usually more important than it would be for an individual, since there are more people involved. Whereas an individual might have difficulty in choosing between two equally attractive holiday destinations, discussions about family holidays are inevitably much more difficult since each family member will have his or her own favourite idea on a holiday destination or activity. There is likely to be a degree of negotiation, and even small children quickly develop skills in negotiating, justifying the benefits of a particular choice, forming coalitions with other family members and compromising where necessary (Thomson *et al.* 2007).

Culture can have a marked effect: African cultures tend to be male-dominated, whereas European and North American cultures show a more egalitarian pattern of decision-making (Green *et al.* 1983). This may be because decision-making becomes more egalitarian when both partners earn money outside the home (Filiatrault and Brent Ritchie 1980).

Decision-making stage also affects the roles of the family in the decision: problem recognition may come from any family member, whereas information search and product evaluation may be undertaken by different members. For example, the father may notice that the teenage son needs new football boots, the son might ask around for types, and the mother might decide which type falls within the family's budget.

Four kinds of marital role specialisation have been identified:

- *wife dominant*, where the wife has most say in the decision;

- *husband dominant*, where the husband plays the major role;

- *syncratic or democratic*, where the decision is arrived at jointly; and

- *autonomic,* where the decision is made entirely independently of the partner (Davies and Rigaux 1974).

Marketers need to know which type of specialisation is most likely to occur in the target market, since this will affect the style and content of promotional messages; for example, some advertising in the United Kingdom has tended to portray men as being incompetent at household tasks, despite evidence that men are taking a more active role in housework (Dwek 1996).

In most industrialised countries the family is undergoing considerable changes because of the rising divorce rate and the increasing propensity for couples to live together without marrying. In the above role specialisations, the terms 'husband' and 'wife' apply equally to unmarried partners.

Children have an increasing role in purchasing decisions: 'pester power' often results in increased family purchases of particular brands of chocolate, pizza, burgers and snack foods (Dwek 1995). Consequently, marketers often try to reach children aged between 5 and 12 through the use of sponsorship of teaching materials, free samples and sponsorship of prizes in schools (Burke 1995).

Children sometimes have greater influence on the family purchasing decisions than do the parents themselves, for the following reasons:

- Often they do the shopping, since both parents are out at work.

- They watch more TV than do their parents, so they are more knowledgeable about products.

- They tend to be more attuned to consumer issues, and have the time to shop around for (for example) environmentally friendly products.

- Parents are often concerned about the image the child presents: poor families, in particular, go to great lengths to ensure that their children are not embarrassed by poverty (Hamilton and Catterall 2006).

Purchasing behaviour is also affected by people's identity – in other words their view of themselves. The more closely the purchasing behaviour fits with the person's identity, the more likely it is to occur; this is particularly important in non-profit marketing such as charitable donations or participation in voluntary work, where the exchange involves individuals and is often based on social exchanges (Arnett *et al.* 2003). For some women, buying things for a new baby reinforces their own role as mother: research shows that purchase of a pram carries a public signal meaning, a private signal meaning, an experiential meaning and a role embrace. Each of these aspects contributes to the mother's self-image (Thomsen and Sorensen 2006).

IMPULSE BUYING

Impulse purchases are not based on any plan, and usually happen as the result of a sudden confrontation with a stimulus.

Pure impulse is based on the novelty of the product. Seeing something new may prompt the consumer to buy it just to try it. **Reminder impulse** acts when the consumer suddenly realises that something has been left off the shopping-list. **Suggestion impulse** arises when confronted with a product that meets a previously unfelt need, and **planned impulse** occurs when the consumer has gone out to meet a specific need, but is prepared to be swayed by what is on special offer.

For example, someone may be on a shopping trip to buy a new jacket for a weekend dinner party. In the shop he notices a rack of bow ties, and buys one because he has never owned one before (pure impulse). Next he remembers that he has not got a suitable summer shirt, so he picks one up from the counter (reminder impulse), and near it he sees a rack of cotton trousers which are on offer (suggestion impulse). Finally he sees a safari jacket which, although it is not the style he was thinking of, is actually ideal for the job so he buys it (planned impulse). Most shoppers are familiar with these situations, and indeed they commonly occur when browsing in supermarkets.

The purchase process itself is an important part of the benefits consumers get from consumption; research has shown that satisfaction with the process relates to the desire to participate in future purchases (Tanner 1996).

INDUSTRIAL BUYER BEHAVIOUR

Industrial buyers differ from consumers in that they are (at least theoretically) more formalised in their buying behaviour. The major areas where organisational buying differs from consumer buying are as follows:

- Bigger order values in terms of finance and quantity.
- Reciprocity; the firms may buy each other's products as part of a negotiated deal.
- Fewer buyers, because there are fewer firms than there are individuals.

- More people in the decision process.
- Fewer sales in terms of the number of deals.
- More complex techniques exist for buying and for negotiating.

Organisational buyers are buying in order to meet the organisation's needs, but it should also be remembered that they have their personal needs. These might be a need for *prestige,* a need for *career security,* for *friendship and social needs,* and other personal factors such as the satisfaction of driving a hard bargain, or the buyer's personality, attitudes and beliefs (Powers 1991). The astute marketer, and particularly the astute salesperson, will not ignore these personal needs of the buyers.

Critical thinking

Are professional buyers really so easily swayed by their personal needs? After all, they have their careers to think about – surely that implies a certain amount of care about how they behave, and showing favouritism to one supplier over another almost smacks of corruption!

Of course, we are all human – and we each bring our humanity to our working day, so maybe we shouldn't expect buyers to be any different from the rest of us.

Regarding the organisation's needs, however, the chief considerations of most buyers appear to revolve around quality, delivery, service and price (Green and Wind 1968). This often means that buyers will be working to a set of *specifications* about the products, and will probably use some or all of the formal techniques shown in Table 3.5.

The industrial purchase task might be a *new task,* in which case the buyer will need to adopt extensive problem-solving behaviour. The vendor has the opportunity of establishing a relationship which might last for many years, however. New-task situations will often involve the greatest amount of negotiation, since there is little (if any) previous experience to draw on.

Straight re-buy tasks are routine; the buyer is simply placing an order for the same products in the same quantities as last time. This requires very little thought or negotiation on the part of either buyer or seller. Often these deals are conducted over the telephone rather than spending time and money on a face-to-face meeting.

Modified re-buy involves some change in the purchase order, for example a larger order value or a different delivery schedule. Sometimes the re-buy can be modified by the salesperson, for example by suggesting that the buyer orders a slightly larger value of goods than usual, or by altering the delivery schedule in some way. In circumstances where the two firms have an ongoing relationship, buyers will often track the performance of their suppliers over a long period of time; buying firms that monitor their suppliers effectively can gain real competitive advantage, because they can control their supply of inputs much better

Table 3.5 Industrial buyers' methods

Method	Explanation
Description	Managers within the organisation lay down exactly what is required and the buyer is given the brief of finding the best supplier. The buyer might, for example, be asked to find a supplier of steel bolts. He or she will then ask manufacturers to quote prices, and will make a judgement based on price and delivery reliability.
Inspection	This is commonly carried out for variable goods, such as second-hand plant and equipment. Car dealers will usually inspect the cars before buying, for example.
Sampling	Commonly used for agricultural products. A buyer might sample, say, wool from an Australian sheep-station and fix a price for it on the basis of its quality. Often these decisions will be made by reference to a very small sample, perhaps only a few strands of wool.
Negotiation	Typically used for one-off or greenfield purchase situations. This involves the greatest input in terms of both the buyer's skills and the salesperson's time, and it is likely that a number of people from the buying organisation will be involved.

(Bharadwaj 2004). Unfortunately, most firms appear reluctant to develop their suppliers (Wagner 2006).

Often the demand for industrial products will be dictated by factors outside the buying organisation's control. For example, **derived demand** occurs because the buyers are using the products either for resale, or to use in making other products. The demand is therefore dictated by the demand for the end product. Frequently the demand for a component will be *inelastic*: for example, the price of wheel nuts will not affect the demand for them much, since they form only a tiny proportion of the price of a car, and also the car cannot be made without them. **Joint demand** occurs because the demand for one type of product dictates the demand for another. For instance, if the demand for guitars rises, so will the demand for guitar strings in the following months.

Fluctuating demand is more extreme in industrial markets because a small reduction in consumer demand for a product will lead to de-stocking by retailers and wholesalers, which causes a big reduction in demand from the manufacturers. A rise in consumer demand is likely to lead to re-stocking, which causes a bigger than expected rise in demand from the producers. In this way the fluctuations in demand for industrial products are more extreme than for consumer products.

Decision-making units

Industrial buying decisions are rarely made in isolation. Usually several people are involved in the process at different stages.

Gatekeepers such as secretaries and receptionists control the flow of information to the decision-makers. Often they will act as a barrier to salespeople, and see their role as being primarily to prevent interruptions to the decision-maker's work pattern.

Influencers are those individuals who 'have the ear' of the decision-makers. They could be people within the firm whom the decision-maker trusts, or they could be golf partners, spouses or even children.

Users are those who will actually use the product. For example, if the organisation is contemplating the purchase of a new computer system, the finance department and the IT department will clearly want to have some say in the decision.

Deciders are the ones who make the real decision. These are usually the hardest to influence, since they are usually the more senior people in the decision-making unit and are surrounded by gatekeepers. They are also sometimes hard to identify. They are not necessarily buyers, but they do hold the real power in the buying decision.

Buyers are the ones given the task of actually going through the process of buying. The buyers may be given a very specific brief by the decider, and may have very little room to negotiate except on areas such as price and delivery schedules. Sometimes they are merely there to handle the mechanical aspects of getting tenders from possible suppliers.

Each of these people has an independent existence outside the organisation; each will bring their own personal needs and aspirations to their role. In some cases this will be a job-related need (for example, career progression or the need to appear professional); in other cases the individual may have personal needs, such as a need to exercise power or the hedonic need to drive a hard bargain. The need to impress others within the firm can be extremely powerful.

From the viewpoint of the industrial marketer, it is essential to get to the deciders in some way rather than wait for the buyers to make the first contact by issuing a tender. The reason for this is that a tender will usually be very specific, and the buyers will then be deciding on the basis of price. The only way to get the order in those circumstances is to be the cheapest, and this inevitably results in reduced profits. If the seller has managed to approach the decision-maker beforehand, the seller can persuade the decision-maker to include certain essential aspects of the product in the tender, and thus ensure that the tender contains specifications that are difficult or impossible for the competition to meet.

Webster and Wind (1972) theorised that four main forces determine organisational buyer behaviour: environmental forces (such as the state of the economy), organisational forces (for example the size of the organisation and therefore its buying power), group forces (internal politics and the relative power of group members), and individual forces (the personality and preferences of the decision-maker). These forces combine in complex ways to influence the final decision.

This means that the role of the salesperson is crucial in industrial markets. Salespeople are able to identify potential customers and approach them with a solution for their specific problem; even in cases where the buyer is going to invite tenders from other firms, the salesperson can often ensure that the tender is drawn up in a way that excludes the competition. Salespeople, and in particular key-account salespeople, are crucially important in relationship marketing, since they negotiate the terms of the relationship and are the human face of the supplying corporation.

In the end, organisations do not make purchases. Individuals make purchases on behalf of organisations, and therefore salespeople are always dealing with human beings who have their own needs, failings, attitudes and blind spots. Purchasing decisions are not made entirely rationally; often the personal relationship between the representatives of the buying and selling companies has the biggest role in the purchase. Buyers will naturally prefer to deal with someone they know and trust (see the section on personal selling in Chapter 9).

Case study 3
Buying a car

The UK has one of the biggest traffic problems in the world. It's a relatively small country to have 22 million cars on the road – more than one car per household on average – and yet owning a car is regarded as almost as important as owning a home. Partly this is due to an expensive and inadequate public transport infrastructure for the bulk of the country, but partly it is a cultural issue – people just love to own a car. Outside London (which does have an efficient public transport system) 70% of people travel to work by car, with about one-third of these trips taking people into already-congested urban centres. In all, people travel 78 billion miles a year, just getting to and from work by car. Each year around two and a half million new cars are sold in Britain, but the used car market is much bigger: according to the Society of Motor Manufacturers and Traders, around seven and a half million used cars change hands every year. This only refers to cars – around another million and a half other vehicles change hands each year as well.

Almost everybody in the UK uses cars (even people who do not drive are regularly driven around by car owners). Buying a used car is a familiar process for most people, yet it is still fraught with risk – a car represents a large investment, and the technical aspects of cars are too complex for most people to grasp fully. A typical car owner might have to make the difficult purchase decision twenty times in a lifetime of motoring: even someone who keeps each car for a long time might make ten or twelve purchases. At the same time, technology is moving forward – vehicles are becoming more complex, new features are added each year, and some favourite features disappear.

It has been said that buying a car is the second most financially important decision you can make. Not true, according to website *Top Gear*. They say that 'You are much more likely to flush cash down the toilet on a used car' than on buying a house. This is because a car is a very visible product – one's choice of car says a lot about one's status, personality, financial security, and so forth. The website, owned by the magazine of the same name, goes on to offer a step-by-step guide to buying a second-hand car, including advice on some tax-efficient ways of buying.

The guide is comprehensive – it advises on what to buy, when to buy, where to buy, and what to look for when checking the car's history and paperwork. It advises on how to negotiate with sellers, how to pay for the car in the most cost-effective and secure way, and even provides a lengthy checklist for inspecting the car. A key piece of advice is to take a friend with you when buying, partly because the extra pair of eyes might spot something the buyer has missed, and partly because having someone else around provides moral support in any negotiating situation.

Top Gear is not alone in offering this type of advice. Yahoo! have their own advice system for used car buying, as have motoring organisations such as the Automobile Association and the Royal Automobile Club. Even *Times Online* has an advice section for used car buying, complete with the obligatory checklist and finance advice.

It seems that almost everybody offers advice on buying cars, despite the huge environmental and financial cost associated with them. Car purchase will continue to be an important part of UK consumer behaviour, and people will continue to be grateful for any help.

Questions

1 What is the role of the peer group in car purchase?

2 Why are there so many websites offering help with buying used cars?

3 How might the average person reduce risk when buying a car?

4 Why is used car purchase so risky?

5 What would you expect the purchase process for a car to encompass?

SUMMARY

In this chapter we have looked at how people behave when faced with buying decisions. We have looked at the decision-making process both for consumers and for organisational buyers, and at the influences and pressures on each group.

Here are the key points from this chapter:

- Consumers buy because they recognise either assortment depletion or assortment extension needs.
- Complaints should be encouraged, because they give the opportunity to cure post-purchase dissonance and create loyal customers.
- Individuals belong to several reference groups, and are also influenced by groups they do not belong to such as aspirational groups and dissociative groups.
- Normative compliance is probably the most powerful factor in attitude formation and decision-making.
- The family is probably the most powerful reference group.
- Industrial buying is complex because of the number of people involved.
- Gatekeepers, users, influencers, deciders and buyers are all involved in organisational decision-making. None of them should be ignored if the deal is to go through.
- The route to success in industrial marketing is to make sure the tender has something in it that the competition cannot match.

CHAPTER QUESTIONS

1 How do family members influence each other's buying behaviour?

2 What are the main differences between industrial buyers and consumers?

3 What is the difference between assortment depletion and assortment extension?

4 How can the use of choice heuristics reduce post-purchase dissonance?

5 How can a marketer use interrupts to influence consumer behaviour?

Further reading

Consumer Behavior by **Roger D. Blackwell, Paul W. Miniard and James F. Engel** (Mason, OH, Southwestern, 2001). A very comprehensive American text, now in its ninth edition; this is a readable and clear coverage of all aspects of consumer behaviour.

Consumer Psychology in Behavioural Perspective by **Gordon Foxall** (London, Routledge, 1990). An in-depth analysis of consumer psychology; a rather academic text, with some interesting insights into some more obscure aspects of consumer behaviour.

Business Marketing Management: A Global Perspective by **Jim Blythe and Alan Zimmerman** (London, Thomson, 2005). This book provides an in-depth view of business-to-business marketing, taking a global perspective. It covers all aspects of marketing to other businesses, including buyer behaviour and strategic issues.

References

Ang, Lawrence and Buttle, Francis: 'Customer retention management processes', *European Journal of Marketing*, **40** (1/2) (2006), pp. 83–9.

Arnett, Dennis B., German, Steve D. and Hunt, Shelby D.: 'The identity salience model of relationship marketing success: the case of non-profit marketing', *Journal of Marketing*, **67** (April 2003), pp. 89–105.

Borgerson, Janet, Schroeder, Jonathan, Blomberg, Britta and Thorssen, Erica: 'The gay family in the ad: consumer responses to non-traditional families in marketing communication', *Journal of Marketing Management*, **22** (9) (2006), 955–78.

Bharadwaj, Neeraj: 'Investigating the decision criteria used in electronic components procurement', *Industrial Marketing Management*, **33** (4) (2004), pp. 317–23.

Bhattacharya, C.B. and Sen, Sankar: 'Consumer-company identification: a framework for understanding consumers' relationships with companies', *Journal of Marketing*, **67** (2) (April 2003), pp. 76–88.

Bolls, Paul D., Muehling, Darrel D. and Yoon, Kak: 'The effects of television commercial pacing on viewers' attention and memory', *Journal of Marketing Communications*, **9** (1) (March 2003), pp. 17–28.

Burke, J.: 'Food firms pester pupils for sales', *Sunday Times* (11 June 1995).

Carrigan, Marylyn and Szmigin, Isabelle: '"Mothers of invention": maternal empowerment and convenience consumption', *European Journal of Marketing*, **40** (9/10) (2006), pp. 1122–42.

Davies, Harry L. and Rigaux, Benny P.: 'Perception of marital roles in decision processes', *Journal of Consumer Research*, **1** (June 1974), pp. 5–14.

Day, Ralph L., Brabicke, Klaus, Schaetzle, Thomas and Staubach, Fritz: 'The hidden agenda of consumer complaining', *Journal of Retailing* (Fall, 1981), pp. 86–106.

Dwek, R.: 'In front of the children', *The Grocer*, **2** (December 1995), pp. 45–9.

Dwek, R.: 'Man trouble', *Marketing Business* (February 1996), p. 18.

Ekstrom, Karin M.: 'Parental consumer learning, or keeping up with the children', *Journal of Consumer Behaviour*, **6** (4) (2007), pp. 203–17.

Engel, James F., Blackwell, Roger D. and Miniard, Paul W.: *Consumer Behaviour*, 8th edn (Fort Worth, TX, Dryden Press, 1995).

Filiatrault, Pierre and Brent Ritchie, J.R.: 'Joint purchasing decisions; a comparison of influence structure in family and couple decision-making units', *Journal of Consumer Research*, **7** (September 1980), pp. 131–40.

Fishbein, Martin: 'The search for attitudinal-behavioural consistency', in Joel E. Cohen (ed.) *Behavioural Science Foundations of Consumer Behaviour* (New York, Free Press, 1972), pp. 257–67.

Goffman, Erving: *The Presentation of Self in Everyday Life* (Harmondsworth, Penguin, 1969).

Green, P., Robinson, P. and Wind, Y.: 'The determinants of vendor selection: the evaluation function approach', *Journal of Purchasing* (August 1968).

Green, Robert T., Leonardi, Jean-Paul, Chandon, Jean-Louis, Cunningham, Isabella C.M., Verhage, Bronis and Strazzieri, Alain: 'Societal development and family purchasing roles; a cross-national study', *Journal of Consumer Research*, **9** (March 1983), pp. 436–42.

Hamilton, Cathy and Catterall, Miriam: 'Consuming love in poor families: children's influence on consumption decisions', *Journal of Marketing Management*, **22** (9/10) (2006), pp. 1031–82.

Holbrook, Morris P. and Hirschmann, Elizabeth C.: 'The experiential aspects of consumption; consumer fantasies, feelings and fun', *Journal of Consumer Research*, **9** (September 1982), pp. 132–40.

Lindredge, Andrew M. and Hogg, Margaret K.: 'Parental gate-keeping in diasporic Indian families: examining the intersection of culture, gender and consumption', *Journal of Marketing Management*, **22** (9/10) (2006), pp. 979–1008.

Macdonald, Emma K. and Uncles, Mark D.: 'Consumer savvy: conceptualization and measurement', *Journal of Marketing Management*, **23** (5/6) (2007), pp. 497–517.

Maxham, James G. III and Netemeyer, Richard G.: 'Firms reap what they sow: the effect of shared values and perceived organizational justice on customers' evaluation of complaint handling', *Journal of Marketing*, **67** (1) (January 2003), pp. 46–62.

Ngai, Eric W.T., Heung, Vincent C., Wong, Y.H. and Chan, Fanny K.Y.: 'Consumer complaint behaviour of Asians and non-Asians about hotel services: an empirical analysis', *European Journal of Marketing*, **41** (11/12) (2007), pp. 1375–91.

Oedekerken-Schroder, Gaby, Ouwersloot, Hans, Lemmink, Jos and Semeijn, Janjaap: 'Consumers' trade-off between relationship, service, package and price: an empirical study in the car industry', *European Journal of Marketing*, **37** (1) (2003), pp. 219–242.

Oliver, Richard L.: 'A cognitive model of the antecedents and consequences of satisfaction decisions', *Journal of Marketing Research*, **17** (November 1980), pp. 460–9.

Powers, T.L.: *Modern Business Marketing: A Strategic Planning Approach to Business and Industrial Markets* (St Paul, MN, West, 1991).

Raju, P.S.: 'Optimum stimulation level; its relationship to personality, demographics, and exploratory behaviour', *Journal of Consumer Research*, **7** (December 1980), pp. 272–82.

Shankar, Avi, Cherrier, Helene and Canniford, Robin: 'Consumer empowerment: a Foucauldian interpretation', *European Journal of Marketing*, **40** (9/10) (2006), pp. 1013-30.

Sijun, Wang and Huff, Leonard C.: Exploring buyers' response to sellers' violation of trust', *European Journal of Marketing*, **41** (9/10) (2007), pp. 1033-52.

Singh, Jagdip: 'Consumer complaint intentions and behaviour: definitions and taxonomical issues', *Journal of Marketing*, **52** (January 1988), pp. 93–107.

Smith, Robert E. and Swinyard, William R.: 'Attitude-behaviour consistency; the impact of product trial versus advertising', *Journal of Marketing Research*, **20** (August 1983).

Tanner, J.F.: 'Buyer perceptions of the purchase process and its effect on customer satisfaction', *Industrial Marketing Management*, **25** (2) (March 1996), pp. 125–33.

Thomsen, Thyra Uth and Sorensen, Elin Brandi: 'The first four-wheeled status symbol: pram consumption as a vehicle for the construction of motherhood identity', *Journal of Marketing Management*, **22** (9/10) (2006), pp. 907–27.

Thomson, Elizabeth S., Laing, Angus W. and McKee, Lorna: 'Family purchase decision making: exploring child influence behavior', *Journal of Consumer Behaviour*, **6** (4) (2007), pp. 182–202.

Wagner, Stephan M.: 'Supplier development practices: an exploratory study', *European Journal of Marketing*, **40** (5/6) (2006), pp. 554–71.

Walsh, Gianfranco, Hennig-Thurau, Thorsten and Mitchell, Vincent-Wayne: 'Consumer confusion proneness: scale development, validation and application', *Journal of Marketing Management*, **23** (7/8) (2007), pp. 697–721.

Wang, Shih-Lun Alex: 'The effects of audience knowledge on message processing of editorial content', *Journal of Marketing Communications*, **12** (4) (2006), pp. 281–96.

Webster, F.E. and Wind, Y.: *Organisational Buying Behaviour* (Englewood Cliffs, NJ, Prentice Hall, 1972).

Zajonc, Robert B. and Markus, Hazel: 'Must all affect be mediated by cognition?', *Journal of Consumer Research*, **12** (December 1985), pp. 363–4.

Birmingham

Marketing a whole city may seem like a tall order, but all cities need to attract industry, tourists, even residents, or it will die. The marketers involved are in a unique position, because they do not own the brand – the brand is owned and developed by the people who live in the city.

Identifying appropriate market segments is far from easy: a city the size of Birmingham contains within it virtually all

segments of both consumer and business markets. The aim of Birmingham's positioning is to place the city as a youthful, lively city, on the basis that nobody believes that they themselves are old.

Repositioning Birmingham as an exciting city to visit means building on what was essentially an industrial past – removing the image of a grimy industrial town and replacing it with a vibrant city where many events happen is a challenge the marketers seek to meet.

The marketers monitor the league tables published by tourism organisations, and carry out their own research to determine how many people visit, how much they spend, how long they stay, and whether they intend to return. Monitoring the market is essential for future decision-making about promotion activities.

Neil Rami, Managing Director

Watch the video clip, then try to answer the following questions. The answers are on the companion website.

Questions

1 What segmentation bases are most appropriate for Birmingham?
2 What positioning problems are apparent for the city?
3 How should Birmingham target potential visitors?

4

Segmentation, targeting and positioning

Objectives

After reading this chapter you should be able to:

- describe the main methods of segmenting markets;
- explain how segmentation aids profitability;
- decide whether a given segment is sufficiently profitable to be worth targeting;
- explain the purpose of segmentation;
- develop ways of assessing the economic viability of segments;
- explain the growth of segmented markets;
- establish strategies for dealing with segmented markets;
- describe perceptual mapping;
- describe the main issues surrounding the positioning of brands.

INTRODUCTION

The segmentation concept was first developed by Smith (1957) and is concerned with grouping consumers in terms of their needs. The aim of segmentation is to identify a group of people who have a need or needs that can be met by a single product, in order to concentrate the marketing firm's efforts most effectively and economically. For example, if a manufacturer produces a standardised product by a mass-production method, the firm would need to be sure that there are sufficient people with a need for the product to make the exercise worthwhile.

The assumptions underlying segmentation are:

- Not all buyers are alike.
- Sub-groups of people with similar behaviour, backgrounds, values and needs can be identified.
- The sub-groups will be smaller and more homogeneous than the market as a whole.
- It is easier to satisfy a small group of similar customers than to try to satisfy large groups of dissimilar customers (Zikmund and D'Amico 1995).

Targeting is concerned with choosing which segments to aim for. Segmentation is essentially about dividing up the market; targeting is about the practicalities of doing business within the market. The two are clearly closely linked, since the segmentation process will usually provide information as to which segments are likely to prove most profitable, or will help the firm achieve its strategic objectives in other ways.

Positioning is concerned with the brand's relationship with other brands aimed at the same segment. Positioning is about the place the brand occupies in the minds of the consumers, relative to other brands.

REASONS FOR SEGMENTING MARKETS

Each consumer is an individual with individual needs and wants. On the face of it, this creates a major problem for the marketer, since it would clearly be impossible to tailor-make or customise each product to the exact requirements of each individual.

Before the Industrial Revolution most products were individually made. This proved to be expensive, and essentially inefficient once mass-production techniques had come into being. Unfortunately, mass-production (taken to the extreme) means a reduction in the available choice of product, since the best way to keep production costs low is to have long production runs, which means standardising the product. Every adaptation costs money in terms of re-tooling and re-packaging the product. In some economies, particularly those in parts of Eastern Europe and in the Third World, there is not sufficient wealth or investment in industry to allow for the production of many different types of product. These economies still rely heavily on mass production and mass marketing.

Mass marketing (or undifferentiated marketing) in which a standard product is produced for all consumers will only be effective if the consumers concerned have little choice and do not already own a product that meets the main needs. For example, in 1930s Germany few families owned cars. Hitler promised the German people that every family would own a car, so Porsche was commissioned to develop the Volkswagen (literally 'people's car') as a basic vehicle, which could be cheaply produced for the mass market.

This approach is less effective in economies where most consumers already own the **core benefits** of the product. Once car ownership was widespread and the core benefit of personal transportation was owned by most families, consumers demanded choices in features and design of their vehicles. Segmentation deals with finding out how many people are likely to want each benefit, roughly how much they will be willing to pay for it, and where they would like to buy it from. In this way, the firm approaching a segmented market is able to offer more functional benefits and more attention to *hedonic needs*, i.e. the products are more fun (see Chapter 3).

In order to make these adaptations worthwhile, marketers need to be reasonably sure that there is a large enough market for the product to be viable economically. On the other hand, concentrating on a smaller segment means that economies can be made in the supplier's communications activities; rather than advertise to a mass market, for example, the marketer would be better off concentrating resources on producing an advertisement that is tailored to the target segment – an ad, in other words, designed for the ideal customer and no other.

The reason for this is that consumers are surrounded by advertising messages. Consequently consumers learn to avoid advertisements, and particularly to avoid ones that are clearly never going to be of any interest. At the same time, consumers will go out of their way to find out about products they have some interest in, often by reading special-interest magazines. Therefore an advertisement that is tailored to a specific group of consumers, and that appears in a medium that those consumers use, is likely to be far more effective than an untargeted advertisement in a general-interest medium.

Companies that aim for small segments usually have much greater credibility with consumers, and can learn to provide exactly what most pleases those consumers.

Overall, the main purpose of segmenting is to enable the company to concentrate its efforts on pleasing one group of people with similar needs, rather than trying to please everybody and probably ending up pleasing nobody. Table 4.1 shows the advantages of segmenting the market.

Table 4.1   Advantages of segmentation

Advantage	Explanation
Customer analysis	By segmenting, the firm can get to understand its best customers better.
Competitor analysis	It is much easier to recognise and combat competition when concentrating on one small part of the overall market.
Effective resource allocation	Companies' scarce resources can be concentrated more effectively on a few consumers, rather than spread thinly across the masses.
Strategic marketing planning	Planning becomes easier once the firm has a clear picture of its best customers.
Expanding the market	Good segmentation can increase the overall size of the market by bringing in new customers who fit the profile of the typical customer, but were previously unaware of the product.

SEGMENTATION VARIABLES

 A segment must fulfil the following requirements if it is to be successfully exploited:

- *It must be measurable, or definable.* In other words, there must be some way of identifying the members of the segment and knowing how many of them there are.
- *It must be accessible.* This means it must be possible to communicate with the segment as a group, and to get the product to them as a group.
- *It must be substantial*, i.e. big enough to be worth aiming for.
- *It must be congruent*, that is to say the members must have a close agreement on their needs.
- *It must be stable.* The nature and membership of the segment must be reasonably constant.

The three key criteria are accessibility, substance and measurability (Kotler 1991) but it is important also to look at the causes underlying the segmentation (Engel *et al.* 1995). This enables the marketer to anticipate changes more easily and sometimes to verify that the segmentation base is correctly defined.

There are many bases for segmenting, but the following are the main ones:

- *Geographic.* Where the consumers live, the climate, the topology, etc. For example, cars in California almost always have air-conditioning; cars in Sweden have headlights that stay on constantly because of the poor quality of the light for much of the year. Geographic segmentation is very commonly used in international marketing, but is equally useful within single nations.
- *Psychographic.* Based on the personality type of the individuals in the segment. For example, the home insurance market might segment into those who are afraid of crime, those who are afraid of natural disasters, and those who are afraid of accidental damage to their property.
- *Behavioural.* This approach examines the benefits, usage situation, extent of use and loyalty. For example, the car market might segment into business users and private users. The private market might segment further to encompass those who use their cars primarily for commuting, those who use their cars for hobbies such as surfing or camping, and those who use the car for domestic duties such as shopping or taking children to school. The business market might segment into 'prestige' users such as managing directors and senior executives, or high-mileage users such as salespeople.
- *Demographic.* Concerned with the structure of the population in terms of ages, lifestyles, economic factors. For example, the housing market can be divided into first-time buyers, families with children, older retired people, and elderly people in sheltered accommodation; equally, the market could be segmented according to lifestyle, with some accommodation appealing to young professionals, some appealing to country-lovers, and so forth.

Geographic segmentation

Geographic segmentation may be carried out for a number of reasons.

■ The nature of the product may be such that it applies only to people living within a specific area, or type of area. Clothing manufacturers know that they will sell more heavy-weather clothing in cold coastal areas than in warm inland areas.

■ If the company's resources are limited, the firm may start out in a small area and later roll out the product nationally.

■ It might be that the product itself does not travel well. This is true of sheet glass, wedding cakes and most personal services such as hairdressing.

Markets may be segmented geographically according to the type of housing in the area. Firms that supply products specifically aimed at elderly people may wish to locate (or at least concentrate their marketing efforts) in retirement areas. Products aimed at young people might be heavily marketed in university towns, and so forth.

Psychographic segmentation

Psychographic segmentation classifies consumers according to their personalities. As the reliability of measures has improved, more evidence has come to light of links between personality and consumer behavior (Lastovicka and Joachimstaler 1988) but psychographic segmentation remains problematical because of the difficulties of measuring consumers' psychological traits on a large scale. This type of segmentation therefore often fails on the grounds of accessibility. For example, researchers might find out that there is a group of people who relate the brand of coffee that they buy to their self-esteem. The problem then is that there is no obvious medium in which to advertise this feature of the coffee: if there were a magazine called *Coffee Makes Me Feel Good* there would be no problem. The advertisers are therefore left with mass media such as TV advertising, which may be far too expensive for the purpose. Some of the most creative ideas in marketing have revolved around ways of gaining access to such segments.

Behavioural segmentation

Behavioural segmentation can be a useful and reliable way of segmenting. At its most obvious, if the firm is marketing to anglers they are not interested in how old the anglers are, what their views are on strong drink, or where they live. All the firm cares about is that they go fishing and might therefore be customers for a new type of rod. Accessing the segment would be easily undertaken by advertising in angling magazines. At a deeper level the firm might be interested in such issues as where they buy their fishing tackle, how much they usually spend on a rod, what kind of fish they are after, and so forth, but this information is easily obtained through questionnaire-type surveys. *Lifestyle* analysis has been widely used for the past 30 years or so, and seeks to segment markets according to how consumers spend their time, what their beliefs are about themselves and about specific issues, and the relative importance of their various possessions (e.g. cars, clothes, homes). The attraction of this approach is that it takes account of a wide range of characteristics of the segment encompassing some psychographic features and some behavioural features (Plummer 1974).

Demographic segmentation

Demographic segmentation is the most commonly used method of segmenting markets, probably because it is easy to pick up the relevant information from government statistics. Demographics is the study of how people differ in terms of factors such as age, occupation, salary and lifestyle stage.

Typically, demographic segmentation revolves around age. While this is relevant in many cases, it is often difficult to see the difference between, say, a 20-year-old's buying pattern and a 30-year-old's buying pattern. Equally, it cannot be said with much reliability that all 10-year-olds share the same tastes. There are undoubtedly 10-year-olds who would not want to visit Disneyland or Luna Park, and 10-year-olds who would prefer duck á l'orange to a hamburger. Age is, of course, relevant but it should be included as part of a range of measures, not relied upon on its own.

Critical thinking

Can we really be pigeonholed this easily? Surely our behaviour cannot be entirely governed by our age, or our gender, or our religious beliefs! As we grow older, or change our jobs, or have children, or become better-educated, do our basic likes and dislikes really change?

If you like chips, you like chips, and no amount of lottery wins will make you suddenly like caviar instead. But then again – how are our tastes determined in the first place? By our upbringing, our friends, our experiences. And these are governed by our age, our gender, our religious beliefs, our education, etc. etc.

Maybe we CAN be pigeonholed that easily!

As we saw in Chapter 2, demographic variables are shifting over time, as the birth rate falls and the average age of the population rises. In addition, the number of single-person households is rising as people marry later and divorce rates increase: in 2001, single-person households represented 30% of UK households (Office of National Statistics 2003). The implications of this one change for marketers are far-reaching; here are some of the possibilities:

- Increase in sales of individual packs of food.

- Increase in sales of recipe products and ready meals.

- Decrease in sales of gardening equipment and children's items.

- Increase in sales of mating-game items.

- Decrease in family-sized cars, packs of breakfast cereal, cleaning products, etc.

In Australia, immigration from South-East Asia is causing major changes in eating habits, religious observances and the linguistic structure of the country. In some cases, marketing activities have themselves contributed to a cross-fertilisation of cultural behaviour, so that individuals from one ethnic group behave in ways more usually associated with another group. This culture swapping means that ethnic and racial segmentation is no longer possible in most cases (Jamal 2003).

Overall, demographic change means that new segments are emerging, some of which offer greater opportunities to marketers than do the segments they replace. Marketers need to monitor these changes in the demography if they are to remain able to segment the market effectively.

Not all segmentation variables will be appropriate to all markets. A pizza company might segment a market geographically (locating in a town centre) but would not segment by religion; the situation would be reversed for a wholesale kosher butcher. This is despite the fact that both firms are in the food business. **Single-variable segmentation** is based on only one variable, for example size of firm. This is the simplest way to segment, but is also the most inaccurate. To achieve **multivariable segmentation**, several characteristics are taken into account. The more characteristics are used, the greater the accuracy and effectiveness, but the smaller the resulting markets.

SEGMENTING INDUSTRIAL MARKETS

Industrial or organisational markets can be, and are, segmented by marketers according to the following criteria:

- *Geographic location.* Probably the commonest method, since most organisational markets are serviced by salespeople, and geographical segmentation enables the salesperson to make best use of drive time. Often firms in the same industry will locate near each other, perhaps because of availability of raw materials, or for traditional reasons to do with availability of local skilled workers.

- *Type of organisation.* IBM segments its market according to the industry the customer is in. This means that some IBM salespeople specialise in banking, others in insurance, others perhaps in local government applications of the equipment.

- *Client company size*. Many companies have separate salesforces to deal with large accounts.
- *Product use*. Oil companies have separate strategies (and sometimes separate subsidiaries) for marketing household central-heating oil, for the plastics industry, for petrochemicals and for automotive sales.
- **Usage rate**. Customers who use large quantities of a given product will expect (and get) different treatment from customers who buy only in small quantities. This is partly because their needs are different, and partly because the supplier will tend to value the large buyer over the small buyer.

Bonoma and Shapiro (1984) suggest a nested approach to organisational market segmentation. This approach entails starting with broad characteristics such as the type of industry and the size of the organisations in it, then narrowing the segment by working through operating variables (processes, product types, etc.), then looking at the purchasing approach of the organisations, followed by situational factors such as delivery lead times and order size, and finally looking at the individual types of buyer in each firm.

For example, a glass manufacturer might begin by segmenting according to type of industry (window glass for construction, toughened glass for cars, bottles and jars for food packaging). Within the food packaging market the industry might break down further to pickles and sauces, wines and beers, and soft drinks. The wine and beer bottle market may further break down into major brewers and bottlers who buy in large quantities, and small privately owned vineyards who buy on a once-a-year basis. Some of the brewers may buy by tender, some may prefer to use a regular supplier, and some may have special requirements in terms of bottle shape or design.

As in consumer markets, it is not necessarily the case that buyers act from wholly rational motives (see Chapter 3), so it would be unreasonable not to include the buyers' personal characteristics in the segmentation plan somewhere. This is likely to be the province of the salesforce since they are dealing with the buyers on a day-to-day basis.

SEGMENTATION EFFECTIVENESS

If a segment is correctly identified, it should be possible for the marketer to meet the needs of the segment members much more effectively than their competitors can. The firm will be able to provide specialist products that are more nearly right for the consumers in the segment, and will be able to communicate better with them. From the consumer's viewpoint, this is worth paying an extra premium for. Rather than putting up with a product that does not quite fit the bill, the consumer will pay a little more for something that more closely approaches the ideal.

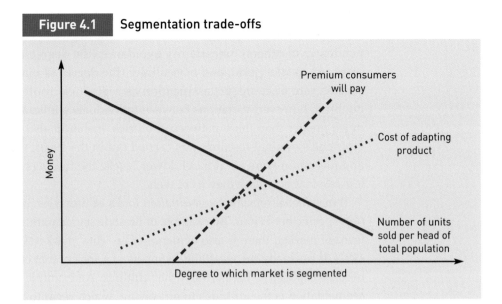

Figure 4.1 Segmentation trade-offs

The segment will be profitable as long as the **premium** the consumer will pay is greater than the cost to the manufacturer of making the modifications. There is therefore a trade-off; the finer-tuned the segmentation, the smaller the market but the greater the premium the target consumers will be prepared to pay. This is illustrated in Figure 4.1.

As the segmentation becomes narrower, fewer units will be sold, so the number of items sold as compared with the population at large will drop. This is partly offset by higher prices, but the profitability of the segment will begin only where the premium line and the cost line diverge. Where the costs of adaptation are higher than the premium, it is not worthwhile to make the adaptations; where the premium is higher than the cost, it may be worthwhile but the firm must still take account of the reduction in unit sales overall.

GLOBAL SEGMENTATION

Although cultural variance (and differences in consumer behaviour) are still major issues for international marketers (Hofstede 1994), transnational segments are still identifiable. The main bases for segmentation are:

■ by country;
■ by individual characteristics (in much the same way as segmentation is handled within one's own country).

Countries can be grouped according to economic development criteria, by cultural variables, or by a combination of factors such as economic, political and R&D factors (Lee 1990). One of the best-known studies is that of Hofstede (1980) in which countries were classified according to power distance (the degree to which power is centralised), individualism (the degree to which people act independently of others), uncertainty avoidance (the degree to which people are prepared to take risks), and masculinity (the degree of male domination). The success rate of country classification as a practical route to segmentation is doubtful, however; variations between individuals within a country are usually much greater than those between countries. It should also be remembered that Hofstede's original research was carried out in the 1960s, when travel, tourism and migration were all at much lower levels: the findings may be a great deal less relevant now than they were then.

Transnational consumer segmentation looks at lifestyles, behaviour and situation-specific behaviour. An example of lifestyle segmentation is the transnational teenage market; there is also evidence of an 'elite' market (Hassan and Katsanis 1991). It is usually the wealthier members of a society that can travel abroad and become exposed to ideas from other cultures. An example of situation-specific segmentation is the attitudes to gift-giving, which seem to be common to many cultures (Beatty *et al.* 1991).

The main difficulty with seeking transnational consumer segments lies in generating adequate research within the target countries.

TARGETING

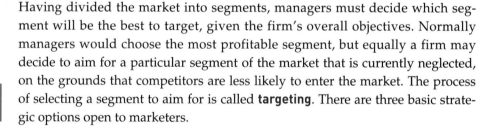

Having divided the market into segments, managers must decide which segment will be the best to target, given the firm's overall objectives. Normally managers would choose the most profitable segment, but equally a firm may decide to aim for a particular segment of the market that is currently neglected, on the grounds that competitors are less likely to enter the market. The process of selecting a segment to aim for is called **targeting**. There are three basic strategic options open to marketers.

1 Concentrated marketing (single segment). This is also known as **niche marketing**; Tie Rack, Sock Shop and Knickerbox follow this approach. The niche marketer concentrates on being the very best within a single tiny segment.

2 **Differentiated marketing** (multisegmented) means concentrating on two or more segments, offering a differentiated marketing mix for each. Holiday Inn aims to attract business travellers during the week, but aims for the leisure market at the weekend, and promotes to families. At the weekend, the hotels often have events for children and special room rates for families.

3 **Undifferentiated marketing** is about using a 'scattergun' approach. The producers who do this are usually offering a basic product that would be used by almost all age groups and lifestyles. For example, the market for petrol is largely undifferentiated. Although oil producers occasionally try to differentiate their products by the use of various additives and detergents, the use of

petrol is much the same for everybody, and there would not appear to be any relationship between segmentation variables and petrol use. It would be difficult to imagine any real adaptation to the product that would meet people's needs sufficiently well to merit a premium price. Such examples of undifferentiated products are increasingly rare; even the producers of such basic commodities as salt and flour have made great strides forward in differentiating their products (i.e. meeting consumers' needs better).

The decision regarding which strategy to adopt will rest on the following three factors:

- the company's *resources*;
- the product's features and benefits; and
- the characteristics of the segment(s).

Clearly if resources are limited the company will tend to adopt a concentrated marketing approach. This approach is taken by Titleist, the golf supply company. Titleist supplies everything the golfer needs, from clubs to golfing clothes, rather than diversifying into a general sporting-products market. This enables the firm to become very close to its market, and to understand the needs of golfers (and intermediaries such as club professionals) better than any other firm.

A higher level of resourcing coupled with a range of segments to approach will lead to a differentiated approach, and a simple made-for-everybody type product will lead to an undifferentiated approach. Table 4.2 shows this in action.

Companies with a small resource base are often unable to make their voices heard in mass markets simply because they cannot afford the level of promotional spend. They therefore need to segment narrowly, perhaps by starting out in a small area of the country (geographical segmentation) and gradually spreading nationwide as resources become available.

Table 4.3 shows the decision matrix for choosing a segment to target. The marketing strategy should be tailored to fit the intended audience: this means that each of the seven Ps, and every element of the promotion mix, needs to be built around the segment.

Table 4.2 **Resourcing and degree of differentiation**

		Type of product	
		High-differentiation consumers	**Low-differentiation consumers**
High-resource company	**Mass market**	Differentiated	Undifferentiated
	Specialist market	Differentiated	Concentrated
Low-resource company	**Mass market**	Concentrated	Differentiated (perhaps geographically)
	Specialist market	Concentrated	Concentrated

Table 4.3 Targeting decisions

Segment size	Profit per unit sold	Number of competitors	Strategic decision rationale
Large	Large	Large	A large market with large profits will attract competitors; prices will fall rapidly, and so will profits.
Large	Small	Large	This is a mature market. A new entrant would have to have something special to dominate the market: perhaps a much-reduced cost base.
Small	Large	Large	A small segment with a high profit per unit and a large number of competitors can be captured entirely by a penetration pricing strategy.
Large	Large	Small	If the segment is both large and profitable competitors will certainly enter the market. A skimming policy is best for this market; as competitors enter, it will be possible to reduce prices to compete effectively.
Large	Small	Small	This is a mature market, but should be low risk; the lack of competition means that it should be easy to capture a share, and the low profit margin will discourage others from entering.
Small	Small	Large	This is a dying market. Really not worth entering at all.
Small	Large	Small	This is a niche market. It should be possible to capture all of this market.
Small	Small	Small	This is clearly not a very profitable segment at all. Unless the firm has something very new to bring to the segment, this is probably not worth targeting.

Accurate targeting is best achieved by carrying out detailed market research into the needs and wants of the target group (see Chapter 5). In this way the company is able to decide what to offer the target audience to improve on the competitors' offering. Note that three factors are being taken into account here. First, what do the consumers in the target segment need? Second, what is already available to them? Third, what can the firm offer that would be better than what is currently available?

The five basic strategies of market coverage were outlined by Derek F. Abell in 1980. They are shown in Table 4.4.

Choosing the right market and then targeting it accurately are possibly the most important activities a marketer carries out. Choosing the wrong segment to target, or still worse not attempting to segment the market at all, leads to lost opportunities and wasted effort. Most firms find that Pareto's Law applies, and the firm obtains 80% of its profits from 20% of its customers: choosing the right group therefore becomes absolutely crucial to success.

Table 4.4 Market coverage strategies

Strategy	Explanation	Example
Product/market concentration	Niche marketing; the company takes over one small part of the market.	Tie Rack, Sock Shop
Product specialisation	Firm produces a full line of a specific product type.	Campbell's Soup
Market specialisation	Firm produces everything that a specific group of consumers needs.	Titleist golf clubs, golf balls, tees, caddies
Selective specialisation	Firm enters selective niches that do not relate closely to each other, but are profitable.	British Telecom sells telephone services to consumers and industry, but also owns satellite time, which it sells to TV broadcasters and others
Full coverage	Firm enters every possible segment of its potential market.	Mitsubishi Industries, which produces everything from musical instruments to supertankers

Accessing the target market is another issue that deserves attention. For a segment to be viable, it needs to be accessible via some communications medium or another: the segment may comprise people who read a particular magazine or watch a particular TV station. If there is no way to reach the segment, it cannot become a target market. In some cases the segment is defined by the medium: for example, *Cosmopolitan* readers represent a group of independently minded women with career aspirations, usually with high disposable incomes or aspirations in that direction, and interests that are more likely to run to business issues than to knitting patterns. These women represent a valuable market segment in their own right, but can probably only be easily identified as a group because they read *Cosmopolitan*.

POSITIONING

Positioning has been defined as: 'The place a product occupies in a given market, as perceived by the relevant group of customers; that group of customers is known as the target segment of the market' (Wind 1984). Usually positioning refers to the place the product occupies in the consumer's **perceptual map** of the market: for instance as a high-quality item, or as a reliable one, or perhaps as a cheap version. The product is positioned in the perceptual map alongside similar offerings; this is a result of the categorisation and chunking processes (see Chapter 3).

Consumers build up a position for a product based on what they expect and believe to be the most pertinent features of the product class. Marketers therefore need to find out first what the pertinent features of the products are in the target consumers' **perceptions**. The marketer can then adjust the mix of features and benefits, and the communications mix, to give the product its most effective position relative to the other brands in the market. Sometimes the positioning process is led by consumers, sometimes by marketers.

Research shows that consumers use a relatively short list of factors in determining the position of a product (Blankson and Kalafatis 2004). These are as follows:

- *Top-of-the-range*. This refers to the product which consumers believe to be the most expensive or 'the best'. In the UK, this is often called 'the Rolls-Royce of . . .' whichever product type is under discussion.
- *Service*. The service levels which surround the product can be an important factor.
- *Value for money*. This is the degree to which the product's benefits represent a fair exchange for the price being asked.
- *Reliability*. Products are often positioned as being more (or less) reliable than their competitors.
- *Attractiveness*. This can refer to factors other than appearance, but implies factors other than the purely practical, performance-related factors.
- *Country of origin*. Some countries have a reputation for producing the best examples of some categories of product. For example, German engineering is highly regarded, whereas the French are known for their food and wine.
- *Brand name*. Branding is a key issue in positioning, as it identifies the product and conveys an impression of its quality (see Chapter 6).
- *Selectivity*. The degree to which the consumer can distinguish between brands and select from the range is a factor in positioning.

Ultimately, product positioning depends on the attitudes of the particular target market, so the marketer must either take these attitudes as they are and tailor the product to fit those attitudes, or must seek to change the attitudes of the market. Usually it is easier and cheaper to change the product than it is to change the consumers, but sometimes the market's attitudes to the product are so negative that the manufacturer feels constrained to reposition the product. For example, Skoda cars had to fight hard to throw off the negative connotations of the vehicle's Eastern European origins. Not wishing to be classed with Ladas, Yugos and Polski Fiats and thus share the perception of poor workmanship and unreliability, Skoda made great efforts to emphasise Volkswagen's takeover of the company and to position the car next to VW in the consumer's mind.

Skoda has pointed out that, under the auspices of VW ownership, the company's quality control and engineering procedures have been greatly improved. Skoda was, in any case, the jewel in the crown of Eastern European car manufacture, so the firm has been able to demonstrate that the cars are made to a high standard.

In order to determine the product's position, research is carried out with the target group of consumers, and a perceptual map such as the one in Figure 4.2 will be produced.

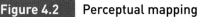

Figure 4.2 Perceptual mapping

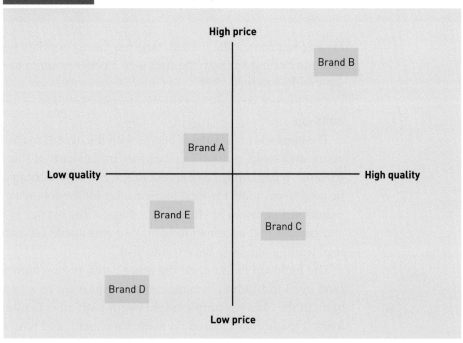

From the diagram it can be seen that Brand B has the image of being both high price and high quality: this is probably the Rolls-Royce of the products (top-of-the-range factor). Brand D is perceived as being low price, but low quality: this would be a cheap, everyday brand. Brand A has a problem: although tending towards a high price, this product is perceived as being below-average quality. Sales are likely to be low, or will take place only when the consumer has no other choice available. Brand C, on the other hand, enjoys a low price and good quality, so is probably the top-selling brand (value-for-money factor).

It should be noted that these positions are based on average responses from consumers in the target groups. They are not objective, nor are they based on the firm's view of the quality of its products. For this reason, they can sometimes be changed by promotional efforts. Far more commonly, though, the firm will need to do something more practical about changing the product or changing its price to make the necessary changes.

In Figure 4.2, the products have been mapped against only two dimensions, but it is perfectly possible (perhaps even advisable) to map the product against more dimensions. This can be done on a computer using multidimensional mapping software.

One of the most useful tactical aspects of positioning maps is that they can be used to identify gaps in the market. Using Figure 4.2 as an example, there is clearly a gap next to Brand A and below Brand B for a medium-to-high quality product at a medium-to-high price. Currently this market seems to be dominated by lower-priced brands; a brand entering this market would need to be perceived as higher quality than Brand C, but at a lower price than Brand B.

SALES FORECASTING

Having segmented the market, targeted the appropriate segments, and decided on a positioning strategy, the firm is in a better position to forecast the expected sales of the product.

Two overall strategic approaches to sales forecasting exist: **break-down** and **build-up**.

The break-down approach begins with the overall market for the product category and seeks to predict what the firm's share of that market will be. For example, a bank may have access to government economic forecasts which can be used to calculate the total loans market for the following year. The bank forecasters will know what the bank's share of the market was in previous years, and can use this information to make a reasonable estimate of what the bank's total lending will be in the ensuing year.

The build-up method, on the other hand, begins with the market segments (and even individual consumers) and builds up to a total market share. The bank in the above example might begin with an estimate of how many home loans it might make (based on market research), and how many business loans, how many car loans, and so forth. By adding these figures together, an overall estimate of the total sales for the following year is arrived at.

Sales forecasts help to determine the viability of a segment, and also help the firm to plan its budgets and indeed virtually all of its other activities. Forecasting the future is always difficult; many firms rely on **executive judgement**, using the skill and experience of its senior people in deciding whether a product is a winner or not. Unfortunately this approach can fail because the executives will favour a product that they would buy as private consumers, rather than a product that the target market segment would buy.

Through a **customer survey** firms are able to ask potential customers how much of a given product they are likely to buy within the next 12 months or so. These intent-to-buy studies work best for existing product categories; for a radically new product it is much more difficult, since only the most innovative of consumers will be able to say with any certainty that they would be prepared to buy the product early in its launch. The main drawback with this method is that customers may intend to purchase, but change their minds during the course of the year, perhaps owing to a competitor's actions. On the other hand, some customers who say in the survey that they will not buy may well do so if their circumstances change.

Other firms may use a **salesforce survey**, asking the salesforce how much of a given product they might expect to sell over the next 12 months. This has the advantage that the salespeople, unlike senior management, are usually close to the customer and are able to make judgements based on this. Also salespeople will be wary about making rash forecasts that they might later be held to. On the other hand, salespeople generally like to be consulted about their own targets and quotas. A variation on the salesforce survey is the **distributor survey**, where the company's distributors are asked how much they expect to sell over a specific period. Since the distributors will be giving the total sales in the product category (e.g. off-licences might be asked how much whisky they expect to sell in the next 12 months) the company will then have to make a judgement regarding the amount of market share they might reasonably expect to capture.

The **Delphi technique** involves taking in the managers' and salespeople's forecasts, combining them centrally, then sending the aggregate forecast back to the individuals concerned for revision. This approach has proved popular with firms because it tends to produce a consensus of opinion that all those concerned can adhere to. A problem with using Delphi might be that individuals will only make forecasts that they are quite sure are achievable: in other words, they might underestimate the possible sales rather than risk being unable to hit targets.

Time-series analysis uses the company's past sales records to predict what will happen in the future. Although this can be quite accurate, it does not take account of the unexpected – a sudden entry by a competitor, a change in legislation, or a change in the company's fortunes through takeover or merger. Few forecasting methods can take account of these factors, of course, and ultimately the company has to plan in some way. Time-series forecasters usually perform four types of analysis, as shown in Table 4.5 (Marino 1986). Having carried out each of these analyses, the forecaster is able to combine the results to develop the sales forecast.

Time-series analysis works best for well-established products with fairly stable purchasing patterns. It is not suitable for new products or for products with erratic demand cycles.

Table 4.5   Time-series analysis

Type of analysis	Description
Trend analysis	Focuses on aggregate sales data collected over a long period to determine whether sales are rising, falling or staying level.
Cycle analysis	Here the forecaster examines the sales figures from a number of years to see whether there is a cyclical pattern; perhaps a response to the economic boom-and-bust cycle. This method has been largely discredited for most markets, since the cycles do not follow a regular pattern.
Seasonal analysis	Sales figures are analysed on a monthly or even weekly basis to see whether there is a seasonal cycle operating.
Random factor analysis	In any analysis there will be figures that do not fit the pattern; random factor analysis seeks to attribute explanations for these abnormal findings. For example, a spell of unseasonal weather might have affected one month's figures.

For new products, a **test marketing** exercise might be carried out. This involves making the product available in one geographical area for a period of time, and monitoring the actual sales of the product in the area. The key to success with test marketing lies in ensuring that the area chosen is an accurate representation of the country as a whole; if not, the predicted sales on national roll-out will not be as expected. The major drawback of test marketing is that it allows the firm's competitors to see the product and possibly develop their own version before the product goes national. For this reason, test marketing exercises are usually short.

Case study 4
The holiday business

In the UK, increased leisure and increased income has meant a huge growth in the travel industry. Fifty years ago most people had only two weeks' holiday a year – only a lucky few had three weeks. Yet in the twenty-first century many people enjoy six weeks' annual leave, or even seven weeks. At the same time disposable income rose 18% between 1997 and 2001 – and there are only so many household items someone can buy. The surplus income often finds a home in paying for ever more exotic holidays.

In the 1950s most British people holidayed within the UK, at resorts such as Blackpool, Brighton, Rhyl, Bognor Regis or Bournemouth. In most cases, these resorts drew their custom from nearby cities – Manchester and Liverpool for Blackpool, London for Bognor Regis and Brighton, and so forth. However, the advent of the jet aircraft made flying much cheaper, and during the late 1950s and early 1960s package holidays to foreign countries began to become popular. Air-inclusive tours (AITs) boomed during the next 20 years, but as travellers became more sophisticated the idea of a package holiday became less appealing – people wanted to set their own agendas on holiday. During the 1990s cheap airlines became established, and the main advantage of the AIT (low overall cost) was eroded.

The range of choice of holiday is now vast, to take account of the variety of customer needs and customer experiences. At one end of the spectrum, there are holidaymakers who look for an organised tour from a knowledgeable firm, where the holiday experience is managed almost entirely by the tour operator. Examples of this include guided tours of Egyptian antiquities, cruises or two-centre holidays where the customers spend part of their time in a major city and part of their time on a beach somewhere. At the other end of the scale, backpackers and independent travellers book themselves a flight, and find their hotels or hostels when they arrive, needing no more than a good guide book and a smattering of the local language.

For firms in the holiday industry, segmenting the market is therefore complex. Package holidays might be AIT or non-AIT (mostly self-drive tours to Ireland or France). The market could be segmented by destination (France, Spain, Greece and North America are the most popular destinations for Brits). The market may be segmented by degree of independence of the holidaymakers. It may even segment by income – backpackers are at the budget end, whereas many people in their 50s and 60s have high disposable incomes and take luxurious holidays.

Some holidaymakers look for specific activities (skiing, sightseeing, surfing, etc.). There were 954,000 ski trips taken from the UK in the 2001/2002 season alone, according to researchers Mintel. Packages aimed at such customers sometimes include tuition or expert guides. Other holidays aim at relaxation – but even here the market can be segmented. There is a great deal of difference between a relaxing holiday aimed at 18- to 30-year-olds and one aimed at families with small children.

The final complication for holiday companies is that individuals often shift from one segment to another. The young people looking for a lively night-life five years ago might be looking for a quiet location where their children can be entertained this year. Equally, someone who backpacked across India five years ago might be a rising executive looking for a honeymoon trip on the Orient Express this year. Even within a shorter space of time, it would not be unusual for someone to take a cheap, self-organised holiday for one chunk of leave and take a more organised package holiday later in the same year. Over a longer period of time, backpackers become family people and eventually become well-off older people – people aged over 50 are among the most affluent in the country, and also frequently have the most spare time available to enjoy foreign holidays.

Undoubtedly the package holiday is not yet dead, but the strongest growth is in the independent sector. How tour operators will counter this trend remains to be seen.

Questions

1 What bases for segmentation might be appropriate in the holiday business?
2 Which segments are likely to show the strongest growth in the next 10 years?
3 Which segments are likely to shrink in the next 10 years?
4 How might tour operators respond to the growth in the independent sector?
5 How might a holiday marketer track people who apparently shift from one segment to another?

SUMMARY

This chapter has been about ways of dividing markets up into manageable portions. Here are the key points from this chapter:

- There are few, if any, mass markets left untouched.
- If most consumers already own the core benefits of a product, the market must be segmented if success is to follow, since there is otherwise no reason for consumers to switch brands.
- Segments must be measurable, accessible, substantial and congruent.
- The profitability of a segment is calculated as the number of people in the segment multiplied by the premium they are willing to pay.
- The narrower the segment the fewer the customers, but the greater the satisfaction and the greater the premium they are willing to pay (provided the segment has been correctly identified).
- There are many ways to segment a market, in fact as many ways as there are groups with congruent needs.
- Targeting is concerned with selecting an appropriate segment or segments, and approaching it in a consistent and effective way.
- Some segments are defined by the media used to target them.

- Sales forecasting is difficult, but can most easily be accomplished where the product is a fairly standard item.
- Forecasting is likely to be self-fulfilling if all the interested parties are involved in the process.

CHAPTER QUESTIONS

1 What might be the segmentation bases for the home computer market?

2 What sales forecasting approaches would be most suitable for the launch of a new family car?

3 When should an industrial market be segmented geographically?

4 When should a consumer market be segmented geographically?

5 How might a TV company assess the viability of a new drama series?

Further reading

Unlike consumer behaviour or marketing communications, there are relatively few texts that cover segmentation in any great detail.

Consumer Behaviour and Marketing Strategy, **4th edn, by J. Paul Peter and Jerry C. Olson** (Chicago, IL, Irwin, 1996) has a good section on segmenting consumer markets in Chapter 16.

Zikmund and D'Amico's *Effective Marketing: Creating and Keeping Customers* (St Paul, MN, West, 2001) has a good account of segmentation methodologies in Chapter 7.

References

Abell, Derek F.: *Defining the Business: The Starting Point of Strategic Planning* (Englewood Cliffs, NJ, Prentice Hall, 1980).

Beatty, S.E., Kahle, L. and Homer, P.: 'Personal values and gift-giving behaviours: a study across cultures', *Journal of Business Research*, **22** (1991), pp. 149–57.

Blankson, Charles and Kalafatis, Stavros P.: 'The development and validation of a scale measuring consumer/customer derived generic typology of positioning strategies', *Journal of Marketing Management*, (1) **20** (February 2004), pp. 5–43.

Bonoma, T.V. and Shapiro, B.P.: 'How to segment industrial markets', *Harvard Business Review* (May/June 1984), pp. 104–10.

Engel, J.F., Blackwell, R.D. and Miniard, P.W.: *Consumer Behaviour*, 8th edn (Fort Worth, Tx, Dryden Press, 1995).

Hassan, S.S. and Katsanis, L.P.: 'Identification of global consumer segments: a behavioural framework', *Journal of International Consumer Marketing*, **3** (2) (1991), pp. 11–28.

Hofstede, G.: *Culture's Consequences: International Differences in Work-Related Values* (Beverly Hills, Sage, 1980).

Hofstede, G.: 'Management scientists are human', *Management Science*, **40** (1) (1994), pp. 4–13.

Jamal, Ahmed: 'Marketing in a multicultural world: the interplay of marketing, ethnicity and consumption', *European Journal of Marketing*, **37** (1) (2003), pp. 1599–1620.

Kotler, P.: *Marketing Management*, 7th edn (Englewood Cliffs, NJ, Prentice Hall, 1991).

Lastovicka, John L. and Joachimstaler, Erich A.: 'Improving the detection of personality–behaviour relationships in consumer research', *Journal of Consumer Research* (March 1988), pp. 583–7.

Lee, C.: 'Determinants of national innovativeness and international market segmentation', *International Marketing Review*, **7** (5) (1990), pp. 39–49.

Marino, Kenneth E.: *Forecasting Sales and Planning Profits* (Chicago, IL, Probus Publishing, 1986), p. 155.

Office of National Statistics: Census 2001, www.statistics.gov.uk/cci/nugget.cisp?id=350, 2003.

Plummer, Joseph T.: 'The concept and application of life style segmentation', *Journal of Marketing* (January 1974), pp. 33–7.

Smith, W.R.: 'Product differentiation and market segmentation as alternative marketing strategies', *Journal of Marketing* (21 July 1957).

Wind, Yoram: 'Going to market: new twists for some old tricks', *Wharton Magazine*, **4** (1984).

Zikmund, William G. and D'Amico, Michael: *Effective Marketing: Creating and Keeping Customers* (St Paul, MN, West, 1995), p. 232.

VIDEO CASE 3
www.pearsoned.co.uk/blythe

HSBC Private Banking

The Hong Kong and Shanghai Banking Corporation started out (not surprisingly) in China, but was founded by British bankers to provide finance for the Hong Kong colonies and British business in the Far East. In the intervening 150 years the company has taken over other banks and has become a global brand: from 1998 the company rebranded all its 'local' banks in each country as HSBC: overnight, the bank became a global brand.

HSBC brands itself as the world's local bank. With branches worldwide, this is no idle boast: the company prides itself on knowing its individual markets, and with understanding local cultural issues.

When HSBC wanted to launch a new private bank venture in India, market research played a vital role. India is a very large market – although the country is often portrayed as poor, there are over 200 million people who would fit into the 'middle class' category, and more millionaires than there are in the UK or even the USA. Tapping into this market was the aim of HSBC Private Banking, and establishing and maintaining relationships with this wealthier group was crucial to the success of the new venture.

Using the image of a butterfly emerging from an egg, HSBC advised customers 'Assume nothing'. This striking image helped put the bank into the forefront of customers' minds.

Chris Meares, Chief Executive Officer, Group Private Banking, HSBC

Watch the video clip, then try to answer the following questions. The answers are on the companion website.

Questions

1 What is the importance of market research for HSBC Private Banking?

2 What research methods might be most appropriate for the bank?

3 How does the company's product offering benefit directly from research?

5 Market research

Objectives

After reading this chapter you should be able to:

- explain the difference between data and information;
- describe the research process;
- explain the difference between qualitative and quantitative research;
- explain the difference between primary and secondary research;
- develop a sampling frame for a given piece of research;
- design a suitable questionnaire;
- explain the importance of correct interview technique.

INTRODUCTION

There is considerable debate over the term 'market research'; many marketers believe that the term 'marketing research' is more appropriate. Market research is usually considered to be research into customer needs, wants and preferences; marketing research is sometimes used to describe all research carried out for the purpose of supporting marketing decisions. Whichever term is used, market research is concerned with the disciplined collection and evaluation of specific data in order to help suppliers understand their customers' needs better (Chisnall 1992).

THE NEED FOR MARKET RESEARCH

Market research is the process of collecting, analysing and presenting useful information about consumers. **Marketing research** also includes more general research into markets, which includes competitive activities and also environmental issues such as government activities and economic shifts. The ability to measure marketing performance has a significant positive impact on firm performance, profitability, stock market valuation, and (of course) the status of marketing within the organisation (O'Sullivan and Abela 2007).

The first question any marketer should ask before embarking on a research exercise is whether the information gained will be worth more than the cost of collecting it. Market research can represent a substantial investment in both time and money terms; in some cases it is undoubtedly cheaper simply to go ahead with the project without carrying out any research at all. For example, if the total cost of sending out a mailing is less than £10 000, but research into finding out whether or not it would be effective would cost £12 000, it is obviously better not to do the research. More subtly, if the managers feel that the risk of the mailshot failing altogether is low, they may still not run the research even if it is much cheaper. If, for example, the management estimated the risk of failure at only 10%, the value of the research would be only £1000. Therefore it might not be worthwhile carrying out research even if the cost of it were, say, £3000.

In general, however, it is not wise to embark on a major commitment (such as launching a new product) without carrying out some market research beforehand. The vast majority of new products fail (see Chapter 6), and this is usually because consumers do not think that the product is worth the money. Good market research will reduce the risk of this happening, and it has been said (wisely) that those who find research expensive should think about what ignorance would cost.

Types of research that are carried out by marketers are as follows:

- customer research;
- promotion research;
- product research;
- distribution research;
- sales research; and
- marketing environment research.

Customer research is intended to produce facts about markets and market segments; it provides information about where customers live, what they do with their time, what their motivations are, what they like to spend money on and what their spending power is, and what the trends are in the market.

Promotion research measures the success of promotions in terms of their objectives. It relies on careful planning of objectives (see Chapter 9) but can provide information about the suitability of the approach used in reaching a target audience. Research is also useful for determining which media should be used; since promotion in general, and advertising in particular, tends to be expensive it is important that the effort is not squandered on advertising in the wrong place.

Product research is used to identify new uses for existing products, or to identify needs for new products. Product research is often used to refine the design of an existing product to produce an improved 'Mark 2' version.

Distribution research is concerned with finding the best channels of distribution for a product; often it overlaps with consumer research, since the location of retail outlets will depend on where the target consumers live and on their habits. For example, many DIY products are distributed through edge-of-town outlets, which means that only those consumers with cars will be able to reach the store and buy the product. This will not matter if the product is an automotive one, but may matter if it is a product for elderly people, who may not own cars (or perhaps prefer not to drive).

Sales research is intended to help the sales management process by ensuring that territories are of equal size or value, that the techniques and approaches being used are effective, that the training of the salesforce is appropriate and sufficient, and that salesforce motivation is appropriate (see Chapter 9).

Finally, **marketing environment research** examines aspects of the micro- and macro-environments (see Chapter 2). The purpose of the exercise is to ensure that the firm can anticipate environmental change and develop responses in advance.

Very often research can be carried out fairly quickly and cheaply, since much of the information needed will probably already exist, either in published form or within the company's own records. Often the company records contain a great deal of useful **data**, or raw facts; analysis of those facts will turn it into usable **information**. The data items themselves are worthless until there has been some kind of thoughtful analysis to convert them to information. Data mining is an important component of database marketing, in which the database drives everything the company does: provided the entire company (from invoicing department to shipping) use the same database, so that all the information about the customer (from whether they are prompt payers through to whether they prefer deliveries on Wednesdays) can be collated to form a complete picture.

Marketing information systems are often set up to provide an automatic flow of data into the firm, with systems for regular analysis of the data. These systems used to be held on paper, with consequent emphasis on form-filling by salespeople, shipping departments, finance staff and others. In recent years, the increased use of computers (particularly desktop PCs) has allowed far more efficient systems to be put in place, and has reduced the amount of time spent on gathering information (Proctor 2000). There is always a trade-off involved between the value of information and the cost in time, effort and money of obtaining it; by reducing the cost element, computers have increased the possibilities for obtaining useful data and converting it into usable information. Computer-based systems such as these are called **decision support systems**: an example is the electronic point-of-sale (EPOS) systems used by large retailers. These record every purchase made in the store so that the retailer can re-order stock in the correct amounts, can automatically analyse trends, and can even (with the use of loyalty cards) track an individual customer's purchases over a period of time.

Decision support systems need to be user-friendly so that managers without training in data analysis can use them; this is the main reason for their popularity over paper-based information systems (Bessen 1994).

THE RESEARCH PROCESS

The purpose of the research is to collect data (and sometimes information) and process it into usable information that can be used to make management decisions. The first stage in any research process is to define the problem and set objectives. Figure 5.1 shows the research process.

After setting the objectives, the process of collecting the data can begin. Data can be collected from either **primary research** sources or **secondary research** sources. Primary sources are original research: questionnaires, interviews, experiments or product tests with consumers. Secondary research (also called *desk research*) comes from already published information in journals, newspapers, commercially published market research, government statistics, directories, yearbooks, CD-ROM databases, the Internet, and other published materials. Secondary data are, in effect, second-hand data.

Figure 5.1   The market research process

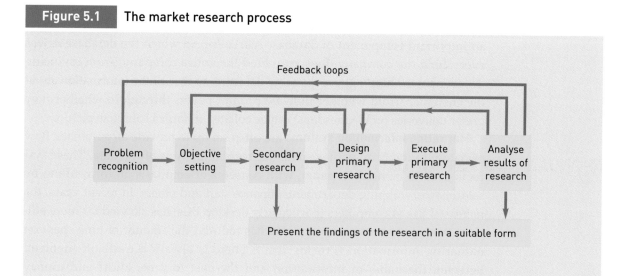

Normally it is sensible to begin the research process by looking at secondary sources. The reasons for this are as follows:

- It is always cheaper.
- It is always quicker.
- Sometimes all the necessary information for making the decision has already been published and is available.
- Even when the published information is incomplete, the researchers will only have to fill in the gaps with primary research rather than gather all the information first-hand.

Secondary research will not necessarily tell the researchers everything they need to know. For example, if the company is planning to launch a new solar-powered personal FM radio set, it is unlikely that anyone will have carried out research specifically into solar-powered FM radio sets. There will probably be research on personal stereos, on radio ownership, on environment-friendly consumers and on solar power, so all these sources should be examined first. This will, at the very least, help with the design of the primary research.

The other main drawbacks with secondary research are that it is often out of date, and that it can be hard for the researcher to be confident of its accuracy, since it is often published without giving details of the methods used in its collection. This is particularly the case with Internet sources, which are notoriously unreliable: there is nothing to stop anyone publishing anything on the Internet, whether it is true or false, and in the absence of any kind of checking there have certainly been some highly biased statements and faked 'research' published. Researchers therefore need to exercise some caution, but that certainly does not mean that secondary sources should be ignored.

Having completed the search for secondary data, it is possible to design the primary research. This will involve deciding: (a) what gaps there are, in terms of the objectives and what is known from the secondary sources; (b) who we need to approach to get the information; and (c) the methods to be used.

Deciding what we need to find out from the primary research means comparing what the secondary research says with the objectives that were originally set. Where there is information lacking, the researchers need to decide how to find it out, and who would have the information.

APPROACHING RESPONDENTS

Respondents are the subjects of research – the people whose behaviour and opinion are of interest to the researchers. The *methodology* will depend on what the researchers are hoping to discover. Methodology is not the same as method; methodology is actually the study of method, and is concerned with the philosophy behind the choice of a specific method.

Qualitative research

Qualitative research is to do with how people feel about the product, advertisement or company; the approach is usually much more probing (and thus time-consuming) than would be the case with quantitative research, and therefore the *sample size* (number of respondents) will be much smaller. Qualitative research will often tell researchers why people behave in the way they do, but since it usually consists of subjective opinions it can be difficult to quantify. Table 5.1 shows some of the methods used in qualitative research.

It is not unusual to carry out qualitative research before designing a quantitative study, to find out the dimensions of the problem; the researcher might then carry out a questionnaire-type survey to find out how many people agree with the statements made in the qualitative study. Because of the cost and time involved, there has been a movement away from this extensive approach, however, and much more research is being done using qualitative methods only.

Table 5.1 Qualitative methods

Method	Explanation
Group depth interview or focus group	A group of six or eight people is recruited and invited to talk about the subject. This method tends to produce a wide range of opinion, because each member of the group will 'trigger' the other members to think of things to say. On the other hand, group pressure may mean that only the most vociferous respondents' views are expressed.
Exploratory groups	A type of focus group used at the initial stages of market research to find the dimensions of the problem. Dimensions are the factors which are of interest to respondents about a particular marketing issue. Exploratory groups usually consist of a cross-section of potential consumers.
Clinical focus groups	On some issues, respondents' attitudes may be hidden below the conscious level. These groups are used in a clinical setting where the researcher can judge whether the person's true feelings are being expressed. Clinical focus groups are also heterogeneous.
Experiencing focus groups	These groups are homogeneous, and allow the researcher to gauge the feelings of a group of actual customers for the product category under consideration.
Teleconferencing	Teleconferencing involves a group discussion conducted over the telephone. Similar to a focus group, this avoids the necessity of bringing people together physically and also can make people feel easier about expressing themselves. The technique is particularly useful for focus groups involving managers in industry.
Video-conferencing	Like teleconferencing, but with vision. This has the major advantage of allowing the researcher to see people's facial reactions, which often say more about a person's true feelings than do words.
Depth interviews	Usually carried out by highly trained interviewers or psychologists, the depth interview uses probing questions to uncover the respondent's deepest feelings.

Method	Explanation
Table 5.1 continued	
Projective techniques	Subjects are presented with ambiguous, unstructured situations and invited to respond. Because the situation is unclear, the respondents must use their imaginations to respond, in the course of which their own true feelings will be revealed. Projective techniques are used when a direct response might be embarrassing for the respondent.
Word association	A projective technique in which the respondent is asked to say the first thing that comes to mind when the researcher says a particular word. The theory is that the respondent does not have time to censor his or her response, so that the respondent's true feelings are revealed.
Cartoon tests	Another projective technique; the respondent is shown a cartoon and asked to supply the captions for it. The respondent will actually put his or her true feelings down; since it is only a cartoon, no blame can attach to the respondent for what the characters are 'saying'.
Third-person techniques	This projective technique is simple to apply: the respondent is asked what he or she thinks another person ('your neighbour' or 'most people') would say or do in a given situation. The respondent would typically give their own opinion as if it were that of the third person.
Analogy	Here the respondent's personality is linked to a prospective purchase. For example, the respondent might be asked to imagine what it would be like to actually be a new BMW car. The respondent might say 'I feel powerful' or 'I feel ready for my new executive owner' (Proctor 2000). Analogies help marketers develop communications strategies targeted at specific groups of consumers.
Experimentation	Respondents are invited to do something, or are shown an item and their responses are monitored. For example, Goodyear Tire and Rubber Company used a virtual shopping computer simulation to examine brand equity issues (Burke 1996).
Observation	The researcher watches the consumers and notes their behaviour. For example, a researcher might stand outside a shopping mall and count how many people go in. At one time, Fisher-Price, the toy manufacturer, ran a free crèche in Chicago and gave the children prototype toys to play with in order to see which ones the children like best, and how they play with the toys (Stewart 1989).
Virtual focus group	Here respondents are recruited for an online chatroom to discuss the subject of interest. This technique has the great advantage that people can respond from their home or workplace, which means they can be recruited from anywhere in the world if need be. Also, they do not have to be on-line at the same time – the focus group can run for days or weeks if necessary. Third, a degree of anonymity can be preserved. Finally, analysis is made much easier because there is no need to prepare a transcript – the responses are already written down.

Quantitative research

Quantitative research methodology deals with areas that can be expressed in numbers. It will tell researchers, for example, what proportion of the population drinks tea in the mornings and what their ages and occupations are; what it will not do very easily is tell researchers why those people prefer tea to coffee.

Surveys

Most people have at some time or other been asked to participate in a survey, and this method remains the commonest method of collecting quantitative data. Surveys can elicit facts about the respondent's behaviour and possessions, can find out opinions about issues and ideas, and can sometimes elicit interpretations of the respondent's actions or opinions. Table 5.2 shows some survey techniques.

A major problem with any survey lies in ensuring that the right questions are asked, and that they are asked in the right way. A typical questionnaire would ask respondents about their behaviour and attitudes, and about themselves; this is important for classification purposes. Obviously the researcher will be unable to say '25% of 25–35-year-olds buy beer at least twice a week' if the questionnaire did not ask the respondents their age, but most questionnaires would need to contain much more detail about the respondents. The questions about the respondents themselves must be discreet as well as relevant, and this requires considerable skill on the part of the researcher in deciding what might or might not be relevant to the study at hand.

Questionnaire design can be a lengthy process for this reason. The criteria for writing survey questions are as follows:

- Questions need to be short, simple and unambiguous.
- Questions should not be leading – in other words they should not direct the respondent towards a particular answer.
- The questionnaire's introduction should be persuasive, and must qualify the respondent as belonging in the sample.
- The answers must be capable of analysis, preferably by computer.
- Questions must be necessary and relevant to the study.
- The respondent must have the information needed to answer the question.
- Respondents must be willing to answer the questions. If the questions get too personal, people will not respond.
- Questions must be specific. Avoid asking two questions at once: e.g. 'Was your holiday pleasant and good value for money?' Holidays can be pleasant without being good value.
- Hypothetical questions should be avoided; they require guesswork on the part of respondents, and also can rarely be worded in such a way that respondents have enough information to answer.

Even experienced researchers have difficulty in writing effective questionnaires; what is a clear and obvious question to one person may have a different meaning to another, so it is usually a good idea to **pilot** all questionnaires. This means testing the first draft of the questionnaire by asking a group of typical respondents to fill it in, then analysing the results. Often (in fact usually) this process will highlight errors in the design; these can be corrected before the finished

Table 5.2 Survey techniques

Method	Explanation
Postal surveys	Questionnaires sent to respondents through the mail. Respondents fill in the answers and mail the survey back. They have the advantages of being cheap, of avoiding interviewer bias and of being capable of containing questions on a broad range of issues. They have the disadvantages of (typically) having a low response rate, of not allowing the researcher control over the respondent, and of the possibility of someone other than the addressee (e.g. a secretary or assistant) filling in the replies.
Personal structured interviews	Here the researcher goes through the questions face-to-face with the respondent. This technique is more expensive than a postal survey, but gives the researcher control over the process (e.g. the order in which questions are asked and answered). The cost is high, and refusal rate (the proportion of people who refuse to participate) is also high.
Telephone surveys	Here the questionnaire is administered over the telephone. This has the advantage of being quick and cheap, with a high response rate, while still allowing the researcher to control the process. The disadvantage is that respondents sometimes suspect that they are about to be subjected to an unwanted sales pitch, and also the list of telephone numbers may be out of date. In recent years, people have been able to opt out of inclusion on telephone lists by registering with the Telephone Preference Service, which means that a large number of potential respondents have been removed from the system.
Self-administered surveys (feedback cards)	This method is often used in service industries such as hotels and restaurants. Questionnaires are left for customers to fill in and put into a box or mail back. The major drawback of this method is that not all customers will fill in the survey; only those who are exceptionally pleased or exceptionally disappointed are likely to fill them in, so the management will get a distorted picture of the customer satisfaction levels. Managers would be well advised to treat any comment other than 'excellent' as a complaint.
Panels	A panel is a group of respondents who regularly respond to surveys. Some panels are set up on a permanent basis and are often made available to researchers by commercial market research companies. Sometimes panels are used by a group of firms to carry out research which is syndicated to the group. Panels are expensive to set up, but relatively cheap to run and have the major advantage of offering a very high response rate.
Omnibus studies	Omnibus surveys are usually carried out by commercial market research agencies who combine several studies into one questionnaire. This reduces the cost for each client, and ultimately reduces effort for respondents since they will need to give their personal details only once. For an omnibus survey respondents will be asked about several unrelated topics; the questionnaires tend to be somewhat long and arduous to complete so respondents are often rewarded with a small gift.
Online surveys	Several online survey systems exist (surveymonkey for example). Researchers can post their questionnaires on the site, then direct respondents to it. The major advantage is that analysis can be conducted virtually instantly: the main disadvantage is ensuring that the sample is representative, though of course this is a problem with all surveys.

version is used on the overall sample of respondents. If several errors are detected at the pilot stage, it may be worth considering piloting a second time; many surveys have been run only to find that there is a major ambiguity in one or more questions, invalidating the entire project.

Critical thinking

This is all very well, but how do we know people are telling us the truth? Even if they want to, might they not misunderstand the question, or have something else on their minds? People often tell lies, especially if they are confronted with something embarrassing – and in any case, almost all of us like to appear in a good light.

Furthermore, there is the widespread view that a nosy question deserves a lying answer – people might appear to be co-operating, but instead will deliberately mislead us. And if that's the case, how can any research be worthwhile?

Sampling

Sampling means choosing who to ask. It is usually not feasible or necessary to ask everybody in the target market to give an opinion on a given issue, but it is important to ask enough of the right type of people to ensure that the data we get are reasonably representative of the market as a whole. In some cases sampling can be very simple: if we want to know what were the key factors in making a purchase, we could arrange for a simple questionnaire to be taken at the point of sale, in other words ask people to provide us with their main reasons for buying while they are still in the shop.

Finding the right mix of respondents is important because the researcher is attempting to draw conclusions about the target market as a whole; for some surveys less than 100 respondents' opinions would be solicited in order to draw conclusions about consumers numbering in the millions. This means that a small sampling error will be multiplied many times when the analysis takes place. In general, the bigger the sample the less likely there will be sampling bias, particularly if the survey is intended to find out the opinions of a small minority of the population.

The **sampling frame** is the list of possible respondents from whom the researcher wishes to draw a **sample**. In some cases this list will be available: for example, if a researcher wants to sample the opinions of doctors, it is possible to obtain a list of names and addresses for every doctor in the country. It would then be relatively simple to construct a sample from the list. It is more likely, though, that the list the researcher wants is unavailable: for example, a list of people who have played squash in the last three months probably does not exist. In those circumstances the researcher would have to construct a representative sample of individuals with the required characteristics. This can be a difficult task (Mouncey 1996).

Table 5.3 shows some sampling methods.

Recently there has been a move away from probability sampling towards quota sampling and a growing use of databases for sampling (Cowan 1991). The reasons for this are that quota sampling is easier and more reliable, and databases provide a quick and easy way of sampling for postal questionnaires.

Table 5.3 Sampling methods

Sampling method	Description	Advantages	Disadvantages
Random sample or probability sample	Each individual in the population at large has an equal chance of being included in the sample.	Will give a clear cross-section of the population.	Almost impossible to achieve. Most so-called 'random' samples are seriously biased: for example, choosing names from the telephone book might seem 'random', but in fact only people with landline telephones will be included, and even then those who are ex-directory will not be included.
Quota sample	An analysis of the population is undertaken first of all, often from the census data. Then a quota for each category (e.g. women aged 35, men aged 20, middle-aged professionals) is drawn up and interviewers are told to fill the quota.	Will produce a clear cross-section of opinion, provided the basis for the quota is correctly set.	Often means that interviewers are rejecting respondents because they do not fit the quota, and towards the end of the day the interviewers might be spending a lot of time looking for that last 35-year-old manual worker with two children.
Stratified sample	Similar to quota sampling in that broad bands of the population are specified, but the final choice of respondent is almost taken by chance.	Less waste of respondents than quota sampling, more flexibility for interviewers and therefore cheaper.	Not as accurate as quota sampling.

Interview technique

When conducting interviews, it is all too easy for the interviewer to 'lead' the respondents into making the 'right' statements. Sometimes respondents will encourage this by asking questions themselves; good interviewers will avoid the temptation to step in and help at this point.

Some ways to avoid this are to use statements such as, 'Well, it's your opinion that's important. What do you think?' or perhaps just to give a questioning look. It is also advisable to explain to the respondents beforehand that you will not be able to help them with the answers.

In the case of a focus group or group depth interview, there is a problem of judging whether to let a particular line of conversation continue or not. What may at first appear to be an entirely irrelevant digression from the subject may eventually turn round and produce something very insightful; on the other hand, if the interview just degenerates into a general chat nothing useful will arise. The moderator could, possibly, just ask how the topic relates to the subject of the research. This will sometimes produce a quick explanation of the relationship, or otherwise a quick return to the point of discussion.

In practice, groups usually do keep to the subject at hand; digressions are few and usually short-lived.

Sources of bias

Bias is the effect whereby the results of a survey are rendered unreliable by some external force. The commonest sources are **sampling bias** and **interviewer bias**.

Sampling bias

This results from taking a sample that is not representative of the population we wish to study. It is easy to fall into the trap of thinking that the sample is representative, when in fact it has been drawn from a small population. For example, a researcher might carry out a survey in a high street, stopping every third shopper. This survey will not be representative, since it includes only those who shop in that high street on that day. A survey of this type undertaken on a Tuesday afternoon, for example, might include a higher proportion of pensioners and unemployed people than there are in the population at large. A similar survey undertaken on a Saturday afternoon might exclude most sports fans. Sample bias is common and difficult to avoid.

Interviewer bias

This often comes about because the interviewer wants to help the respondent to answer the question. Interviewers naturally want to get through the questionnaire with the minimum of problems, and they are also acutely aware that the respondent probably has better things to do than answer awkward or badly phrased questions. If the interviewer finds that respondents are showing a negative reaction to some questions, he or she might skip past those questions in future, and 'guess' the answers. Sadly, it has been known for some unscrupulous interviewers to fake the answers altogether if they are having difficulty in finding enough respondents to fill the quota (Kieker and Nelson 1996).

Interviewer bias can be subtle; in one-to-one open-ended interviews the interviewer's body language (facial expressions, movements, etc.) can convey a message to the respondent that leads to a specific answer being given, or to some information being withheld. Likewise, people tend to answer differently when the interviewer is male rather than female, or older rather than younger.

ANALYSING THE RESULTS

Analysis has three distinct stages: **editing**, which means discarding any inconsistent or spoiled responses; **tabulating**, which means totalling the various responses and cross-tabulating them; and **interpreting**, which means saying what the figures mean.

Qualitative data analysis

Until relatively recently the analysis of *qualitative data* was heavily reliant on the judgement of the researcher. The traditional approach has been to make transcripts of recordings made during focus groups or depth interviews, then make an overall judgement of the views expressed using quotes to support the argument. This approach has been criticised on the grounds that it lacks the rigour of quantitative methods.

With the widespread use of computers, programs have become available for the analysis of qualitative data. Programs are available to carry out the following operations:

■ Find individual words or phrases. Having decided which are the key phrases or words that are significant in the study, the researcher can tell the computer to find and count such words and phrases.

■ Create *indexes* to show where and in what context the words and phrases have been used. Rather like a book index, this allows the researcher to attribute phrases to types of individual.

■ Attach key words or codes to segments of text. Sometimes respondents will be talking about a particular issue without using the actual words that the researcher believes are the key ones. Some programs allow the researcher to add relevant codes and key words to identify subject areas in the text.

■ Connecting the categories. This allows the researcher to see whether some types of statement are associated with other types of statement: for example, whether those respondents who make right-wing comments also prefer powerful cars.

Table 5.4 gives some examples of computer programs for analysis of qualitative data. The list is by no means exhaustive; there are many other programs available to help in qualitative analysis, and more are being developed. Such programs can only help take the tedium out of the analysis; they will not do the thinking for the researcher, and a great deal of judgement is still needed in qualitative analysis (Catterall and Maclaran 1995).

Presentation of the data is not numeric. It is not appropriate to ascribe percentages to the comments made, since the sample used is small and the process of ascribing key words and codes to the data is not precise. Typically, qualitative data analysis results in a set of **matrices**, or a **network**. A matrix is the cross-tabulation of two lists, set up as rows and columns; a network is a diagram showing the relationship between concepts.

For example, a *tree* **taxonomy** is a network showing how concepts relate; it is rather like a family tree. A tree taxonomy for eating out is shown in Figure 5.2.

The final stage in qualitative analysis is to interpret the findings into something usable by managers. Again, this requires a degree of judgement on the part of the researcher, and (in common with quantitative analysis) researchers can

Table 5.4 Analysis tools for qualitative data

Program	Description
QSR NUD*IST	Indexes, searches and supports theorising; will handle text or non-textual records such as photographs and tape-recordings. Connects categories, and is good at generating taxonomies (see below).
QUALPRO	Researcher has to segment and code, then QUALPRO will find and assemble the indicated segments.
ETHNOGRAPH	Does what QUALPRO does, but can also find text that has been coded two or more ways.
Longman Concordance	Creates a KWIC (key word in context) file by searching for the key word identified by the researcher and abstracting it with the words around it so as to develop a list of places where the key word appears.

usually only draw inferences about what is probably happening, rather than make categorical statements about what is happening. For this reason most market research reports tend to be lengthy and contain details on the reasoning behind the statements made.

Figure 5.2 Tree taxonomy for eating out

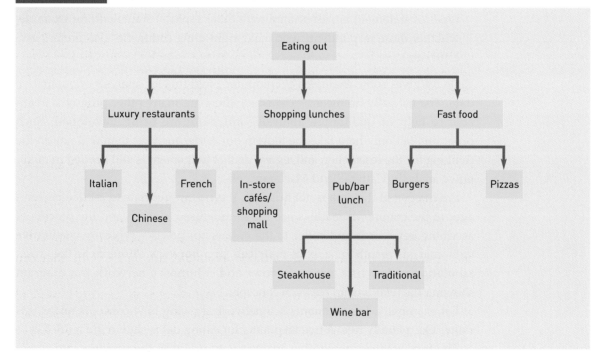

Critical thinking

If so much of this research analysis depends on judgement, what's the point? We might as well just sit down and make it up, might we not? Turning everything into numbers might seem very scientific, but what happens if the basis for the calculations starts from the wrong place?

Maybe, though, just going through the process helps to focus our thinking. Is it the formal process that is important, then, or the results?

Quantitative data analysis

Quantitative data analysis follows the editing, tabulating and interpreting format described earlier. Putting the data into tables needs to be considered at the design stage of the research; projects have been known to collapse because the questionnaire proved impossible to analyse. Normally the data would be cross-tabulated so that the researcher can identify which type of respondent gives each type of answer. For example, research into soft drink consumption might show that 40% of the respondents buy soft drinks at least four times a week, and 5% buy soft drinks every day. The researcher would now need to identify which of the respondents do this, and what else they have in common: Are they all young? What are their incomes? Which newspapers and magazines do they read? This enables the marketers to target that segment of the market.

One of the problems of quantitative analysis is determining how reliable the information is. Because only a small number of people have been surveyed (compared with the population at large), errors can easily be multiplied. The larger the sample, the more reliable it will be, and the more confident the researcher will be that the data reflect a true state of affairs in the population.

The mathematics of analysing the data is beyond the scope of this book, but statistical techniques exist that will enable the researcher to say how reliable the results are likely to be, and also to say which are the relevant factors in the research (see Further Reading at the end of the chapter). Figure 5.3 shows a broad overview of the quantitative methods used in marketing.

Statistical testing should, if carried out correctly, tell us whether this year's results are following a similar pattern to last year's, and whether this relationship actually means something, or merely came about by accident. Table 5.5 shows some of the statistical methods available, and the results that can be obtained.

There are, of course, a great many more statistical tools available, most of which are easily available on computer programs such as SPSS or Windows Excel. This means that the hard work of doing the calculations is taken away, but researchers still need to understand the principles behind the statistical tools if they are to be able to draw sensible conclusions from the answers.

Figure 5.3	Statistical methods chart: PERT, program evaluation and review technique; CPM, critical path method

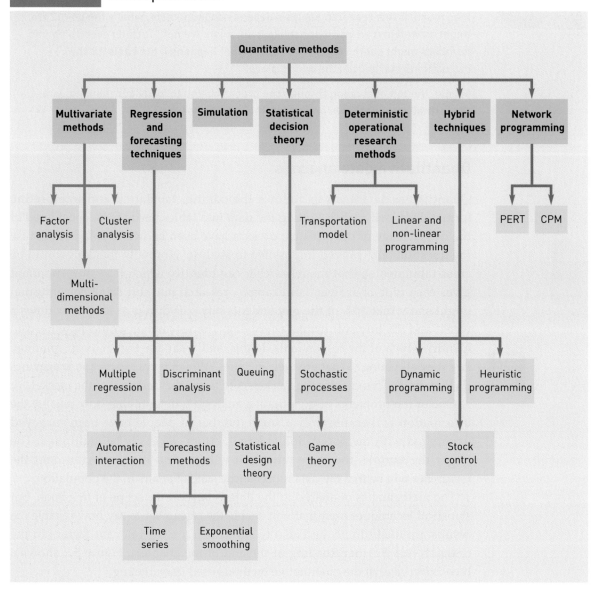

Source: Adapted from Meidan, 1987

For example, a researcher might have surveyed 100 people to find out how many of them would be prepared to buy a new brand of beer. The researcher finds that 42% of them, having tasted the beer, say that they would buy the beer, and on looking at the results for those people it turns out that three-quarters of them are manual workers. This seems to show that manual workers are much more likely to try the beer than are white-collar workers, but it is possible that the researcher just happened to ask an unusual group of manual workers, and most manual workers in the population at large would stay loyal to their current brand of beer.

Table 5.5 Common statistical methods

Statistical method	Explanation
Exponential smoothing	Detects trends in the data by smoothing out the peaks and troughs. Gives more weight to recent data.
Regression analysis	Compares one set of data with another to show whether a trend in one set relates to a trend in the other.
Correlation	Shows the degree to which one set of data relates to another.
Factor analysis	Shows which factors relate to each other by relating them to a set of (theoretical) extra factors.
Significance testing, e.g. *t*-tests	Tests whether the results of a survey can be relied on, or whether they could simply have come about by chance.

A *t*-test might show that the results of the survey are significant at the 95% confidence interval. This means that the researcher is 95% confident that the results can be relied upon; there is still, however, a 5% chance that the results have come about by a fluke. Unless the researcher talks to everybody in the country, there will always be some chance that the sample chosen is not typical; in practice, of course, it is impossibly expensive to question the entire population of the country, so researchers will always be working with samples of the population. In general the larger the sample, the more reliable the results, but this is what a *t*-test will show. By comparing the size of the difference between the groups with the overall sample size, a *t*-test will show whether the sample was large enough to be confident that the difference is a real one, and not one that has appeared by chance.

Statistical methods are relatively easy to apply with the use of a computer, but the most exacting part of the analysis is interpreting the results. For example, the research may show that 40% of people under 35 say that they prefer one type of washing powder to another. This is an interesting piece of information, but it still begs the question of why this should be so. Often research of this nature generates as many questions as it answers, and the researchers may find themselves going back to the beginning and re-designing the research to answer a different set of questions. Usually qualitative research is more useful than quantitative research in finding out why people behave the way they do.

Overall, market research is not a simple proposition. There are many pitfalls for the unwary, but the alternative is almost always worse: examples abound of companies who failed to carry out appropriate market research, launched their products and lost millions before their mistakes could be corrected. Because of the subjective nature of consumer behaviour, no market research is ever going to be fully accurate, but good research will always improve the marketer's 'batting average.

For example, in Denmark there was a steady decline in the consumption of fresh fish during the 1980s and 1990s. Research showed that consumers thought that fish was difficult to prepare, and awkward to eat because of the number of bones. The Danish fishing industry developed a series of advertisements that showed easy recipes for fish, and also packaged a range of fish guaranteed to be bone-free. The result has been a doubling of the consumption of fish in Denmark; a similar campaign in the United Kingdom has yielded equally impressive results.

Case study 5
Mintel

Commercial market research is the cornerstone of business decision-making, and Mintel is at the sharp end of providing it. The company produces detailed industry reports at regular intervals, and few marketing departments are without at least one Mintel report.

Since the late 1970s, when Mintel began by researching the food and drinks industries, the company has produced regular reports on all industries. These reports are sold to interested parties: regular subscribers include SmithKlineBeecham, Air Miles and Associated Newspapers.

As time has gone on, Mintel have expanded from providing 'blanket', one-size-fits-all industry reports which, useful as they are as secondary research, often do not provide the detail some companies need. Mintel can provide tailored advice to marketing departments through their research consultancy, and have specialist databases such as the Global New Products Database, which covers food, beverages, toiletries, over-the-counter pharmaceuticals and household goods in all major global markets. The site offers more than just a brief description: each product is accompanied by an informative editorial on the market and the product's fit within it.

Mintel Menu Insights tracks 350 restaurant chains, 150 independent restaurants 50 top chefs, 25 beverage-based restaurants and 5 buffet restaurants to provide an overview of trends in the restaurant industry. The site provides information on prices, menu changes, ingredients and even preparation methods to give a comprehensive overview of trends in eating out. One recent highlight is the launch of Brix chocolate, specially made to go with specific wines: Mintel report that Brix (a Gia Brands product) has a different formula for each type of wine, and will be sold through off-licences.

Of course, none of this comes cheap – information is expensive to create, because the cost of the original research is high, and the reports are very comprehensive. A typical report costs around £1500, but this is a small price to pay considering that the cost of running a dedicated primary research exercise to find out the same information is likely to cost upwards of £30 000. Granted, the Mintel report may not provide exactly the answer the firm needs, but it often provides most of them, and many firms can easily make up the shortfall from their internal sources, without ever using primary research.

Data is collected through interviews, questionnaires and trawls of secondary sources such as Government statistics. Trade research includes interviews with senior managers in the industry and trawls of the trade press. Analysis is carried out by Mintel's own core of statisticians and analysts to create the final report, which includes informed editorial analysis as well as statistical tables. The reports all follow the same basic format, as follows:

- Executive summary
- Market drivers.
- Market size and trends.

- Market segmentation.
- The supply structure.
- Advertising and promotion.
- New product trends.
- Retail distribution.
- Consumer attitudes and purchasing habits.
- Forecast and future.

Reports are designed to cover the next five years, so the data should remain usable for a long enough period for most firms' planning. From the viewpoint of almost any major firm, using Mintel reports really does not require much thinking time – they are an obvious asset in any firm's planning. Using other Mintel services to fine-tune the information is also likely to be a great deal more cost-effective than running a dedicated primary research exercise – after all, Mintel's staff are extremely highly skilled in the collection of data and the creation of information.

Questions

1 What are the main advantages of using Mintel reports?
2 What disadvantages might there be in using Mintel reports?
3 Why would a firm carry out primary research, even after buying a report?
4 How might Mintel expand its market?
5 What research methods might complement Mintel's own approach?

SUMMARY

Market research is the starting-point of marketing planning, since it focuses on the needs of the customer and provides information that supports decisions designed to meet those needs. Without good information systems, the marketing planning and strategy activities have little hope of success, and will almost always focus on the beliefs of the senior management, which may bear no relationship to the real needs of customers.

Here are the key points from this chapter:

- Data (raw facts) are useless until analysed and interpreted.
- Secondary research should always be conducted before embarking on primary research.
- Self-completion questionnaires need to be simple and unambiguous.
- All questionnaires should be piloted at least once.
- Careful training is needed to avoid interviewer bias.
- Quantitative research is about the how and the what; qualitative research is about the why.
- Market research is never 100% reliable.

CHAPTER QUESTIONS

1 What steps would you take to research the market for a new computer game?

2 Questionnaires can sometimes be ambiguous or ask irrelevant questions. How can these sources of error be reduced?

3 What can be done to overcome interviewer bias?

4 Under what circumstances would qualitative research be more appropriate than quantitative research?

5 What are the main drawbacks of questionnaires?

6 What type of focus group would be best suited to an investigation of working women's food shopping habits?

Further reading

Ian Dey's *Qualitative Data Analysis: A User-friendly Guide for Social Scientists* (London, Routledge, 1993) offers a very entertaining and readable guide to some of the issues surrounding qualitative data analysis, as well as some techniques for carrying it out.

Essentials of Marketing Research, **2nd edn, by Tony Proctor** (Harlow, Financial Times Prentice Hall, 2000) gives a concise yet comprehensive guide to marketing research techniques. In particular, Chapter 10 gives a straightforward guide to data analysis and the mathematical tools used by market researchers.

Contemporary Marketing Research **by Carl McDaniel and Roger Gates** (St Paul, MN, West, 1996) is a comprehensive American text with a wealth of examples. The explanations are clear and the examples are realistic, although the whole book is geared to a US audience.

References

Bessen, Jim: 'Riding the marketing information wave', *Harvard Business Review* (September–October 1994), pp. 150–60.

Burke, R.R.: 'Virtual shopping; breakthrough in marketing research', *Harvard Business Review* (March–April, 1996), p. 120.

Catterall, M. and Maclaran, P.: 'Using a computer to code qualitative data', Proceedings of the 1995 Annual Conference of the Marketing Education Group 'Making Marketing Work', Bradford University, July 1995, pp. 133–42.

Chisnall, P.: *Marketing Research*, 4th edn (Maidenhead, McGraw-Hill, 1992).

Cowan, Charles D.: 'Using multiple sample frames to improve survey coverage, quality and costs', *Marketing Research* (December 1991), pp. 66–9.

Kieker, P. and Nelson, J.E.: 'Do interviewers follow telephone survey instructions?', *Journal of the Market Research Society* (April 1996), pp. 161–76.

Meidan, A.: 'Quantitative methods in marketing', in M.J. Baker (ed.) *The Marketing Book* (London, Heinemann/Chartered Institute of Marketing, 1987).

Mouncey, Peter: 'With growing demands for data, will purity prove only theoretical?', *Research Plus* (May 1996), p. 9.

O'Sullivan, Don and Abela, Andrew V.: 'Marketing performance measurement ability and firm performance', *Journal of Marketing*, **71** (2) (2007), pp. 79–93.

Proctor, Tony: *Essentials of Marketing Research*, 2nd edn (Harlow, Financial Times Prentice Hall, 2000).

Stewart, Doug: 'In the cut-throat world of toy sales, child's play is serious business', *Smithsonian* (December 1989), pp. 76–8.

Acme Whistles

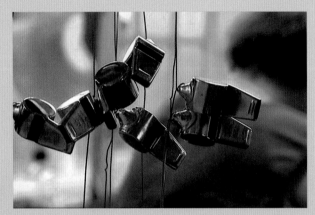

Normally, whistles are not things we think about a great deal. Yet a great many whistles are sold each day – some for sporting events, some for emergency purposes (whistles on lifejackets, for example) and some for entertainment purposes – no carnival would be complete without dancers blowing whistles.

Acme Whistles are the world leaders in making whistles. The company prides itself on the reliability of its products – each whistle is individual tested before it leaves the factory (by using an air line – the days of the company's founder blowing every whistle before it left are long gone). New products are developed at the rate of two a year – even whistles eventually date, since every product has its life cycle. NPD also keeps the company ahead of its competitors. The company aims to develop patentable whistles, as a way of protecting its intellectual property from competitors.

The company is well aware of the needs of its customers. For business to business customers, who may be adding the whistles to an existing product such as a fire safety kit, the company emphasises the reliability of the whistle, since this will reduce returns of faulty products. For consumer markets, the company produces a range of specialist whistles, such as the Titanic Mate's Whistle, a replica of the whistles the company made for the crew of the Titanic. Overall, the company has a surprisingly wide range of whistles!

Simon Topman, Managing Director

Watch the video clip, then try to answer the following questions. The answers are on the companion website.

Questions

1 What is the significance of the company's brand?

2 What type of NPD strategy does Acme have?

3 Why does the company aim to produce two patentable new products a year?

6 Products, branding and packaging

Objectives

After reading this chapter you should be able to:

- describe the stages a product goes through from introduction to obsolescence;
- assess products in a given range and decide which ones are worth keeping and which should be dropped from the range;
- decide on an appropriate policy for developing and introducing new products to the market;
- identify some of the risks inherent in new product development;
- understand what a marketer means by 'product'.

INTRODUCTION

This chapter is about developing new products, and about product policy. The success of an organisation will depend, ultimately, on what bundles of benefits it offers to consumers; the decisions about what the firm should be offering need to be made in the light of the consumer's needs and wants.

There is a strong positive relationship between a firm's innovative activities and its ability to survive and prosper (Hart 1993), so many companies place a strong emphasis on developing new products to replace those which become obsolete, or which are superseded by competitors' offerings.

DEFINING PRODUCTS

Marketers define a *product* as being a *bundle of benefits*. This means that the product is more than just the sum of its physical characteristics; it includes fringe elements such as the brand image, the way the product is packed and delivered, even the colour of the box it comes in. **Primary characteristics** are those core benefits of the product that it has in common with its competitors; **auxiliary characteristics** are the features and benefits that are unique to the product. For instance, consider the contrast between a pizza from a delivery service and a pizza from the supermarket freezer. The primary characteristics of each are the same: a dough base with tomato sauce and cheese on top, with other ingredients included. The primary benefit is that each provides a tasty and filling meal; the auxiliary characteristics are where the two products diverge.

Apart from the differences in flavour, ingredients and so forth, the delivery service is more expensive (perhaps double the price of the supermarket version). The supermarket pizza can be kept in the freezer and heated when needed, and can even be 'customised' by adding extra cheese or other ingredients. On the other hand, the delivery-service pizza includes the service element of delivery, and is already heated and ready to eat. Clearly the benefits are different, and therefore a marketer would say that the products are different.

Marketers need to be aware of the ways in which the needs and wants of consumers are changing, so that the benefits offered by the product range can be tailored to fit those needs and wants. This is the function of market research (see Chapter 5) but it is important to make good use of the information gathered to see which new products might be developed, or which old products might be adapted, and also to see which products are nearing the end of their useful lives.

CLASSIFYING PRODUCTS

Products bought to satisfy personal and family needs are **consumer products**; products bought for the purposes of resale or to be used to make other products are **industrial products**. As in any other question of marketing, the subdivision of these broad categories into smaller, more convenient categories is carried out by reference to the consumer or the customer. In the case of consumer goods, the classification will be as shown in Table 6.1.

Likewise, industrial products can be categorised according to the use the purchasers intend to make of them. Table 6.2 illustrates this. In some ways, industrial buying has parallels with consumer buying behaviour (see Chapter 3), so parallels can also be drawn with the types of product purchased. First of all the company must develop a clear view of what the customer is buying. Levitt (1986) has suggested the following hierarchy of levels:

Table 6.1	Classification of consumer products
Classification	**Explanation**
Convenience products	*Cheap, frequently purchased items that do not require much thought or planning.* The consumer typically buys the same brand or goes to the same shop. Examples are newspapers, basic groceries and soft drinks. Normally convenience products would be distributed through many retail outlets, and the onus is on the producer to promote the products, because the retailer will not expend much effort on such low-priced items.
Shopping products	*Products people shop around for.* Usually infrequently purchased items such as computers, cars, hi-fi systems or household appliances. From the manufacturer's viewpoint, such products require few retail outlets, but will require much more personal selling on the part of the retailer: so there is usually a high degree of co-operation between manufacturer and retailer in marketing the products.
Speciality products	*People plan the purchase of these products with great care, know exactly what they want and will accept no substitutes.* Here the consumer's efforts bend towards finding an outlet that can supply exactly the item needed: this accentuates the exclusivity of the product, so some marketers deliberately limit the number of outlets that are franchised to sell the products. An example of this is the American hair-product manufacturer Redken, which appoints a limited number of hair salons to carry its products.
Unsought products	*These products are not bought; they are sold.* Examples are life insurance, fitted kitchens and encyclopaedias. While most people would recognise the need for these items, it is rare for consumers to go out looking for them; far more commonly the products are sold either by salespeople, or are bought as the result of a sudden change of circumstances (for example, most mortgage lenders require house buyers to take out life insurance).

1 *Core or generic.* This is the basic physical product, or the minimum features that the customer would expect it to have. For example, a microwave oven would be expected to have a timer and a space inside to put the food, and would be expected to heat things up effectively.

2 *Expected.* This is the generic product plus some extra features that the customer would reasonably expect to see. In the microwave example, the customer would expect there to be an instruction book, a guarantee and some kind of servicing network in case of breakdowns.

3 *Augmented.* These are the factors that differentiate the product. For the microwave, this could be a sensor to say when the food is cooked, a defrost facility, free delivery or an after-sales call to check the product is functioning well. These are the features that make the customer buy one brand rather than another.

4 *Potential.* This is all the possible features and benefits that could be wanted by customers. It is unlikely that any product could have all the necessary features (and it would be too expensive to buy anyway), but this list still needs to be developed so that the company can produce different models of the product for different customer needs. If a microwave oven manufacturer knows who the end buyer of the microwave is, it would be possible to keep the customer

Table 6.2 Categorisation of industrial products

Categorisation	Explanation
Raw materials	*Basic products that will be transformed entirely into something else.* These are usually bought in large quantities, and usually have a standardised quality range and prices: this makes it hard for the producer to differentiate the product from those of the competitors.
Major equipment	*The capital machinery and tools used for running the buyer's business.* These are equivalent to shopping goods: the purchasers spend considerable time and effort in choosing which to buy, and therefore there is considerable emphasis on personal selling and on product differentiation. After-sales service is also crucial to success in this market.
Accessory equipment	*Equipment used for the peripheral needs of the firm.* Examples are office equipment and health and safety equipment. Often these are distributed through many outlets, and are more standardised than the major equipment items. This means there is more competition, but also a bigger market for such items as fire extinguishers or PCs.
Component parts	*Manufactured items which will be assembled into the finished product.* These are usually bought by negotiation or tender; often the purchaser has the most power in the relationship, as with car manufacturers.
Process materials	Rather more advanced than raw materials, process materials might be the special alloys used in aircraft construction, or specially tailored plastics. From a marketing viewpoint, process materials are similar to component parts, but with more opportunity for differentiation.
Consumable supplies	*Materials that are used by the purchasers but that do not become part of the finished product:* for example, industrial cleansing products. Consumable supplies are used for maintenance, repair and operation, so they are sometimes called MRO items.
Industrial services	*The intangible products used by firms:* for example, industrial cleaning services, accountancy and legal services, and some maintenance services. Some firms provide these for themselves; for others it is cheaper to buy in the services as needed (for instance, a ten-person light engineering firm would not need a full-time lawyer on the staff).

informed of new models coming onto the market in, say, three years' time when the old microwave is beginning to show signs of wear. The idea behind this is to encourage the customer to remain loyal to the original manufacturer.

From the consumer's viewpoint, some of those benefits are essential requirements, others are less important but still good to have, still others are not really relevant. Each consumer will have a different view as to which benefit belongs to which category.

MANAGING THE PRODUCT RANGE

The **product life cycle (PLC)** is a useful concept to describe how products progress from introduction through to obsolescence. The theory is that products, like living things, have a natural life cycle beginning with introduction, going through a growth phase, reaching maturity, then going into decline, and finally becoming obsolete. Figure 6.1 illustrates this in graphical form.

In the introduction phase, the product's sales grow slowly, and the profit will be small or negative because of heavy promotion costs and production ineffi- ciencies. If the product is very new, there will also be the need to persuade retailers and others to stock the product.

In the growth stage, there will be a rapid increase in sales as the product becomes better known. At this stage profits begin to grow, but competition will also be entering the market so the producer may now need to think about adapt- ing the product to meet the competitive threat.

In the maturity phase the product is well known and well established: at this point the promotional spend eases off and production economies of scale become established. By this time competitors will almost certainly have entered the market, so the firm will need to develop a new version of the product.

In the decline phase, the product is losing market share and profitability rap- idly. At this stage the marketer must decide whether it is worthwhile supporting the product for a little longer, or whether it should be allowed to disappear; supporting a product for which there is little natural demand is very unprofitable, but sometimes products can be revived and relaunched, perhaps in a different market.

Figure 6.1	Product life cycle

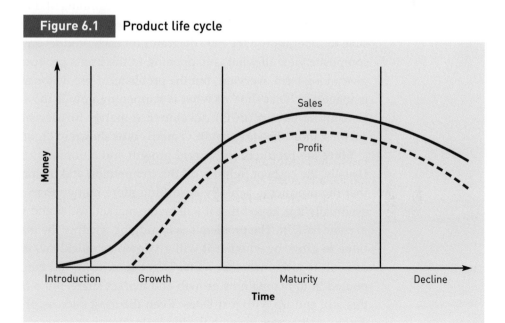

The assumption is that all products exhibit this life cycle, but the timescale will vary from one product to the next. Some products, for example computer games, may go through the entire life cycle in a matter of months. Others, like pitta bread, have a life cycle measured in thousands of years, and may never become obsolete.

The product life cycle concept is a useful way of looking at product development, but like many simple theories it has a number of flaws:

- The theory assumes that changes in consumer preference go only one way, and that there is no swing back to an earlier preference. Some clothing fashions return after a few years, and some styles of music enjoy periodic revivals, but also some traditional products can suddenly become popular again, often following advertising campaigns based on nostalgia.

- The model assumes that nobody does anything to revive the product when it begins to decline or be superseded by other products. Most marketers would look at their declining products and decide whether a revival is possible, or worthwhile.

- The model looks at only one product, whereas most marketing managers are having to balance the demands of many differing products, and decide which ones are most likely to yield the best return on investment.

Note here that the PLC concept is useful to describe what is happening, but is not much use for predicting what is going to happen, since it is virtually impossible to tell how long the maturity phase will continue. This makes it difficult to use as a decision-making device; marketers are not easily able to tell which part of the product life cycle the product currently occupies. A temporary fall-off in sales might be caused by extraneous factors such as recessions or new competitive activity, without actually heralding the beginning of the decline phase.

Most firms produce several different products at the same time, and it is possible to superimpose the PLC diagrams for each product onto the graph to give a composite view of what is happening to the firm's product portfolio. This will give a long-term overview, but the problems of prediction still remain; for many managers, a 'snapshot' of what is happening now is more useful. The Boston Consulting Group (BCG) developed a matrix for decision-making in these circumstances. The original BCG matrix is as shown in Figure 6.2.

Stars are products with rapid growth and a dominant share of the market. Usually, the costs of fighting off the competition and maintaining growth mean that the product is actually absorbing more money than it is generating, but eventually it is hoped that it will be the market leader and the profits will begin to come back in. The problem lies in judging whether the market is going to continue to grow, or whether it will go down as quickly as it went up. It may be difficult to judge whether a Star is going to justify all the money that is being poured in to maintain its growth and market share, but a firm that does not do this will end up with just Dogs. Even the most successful Star will eventually decline as it moves through the life cycle.

| Figure 6.2 | Boston Consulting Group matrix |

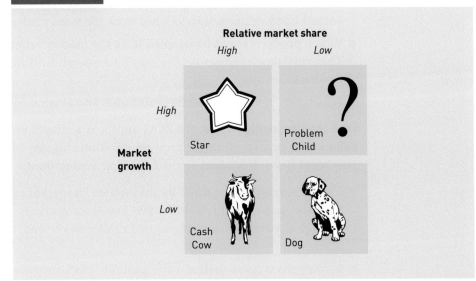

Source: Reprinted by permission of the Boston Consulting Group

Cash Cows are the former Stars. They have a dominant share of the market, but are now in the maturity phase of the life cycle and consequently have low growth. A Cash Cow is generating cash, and can be 'milked' of it to finance the Stars. These are the products that have steady year-in year-out sales and generate much of the firm's profits: examples might be the Big Mac hamburger, Coca-Cola and the Ford Mondeo.

Dogs have a low market share and low growth prospects. The argument here is not whether the product is profitable; it almost always is. The argument is about whether the firm could use its resources to make something that would be more profitable, and this is also almost always the case.

The **Problem Child** (also sometimes shown as a question mark) has a small share of a growth market, and causes the marketer the most headaches since it is necessary to work out a way of building market share so as to turn the product into a Star. This means finding out why the share is so low, and developing strategies to increase market share rapidly. The Problem Child could be backed with an even bigger promotion campaign, or it could possibly be adapted in some way to fit the market better. Market research plays a crucial role in making these decisions; finding out how to adapt a product is a difficult area of research, but the potential rewards are huge, and adapting the product to meet people's needs better is almost always cheaper than increasing the advertising spend.

The policy decisions that arise from this view of the firm's product portfolio lie in the following areas:

■ Which products should be dropped from the range entirely? This question not only hinges on how profitable the product itself is; sales of one product often indirectly generate sales of another more profitable product. For example, Black and Decker sell the Scorpion electric saw cheaply, but make the profit on sales of replacement saw blades.

■ Which products should be backed with promotion campaigns? Backing the wrong product can be extremely expensive; advertising campaigns have no second-hand value, so if it does not work the money is lost for ever.

■ Which products could be adapted to fit the market better, and in what ways? This very much hinges on the market research findings, and on customer feedback.

■ Which new products could be introduced, and at what cost?

Like the product life cycle, the BCG matrix is a simple model that helps marketers to approach strategic product decisions; again, like the PLC, it has a number of flaws. It is based on the following assumptions:

■ Market share can be gained by investment in marketing. This is not always the case: some products will have lost their markets altogether (perhaps through environmental changes) and cannot be revived, no matter how much is invested.

■ Market share gains will always generate cash surpluses. Again, if market share is gained by drastic price cutting, cash may actually be lost.

■ Cash surpluses will be generated when the product is in the maturity stage of the life cycle. Not necessarily so; mature products may well be operating on such small margins due to competitive pressure that the profit generated is low.

■ The best opportunity to build a dominant market position is during the growth phase. In most cases this would be true, but this does not take account of competition. A competitor's product might be growing even faster.

Barksdale and Harris (1982) proposed two additions to the BCG matrix. **War Horses** have high market share, but the market has negative growth; the problem for management is to decide whether the product is in an irreversible decline, or whether it can be revived, perhaps by repositioning into another market. **Dodos** have a low share of a negative growth market, and are probably best discontinued (Figure 6.3).

The BCG matrix has proved a useful tool for analysing product portfolio decisions, but it is really only a snapshot of the current position with the products it describes. Since most markets are to a greater or lesser extent dynamic, the matrix should be used with a certain degree of caution.

Critical thinking

The BCG Matrix is all very well, but how do we decide whether a market is 'high growth' or 'low growth?' Is 5% per annum high growth? It would be in the car industry – but not in mobile telephones. Likewise, what is a high market share? 5%? 50%? 2%? Any of these might be regarded as a respectable share in some markets.

Maybe we are back to executive judgement as the key factor in decisions – or maybe the BCG matrix just helps to focus our thinking!

Figure 6.3	Expanded Boston Consulting Group matrix

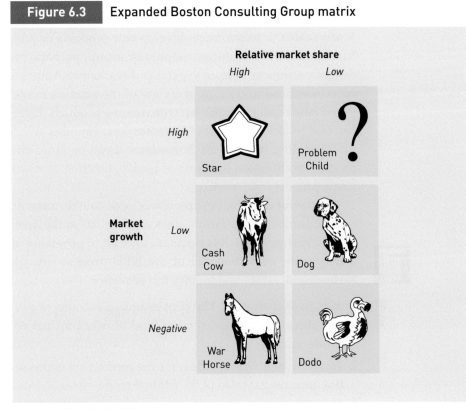

Source: Barksdale and Harris, 1982

The size of the product portfolio and the complexity of the products within it can have further effects on the firm's management. For example, it has been shown that manufacturing a wide range of products with many options makes it difficult for the firm to use just-in-time purchasing techniques, and complicates the firm's supply activities (Benwell 1996).

DEVELOPING BETTER PRODUCTS

There is often debate within firms as to what constitutes a 'better' product. For marketers, the definition must be 'a product that more closely meets our customers' needs than does the product it supersedes'. Engineers, accountants and managers may have differing definitions; there is, however, general agreement that firms must introduce new products if they are not to be left with a range of obsolete, dying products. **New product development (NPD)** is therefore a crucial area of marketing activity, and a great deal has been published on the subject.

New product development

Venture teams or *project teams* develop new products or projects. Typically a venture team will be an interdisciplinary group, perhaps comprising engineers, research scientists, finance experts and marketers. Among other considerations, marketers need to take an overview of the product range to see how the proposed new products match up with existing products. Sometimes a new product can lead to cannibalism of old product lines (in other words, the company ends up competing with itself). Sometimes it can be more effective to carry out a product modification (in terms of quality, function or style) rather than develop a new product from scratch.

The task of creating new products is, of course, more art than science: however, customer orientation does appear to make firms more innovative (Tajeddini *et al.* 2006). It is therefore difficult to generalise about the process, but a frequently quoted model of the NPD process was given by Cooper and Kleinschmidt (1986) and follows this sequence:

1 *New product strategy.* The firm examines its current portfolio, opportunities and threats and decides what kind of new product would best fit in with future strategy.

2 *Idea generation.* Specific ideas for the product are expressed, perhaps through a brainstorming session of the venture team.

3 *Screening and evaluation.* The ideas are checked for feasibility and marketability.

4 *Concept testing.* Having selected the ideas which show promise, discussions take place with customers, production engineers, and anyone else who may have something to contribute, to develop the ideas further.

5 *Business analysis.* The feasibility of the product is estimated in terms of its potential profitability, effects on sales of other products, possible competitive responses, and so forth.

6 *Technical development.* The engineering aspects of the product are investigated, and a prototype is developed. The final design of the product needs to reflect the results of the concept testing stage.

7 *Market testing.* Formal market research is carried out to assess the product's viability in the market.

8 *Commercialisation.* Assuming the market research is positive about the product, the firm puts it into production.

All of these stages are likely to be covered in one form or other, but in many cases the methods used are likely to be subjective, or carried out ineffectively. This can often be a source of problems following the launch: for example, a proper market appraisal may not be carried out because the venture team fall in love with the project and champion it through the process. *Product champions* within firms often perform a valuable function in ensuring that the new product actually comes into existence rather than being sidelined by the routine tasks of making existing products; this is sometimes encouraged by firms, but is believed by some researchers to be a sign of a failed management who have abdicated their responsibility for keeping the firm up to date (Johne and Snelson 1990).

There are six broad types of innovation strategy:

1 *Offensive*. Pride in being the first. This is very much the strategy of firms such as Sony and 3M.

2 *Defensive*. 'Me-toos', copies of other companies' products, but slightly better.

3 *Imitative*. Straight copies of other companies' products.

4 *Dependent*. Led by bigger companies, perhaps customers or suppliers. For example, Microsoft produces new computer software, so it is dependent on new technology developed by computer chip manufacturers.

5 *Traditional*. Not really innovative at all; the firm is merely resurrecting old-fashioned designs.

6 *Opportunist*. Selling and marketing of inventions.

Launch decisions might revolve around areas such as test marketing (see Chapter 5); if the firm *test markets* the product (i.e. launches the product in a small geographical area to see whether it will be successful), this may save money on promotion but loses the advantage of surprise. On the other hand, if the firm goes for a national launch, this means committing large amounts of money, and mistakes are much harder to correct afterwards. The process of launching in one area at a time is called *roll-out*. The promotion policy will be affected by the customer category the firm is aiming for: innovators, early adopters, early majority, late majority or laggards.

Whether to go ahead or not with a new product is a decision which revolves around five dimensions (Carbonell-Foulquie *et al.* 2004). These are as follows:

1 *Strategic fit*. The degree to which the new product fits in with the company's overall marketing strategy.

2 *Technical feasibility*. Whether an effective product can be made economically.

3 *Customer acceptance*. Whether customers like the product.

4 *Market opportunity*. The level of competition the firm might be expected to face, and the current state of the external environment.

5 *Financial performance*. Whether the product will prove sufficiently profitable to be worth launching.

Of these, customer acceptance should be the most important consideration throughout the new-product development process.

Success and failure in NPD

NPD is extremely risky; eight out of ten new products eventually fail (i.e. do not recover their development costs) and the remaining two out of ten thus have to fund all the others (Clancy and Shulman 1991). Great effort has been expended on trying to find better ways of forecasting a product's prospects in the market, with only limited results.

First of all, though, it is necessary to define what a new product is, and the researchers Calentone and Cooper (1981) have identified nine categories of new product, as shown in Table 6.3. The clusters were identified according to whether the product was new to the firm or new to the world, and whether there was a production or marketing *synergy* with the firm's existing products.

Success rates for each cluster were as laid out in Table 6.4. Data were obtained on 102 successes and 93 failures. Some 177 firms were surveyed, and there were 103 usable replies.

Table 6.3 New product clusters

Clusters	Description
Cluster 1 **The Better Mousetrap with No Synergy**	This is a product that, while being an improvement over existing offerings, does not fit in with the firm's existing product lines.
Cluster 2 **The Innovative Mousetrap that Really Wasn't Better**	This might be a product that, while being technically excellent, has no real advantage for the consumer over existing products.
Cluster 3 **The Close-to-Home Me-Too Product**	A copy of a competitor's offering. Not likely to be perceived as new by consumers.
Cluster 4 **The Innovative High-Tech Product**	A truly new-to-the-world product.
Cluster 5 **The Me-Too Product with No Technical/Production Synergy**	A copy of a competitor's product, but with no real connection with existing product lines.
Cluster 6 **The Old But Simple Money-Saver**	Not a new product at all, except to the firm producing it.
Cluster 7 **The Synergistic Product that was New to the Firm**	A product that fits the product line, but is new.
Cluster 8 **The Innovative Superior Product with No Synergy**	A product that does not fit the existing product line, but is new.
Cluster 9 **The Synergistic Close-to-Home Product**	A product line extension; perhaps a minor improvement over the firm's existing products.

Table 6.4	Success rates of new products		
Cluster	**Success ratio**	**% successes**	**% of cases**
9 The Synergistic Close-to-Home Product	1.39	72	12.82
8 The Innovative Superior Product with No Synergy	1.35	70	10.26
6 The Old But Simple Money-Saver	1.35	70	10.26
7 The Synergistic Product that was New to the Firm	1.2	67	10.76
4 The Innovative High-Tech Product	1.23	64	14.35
3 The Close-to-Home Me-Too Product	1.08	56	8.20
1 The Better Mousetrap with No Synergy	0.69	36	7.17
5 The Me-Too Product with No Technical/Production Synergy	0.27	14	10.26
2 The Innovative Mousetrap that Really Wasn't Better	0.00	0	10.26

Source: Calentone and Cooper, 1981

Clusters 9, 8 and 6 were the most successful by far, perhaps indicating that the safest course is not to be too innovative. In recent years, many new products have been introduced which are reproductions of old designs: the Chrysler PSV, Volkswagen Beetle and Mini Cooper are all examples from the motor industry, and there are many household appliances which have been designed with a 'retro' image. These products rely on the following factors for their success (Brown *et al.* 2003):

- *Allegory*. This is the brand 'story', the history of the original product.
- *Aura*. This is the 'essence' of the brand, the mystique surrounding it.
- *Arcadia*. This is the idealised community in which such products might be used. Based on nostalgia, Arcadia is the place people would like to return to (for example, the 1960s, when they owned their first VW Beetle).
- *Antinomy*. This is brand paradox. New technology is viewed as unstoppable and overpowering, yet at the same time is responsible for people's desire to return to a simpler, less high-tech past.

Although not all products in Cluster 6 are retro, the advent of a significant interest in retro styling has certainly changed the success rate of such products.

Cluster 8 contains the truly innovative, new-to-the-world product, but until it is actually launched it may be difficult to distinguish from Cluster 2, the Innovative Mousetrap that Really Wasn't Better. This category had no successes at all.

What the above research does not show is the degree to which new products are successful. The innovative, new-to-the-world product may carry the highest risks, but potentially it also carries the highest rewards if successful. The evidence is, therefore, that the safest route is to produce 'me-too' products (minor adaptations of existing market leaders), but that the much riskier route of producing real innovations (e.g. the Nintendo Wii) is the only way to become a world-leading company. Producing retro products may well be a useful strategy, combining the success factors of both approaches.

The research also does not consider what a firm might use as a measure of success. Is it profitability? Or is it market share? This will depend on the firm's overall strategy, which may or may not put profitability first. Research shows that the most commonly used measures of success in NPD are customer acceptance, customer satisfaction, product performance and quality (Huang *et al*. 2004).

Another aspect not addressed by the Calentone and Cooper research is that of the consumer's view of new products. Although a given product may be new to the firm, and may even involve a radical re-think of the company's production and marketing methods, consumers may not see the product as being significantly different from what is already available. If consumers do not see any advantage in using the new product, they will not buy it; this re-emphasises the importance of good market research and analysis.

Calentone and Cooper's research was borne out by research published in 2006, in which the authors found that incremental innovations (those which are a small improvement on existing products) carry the least risk for firms who are first to bring them to market. Discontinuous innovation (truly new-to-the-world products) carry the greatest risk for firms first into the market, and for firms which follow later: in other words, being first to market only carries risks, not rewards (Min *et al*. 2006).

Overall, new product development is concerned with replacing the firm's existing product range with fresh products that come even closer to meeting customer needs. Firms that do not innovate will, eventually, lose market share to firms that do, since the competitor firms will be offering better products. This places a heavy premium on new product development. Having said that, new products do not sell themselves – unsurprisingly, firms which provide high levels of marketing and technological support for their new products experience greater financial rewards from their innovations (Sorescu *et al*. 2003).

DIFFUSION OF INNOVATION

New products are not immediately adopted by all consumers. Some consumers are driven to buy new products almost as soon as they become available, whereas others prefer to wait until the product has been around for a while before risking their hard-earned money on it. Innovations therefore take time to filter through the population: this process is called diffusion, and is determined partly by the nature of consumers and partly by the nature of the innovation itself.

Everett M. Rogers (1962) classified consumers as follows:

- **Innovators**: those who like to be first to own the latest products. These consumers predominate at the beginning of the product life cycle.

- **Early adopters**: those who are open to new ideas, but like to wait a while after initial launch. These consumers predominate during the growth phase of the PLC.

- **Early majority**: those who buy once the product is thoroughly tried and tested. These consumers predominate in the early part of the maturity phase of the PLC.

- **Late majority**: those who are suspicious of new things, and wait until most other people already have one. These consumers predominate in the latter part of the maturity phase of the PLC.

- **Laggards**: those who adopt new products only when it becomes absolutely necessary to do so. These consumers predominate in the decline phase of the PLC.

The process of diffusion of innovation is carried out through reference-group influence (see Chapter 3). Theories concerning the mechanisms for this have developed over the past hundred years, the three most important ones being trickle-down theory, two-step flow theory and multistage interaction theory.

Trickle-down theory says that the wealthy classes obtain information about new products, and the poorer classes then imitate their 'betters' (Veblen 1899). This theory has been largely discredited in wealthy countries because new ideas are disseminated overnight by the mass media and copied by chain stores within days.

Critical thinking

Perhaps nowadays we don't blindly copy the doings of the aristocracy, or even the upper middle class, but does that mean we are entirely uninfluenced by our betters? We seem to have developed a new aristocracy, largely composed of entertainers such as footballers and singers, who set the fashions for us in many ways.

Even without celebrity endorsement, where such people are paid to say they use a particular brand of perfume or use a particular set of golf clubs, we watch avidly to see what they are wearing, buying and doing. So maybe Veblen was stating a universal truth, back in 1899!

Two-step flow theory is similar, but this time it is 'influentials' rather than wealthy people who are the start of the adoption process (Lazarsfield *et al.* 1948). This has considerable basis in truth, but may be less true now than it was in the 1940s, when the theory was first developed; access to TV and other information media has proliferated and information about innovation is disseminated much faster.

The multistage interaction model (Engel *et al.* 1995) recognises this and allows for the influence of the mass media. In this model the influentials emphasise or facilitate the information flow (perhaps by making recommendations to friends or acting as advisers).

Consumers often need considerable persuasion to change from their old product to a new one. This is because there is always a cost of some sort. For example, somebody buying a new car will lose money on trading in the old car (a *switching cost*), or perhaps somebody buying a new computer will also have to spend money on new software, and spend time learning how to operate the new equipment (an *innovation cost).*

On the other hand there is strong evidence that newness as such is an important factor in the consumer's decision-making process (Haines 1966). In other words, people like new things, but there is a cost attached. Provided the new product offers real additional benefits over the old one (i.e. fits the consumer's needs better than the old product), the product will be adopted.

Consumers must first become aware of the new product, and then become persuaded that there is a real advantage in switching from their existing solution. A useful model of this adoption process is as follows:

- *Awareness.* This will often come about as a result of promotional activities by the firm.

- *Trial.* For a low-price item (e.g. a packet of biscuits) this may mean that the consumer will actually buy the product before trying it; for a major purchase, such as a car, the consumer will usually need to have a test-drive. Increasingly, supermarkets hold tasting sessions to allow customers to try new products.

- *Adoption.* This is the point at which the consumer decides to buy the product, or make it part of the weekly shopping list.

Rogers (1962) identified the following perceived attributes of innovative products, by which consumers apparently judge the product during the decision-making process:

- **Relative advantage**. The degree to which the innovation is perceived as better than the idea it supersedes.

- **Compatibility**. Consistency with existing values, past experiences and needs of potential adopters.

- **Complexity**. Ideas that are easily understood are adopted more quickly.

- **Trialability**. Degree to which a product can be experimented with.
- **Observability**. The degree to which the results of an innovation are visible to others.

Apart from the issue of adopting a product as it stands, there is the concept of **re-invention**. Sometimes users find new ways to use the product (not envisaged by the designers) and sometimes this leads to the creation of whole new markets. For example, in the 1930s it was discovered that baking soda is good for removing stale smells from refrigerators, a fact that was quickly seized on by baking soda manufacturers. Deodorising fridges is now a major part of the market for baking soda.

BRANDING

Many products are so similar to other manufacturers' products that consumers are entirely indifferent as to which one they will buy. For example, petrol is much the same whether it is sold by Shell, Esso, BP, Statoil, Elf or Repsol: such products are called commodity products because they are homogeneous commodities rather than distinct products with different benefits from the others on offer.

At first sight, water would come into the category of a commodity product. Yet any supermarket has a range of bottled waters, each with its own formulation and brand name, and each with its loyal consumers. In these cases the original commodity product (water) has been converted into a brand. Branding is a process of adding value to the product by use of its packaging, brand name, promotion and position in the minds of the consumers. Even non-profit making firms are more successful if they are brand-oriented (Napoli 2006).

DeChernatony and McDonald (1998) offer the following definition of brand:

> A successful brand is an identifiable product, service, person or place, augmented in such a way that the buyer or user perceives relevant, unique added values which match their needs most closely. Furthermore, its success results from being able to sustain those added values in the face of competition.

This definition emphasises the increased value that accrues to the consumer by buying the established brand rather than a generic or commodity product. The values that are added may be in the area of reassurance of the brand's quality, they may be in the area of status (where the brand's image carries over to the consumer), or they may be in the area of convenience (making search behaviour easier).

Figure 6.4 shows the relationship between commodity products and branded products in terms of image and price. Commodity products tend to be undifferentiated in price (for example, petrol tends to be much the same price in petrol stations within a given geographical area. A differential of even 10% would be very noticeable). They also tend to have a low degree of differentiation in the product characteristics and the image. Branded goods, on the other hand, score

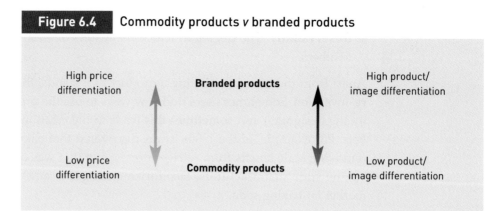

Figure 6.4 Commodity products *v* branded products

high on both factors; since they command a premium price, this is likely to lead to an increased profit, which strengthens the case for developing a strong brand.

Brand names

When a new product has been developed, the producer will usually give it a *brand name*. A brand name is a term, symbol or design that distinguishes one seller's product from its competitors. The strategic considerations for brand naming are as follows:

- *Marketing objectives*. The brand name should fit the overall marketing objectives of the firm: for example, a firm intending to enter the youth market will need to develop brand names that appeal to a young audience.
- *Brand audit*. An estimate of the internal and external forces such as critical success factor (also known as the unique selling proposition).
- *Brand objectives*. As with the marketing objectives, the overall intentions about the brand need to be specified.
- *Brand strategy alternatives*. The other ways of achieving the brand's objectives, and the other factors involved in its success, have a bearing on the choice of brand name.

Brand names can be protected in most countries by *registration*, but there is some protection for brands in that it is illegal to try to 'pass off' a product as being a branded one when it is not. For example, using a very similar brand name to a famous brand, or even using similar package design, could be regarded as passing off. This is a civil offence, not a criminal one, so it is up to the offended brand owner to take legal action.

Ries (1995) suggests that brand names should have some, or all, of the following characteristics:

- They should shock, i.e. catch the customer's attention. French Connection United Kingdom use their FCUK acronym for this purpose.

- They should be alliterative: this helps them to be memorable. For example, West'n'Welsh double-glazing is a more memorable name than BJ double glazing.
- They should connect to the product's positioning in the consumer's perceptual map. UK biscuit brand Hob Nobs conveys an image of a warm kitchen (the hob) with friendliness (hob-nobbing).
- They should link to a visual image: again, this helps the memorability. Timberland outdoor clothing conjures a visual image of mountain country.
- They should communicate something about the product, or be capable of being used to communicate about the product. Duracell conveys the main advantage of the batteries – they are durable.
- They should encourage the development of a nickname (for example, Bud for Budweiser Beer).
- They should be telephone- and directory-friendly. Words often seem muffled on the telephone, so that 'Bud' becomes 'Mud'.

Brands and semiotics

Semiotics is the study of meaning, and is concerned with the symbolism conveyed by objects and words. Semiotics refers to systems of signs; the most obvious system is words, but other systems exist. For example, a film would use the sign systems of the spoken word, the gestures of the actors, the music of the soundtrack, and the conventions of movie direction and production to generate an overall meaning. The overall meaning is generated as a result of an interaction between the sign system and the observer or reader: the viewer interprets the information in the light of existing knowledge and attitudes, later including it in an overall perceptual map of reality (see Chapter 3).

Brands are important symbols, often using more than one sign system to create meaning; the brand name, the logo, the colour and the design of the packaging all contribute. In terms of semiotics brands have four levels:

1 *A utilitarian sign.* This is about the practical aspects of the product, and includes meanings of reliability, effectiveness, fitness for the purpose and so forth.

2 *A commercial sign.* This is about the exchange values of the product, perhaps conveying meanings about value for money or cost-effectiveness.

3 *A socio-cultural sign.* This is about the social effects of buying (or not buying) the product, with meanings about membership of aspirational groups or about the fitness of the product for filling social roles.

4 *A sign about the mythical values of the product.* Myths are heroic stories about the product, many of which have little basis in fact: for example, the Harley Davidson motorcycle brand has a strong mythical value due (in part) to its starring role in the film *Easy Rider*. The same is true of James Bond's Aston Martin, and several brands of beer.

Myths provide a conceptual framework through which the contradictions of life can be resolved, and brands can build on this. For example, modern industrial life is, presumably, the antithesis of frontier adventure. Yet the Harley Davidson, a product of twentieth-century industry, was used to represent the (probably mythical) freedom and adventure of the American West. Most powerful brands have at least some mythical connotations – in the United Kingdom, the Hovis bread brand has mythical connotations centred around corner bakery shops at the turn of the century; in Malaysia and Singapore Tiger Balm carries mythical connotations about ancient Chinese apothecaries; in Australia Vegemite carries mythical connotations about Australian family life that its main competitor, Promite, has never tapped into.

The association of different values with the brand name can be extremely useful when researching the acceptability of a brand's image. The importance that consumers place on these values can be researched using focus groups, with a subsequent analysis of the key signs contained within the brand, and consumers can be segmented according to their responsiveness to the particular signs contained within the brand and their relevance to the consumer's own internal values.

Research carried out by Gordon and Valentin (1996) into retail buying behaviour showed that different retail outlets convey different meanings to consumers in terms of a continuum from planned, routine shopping through to impulse buying. Each store type met the needs differently and conveyed different meanings in terms of appropriateness of behaviour. Convenience stores conveyed an image of disorder and feelings of guilt and confusion (perhaps associated with having forgotten to buy some items in the course of the regular weekly shop). Supermarkets represented planned shopping and conveyed an image of efficient domestic management and functionality. Petrol stations carried a dual meaning of planned purchase (for petrol) and impulse buying (in the shop). Business travellers seeking a break from work and pleasure travellers seeking to enhance the 'holiday' feeling both indulged in impulsive behaviour motivated by the need for a treat. Finally, off-licences legitimated the purchase of alcohol, allowing shoppers to buy drinks without the uneasy feeling that other shoppers might disapprove. Off-licences also provided an environment in which people felt able to experiment with new purchases.

These signs are relevant not only for the retailers themselves in terms of their own branding, but also for branded-goods manufacturers who need to decide which outlets are most appropriate for their brands and where in the store the brand should be located. For example, snack foods and chocolate are successfully sold in petrol stations, where travellers are often looking for a treat to break up a boring journey.

STRATEGIC ISSUES IN BRANDING

Adding value to the product by branding involves a great deal more than merely giving the product a catchy name. Branding is the culmination of a range of activities across the whole marketing mix, leading to a brand image that conveys a whole set of messages to the consumer (and, more importantly, to the consumer's friends and family) about quality, price, expected performance and status. For example, the Porsche brand name conveys an image of engineering excellence, reliability, sporty styling, high speed and high prices, and of wealth and success on the part of the owner. People do not buy Porsches simply as a means of transport.

Because branding involves all the elements of the marketing mix it cannot be regarded simply as a tactical tool designed to differentiate the product on the supermarket shelves. Instead, it must be regarded as the focus for the marketing effort, as a way of directing the thought processes of the management towards producing consumer satisfaction. The brand acts as a common point of contact between the producer and the consumer, as shown in Figure 6.5.

As the figure shows, the consumer benefits from the brand in terms of knowing what the quality will be, knowing what the expected performance will be, gaining some self-image values (for example, a prestigious product conveys prestige to the consumer by association – conversely, a low-price product might enhance a consumer's sense of frugality and ability to find good value for money).

In many cases the core product has very little to differentiate it from other products, and the brand is really the only differentiating feature. A famous example is the rivalry between Pepsi Cola and Coca-Cola; in blind taste tests, most people prefer the flavour of Pepsi but Coca-Cola outsells Pepsi in virtually every market. This apparent discrepancy can only be explained by the brand image which Coca-Cola has, and in taste tests where consumers are able to see the can the drink comes out of, Coca-Cola is the preferred brand.

Despite the apparently artificial nature of differentiation by branding, the benefits to the consumer are very real; experiments show that branded analgesics work better than generic analgesics at relieving pain, even though the chemical formula is identical. This is because of the psychosomatic power of the brand. Someone driving a prestige car gains very real benefits in terms of the respect and envy of others, even if the performance of the car is no better than that of its cheaper rival.

Brands can be looked at in a number of different ways. Table 6.5 shows eight different strategic functions of brands.

Branding clearly has advantages for the manufacturer and the retailer, since it helps to differentiate the product from the competitor's product. Economies of scale and scope are attributed to branding, and a brand with high sales will generate production economies. A successful brand also creates a *barrier to entry*, so

Figure 6.5	Brands as a contact point

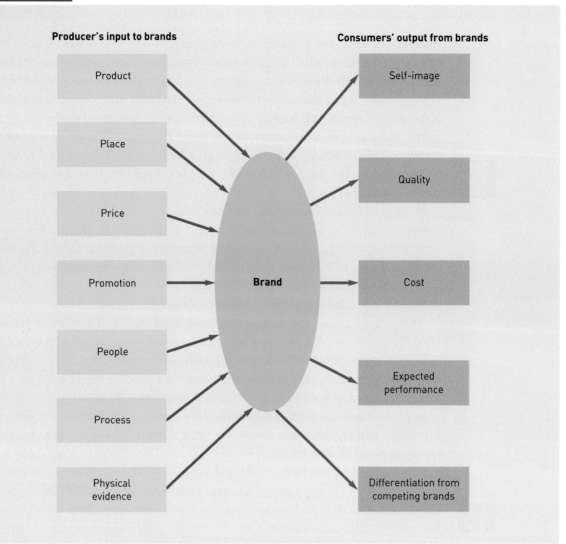

that competitors find it harder to enter the market (Demsetz 1982). Brands also allow firms to compete other than on price, which clearly has advantages since the firm does not have to cut its profit margins in order to compete.

Furthermore, brands that are held in high esteem tend to be more consistent in their sales, riding over the ups and downs of the marketplace (Png and Reitman 1995). Not all brands are priced at a premium; many brands are competitively priced in order to take advantage of consistent sales.

Branding has advantages for the consumer: it is easy to recognise the product, and easy to identify with it. Messages about the formulation and benefits are clearly conveyed, and in most cases the use of a particular brand says something about the consumer (for example, wearing designer clothes) (Bagwell and Bernheim 1996). Because most purchases involve only limited problem-solving

Table 6.5	Strategic functions of brands

Function	Explanation
Brand as a sign of ownership	Brands were at one time a way of showing who had instigated the marketing activities for the brand. This was an attempt to protect the formulation of the product in cases where intellectual property protection was insufficient, and also to ensure that customers knew whether they were buying a manufacturer's brand or a retailer's brand.
Brand as a differentiating device	A strong brand undoubtedly does differentiate the product from similar products, but having a strong brand name is not enough. The product itself also needs to be different in some way; the brand image is the communicating device that conveys the difference to the consumer.
Brand as a functional device	Branding can be used to communicate functional capability. In other words, the brand conveys an image of its quality and expected performance to the consumer.
Brand as a symbolic device	The symbolism of some brands enables the consumer to say something about themselves. This is particularly apparent in the 'designer' clothes industry – a very ordinary T-shirt acquires added value because the name of the designer is printed on the front. If the consumers believe that the brand's value lies in its communication ability they will spend considerable time and effort in choosing the brand that conveys the appropriate image.
Brand as a risk reducer	Every purchase involves a degree of risk; the product might not perform as expected, and if it fails to do so then the vendor might not be prepared to make restitution. Buying a strongly branded product offers the consumer a degree of reassurance about both the product and the producer. Astute marketers find out what types of risk are of most concern to the customers or consumers and develop a brand presentation which addresses those risks.
Brand as a shorthand device	Brands are used as a way of 'tagging' information about a product in the consumers' memories. This is particularly relevant when the brand is extended to other product categories, since the consumer's view of the parent brand is transferred to the new brand. For example, Virgin has successfully extended the brand image from records to retailing to airlines to financial services, all offering the same innovative approach and serving similar market segments.
Brand as a legal device	Brands give a certain amount of legal protection to the producer, since pack design and name can be protected where (often) the formulation of the product cannot. Strong branding offers some protection for the firm's intellectual property.
Brand as a strategic device	The assets constituting the brand can be identified and managed so that the brand maintains and builds on the added value that it represents.

behaviour, branding helps to reduce the decision-making time and also the effort of evaluating competing products: brands do not necessarily need to have unique features for this to happen (Romaniuk and Gaillard 2007). Consumers who either do not want to spend time on an extended information search, or do not have the expertise to do so, can use the brand as an implicit guarantee of quality. These positive feelings about the brand are called consumer brand equity, and can be affected by all aspects of the brand, including country of origin (Pappu *et al.* 2006).

Information storage and retrieval in humans are carried out by a process of 'chunking' or collecting information in substantial quantities and storing them under a single 'file name' (Buschke 1976). In effect, the brand name provides an informational chunk: the individual is able to summon up a huge amount of information from memory using the brand name as the trigger.

From a strategic viewpoint, the brand image provides a focus for the creative energies of the marketing team. Koestler (1964) suggested that creativity involves the bringing together of hitherto unrelated, yet familiar, objects to generate a creative insight. The difficulty for marketers is that product and brand development is often a team process, and as such the team needs to keep a firm picture of what the product is intended to convey – the 'personality' of the product – if they are to maintain consistency in their creative activities. One way of doing this is to use a metaphor for the product. For example, the Honda Accord developers used the metaphor 'Rugby player in a dinner suit' to achieve product coherence across the team, even though the entire creative team consisted of hundreds of people, from automotive stylists through to ad designers (Clark and Fujimoto 1990).

Brand planning is important, but time-consuming; often the job is given to a brand manager, many of whom are young and inexperienced. Developing the brand is a process of integrating a number of strands of business activity, so a clear idea of the brand image is essential, as is a long-term view. To see branding as merely being about design or advertising or naming is inadequate and short-sighted; successful brands are those that act as a lens through which the consumer sees the corporation and the product. Constant evaluation of the image seen through the lens is essential if the brand is to retain its status.

Occasionally products need to be rebranded, sometimes because of a bad association (for example, after the Zeebrugge ferry disaster the company rebranded itself from Townsend Thoresen to P&O Ferries), but more commonly because of a structural change in the firm, perhaps caused by a merger or a takeover (Muzellec and Lambkin 2006). Within the European Union, rebranding has often occurred in recent years in order to develop a Europe-wide identity (as in the case of Jif cleaners, which became Cif). Such rebranding needs to be handled carefully, and invariably involves added promotional expenditure to establish the new brand.

EXTENDING THE BRAND

A **brand extension** is another product in the company's range that uses a similar brand name. For example, Cherry Coke is a brand extension of the original Coca-Cola. Overall **family branding** is where one brand name is used for a range of products, such as Heinz 57 Varieties, and **line family branding** is where a smaller group of brands carries a single identity.

In each case the aim is to convey a message of quality to the consumer by borrowing from the established reputation of the parent brand, and to appeal to the target market, who are already familiar with the parent brand. Properly carried out, the establishment of a brand is a long-term project, which can be expensive: this leads to an emphasis by some firms on brand extensions that are intended to maximise the return on the investment made in establishing the brand. In some cases, brands have been extended to the breaking-point; relatively few brands (Virgin being one example) can be extended apparently indefinitely, and even as well-established a brand as Levi Strauss jeans could not extend itself to smart suits (the company's attempt to do so in the early 1980s turned to disaster). The most important driver for brand extension success is the fit between the present brand and the extension product (Volckner and Sattler 2006); Virgin's ability to extend relies on the brand's image as being original and fresh-thinking, coupled with a combination of solidity and practicality. Even so, the bad publicity which surrounded Virgin Trains at the beginning of the century is thought to have damaged the brand, and the company has been forced to make major investments in their rolling stock in order to recover some of the lost ground.

A more recent development has been **compositioning**, in which products are grouped under a brand name to create a composite value greater than that of the components (Ruttenberg *et al.* 1995). Joint marketing and distribution alliances come under this heading. The products concerned do not necessarily come from the same producer, and may not even be in the same general category: for example, Disneyland has 'official airlines' or 'official ferry companies' to transport visitors to its theme parks. A further extension of this concept is **brand architecture** (Uncles *et al.* 1995) which is concerned with setting up 'partner' brands and creating a balance between branding at the product level and corporate or banner levels.

Within the international arena, firms have the opportunity to extend the brand across international frontiers. This raises fundamental strategic issues: for example, should the brand be globalised, with the firm offering a standard package throughout the world (as does Coca-Cola), or should the brand be adapted for each market (as does Heinz)? Some firms brand globally, but advertise locally (Sandler and Shani 1992) while others organise task groups to handle the brand on a global scale (Raffee and Kreutzer 1989).

RETAILERS' OWN-BRANDS

Retailer power has grown considerably since 1980, with a proliferation of own-brand products. In the past, the retailer's own-brand products were usually of poorer quality than manufacturers' brands, but they are now often of equal or even superior quality. These brands now account for up to 60% of the sales in some major retail stores such as Tesco and Sainsbury in the United Kingdom, and Carrefour in France (slogan: *'Carrefour – c'est aussi une marque'*, which translates as 'Carrefour – it's also a brand') (Hankinson and Cowking 1997). For manufacturers this creates a problem of response: should the manufacturer try to invest in the firm's brands more heavily in order to overcome the retailer's brand, or should he or she capitulate entirely and produce on behalf of the retailer (Quelch and Harding 1995). Often manufacturers will become suppliers of retailer-brand products which compete with their own branded goods. Reasons for doing this are as follows:

- *Economies of scale*. The manufacturer may be able to buy raw materials in greater quantities, or may be able to invest in more efficient production methods, if the throughput of product is increased.
- *Utilise excess capacity*. Seasonality or production synergies may make production of own-brand products attractive in some cases.
- *Base for expansion*. Supplying a retailer with own-brand goods may lead to other opportunities to supply the retailer with other products in future.
- *No promotion costs*. The retailer bears all the investment in the brand (which is, of course, a brand extension of the retailer's trading name in any case).
- *No choice*. Some retailers (the UK's Marks & Spencer being an example) only trade in their own-brands. Manufacturers who wish to trade with these retailers have no choice but to produce under the retailer's brand name.
- *To shut out the competition*. If the manufacturer does not produce goods under the retailer's brand name, another manufacturer will and will thus gain ground.

Manufacturers with very strong branding often refuse to produce own-brand goods, Kellogg's breakfast cereals being a notable example. If the brand is strong enough this allows the firm to promote on an 'accept no substitutes' platform.

In the past, own-brand products were cheap versions of the leading brands, but in more and more cases the retailers now have enough financial strength to fund the development of entirely new versions of products, some of which are superior to the proprietary brands and have achieved substantial market shares.

In many cases this is achieved by producing *'lookalike'* branding, where the product looks very similar to the brand leader. In the United Kingdom this led to the formation of the British Producers and Brand Owners Group, which lobbied Parliament to regulate the visual and physical simulation of successful brands. In fact, research showed that few if any consumers accidentally pick up the wrong brand (Balabanis and Craven 1997) but some confusion is engendered. Retailers (perhaps disingenuously) claim that using similar packaging helps consumers identify products, whereas manufacturers claim that lookalikes give the impression that the products are identical. In other words, the confusion arises not at the level of picking up the wrong pack, but at the more subtle level of forming inaccurate beliefs about the lookalike's attributes based on the attributes of the leading brand (Foxman *et al.* 1992).

A further argument advanced by retailers is that the strong manufacturers' brands have created generic product categories of their own – 'Gold Blend-type' instant coffees, for example. The retailers argue that products with similar quality and specifications should look as similar as possible to the brand that first created those values – an argument that is particularly galling to manufacturers who have invested large sums of money in creating those brand values in the first place.

PACKAGING

Packaging of the product is equally part of the product, since the packaging can itself convey benefits. The main purpose of packaging is to protect the contents from the outside environment and vice versa, but packaging also carries out the following functions:

- informs customers;
- meets legal information requirements;
- sometimes aids the use of the product (e.g. ring pulls on drinks cans make it easier to open the can).

Packaging decisions might include such areas as **tamper resistance** (paper strips around caps to prevent bottles being opened while on supermarket shelves) and *customer usage* (e.g. the resealable nipples on mineral water bottles, making it easier to drink the water while participating in sports such as running or cycling). The protection of the environment has become important to consumers in recent years, so much packaging is either recyclable or biodegradable. Customer acceptability is of obvious importance; packaging must be hygienic and convenient for the consumer. Within the United Kingdom there has been a growing trend to develop packaging designs that can be legally protected under the 1994 Trade Marks Act; the purpose of this is to prevent imitators from making close copies of the packaging. In some cases the package design has been made expensive to copy, requiring re-tooling for unusual pack shapes, or expensive printing processes (Gander 1996). 'Me-too' packaging has become particularly common among supermarket own-brand versions of popular products, and there has been some debate about the ethics of this. In some countries these close copies infringe copyright or patent laws (Davies 1995).

Colour can also be important: for example, Heinz's use of a turquoise label for their baked beans tin emphasises the orange colour of the beans when the can is opened. Even the proportions of the package make a difference: the ratio of the sides of the package affect perception (Raghubir and Greenleaf 2006).

In recent years, because of the huge upsurge in world trade, it has also become necessary to consider the legal requirements of labelling, which differ from one country to the next; nutritional information may have to be in a different form for each country (for example, in the United States food has to be labelled with the amount of fat it contains expressed as a percentage of a 2000 calorie daily intake). There has recently been a dispute within the EU regarding the labelling of recipe products. The EU officials wanted manufacturers to label products with the proportions of each ingredient, so that consumers could judge (for example) how much sugar or fat is contained in the product. Manufacturers pointed out that this was tantamount to giving their competitors their recipes, which in many cases are carefully guarded trade secrets. Eventually the manufacturers won this argument.

Packaging can often be used for promotion of other products in the manufacturer's range (via recipe instructions, for example) or for joint promotions with non-competing companies.

Case study 6
Gadgets

People certainly love a gadget – and NPIONLINE sets out to meet that need. The company name is an acronym of New Products International, and since 1976 the company has been dedicated to providing something new, in whatever product category one might care to mention.

At the time of writing, NPIONLINE was offering the George Foreman Grill, the Hulk Hogan Grill (looking surprisingly like the George Foreman Grill), an atomic travel clock, a spinning desk clock and weather instrument, and a talking pedometer with a built-in panic alarm (presumably for people who are mugged while out for a stroll).

All the products can be personalised, or printed with a corporate logo and message and used as a business gift. New Products International is very much into the business gifts market – novelties which can carry a message, or be printed with a company logo, are very much in the forefront of their thinking, and therefore most of the products on offer are fairly standard – although if you fancy owning a model skeleton hand, NPIONLINE is your place to go, because they do have a brisk trade in supplies for the medical profession (printed with pharmaceutical company logos as necessary).

The UK company, Innovations, is a different story altogether. Originally, this company used a paper catalogue which was delivered with newspapers or credit card statements, and it became a UK institution. Innovations pioneered the radio-controlled clock, the treeless hammock, and the extending window-cleaning device: in the category of the less immediately useful, they also offered fur-lined golf club covers and lip-shaped pillows. The paper catalogue disappeared in 2003, to be replaced by a website (clearly the way forward for a firm dedicated to the innovative).

Gadget lovers and novelty seekers are clearly attracted by the Innovations range. Currently, the firm is offering such exciting items as a robot vacuum cleaner, the 'cold carafe' water cooler, a patented wine server which avoids drips going down the side of the bottle, and a remote control key finder. In the weird department, the catalogue offers a motorised tie rack, a set of eye-massaging goggles, and an electric broom with a triangular head for getting into remote corners.

Innovations is dedicated to the lone inventor, working in his or her garage to come up with an idea that will revolutionise our lives. However, it is difficult to see the appeal of the catalogue – the company simply offers a wide variety of products to a wide variety of possible markets, with no clear customer focus. While many people read the old catalogue, and now visit the website, it is difficult to imagine why anyone would actually buy anything – the demand for the Aqua FM snorkel with a built-in radio must be somewhat limited, to take just one example.

Finally, well out on the lunatic fringe are the products listed on the Strange New Products website. This is not a marketing website as such – it is just a site dedicated to the weird and wacky. Climate Change Chocolate (each purchase includes a contribution which offsets one day's worth of carbon) sounds at first to be a great idea – but would people seriously seek it out? Likewise, the Doggie Thong, a thong containing activated charcoal to absorb the dog's farts may not be a product everyone would rush out to buy, even though it is washable (who would want to wash it, one might ask). Earth Dog Tags, which are for humans to wear in case of abduction by aliens, show where Earth is and identify the person so that he or she can be returned home by friendly aliens.

Golfers might like to buy the Big Daddy Driver, a golf club with a grass cutter built in, in case the ball lands in the rough, and motorcyclists might feel attracted to the EMF Shield which protects the rider from electromagnetic radiation generated by the bike's engine. The inventor has written a book about the dangers from radiation – although it is hard to imagine the average big hairy biker worrying too much about this, considering the other safety issues surrounding motorbikes.

Most of the products have a spurious logic attached to them. Throx, the company that sells socks in threes in case you lose one, is certainly addressing a common problem but a moment's further thought usually reveals a better solution (in this case, buy two pairs the same, thus having two spare socks, and give oneself a wider choice). Yet the fascination with novelty continues.

Questions

1 How might Innovations overcome the problem of segmentation?
2 Why would anyone want to buy an Earth Dog Tag?
3 What is the appeal of the Innovations catalogue?
4 Why would a company use innovative products as corporate gifts?
5 What factors have enabled Innovation's catalogue to survive?

SUMMARY

This chapter has been about those decisions that are closest to the product. The main issues revolve around managing the product portfolio to ensure that the firm continues to offer relevant products to meet the needs of consumers, knowing when to drop a product from the mix and knowing when to introduce a new product.

Branding is concerned with communicating the unique selling proposition of the product to the consumers, and is the focus of all the firm's marketing activities relating to the product. The brand is the 'personality' of the product, communicating subtle messages about quality and performance.

Here are the key points from this chapter:

■ The product life cycle is a useful description, but not much help in prediction.

- Products in the Star stage will cost more money to maintain than they bring in, but are an investment for the future.

- Dogs may still be profitable, but are probably a poor use of resources and could be replaced by more profitable products.

- War Horses and Dodos will eventually disappear unless they can be repositioned into new, growing markets.

- Most products will decline and must be replaced eventually.

- The safe route in NPD is the me-too; the high-growth route is innovation.

- A product is a bundle of benefits, not merely the sum of its physical characteristics.

CHAPTER QUESTIONS

1 What are the stages of new product development?

2 Why should firms innovate?

3 How might a firm use re-invention when repositioning a product?

4 From the BCG matrix, which products would probably be bought by the late majority of adopters?

5 What disadvantages might family-line branding have over individual branding?

Further reading

Successful Product Development by **Axel Johne and Patricia Snelson** (Oxford, Basil Blackwell, 1990) is a book based on research conducted among British and American firms during the 1980s to find the best-practice approaches to NPD. It is a readable and interesting text, and contains numerous quotes from managers and others involved in the NPD process.

Services Marketing by **Helen Woodruffe** (London, Pitman Publishing, 1995) gives a very thorough and readable account of the special aspects of the marketing of services.

Building Strong Brands by **David A. Aaker** (New York, The Free Press, 1996) gives a good, practitioner-orientated guide to developing brands.

References

Bagwell, L.S. and Bernheim, B.D.: 'Veblen effects in a theory of conspicuous consumption', *The American Economic Review*, **86** (1996), pp. 349–73.

Balabanis, G. and Craven, S.: 'Consumer confusion from own-brand lookalikes: an exploratory survey', *Journal of Marketing Management*, **13** (4) (May 1997), pp. 299–313.

Barksdale, H.C. and Harris, C.E.: 'Portfolio analysis and the PLC', *Long Range Planning*, **15** (6) (1982), pp. 74–83.

Benwell, M.: 'Scheduling stocks and storage space in a volatile market', *Logistics Information Management*, **9** (4) (1996), pp. 18–23.

Brown, Stephen, Sherry, John F. and Kozinetts, Robert V.: 'Teaching old brands new tricks: retro branding and the revival of brand meaning', *Journal of Marketing*, **67** (3) (July 2003), pp. 19–33.

Buschke, H.: 'Learning is organised by chunking', *Journal of Verbal Learning and Verbal Behaviour*, **15** (1976), pp. 313–24.

Calentone, Roger J. and Cooper, Robert G.: 'New product scenarios: prospects for success', *American Journal of Marketing*, **45** (Spring 1981), pp. 48–60.

Carbonell-Foulquie, Pilar, Munuera-Aleman, Jose L. and Rodriguez-Escudero, Ana I.: 'Criteria employed for go/no-go decisions when developing successful highly innovative products', *Industrial Marketing Management*, **33** (4) (April 2004), pp. 307–16.

Clancy, Kevin J. and Shulman, Robert S.: *The Marketing Revolution* (New York, Harper Business, 1991), p. 6.

Clark, K. and Fujimoto, T.: 'The power of product integrity', *Business Review* (November/December 1990), pp. 107–18.

Cooper, R.G. and Kleinschmidt, E.J.: 'An investigation into the new product process: steps, deficiencies and impact', *Journal of Product Innovation Management*, (June 1988), pp. 71–85.

Davies, I.: 'Look-alikes; fair or unfair competition?', *Journal of Brand Management* (October 1995), pp. 104–20.

DeChernatony, L. and McDonald, M.: *Creating Powerful Brands*, 2nd edn (Oxford, Butterworth Heinemann, 1998).

Demsetz, H.: 'Barriers to entry', *American Economic Review*, **72** (1982), pp. 47–57.

Engel, James F., Blackwell, Roger D. and Miniard, Paul W.: *Consumer Behaviour*, 8th edn (Fort Worth, TX, Dryden Press, 1995).

Foxman, E.R., Berger, P.W. and Cote, J.A.: 'Consumer brand confusion: a conceptual framework', *Psychology and Marketing*, **19** (1992), pp. 123–41.

Gander, P.: 'Patently obvious', *Marketing Week* (28 June 1996), pp. 51–5.

Gordon, W. and Valentin, V.: 'Buying the brand at point of choice', *Journal of Brand Management*, **4** (1) (1996), pp. 35–44.

Haines, George H.: 'A study of why people purchase new products', *Proceedings of the American Marketing Association* (1966), pp. 685–97.

Hankinson, G. and Cowking, P.: 'Branding in practice: the profile and role of brand managers in the UK', *Journal of Marketing Management*, **13** (4) (May 1997), pp. 239–64.

Hart, Susan: 'Dimensions of success in new product development; an exploratory investigation', *Journal of Marketing Management*, **9** (1) (January 1993), pp. 23–42.

Huang, Xueli, Soutar, Geoffrey N. and Brown, Alan: 'Measuring new product success: an empirical investigation of Australian SMEs', *Industrial Marketing Management*, **33** (2) (February 2004), pp. 101–23.

Johne, A. and Snelson, P.: *Successful Product Development: Management Practices in American and British Firms* (Oxford, Basil Blackwell, 1990).

Koestler, A.: *The Act of Creation* (London, Pan Books Ltd, 1964).

Lazarsfield, Paul F., Bertelson Bernard R. and Gaudet, Hazel: *The People's Choice* (New York, Columbia University Press, 1948).

Levitt, T.: *The Marketing Imagination* (New York, The Free Press, 1986).

Min, Sungwook, Kauwani, Manohar U. and Robinson, William T.: 'Market pioneer and early follower survival risks: a contingency analysis of really new vs. incrementally new products', *Journal of Marketing*, **70** (1) (2006), pp. 15–33.

Muzellec, Laurent and Lambkin, Mary: 'Corporate rebranding: destroying, transferring or creating brand equity?' *European Journal of Marketing*, **40** (7/8) (2006), pp. 803–24.

Napoli, Julie: 'The impact of non-profit brand orientation on organizational performance', *Journal of Marketing Management*, **22** (7/8) (2006), pp. 673–94.

Pappu, Ravi, Quester, Pascale and Cooksey, Ray W.: 'Consumer-based brand equity and country of origin relationships', *European Journal of Marketing*, **40** (5/6) (2006), pp. 696–717.

Png, J.P. and Reitman, D.: 'Why are some products branded and others not?', *Journal of Law and Economics*, **38** (1995), pp. 207–24.

Quelch, J. and Harding, D.: 'Brands versus private labels: fighting to win', *Harvard Business Review* (January–February 1995), pp. 99–109.

Raffee, H. and Kreutzer, R.: 'Organisational dimensions of global marketing', *European Journal of Marketing*, **23** (5) (1989), pp. 43–57.

Raghubir, Priya and Greenleaf, Eric A.: 'Ratios in proportion: what should the shape of the package be?', *Journal of Marketing*, **70** (2) (2006), pp. 95–107.

Ries, A.: 'What's in a name?', *Sales and Marketing Management* (October 1995), pp. 36–7.

Rogers, Everett M.: *Diffusion of Innovations* (New York, Macmillan, 1962).

Romaniuk, Jenni and Gaillard, Elise: 'The relationship between unique brand associations, brand usage and brand performance: analysis across eight categories', *Journal of Marketing Management*, **23** (3/4) (2007), pp. 267–84.

Ruttenberg, A., Kavizky, A. and Oren, H.: 'Compositioning – the paradigm-shift beyond positioning', *Journal of Brand Management* (December 1995), pp. 169–79.

Sandler, D. and Shani, D.: 'Brand globally but advertise locally? An empirical investigation', *Marketing Review* (1992), pp. 18–31.

Sorescu, Alina B., Chandy, Rajesh K. and Prabhu, Jaideep C.: 'Sources and financial consequences of radical innovation: insights from pharmaceuticals', *Journal of Marketing*, **67** (4) (October 2003), pp. 82–102.

Tajeddini, Kayhan, Trueman, Myfanwy and Larsen, Gretchen: 'Examining the effect of marketing orientation on innovativeness', *Journal of Marketing Management*, **22** (5/6) (2006), pp. 529–51.

Uncles, M., Cocks, M. and Macrae, C.: 'Brand architecture: reconfiguring organisations for effective brand management', *Journal of Brand Management* (October 1995), pp. 81–92.

Veblen, T.: *The Theory of the Leisure Class* (New York, Macmillan, 1899).

Volckner, Franziska and Sattler, Henrik: 'Drivers of brand extension success', *Journal of Marketing*, **70** (2) (2006), pp. 18–34.

www.pearsoned.co.uk/blythe

Tata

Tata is India's largest industrial company, generating more than 3% of the country's gross national product. The company's motor division manufactures trucks, buses, scooters and three-wheel motor rickshaws. India is a large country, but most people are poor, in fact too poor to own cars at all.

Tata's promise was to build a car for 1 lakh rupees (a lakh is 100,000). This price equates to around £1500, a price which the company thought was realistic for many Indians (although still out of reach of the poorest, many of whom would struggle to afford a bicycle).

Most major car manufacturers thought that this target was entirely unrealistic, given the cost of raw materials: even with the low wage structure of India, producing even a very small car for £1500 seemed out of the question. No matter how basic, the task seemed impossible.

The Tata Nano was eventually unveiled and, true to his promise, Ratan Tata, the company's chairman, put the car on the market for 1 lakh. The car has a 600 cc engine, continuous transmission (no gearbox or clutch), no passenger mirror, no radio, and only one windscreen wiper. The car meets all safety standards for India, but might need adapting for Europe or the United States – but it is still a remarkable feat of engineering.

Ratan Tata, Chairman

Watch the video clip, then try to answer the following questions. The answers are on the companion website.

Questions

1 What type of pricing is Tata using for the Nano?
2 What should be the company's pricing policy for Europe?
3 Should the car meet the European safety standards?
4 What are the drawbacks of charging such a low price?

7

Pricing strategies

Objectives

After reading this chapter you should be able to:

- explain the advantages and disadvantages of different pricing methods;
- calculate prices using different approaches;
- choose the correct pricing strategy to fit a firm's overall objectives;
- explain some of the economic theories underlying the marketer's view of price and value.

INTRODUCTION

Pricing may not be exciting, but it is one of the most important issues for marketers; it is crucial not only to the profit that is to be made, but also to the quantity of the products that will be sold. It also touches on all the other elements of the marketing mix, because it clarifies the offer of exchange being made – it is the signal to the customer of what we expect in exchange for what we are offering. This chapter examines the different ways of pricing that are used, and offers some ideas on how to choose a pricing strategy.

ECONOMIC THEORIES OF PRICING AND VALUE

Classical economists assumed that prices would automatically be set by the laws of *supply and demand*. Figure 7.1 shows how this works.

As prices rise, more suppliers find it profitable to enter the market, but the demand for the product falls because fewer customers think the product is worth the money. Conversely, as prices fall there is more demand, but fewer suppliers feel it is worthwhile supplying the product so less is produced. Eventually a state of equilibrium is reached where the quantity produced is equal to the quantity consumed, and at that point the price will be fixed.

Unfortunately this neat model has a number of drawbacks.

■ The model assumes that customers know where they can buy the cheapest products (i.e. it assumes perfect knowledge of the market).

■ Second, it assumes that all the suppliers are producing identical products, which is rarely the case.

■ Third, it assumes that price is the only issue that affects customer behaviour, which is clearly not true.

■ Fourth, it assumes that customers always behave completely rationally, which again is substantially not the case.

■ Fifth, there is an assumption that people will always buy more of a product if it is cheaper. This is not true of such products as wedding rings or artificial limbs.

■ Finally, the model assumes that the suppliers are in perfect competition – that none of them has the power to 'rig' the market and set the prices (see Chapter 2).

Figure 7.1 Supply and demand

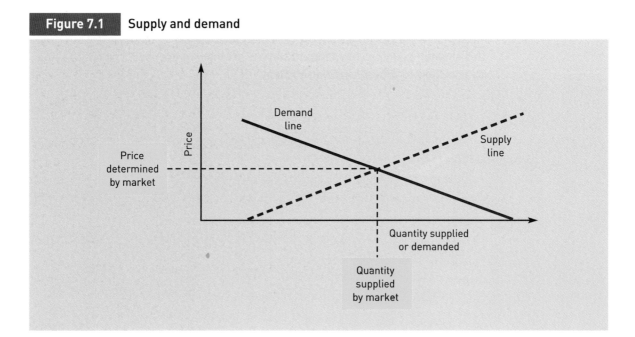

The model does, at least, take account of customers, and it was the pioneer economist Adam Smith who first said that 'the customer is king' (Smith 1776). Unfortunately the shortcomings of the model mean that it has little practical use, no matter how helpful it is in understanding a principle. Economists have therefore added considerably to the theory.

Elasticity of demand

This concept states that different product categories will show different degrees of sensitivity to price change.

Figure 7.2(a) shows a product where the quantity sold is affected only slightly by price fluctuations, i.e. the demand is **inelastic**. An example of this is salt. Figure 7.2(b) shows a product where even a small difference in price leads to a very substantial shift in the quantity demanded, i.e. the demand is **elastic**. An example of this is borrowed money, e.g. mortgages, where even a small rise in interest rates appears to affect the propensity to borrow. Although these examples relate to consumers, the same is true for suppliers: in some cases suppliers can react very quickly to changes in the quantities demanded (for example, banking), whereas in other cases the suppliers need long lead times to change the production levels (for instance, farming).

The **price elasticity of demand** concept implies that there is no basis for defining products as necessities or luxuries. If a necessity is defined as something without which life cannot be sustained, then its demand curve would be entirely inelastic: whatever the price was, people would have to pay it. In practice, no such product exists.

Figure 7.2 Price elasticity of demand

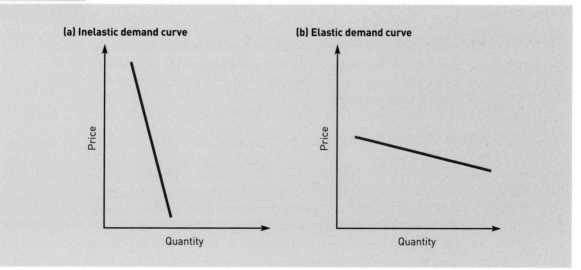

Economic choice

Economists have demonstrated that there can never be enough resources in the world to satisfy everybody's wants, and therefore resources have to be allocated in some way (which will probably mean an equality of dissatisfaction). Resources used for one purpose cannot, of course, be used for another: this is the concept of the **economic choice**.

For example, a clothing manufacturer has only a certain number of machinists who work a certain number of hours. This means that it may be possible to produce either 8000 shirts with the available resources, or 4000 pairs of trousers. If the manufacturer has two orders, one for each type of product, he or she will have to choose which order to supply, and disappoint the other customer.

From the customer's viewpoint, the economic choice means having to choose between going to the cinema or going to the pub; there may not be the time or the money to do both. Because of this, customers may also take into account the price of activities other than those the prospective supplier is providing; the pub, for example, may not be aware that the cinema is competition, and that a fall in the price of going to the cinema may affect the takings over the bar.

Although the economists' view of pricing offers some interesting insights, there is little practical value in the theories offered because they do not take account of the consumer decision-making process (see Chapter 3). Consumers are not always rational; marketers are aware of this.

Critical thinking

Are we really that illogical when we buy things? It's a rather bleak comment on human beings – after all, we are the most intelligent creature so far discovered! If we don't use our brains to decide how to spend our hard-earned money, doesn't that imply that we don't use our brains much for anything else?

Of course, maybe we do think about things sometimes. If it's an important purchase, or if we are short of money, we might make more effort – but who bothers to spend time thinking about the price of a bar of chocolate? Apart, of course, from marketers!

PRICING AND MARKET ORIENTATION

As in any other question of marketing, pricing is dependent on how customers will react to the prices set. Customers do not usually buy the cheapest products; they buy those that represent good value for money. If this were not so, the most popular cars in Britain would be Citroen 2CVs, or cheap Eastern European models, rather than Vauxhalls and Fords. Typically, customers will assess the promises the supplier has made about what the product is and will do, and will measure this against the price being asked (Zeithaml 1988).

This leaves the marketer with a problem. Marketers need to decide what price will be regarded by customers as good value for money, while still allowing the company to make a profit.

The main methods of pricing used by firms are cost-based, customer-based and competition-based.

Cost-based pricing

Cost-based methods are the least customer-orientated; two still used are **cost-plus pricing** and **mark-up pricing**.

Cost-plus pricing

Cost-plus pricing is commonly advocated by accountants and engineers, since it is simple to use and appears to guarantee that the company meets a pre-determined profit target. The method works by calculating the cost of manufacturing the product, including distributed overhead costs and research and development costs, then adding on a fixed percentage profit to this figure in order to arrive at the price. Such a calculation might look like Table 7.1.

A variant of cost-plus pricing is absorption costing, which works by calculating the costs of each unit of production including an allowance for overheads within the unit price. This allows the firm to calculate a break-even point at which further sales will be profitable.

On the face of it, this type of pricing seems logical and straightforward; unfortunately, it does not take account of how customers will react to the prices quoted. If customers take the view that the price does not represent value for money, they will not buy the product, and the result will be that the company will have made 20 000 units of a product for which there will be no sales.

Table 7.1   Cost-plus pricing

Item	Cost per unit
Labour costs	£2.52
Raw materials	£4.32
Electricity	£0.27
Tooling costs (assuming production run of 20 000 units)	£1.78
Overheads	£3.43
Total production cost per unit	£12.32
Plus profit of 20%	£2.46
Net price	**£14.78**

Conversely, if customers take the view that the price is incredibly good value for money, the company may not have enough stocks on hand to meet demand, and competitors will be able to enter the market easily (not to mention that the company could have charged more for the product and therefore made more money).

Some government contracts are awarded on a cost-plus basis, but experience in the United States has shown that allowing cost-plus contracts to be granted will often result in the supplier inflating the costs to make an extra profit.

Mark-up pricing

Mark-up pricing is similar to cost-plus pricing, and is the method used by most retailers. Typically, a retailer will buy in stock and add on a fixed percentage to the bought-in price (a mark-up) in order to arrive at the **shelf price**. The level will vary from retailer to retailer, depending on the type of product; in some cases the mark-up will be 100% or more, in others it will be near zero (if the retailer feels that stocking the product will stimulate other sales). Usually there is a standard mark-up for each product category.

Here the difference needs to be shown between a **mark-up** and a **margin**. Mark-up is calculated on the price the retailer pays for the product; margin is calculated on the price the retailer sells for. This means that a 100% mark-up equals a 50% margin; a 25% mark-up equals a 20% margin (Table 7.2).

Retailers use this method because of the number of lines the shop may be carrying. For a hypermarket, this could be up to 20 000 separate lines, and it would clearly be impossible to carry out market research with the customers for every line. The buyers therefore use their training and knowledge of their customer base to determine which lines to stock, and (to some extent) rely on the manufacturers to carry out formal market research and determine the recommended retail prices.

This method is identical to the cost-plus method except for two factors: first, the retailer is usually in close contact with the customers, and can therefore develop a good 'feel' for what customers will be prepared to pay; and second, retailers have ways of disposing of unsold stock. In some cases, this will mean discounting the stock back to cost and selling it in the January sales; in other cases, the retailer will have a sale-or-return agreement with the manufacturer, so that unsold stock can be returned for credit. This is becoming increasingly

Table 7.2 Mark-up *v* margin

Bought-in price	£4.00
Mark-up at 25% of £4.00	£1.00
Price on the shelf	£5.00
Margin of 20% of £5.00	£1.00
Bought-in price	£4.00

common with major retailers such as Toys 'R' Us who have sufficient 'clout' in the market to enforce such agreements. In a sense, therefore, the retailer is carrying out market research by test-marketing the product; if the customers do not accept the product at the price offered, the retailer can drop the price to a point that will represent value for money, or can return it to the manufacturer for credit.

Customer-based pricing methods

The various approaches to *customer-based pricing* do not necessarily mean offering products at the lowest possible price, but they do take account of customer needs and wants.

Customary pricing

Customary pricing is customer-orientated in that it provides the customer with the product for the same price at which it has always been offered. An example is the price of a call from a coin-operated telephone box. Telephone companies need only reduce the time allowed for the call as costs rise. For some countries (e.g. Australia) this is problematical since local calls are allowed unlimited time, but for most European countries this is not the case.

The reason for using customary pricing is to avoid having to reset the call-boxes too often. Similar methods exist for taxis, some children's sweets, and gas or electricity pre-payment meters. If this method were to be used for most products there would be a steady reduction in the firm's profits as the costs caught up with the selling price, so the method is not practical for every firm.

Demand pricing

Demand pricing is the most market-orientated method of pricing. Here, the marketer begins by assessing what the demand will be for the product at different price levels. This is usually done by asking the customers what they might expect to pay for the product, and seeing how many choose each price level. This will lead to the development of the kind of chart shown in Table 7.3.

Table 7.3   Demand pricing

Price per unit	Number of customers who said they would buy at this price
£3 to £4	30 000
£4 to £5	25 000
£5 to £6	15 000
£6 to £7	5 000

As the price rises, fewer customers are prepared to buy the product, as fewer will still see the product as good value for money. In the example given in Table 7.3, the fall-off is not linear, i.e. the number of units sold falls dramatically once the price goes above £5. This kind of calculation could be used to determine the stages of a skimming policy (see below), or it could be used to calculate the appropriate launch price of a product.

For demand pricing, the next stage is to calculate the costs of producing the product in the above quantities. Usually the cost of producing each item falls as more are made (i.e. if we make 50 000 units, each unit costs less than would be the case if we made only 1000 units). Given the costs of production it is possible to select the price that will lead to a maximisation of profits. This is because there is a trade-off between quantity produced and quantity sold: as the firm lowers the selling price, the amount sold increases but the income generated decreases.

The calculations can become complex, but the end result is that the product is sold at a price that customers will accept, and that will meet the company's profit targets. Table 7.4 shows an example of costings to match up with the above figures. The tooling-up cost is the amount it will cost the company to prepare for producing the item. This will be the same whether 1000 or 30 000 units are made.

Table 7.4 Costings for demand pricing

Number of units	Unit cost (labour and materials)	Tooling-up and fixed costs	Net cost per unit
30 000	£1.20	£4000	£1.33
25 000	£1.32	£4000	£1.48
15 000	£1.54	£4000	£1.81
5 000	£1.97	£4000	£2.77

Table 7.5 shows how much profit could be made at each price level. The price at which the product is sold will depend on the firm's overall objectives; these may not necessarily be to maximise profit on this one product, since the firm may have other products in the range or other long-term objectives that preclude maximising profits at present.

Table 7.5 Profitability at different price bands

Number of units sold	Net profit per unit	Total profit for production run	Percentage profit per unit
30 000	£2.17	£65 100	62
25 000	£3.02	£75 500	67
15 000	£3.61	£54 150	66
5 000	£3.73	£18 650	57

Based on these figures, *the most profitable* price will be £4.50. Other ways of calculating the price could easily lead to making a lower profit from this product. For instance, the price that would generate *the highest profit per unit* would be £6.50, but at this price they would sell only 5000 units and make £18 650. The price that would generate *the highest sales* would be £3.50, but this would (in effect) lose the firm almost £10 000 in terms of forgone profit.

A further useful concept is that of *contribution*. Contribution is calculated as the difference between the cost of manufacture and the price for which the product is sold – in other words it does not take account of overheads. Sometimes a product is worth producing because it makes a significant extra contribution to the firm's profits, without actually adding to the overheads. It is not difficult to imagine a situation where a product carries a low profit margin, and is therefore unable to support a share of the overheads, but is still worth producing (perhaps because it supports sales of something else, or is bought by our most loyal customers). A calculation which included an overall share of the overheads might not give a fair picture, since the contribution would be additional to existing turnover.

Demand pricing works by knowing what the customers are prepared to pay, and what they will see as value for money.

Product-line pricing

Product-line pricing means setting prices within linked product groups. Often sales of one product will be directly linked to the sales of another, so that it is possible to sell one item at a low price in order to make a greater profit on the other one. Gillette sells its razors at a very low price, with the aim of making up the profit on sales of the blades. In the long run, this is a good strategy because it overcomes the initial resistance of consumers towards buying something untried, but allows the firm to show high profits for years to come (incidentally, this approach was first used by King C. Gillette, the inventor of the disposable safety razor blade).

Polaroid chose to sell its instant cameras very cheaply (almost for cost price) for the US market and to take their profit from selling the films for a much higher price. For Europe, the firm chose to sell both films and cameras for a medium level price and profit from sales of both. Eventually this led Kodak to enter the market with its own instant camera, but this was withdrawn from sale in the face of lawsuits from Polaroid for patent infringement.

Skimming

Skimming is the practice of starting out with a high price for a product, then reducing it progressively as sales level off. It relies on two main factors: first, that not all customers have the same perception of value for money, and second that the company has a technological lead over the opposition which can be maintained for long enough to satisfy the market.

Skimming is usually carried out by firms which have developed a technically advanced product. Initially the firm will charge a high price for the product, and at this point only those who are prepared to pay a premium price for it will buy. Profit may not be high, because the number of units sold will be low and therefore the cost of production per unit will be high. Once the most innovative customers have bought, and the competition is beginning to enter the market, the firm can drop the price and 'skim' the next layer of the market, at which point profits will begin to rise. Eventually the product will be sold at a price that allows the firm only a minimum profit, at which point only replacement sales or sales to late adopters will be made.

The advantage of this method is that the cost of developing the product is returned fairly quickly, so that the product can later be sold near the marginal cost of production. This means that the competitors have difficulty entering the market at all, since their own development costs will have to be recovered in some other way.

Skimming is commonly used in consumer electronics markets. This is because firms frequently establish a technological lead over the competitors, and can sometimes even protect their products by taking out patents, which take some time for competitors to overcome. An example of this is the MP3 player, which sold at a premium price when it was first launched. As competitors entered the market with cloned products, the price dropped dramatically. Recent research shows that customers are aware of skimming in electronics markets, and are delaying purchases of new electronic devices until the prices drop. This may affect the way firms view skimming in the future.

Skimming requires careful judgement of what is happening in the marketplace, in terms both of observing customer behaviour, and of observing competitive response. Market research is therefore basic to the success of a skimming policy, and very careful monitoring of sales is needed to know when to cut the price again.

Critical thinking

Skimming seems like a bit of a cheat. The firm makes the product for a low price, then sells it at a high price, knowing that the price is going to fall later. Isn't this a bit like cheating the first few customers by overcharging them?

Or maybe they are enjoying the fun of being the first to own the product, and the firm is making them pay for the privilege. It seems an expensive bit of fun to have, though – and anyway, people know about skimming.

On the other hand, of course, firms are not in business for the fun of it. They are entitled to make a profit, and of course recover the rather expensive research and development costs they incur in producing new products for us!

Psychological pricing

Psychological pricing relies on emotional responses from the consumer. Higher prices are often used as an indicator of quality (Erickson and Johansson 1985) so some firms will use **prestige pricing**. This applies in many service industries, because consumers are often buying a promise; a service that does not have a high enough quality cannot be exchanged afterwards. Consumers' expectations of high-priced restaurants and hairdressers are clearly higher in terms of the quality of service provision; cutting prices in those industries does not necessarily lead to an increase in business. Interestingly, there is evidence that the price-quality relationship was affected considerably by the introduction of the Euro. Prices previously expressed in Deutschmarks appeared higher than the new price in Euros because there were approximately two Euros to the Deutschmark – people's perception was that the price had 'halved' which lowered their expectations of quality (Molz and Gielnik 2006).

Odd–even pricing is the practice of ending prices with an odd number, for example £3.99 or $5.95 rather than £4 or $6. It appears that consumers tend to categorise these prices as '£3 and a bit' or '$5 and change' and thus perceive the price as being lower. The effect may also be due to an association with discounted or sale prices; researchers report that '99' endings on prices increase sales by around 8% (Schindler and Kirby 1997). Paradoxically, some recent research shows that people are more likely to try a new product for the first time if the price is a round number (Bray and Harris 2006).

This apparent discrepancy may be due to cultural differences. Research has shown that odd–even pricing does not necessarily work in all cultures (Suri *et al*. 2004). In Poland, for example, the effects are negligible. Odd–even pricing also has effects on perceptions of discounts during sales. Rounding the price to (say) £5 from £4.99 leads people to overvalue the size of the discount, which increases the perception of value for money (Gueguen and Legoherel 2004). Thus the positive effect on sales of using a 99-ending can be negated by the effect when the product is on offer in a sale.

Second-market discounting

Second-market discounting is common in some service industries and in international markets. The brand is sold at one price in one market, and in a lower price in another: for example, museums offer discounts to students, some restaurants offer discounts to elderly people on week-nights, and so forth. Often these discounts are offered to even out the **loading** on the firm; week-night discounts fill the restaurant on what would otherwise be a quiet night, so the firm makes more efficient use of the premises and staff.

In international markets products might be discounted to meet local competition. For example, Honda motorcycles are up against strong local competition in India from Royal Enfield, so the price of their basic 100 cc motorcycle is around Rs39 000 (about £600). A similar Honda motorcycle in the UK costs around

£2000. The specifications of the motorcycles do differ somewhat, and the import duty structures are different – but it is difficult to see any difference that would account for a £1400 price differential.

Competitor-based pricing

Competitor-based pricing recognises the influence of competition in the market-place. Strategically, the marketer must decide how close the competition is in providing for the consumers' needs; if the products are close, then prices will need to be similar to those of the competition. A **meet-the-competition strategy** has the advantage of avoiding price wars and stimulating competition in other areas of marketing, thus maintaining profitability. An **undercut-the-competition strategy** is often the main plank in the firm's marketing strategy; it is particularly common among retailers, who have relatively little control over product features and benefits and often have little control over the promotion of the products they stock. Some multinational firms (particularly in electronics) have the capacity to undercut rivals since they are able to manufacture in low-wage areas of the world, or are large enough to use widespread automation. There is a danger of starting price wars when using an undercutting policy (see penetration pricing below). Undercutting (and consequent price wars) may be becoming more common (Mitchell 1996).

Firms with large market shares often have enough control over their distribution systems and production capacity within their industries to become **price leaders**. Typically, such firms can make price adjustments without starting price wars, and can raise prices without losing substantial market share (see Chapter 2 for monopolistic competition) (Rich 1982). Sometimes these price leaders become sensitive to the price and profit needs of their competitors, in effect supporting them, because they do not wish to attract the attention of monopoly regulators by destroying the competition. Deliberate price fixing (managers colluding to set industry prices) is illegal in most countries.

Penetration pricing

Penetration pricing is used when the firm wants to capture a large part of the market quickly. It relies on the assumption that a lower price will be perceived as offering better value for money (which is, of course, often the case).

For penetration pricing to work, the company must have carried out thorough research to find out what the competitors are charging for the nearest similar product. The new product is then sold at a substantially lower price, even if this cuts profits below an acceptable level; the intention is to capture the market quickly before the competitors can react with even lower prices. The danger with this pricing method is that competitors may be able to sustain a price war for a long period and will eventually bankrupt the incoming firm. It is usually safer to compete on some other aspect of the offering, such as quality or delivery.

Predatory pricing

In some cases, prices are pitched below the cost of production. The purpose of this is to bankrupt the competition so that the new entrant can take over entirely; this practice is called **predatory pricing** and (at least in international markets) is illegal. Predatory pricing was successfully used by Japanese car manufacturers when entering European markets in the 1970s, and is commonly used by large firms who are entering new markets. For the strategy to be successful, it is necessary for the market to be dominated by firms that cannot sustain a long price war. It is worth doing if the company has no other competitive edge, but does have sufficient financial reserves to hold out for a long time. Naturally, this method is customer-orientated since it can work only by providing the customers with very much better value for money than they have been used to. The company will eventually raise prices again in order to recoup the lost profits once the market presence has been established, however.

The ultimate in predatory pricing is dumping. This is the practice of selling goods at prices below the cost of manufacture, and was at one time commonly practiced by Communist countries desperate for hard currency. Dumping is illegal under international trade rules, but is difficult to prove, and by the time the victim countries have been able to prove their case and have the practice stopped, it is usually too late.

Competitor-based pricing is still customer-orientated to an extent, since it takes as its starting-point the prices that customers are currently prepared to pay.

SETTING PRICES

Price setting follows eight stages, as shown in Table 7.6.

Price setting can be complex if it is difficult to identify the closest competitors, but it should be borne in mind that no product is entirely without competition; there is almost always another way in which customers can meet the need supplied by the product. Also, different customers have different needs and therefore will have differing views on what constitutes value for money – this is why markets need to be segmented carefully to ensure that the right price is being charged in each segment. As in any question of marketing, it is wise to begin with the customer.

Table 7.6	Eight stages of price setting

Stage	Explanation
Development of pricing objectives	The pricing objectives derive from the organisation's overall objectives; does the firm seek to maximise market share or maximise profits?
Assessment of the target market's ability to purchase and evaluation of price	Buyers tend to be more sensitive to food prices in supermarkets than to drinks prices in clubs. Also, a buyer's income and availability of credit directly affect the ability to buy the product at all.
Determination of demand	For most products demand falls as price rises. This is not necessarily a straight-line relationship, nor is the line necessarily at forty-five degrees; for some products even a small price rise results in a sharp fall in demand (e.g. petrol) whereas for other products (e.g. salt) even a large price rise hardly affects demand at all.
Analysis of demand, cost and profit relationships	The firm needs to analyse the costs of producing the item against the price that the market will bear, taking into account the profit needed. The cost calculation will include both the fixed costs and the unit costs for making a given quantity of the product; this quantity will be determined by the market, and will relate to the selling price.
Evaluation of competitors' prices	This will involve a survey of the prices currently being charged, but will also have to consider the possible entry of new competitors. Prices may be pitched higher than competitors in order to give an impression of exclusivity or higher quality; this is common in the perfume market, and in services such as restaurants and hairdressing.
Selection of a pricing policy	The pricing policy needs to be chosen from the list given in the early part of the chapter.
Development of a pricing method	Here the producer develops a simple mechanism for determining prices in the future. The simplest method is to use cost-plus or mark-up pricing; these do not take account of customers, however, so something a little more sophisticated should be used if possible.
Determining a specific price	If the previous steps have been carried out in a thorough manner, determining the actual price should be a simple matter.

Source: Adapted from Dibb *et al.* 1994.

Case study 7
Petrol prices

One of the more irritating aspects of car ownership is the ever-rising cost of fuel. Although, in real terms, petrol is cheaper now than it was forty years ago, people perceive the price as being exceptionally high: governments worldwide tend to tax petrol highly, partly as a way of generating revenue and partly as a way of discouraging motoring. Trying to price motorists off the road has been singularly unsuccessful, but it does at least allow finance ministers to adopt the moral high ground on environmental issues.

In some countries, fuel prices fluctuate fairly dramatically as a result of local competition. Petrol is a homogeneous product – it works just as well whichever company supplies it, and despite attempts by petrol companies to differentiate the product by introducing additives intended to clean the engine, improve mileage, and so forth most motorists do not care which brand of petrol they put into their cars. Indeed, petrol needs to be homogeneous: car engines have to be able to run on any brand. The result is that competition between service stations can become cut-throat.

The petrol market in Australia is a prime example. Petrol stations are independently owned in Australia, so although they may carry the Shell or BP logo, they operate as individual businesses. Each filling station operator keeps a careful eye on every other operator in the area – if one station cuts prices, the others have to follow suit, but eventually the price is too low to make any money, so one or other operator will try raising the price again. If the others also raise their prices (no doubt relieved that someone has taken the plunge) then all is well and good, but if the others keep their prices the same, then the station will have to drop the price back down. Since most of the filling stations employ someone solely to watch what the other stations are doing, prices can fluctuate rapidly and over a wide range – it is not unusual to see price shifts of 10c a litre within a few hours.

Shell Australia operate a section of their website dedicated solely to advising motorists on how to buy petrol. They advise filling the tank if there is a bargain price, because the price may not be the same even minutes later – they recommend that motorists do not wait until the tank is nearly empty before filling up. They even have a price indicator on the website, showing how the prices have shifted in various regions of Australia, so that motorists can try to predict what is going to happen next, and when would be the best time to buy. The website has detailed graphs of average petrol prices in Sydney, Canberra, Melbourne, Adelaide, Perth, Darwin, Hobart and Brisbane, each of which shows sharp daily fluctuations. In just one week in February 2008, the average price of fuel in Brisbane fluctuated by 17c a litre – almost 15% of the lowest price.

In other countries petrol prices can vary dramatically even within the same country. In Morocco, petrol prices in the north of the country are around the same level as in Europe, but south of Tan Tan in the Western Sahara the price halves. This is due to a government subsidy intended to ease the chronic transportation problems in this remote desert area.

Protests have grown in the UK in recent years about the very high levels of taxation on fuel. During the 1980s the government reduced the tax on unleaded petrol to encourage people to use it rather than the environmentally damaging four-star leaded petrol. This gave a dramatic boost to sales of unleaded, but there is no particular reason for the present government to reduce petrol taxation, unless forced to do so by the European Union, a scenario which is extremely unlikely, despite the fact that petrol prices across the EU vary by as much as 30%.

At first sight, the pricing of a product such as petrol should be simple – it is a simple, basic, homogeneous product with a large number of buyers and a large number of sellers. In practice, it is a great deal more complex than at first appears.

Questions

1 What pricing strategy do Australian petrol stations appear to be using?
2 What is the role of psychological pricing in the pricing of petrol?
3 Why is petrol pricing so complex?
4 Why do people perceive the price of petrol as high?
5 Why might petrol prices vary within the European Union?

SUMMARY

Value for money is a subjective concept; each person has a differing view of what represents value for money, and this means that different market segments will have differing views on whether a given price is appropriate. Marketing is about encouraging trade so that customers and manufacturers can maximise the satisfaction gained from their activities; to this end, marketers always try to make exchanges easier and pleasanter for customers.

Here are the key points from this chapter:

- Prices, ultimately, are fixed by market forces, not by suppliers alone. Therefore suppliers would be ill-advised to ignore the customer.
- There is no objective difference between necessities and luxuries; the distinction lies only in the mind of the customer.
- Customers cannot spend the same money twice, so they are forced to make economic choices. A decision to do one thing implies a decision not to do another.
- Customers have a broad and sometimes surprising range of choices when seeking to maximise utility.
- Pricing can be cost-based, competition-based or customer-based; ultimately, though, consumers have the last word because they can simply spend their money elsewhere.

CHAPTER QUESTIONS

1 What is the difference between margin and mark-up?
2 When should a skimming policy be used?
3 How can penetration pricing be used in international markets?
4 Why should a firm be wary of cost-plus pricing?
5 How does customary pricing benefit the supplier?

Further reading

For a fairly readable text on the economic aspects of pricing, *Richard Lipsey's Introduction to Positive Economics*, **6th edn** (London, Weidenfeld and Nicholson, 1983) is worth looking at.

Len Rogers' *Pricing for Profit* (Oxford, Basil Blackwell, 1990) is a practitioner-style book which contains a very comprehensive 'how-to' guide to pricing.

Hermann Simon's *Price Management* (Amsterdam, Elsevier Science Publishers BV, 1989) gives an in-depth analysis of pricing strategy, with plenty of supporting mathematics.

References

Bray, Jeffrey Paul and Harris, Christine: 'The effect of 9-ending prices on retail sales: a quantitative UK-based field study', *Journal of Marketing Management*, **22** (5/6) (2006), pp. 601–7.

Dibb, S., Simkin, L., Pride, W. and Ferrell, O.C.: *Marketing; Concepts and Strategies*, 2nd edn (London, Houghton Mifflin, 1994).

Erickson, G.M. and Johansson, J.K.: 'The role of price in multi-attribute product evaluation', *Journal of Consumer Research*, **12** (1985), pp. 195–9.

Gueguen, Nicolas and Legoherel, Patrick: 'Numerical encoding and odd-ending prices: The effect of a contrast in discount perception', *European Journal of Marketing*, **38** (1) (2004), pp. 194–208.

Mitchell, A.: 'The price is right', *Marketing Business*, **50** (May 1996), pp. 32–4.

Molz, Gunter and Gielnik, Michael: 'Does the introduction of the Euro have an effect on subjective hypotheses about the price-quality relationship?', *Journal of Consumer Behaviour*, **5** (3) (2006), pp. 204–10.

Rich, Stuart A.: 'Price leaders: large, strong, but cautious about conspiracy', *Marketing News* (25 June 1982), p. 11.

Schindler, R.M. and Kirby, P.N.: 'Patterns of right-most digits used in advertised prices: implications for nine-ending effects', *Journal of Consumer Research* (September 1997), pp. 192–201.

Smith, Adam: *An Inquiry into The Wealth of Nations* (1776).

Suri, Rajneesh, Anderson, Rolph E. and Kotlov, Vassili: 'The use of 9-ending prices: contrasting the USA with Poland', *European Journal of Marketing*, **38** (1) (2004), pp. 56–72.

Zeithaml, Valerie A.: 'Consumer perceptions of price, quality and value', *Journal of Marketing*, **52** (July 1988), pp. 2–22.

Friday's

Friday's is a family business in the egg-producing business. Although the company produces foods other than eggs, fresh egg production and selling is the core of the business. The company has grown from a small chicken farm: it produces 4 billion eggs a year, which is about 6% of the UK market. Sixty per cent of the eggs are produced intensively, but free-range and barn eggs are also sold. Most of the eggs are sold under the supermarkets' own brands: the company is happy to help the supermarkets to brand the eggs appropriately. About 40% of the free-range eggs produced in Europe are produced in the UK.

Eggs are labelled with the Red Lion mark, which indicates that the eggs are British and the chickens are vaccinated against diseases such as salmonella. The lion mark was originally used in the 1950s and 1960s but fell out of use. Consumer confidence was shaken in the 1980s by a salmonella scare, but the brand has now been re-established via a series of TV advertisements.

Friday's is a price taker rather than a price maker: either the supermarkets set the price, or prices are set by supply and demand. Feed prices create a problem for producers – consumers have already moved away from organic eggs due to the cost, and clearly supermarkets are driven by what consumers are prepared (or able) to pay.

Distribution is a problem with such a fragile and perishable commodity. Friday's seek to minimise the distance from farm to retailer, and are the only egg producer able to deliver local eggs in the south east of Britain.

David Friday, Managing Director

Watch the video clip, then try to answer the following questions. The answers are on the companion website.

Questions

1 What are the main logistical problems for Friday's?

2 Why do Friday's distribute mainly through supermarkets?

3 Why does the company produce a mix of free-range and intensively farmed eggs?

8

Distribution

Objectives

After reading this chapter you should be able to:

- understand the role of distribution as providing an integral part of the product's benefits;
- explain the way agents, wholesalers and retailers work in the distribution system;
- choose the best distribution channel for a given market segment and product;
- explain some of the challenges facing retailers;
- know what to expect of different types of wholesaler;
- understand the difference between logistics and distribution.

INTRODUCTION

Producing something that consumers would like to buy is only part of the story; people can only buy products that are available and easily obtained. In terms of the seven Ps distribution is the means by which place is determined. Marketers therefore spend considerable effort on finding the right channels of distribution, and on ensuring that the products reach consumers in the most efficient way.

In business-to-business marketing, distribution is often the real key to success. Business buyers may buy through agents or wholesalers rather than direct from producers, so that tapping into a good distribution network is the most important step a company can take.

Physical distribution is concerned with the ways organisations get physical products to a point where it is most convenient for consumers to buy them. *Logistics* takes a wider view: originally based on military terminology, logistics is concerned with the process of moving raw materials through the production and distribution processes to the point at which the finished product is needed. This involves strategic decision-making about warehouse location, materials management, stock levels and information systems. Logistics is the area in which purchasing and marketing overlap.

In some ways the physical distribution of a product is part of the bundle of benefits that make up that product. For example, a jacket bought through mail order offers convenience benefits which a chain-store jacket does not. Conversely, the chain-store purchase may include hedonic benefits (the fun of shopping around, the excitement of finding a real bargain), which the mail-order company does not supply. Even when the actual jacket is identical, the benefits derived from the distribution method are different.

The purpose of any physical distribution method is to get the product from its point of production to the consumer efficiently and effectively. The product must arrive in good condition, and fit the consumer's need for convenience, or cheapness, or choice, or whatever else the particular target market thinks is important. Thus, from a marketing viewpoint, the subject of distribution covers such areas as transportation methods, wholesaling, high street retailing, direct mail marketing and even farm-gate shops.

Physical distribution is to do with transportation methods; **distribution strategy** decisions are about which outlets should be used for the product.

Transportation methods

Transportation methods vary according to speed, cost and ability to handle the type of product concerned. As a general rule, the quicker the method the more expensive it is, but in some cases it may be cheaper to use a faster method because the firm's capital is tied up for less time. For perishable goods such as fruit, **standby airfreight** can be as cheap as sea transport, when the lower incidence of wastage is taken into account.

The transportation method chosen for a particular product will depend on the factors listed in Table 8.1. In all these cases, there will be trade-offs involved. Greater customer service will almost always be more expensive; greater reliability may increase transit time, as will greater traceability because in most cases the product will need to be checked on and off the transport method chosen. As with any other aspect of marketing activity, the customer's overall needs must be taken into account, and the relative importance of those needs must be judged with some accuracy if the firm is to remain competitive.

Table 8.1 Choosing a transportation method

Factor	Explanation and examples
The physical characteristics of the product	If the product is fragile (e.g. sheet glass) distribution channels need to be short and handling minimised. For perishable goods (e.g. fruit) it may be cheaper to use standby airfreight than to ship by sea, because there will be less spoilage en route.
The methods used by the competition	It is often possible to gain a significant competitive edge by using a method which is out of the ordinary. For example, most inner-city courier companies use motorbikes to deliver urgent documents, but a few use bicycles. In heavy traffic bicycles are often quicker, and can sometimes use routes that are not open to powered vehicles, so deliveries are quicker.
The costs of the various channels available	The cheapest is not always the best: for example, computer chips are light, but costly, and therefore it is cheaper to use airfreight than to tie up the company's capital in lengthy surface transportation.
The reliability of the channel	Emergency medical supplies must have 100% reliable transportation, as must cash deliveries.
The transit time	This also applies to fruit and computer chips.
Security	Highly valuable items may not be easily distributed through retailers. Direct delivery may work much better.
Traceability	The ease with which a shipment can be located or redirected. For example, oil tankers can be diverted to deliver to different refineries at relatively short notice. This allows the oil companies to meet demand in different countries.
The level of customer service required	Customers may need the product to be delivered in exact timings (for example, in just-in-time manufacturing). The Meals on Wheels service is another example; it is essential that deliveries are 100% reliable.

Source: Adapted from *The Management of Business Logistics*, 4th edn, by Coyle, Bardi and Langley. © 1988. Reprinted with permission of South Western, a division of Thomson Learning: www.thomsonrights.com. Fax 800 730 2215.

Distribution channels

Transportation method is also affected by the **channel of distribution**, or marketing channel. Figure 8.1 shows some of the possible channels of distribution a consumer product might go through.

Products are rarely delivered directly from producer to consumer, but instead pass through the hands of wholesalers, agents, factors or other middle men. For example, it is hardly likely to be very efficient for a tuna importer to deliver directly to every small grocery business in the country. (It would be even less efficient to deliver to each consumer.) The importer will probably employ an **agent** (who will be working for several manufacturers) to take orders from wholesalers. The importer will bulk-deliver the tuna to the **wholesalers**, who will then break the delivery down to send out to the **retailers**. The wholesaler

Figure 8.1	Channels of distribution

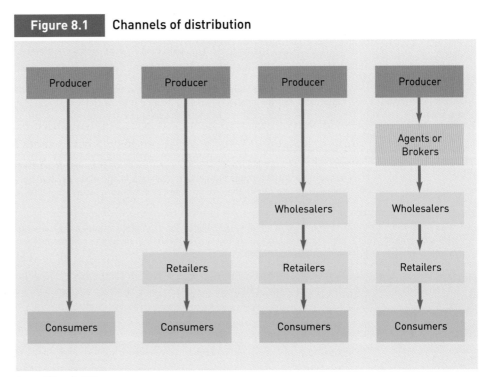

Source: Dibb *et al.,* 1998

either will deliver to the retailers along with the products of many other importers and manufacturers, or will offer a cash-and-carry service so that the retailers can make all their supplies purchases in one trip. The net result is a

Table 8.2	Functions of channel members

Function	Explanation
Sorting out	Separating out heterogeneous deliveries into homogeneous ones. For example, sorting a tomato crop into those suitable for retail sale and those suitable only for juice production.
Accumulation	Aggregating small production batches into amounts big enough to be worth shipping. Forwarding agents will arrange for small exporters to share a container, for example.
Allocation	Breaking down large shipments into smaller amounts. A wholesaler receiving a truckload of baked beans will sell them on a case at a time. This is also called bulk breaking.
Assorting	Combining collections of products that will appeal to groups of buyers. For example, clothes shops stock clothes from many manufacturers; food cash-and-carry wholesalers will specialise in all the products needed by caterers and grocers, including shop signs and plastic knives and forks.

great saving in time, since the trucks are not going perhaps hundreds of miles with one case of tuna on board.

In fact, food frequently passes through lengthy and complex distribution systems. Each intermediary in the process performs a useful function, increasing the efficiency of the exchanges. Table 8.2 shows some of the functions carried out by intermediaries.

'Cutting out the middleman' is popularly supposed to be a way of buying things cheaper. In fact, for most products where agents and wholesalers are used, the savings made by greater efficiency more than cover the cost of the extra mark-up on the product. This means that cutting out the middleman is more likely to increase the cost of the product.

Critical thinking

If cutting out the middle man is such a bad idea, why do companies often advertise it as if it's an advantage? And if it reduces efficiency, why have so many developed interactive websites so that people can order online?

Is it actually cheaper to order online (taking account of delivery costs) or is it more about convenience? And how convenient is it, in fact, when one may have to visit several websites to buy items which are available in one convenient retail store – why not just stop on the way home from work and browse?

Perhaps it depends on one's personal circumstances!

Direct producer-to-consumer channels are typical of personal services such as hairdressing, where use of intermediaries would be impossible, and of major capital purchases such as houses or home improvements. This is because these products cannot be broken down into smaller units, or assorted, or accumulated. There is therefore no function for the middlemen to fulfil.

If the distribution network is efficiently managed, goods come down the channel and information goes up. Retailers can feed back information about what consumers need, either *formally* (by carrying out a monitoring exercise and passing the information to the manufacturer or wholesaler) or *informally* (since retailers order only what is selling, producers can infer what is required by the consumers). A good salesperson will also act as an information channel, and will find out from the retailers what they think consumers want, as well as convey information from the manufacturers to the retailer.

Major manufacturers often have several distribution channels, catering for different market segments. Food processing firms will usually have separate channels for caterers and for retailers, car manufacturers may deal directly with large fleet operators rather than operating through their retail dealer network, and electronics manufacturers may have one channel for consumer products and another for defence products.

Table 8.3 shows the functions of some of the members of a channel of distribution.

Table 8.3	Categories of channel members
Channel member	**Function**
Agents	Agents usually act purely as a sales arm for the manufacturer, without actually buying the products. The agent never takes title to the goods; agency sales representatives call on major retailers and on wholesalers on behalf of a number of manufacturers, and take orders and arrange delivery. This saves the manufacturer the cost of operating a large salesforce to carry perhaps only a small product range.
Wholesalers	Wholesalers actually buy the goods from the manufacturers, often through an agent, then sell the goods on to the retailers or sometimes the final consumers.
Retailers	A retailer is any organisation that offers goods directly to consumers. This includes mail order companies, door-to-door salespeople and e-commerce organisations selling over the Internet.

WHOLESALERS

Wholesalers carry out the following functions:

- Negotiate with suppliers.
- Some promotional activities: advertising, sales promotion, publicity, providing a salesforce.
- Warehousing, storage and product handling.
- Transport of local and sometimes long-distance shipments.
- Inventory control.
- Credit checking and credit control.
- Pricing and collection of pricing information, particularly about competitors.
- Channel of information up and down the distribution network, again particularly with regard to competitors' activities.

All of these functions would have to be carried out by each manufacturer individually if the wholesaler did not exist; by carrying them out on behalf of many manufacturers the wholesaler achieves economies of scale, which more than cover the profit taken.

The wholesaler also provides services to the retailers, as follows:

- Information gathering and dissemination.
- One-stop shopping for a wide range of products from a wide range of manufacturers.
- Facilities for buying relatively small quantities.

- Fast deliveries – often cash-and-carry.
- Flexible ordering – can vary amounts as demand fluctuates.

Again, from the retailer's viewpoint it is much more convenient and cheaper to use a wholesaler. Only if the retailer is big enough to order economic quantities direct from the manufacturer will it be worthwhile to do so. For example, few hairdressers are big enough to order everything direct from the manufacturers, so a large part of a salon's stock-in-trade is bought from wholesalers.

There are many different types of wholesalers:

- **Merchant wholesalers** buy in goods and sell directly to the retailers, usually delivering the goods and having a salesforce calling on retailers in their area.

- **Full-service merchant wholesalers** provide a very wide range of marketing services for retailers, including shop design, sales promotion deals, advertising (sometimes nationally), coupon redemption, own-brand products, and so forth. A good example is Spar, the grocery wholesaler, which supplies corner shops throughout the UK and parts of the rest of Europe. The shops carry the Spar logo and stock Spar's own-brand products, but each shop is individually owned and managed.

- **General-merchandise wholesalers** carry a wide product mix, but little depth, dealing mainly with small grocery shops and general stores. They operate as a one-stop shop for these retailers. Cash-and-carry warehouses are a good example.

- **Limited-line wholesalers** offer only a limited range of products, but stock them in depth. They are often found in industrial markets, selling specialist equipment (such as materials handling equipment) and offering expertise in the field.

- **Speciality line wholesalers** carry a very narrow range, for example concentrating on only one type of food (e.g. tea). They are typically found dealing in goods that require special knowledge of the buying, handling or marketing of the product category.

- **Rack jobbers** own and maintain their own stands or displays in retail outlets. Typical products might be cosmetics, tights or greetings cards. The retailer pays only for the goods sold, and usually does not take title to the goods – this can be a big saving in terms of capital, and since the rack jobber undertakes to check the stock and restock where necessary, the retailer also saves time.

- **Limited-service wholesalers** take title to goods, but often do not actually take delivery, store inventory or monitor demand. A typical example might be a coal wholesaler, who buys from a producer and arranges for the coal to be delivered direct to coal merchants, without the coal first being delivered to the wholesaler.

- **Cash-and-carry wholesalers** offer a way for wholesalers to supply small retailers at minimum cost. The cash-and-carry wholesaler operates like a giant supermarket: retailers call, select the cases of goods needed, and pay at a checkout, using their own transport to take the goods back to their shops. This is an extremely flexible and efficient system for both parties.

- **Drop shippers** (or *desk jobbers*) obtain orders from retailers and pass them on to manufacturers, buying the goods from the manufacturer and selling to the retailer without ever actually seeing the goods. The drop shipper provides the salesforce and takes on the credit risk on behalf of the manufacturer, but does not have the storage costs or the overheads of a merchant wholesaler.

- *Mail order wholesalers* use catalogues to sell to retailers and industrial users. This avoids the use of an expensive salesforce, and works best for dealing with retailers in remote areas. Goods are despatched through the post or by commercial carriers; these wholesalers take title to the products.

To summarise, wholesalers perform a wide variety of functions, all aimed at making the exchange of goods easier and more efficient. This leaves the manufacturer free to concentrate resources on improving production efficiencies and the physical product offering, and retailers to concentrate on providing the most effective service for the consumer.

RETAILERS

Retailers deal with any sales that are for the customer's own use, or for the use of family and friends. In other words, any purchases that are not for business needs are the domain of the retailer.

Therefore, a retailer is not necessarily a high street shop, or a market trader; mail order catalogues, TV phone-in lines, online retailers such as Amazon, even door-to-door salesmen are all retailers. Tupper Corporation (which sells Tupperware on the party plan) is as much a retailer as Aldi, Makro or Coles, even though the product is sold in the customer's own home.

Traditionally most retail outlets have been in city centres or suburban high streets. Partly this was for convenience, so that shoppers had a central area to visit for all their shopping requirements, and partly it was due to planning regulations which zoned most retail shops in traditional retail areas, away from industrial parks and housing estates.

More recently out-of-town hypermarkets and shopping parks have been growing up. This is in response to the following factors:

- Greater car ownership means an increase in **outshopping** (shopping outside the area where the consumer lives).

- High city-centre rents and property taxes make out-of-town sites more attractive for retailers.

- Town planners have used retail parks as a way of regenerating decaying industrial sites on the edges of towns.

Such out-of-town sites have not necessarily damaged all town-centre retailers, although there has been a shift in the composition of city-centre retail districts.

For example, food retailers have largely gone from central sites in major cities, except for delicatessens and speciality food outlets. In the United Kingdom, supermarket chain Tesco has begun to reverse this trend with the establishment of Tesco Metro stores in city centres. These stores carry a limited range of products, usually in smaller pack sizes, and aim at office workers shopping in their lunch hours or convenience shopping.

Here are some descriptions of different types of retail outlet:

- **Convenience stores**, or corner shops, offer a range of grocery and household items. These local shops often open until late at night. They are usually family-run, often belong to a trading group such as Spar, Circle K or 7-Eleven, and cater for last-minute and emergency purchases. In recent years, the Circle K and 7-Eleven franchises have expanded internationally from the United States and are making inroads into the late-night shopping market. Convenience stores have been under threat from supermarkets as later opening has become more common, and as the laws on Sunday trading in many countries have been relaxed.

- **Supermarkets** are large self-service shops, which rely on selling at low prices. Typically they are well-laid-out, bright, professionally run shops carrying a wide range of goods.

- **Hypermarkets** are even bigger supermarkets, usually in an out-of-town or edge-of-town location. A typical hypermarket would carry perhaps 20 000 lines. The true hypermarket sells everything from food to TV sets.

- **Department stores** are located in city centres and sell everything; each department has its own buyers, and functions as a separate profit centre. Examples are Harrods of London, El Corte Ingles in Spain and Clery's in Dublin. Within department stores, some functions are given over to **concessionaires**, who pay a rental per square foot plus a percentage of turnover to set up a store-within-a-store. Miss Selfridge, Brides and Principles all operate in this way within department stores. The trend is towards allowing more concessionaires, and around 70% of Debenham's floor space is allocated this way.

- **Variety stores** offer a more limited range of goods, perhaps specialising in clothes (e.g. Primark) or in housewares and music (e.g. Woolworths).

- **Discounters** (sometimes called baby sharks) are grocery outlets offering a minimum range of goods at very low prices. Often the decor is basic, the displays almost non-existent, and the general ambience one of pile-it-high-and-sell-it-cheap. German retailers Lidl and Aldi are examples of this approach; such stores typically carry only 700 lines or so.

- **Niche marketers** stock a very limited range of products, but in great depth. Examples are Sock Shop and Tie Rack. They frequently occupy tiny shops (even kiosks at railway stations) but offer every possible type of product within their very narrow spectrum. Niche marketers were the success story of the 1980s, but declined somewhat during the 1990s.

- **Discount sheds** are out-of-town DIY and hardware stores. They are usually businesses requiring large display areas, but with per-square-metre turnovers and profits that do not justify city-centre rents. Service levels are minimal, the stores are cheaply constructed and basic in terms of decor and ambience, and everything is geared towards minimising the overhead.

- **Catalogue showrooms** have minimal or non-existent displays, and are really an extension of the mail order catalogue. Customers buy in the same way as they would by mail order, by filling in a form, and the goods are brought out from a warehouse at the rear of the store. These outlets usually have sophisticated electronic inventory control.

- **Non-store retailing** includes door-to-door selling, vending machines, telemarketing (selling goods by telephone), mail order and catalogue retailing. **Telemarketing** may be inbound or outbound: inbound means that customers telephone the retailer to place an order, whereas outbound means the retailer telephones potential customers to ask them to buy. Outbound telemarketing has grown in the UK in recent years; it is often used to make appointments for sales representatives to call, for products such as fitted kitchens or double glazing, and is also used for direct selling of some items which are then delivered by mail. In general, it is unpopular with customers, and in both the United States and the UK systems have been set up to allow people to be removed from the lists of telesales companies. In the UK, the system is the Telephone Preference Service (TPS): firms which continue to call after someone has registered with the TPS can be fined, although in practice this is rare. The TPS has no power to prevent people being telephoned from outside the UK, nor does it have any power to curb companies with whom the person has an existing relationship, for example the individual's bank or telephone company.

E-commerce refers to retailing over the Internet. In its early days, e-commerce was dominated by business-to-business marketing, but dot.com firms such as Amazon.com, Lastminute.com and Priceline.com are making inroads into consumer markets. The growth of such firms is limited mainly by the growth in Internet users; as more people go online, the potential market increases and is likely to do so for the foreseeable future. The other main limiting factor is the degree to which people enjoy the process of shopping – factors such as a social experience outside the home, the pleasure of bargaining, diversion and sensory stimulation are all likely to ensure that people will continue to enjoy visiting traditional retail stores. Traditional retailers have not been slow to respond to the perceived threat, however: many retailers now offer an Internet service, with free delivery. There is more on this in Chapter 12.

Because consumer needs change rapidly, there are fashions in retailing (the rise and fall of niche marketing demonstrates this). Being responsive to consumer needs is, of course, important to all marketers but retailers are at the 'sharp end' of this process, and need to be able to adapt quickly to changing trends. The following factors have been identified as being crucial to retail success:

- *Location.* Being where the consumer can easily find the shop – in other words, where the customers would expect such a shop to be. A shoe shop would typically be in a high street or city-centre location, whereas a furniture warehouse would typically be out of town.

- *Buying the right goods in the right quantities* to be able to supply what the consumer wants to buy.

- *Offering the right level of service.* If the service level is less than the customer expects, he/she will be dissatisfied and will shop elsewhere. If the service level is too high, the costs increase, and also the customer may become suspicious that the prices are higher than they need be. Discount stores are expected to have low service levels, and consumers respond to that by believing that the prices are therefore lower.

- *Store image.* If the shop and its goods are upmarket, so must be the image in the consumer's mind. As with any other aspect of the product, the benefits must be as expected, or post-purchase dissonance will follow.

- *Atmospherics.* The physical elements of the shop design that encourage purchase. Use of the right colours, lighting, piped music and even odours can greatly affect purchasing behaviour (Bitner 1992). For example, some supermarkets use artificially generated smells of fresh bread baking to improve sales of bakery goods.

- *Product mix.* The retailer must decide which products will appeal to his/her customers. Sometimes this results in the shop moving away from its original product range into totally unrelated areas.

Recent trends in retail include the greater use of EPOS (electronic point-of-sale) equipment and laser-scanners to speed checkout queues through (and, incidentally, to save staffing costs), and the increasing use of **loyalty cards**. These cards give the customer extra discounts based on the amount spent at the store over a given period. The initial intention is to encourage customers to buy at the same store all the time in order to obtain the discounts, and in this sense the cards are really just another sales promotion. This type of loyalty programme, involving economic benefits, does have a positive effect on customer retention. The schemes also tend to help in terms of increasing the retailer's share of the customers (Verhoef 2003).

There is a further possibility inherent in EPOS technology, however. It is now possible to keep a record of each customer's buying habits and to establish the purchasing pattern, based on the EPOS records. Theoretically, this would mean that customers could be reminded at the checkout that they are running low on certain items, since the supermarket computer would know how frequently those items are usually bought. The phrase Domesday marketing has been coined by Professor Martin Evans to describe this; whether it could be seen as a useful service for consumers, or as an unwarranted invasion of privacy, remains as a topic for discussion (Evans 1994). EPOS systems in the UK were redesigned in 2004 to allow for the introduction of chip-and-pin credit cards, which require customers to enter a personal identity number (PIN) rather than sign a receipt. These have been used in France and Spain for many years to reduce credit card fraud and reduce time spent at the checkouts.

Perception is important in the retail environment. Store atmospherics have already been mentioned, but people also like to be able to touch products, open the boxes, and see what they are buying. This can cause problems, since people will tend to open the box to examine the product, but then take an unopened box to the checkout. The opened box will probably not sell until it is the last one, since people tend to believe that the product is contaminated and no longer new if other people have handled it. This phenomenon is known as shop soiling, but is explained by anthropologists in terms of magic: the 'contaminated' product has had part of the essence of the other shopper transferred to it (Argo *et al*. 2006).

SELECTING CHANNELS

Choosing a channel involves a number of considerations. These are as follows:

- whether to use a single channel, or several channels;
- location of customers;
- compatibility of the channels with the firm;
- nature of the goods;
- geographic, environmental and terrain decisions;
- storage and distribution issues;
- import and export costs.

Above all, of course, the firm must begin by considering the customers' needs. Having said that, the needs of channel members will also be involved, since they are unlikely to co-operate if their needs are not considered.

Using a single channel clearly provides the channel members with the security of knowing that they will not be competing with other firms carrying the same product line. Some retailers insist on being given exclusive rights to the products they carry, so that they can make 'price promises' without fear of consumers actually being able to buy the identical product anywhere else, whether at a lower price or not. On the other hand, the needs of consumers are best met by having the product widely available.

Location of customers influences the channel as well as the physical distribution. Some channels might be unavailable in some countries – for example, distribution via the Internet is not viable in many African countries because few people are online, and the road infrastructure makes delivery difficult.

Channels need to be compatible with the firm's capability and size: small manufacturers can become overwhelmed by dealing with large retailers, for example.

The nature of the goods determines which type of retailer would be best. Sometimes firms have obtained a competitive advantage by using unusual routes to market – jewellery firms have distributed through hairdressing salons, for example.

Geographic and environmental (in the sense of business environment) considerations can render some routes unviable. For example, mail order in the United States became popular with people living in remote regions during the nineteenth century (a geographical consideration). Such people were unable to reach major stores easily, and local stores were unable to carry all the products people might need. Mail order grew in Germany for a different reason: at one time, the business environment required retail stores to close at 5 p.m., and prohibited weekend opening except for one Saturday a month. This meant that most working people had serious difficulty in getting to shops, and mail order became a favourite way of buying almost everything.

Storage and distribution costs, particularly for overseas markets, may mean that a wholesaler becomes necessary simply because of the need to make few large deliveries rather than many small ones. Likewise, if storage is expensive, an on-demand service such as that supplied by motor factors to small garages might be necessary.

Import and export costs, especially duties and tariffs, might mean that a local agent (or even a local assembly plant) might need to be used. Shipping costs are likely to make it more efficient to fill a shipping container rather than send small quantities at a time, but the nature of the product needs to be considered – perishable or expensive products might need to be sent immediately, rather than waiting until there are enough to fill a container.

MANAGING DISTRIBUTION CHANNELS

Channels can be led by any of the channel members, whether they are producers, wholesalers or retailers, provided the member concerned has **channel power**. This power comes from seven sources, as shown in Table 8.4 (Michman and Sibley 1980).

Channel co-operation is an essential part of the effective functioning of channels. Since each member relies on every other member for the free exchange of goods down the channel, it is in the members' interests to look after each other to some extent. Channel co-operation can be improved in the following ways:

- The channel members can agree on target markets, so that each member can best direct effort towards meeting the common goal.
- The tasks each member should carry out can be defined. This avoids duplication of effort, or giving the final consumer conflicting messages.

Table 8.4	Sources of channel power		
Economic sources of power	**Non-economic sources of power**	**Other factors**	
Control of resources. The degree to which the channel member has the power to direct goods, services or finance within the channel.	Reward power. The ability to provide financial benefits, or otherwise favour channel members.	Level of power. This derives from the economic and non-economic sources of power.	
Size of company. The bigger the firm compared with other channel members, the greater the overall economic power.	Expert power. This arises when the leader has special expertise which the other channel members need.	Dependency of other channel members.	
Referent power emerges when channel members try to emulate the leader.		Willingness to lead. Clearly some firms with potential for channel leadership prefer not to have the responsibility, or are unable to exercise the potential for other reasons.	
Legitimate power arises from a superior–subordinate relationship. For example, if a retailer holds a substantial shareholding in a wholesaler, it has legitimate power over the wholesaler.			
Coercive power exists when one channel member has the power to punish another.			

A further development is **co-marketing**, which implies a partnership between manufacturers, intermediaries and retailers. This level of co-operation involves pooling of market information and full agreement on strategic issues (Marx 1995).

Channel conflict arises because each member wants to maximise its own profits or power. Conflicts also arise because of frustrated expectations: each member expects the other members to act in particular ways, and sometimes these expectations are unfulfilled. For example, a retailer may expect a wholesaler to maintain large enough stocks to cover an unexpected rise in demand for a given product, whereas the wholesaler may expect the manufacturers to be able to increase production rapidly to cover such eventualities.

An example of channel conflict occurred when EuroDisney (now Disneyland Paris) first opened. The company bypassed travel agents and tried to market directly to the public via TV commercials. Unfortunately, this did not work, because European audiences were not used to the idea of booking directly (and also were not as familiar with the Disney concept as American audiences) so few bookings resulted. At the same time Disney alienated the travel agents, and have had to expend considerable time and money in wooing them back again. This is a general problem for companies seeking to use multiple channels of distribution: if the company decides to deal direct with the public via its website, or uses several different routes, existing channel members may feel that the relationship is being undermined. This does not mean that using multiple channels is impossible; it simply means that marketers need to be cautious not to damage the interests of existing channel members. In general, there is unlikely to be a problem if the new channels approach a segment of the market which the existing channels do not reach.

Channel management can be carried out by co-operation and negotiation (often with one member leading the discussions) or it can be carried out by the most powerful member laying down rules that weaker members have to follow. Table 8.5 shows some of the methods which can be used to control channels. Most attempts to control distribution by the use of power are likely to be looked on unfavourably by the courts, but of course the abuse of power would have to be fairly extreme before a channel member would be likely to sue.

Table 8.5 Channel management techniques

Technique	Explanation	Legal position
Refusal to deal	One member refuses to do business with one or more other members: for example, hairdressing wholesalers sometimes refuse to supply mobile hairdressers, on the grounds that this is unfair competition for salons.	In most countries suppliers do not have to supply anybody they do not wish to deal with. However, grounds may exist for a lawsuit if the refusal to deal is a punishment for not going along with an anti-competitive ruling by a supplier, or is an attempt to prevent the channel member from dealing with a third party with whom the manufacturer is in dispute.
Tying contracts	The supplier (sometimes a franchiser) demands that the channel member carries other products as well as the main one. If the franchiser insists that all the products are carried, this is called *full-line forcing*.	Most of these contracts are illegal, but are accepted if the supplier alone can supply goods of a given quality, or if the purchaser is free to carry competing products as well. Sometimes they are accepted when a company has just entered the market.
Exclusive dealing	A manufacturer might prevent a wholesaler from carrying competitors' products, or a retailer might insist that no other retailer be supplied with the same products. This is often used by retailers to ensure that their 'price guarantees' can be honoured – obviously consumers will not be able to find the same product at a lower price locally if the retailer has prevented the manufacturer from supplying anybody else.	Usually these are legal provided they do not result in a monopoly position in a local area: in other words, provided the consumer has access to similar products, there will not be a problem.
Restricted sales territories	Intermediaries are prevented from selling outside a given area. The intermediaries are often in favour of this idea, because it prevents competition within their own area.	Courts have conflicting views about this practice. On the one hand, these deals can help weaker distributors, and can also increase competition where local dealers carry different brands; on the other hand, there is clearly a restraint of trade involved.

Critical thinking

If controlling the channel is regarded as unfair, how about buyers who specify particular ways in which potential suppliers can approach them? Is it unreasonable to ask for salespeople to call on a particular day, or only by appointment? Clearly not. But then, would it be unreasonable to expect suppliers to draw up detailed reports on their ability to meet delivery schedules and quality standards? Hmmm ... Perhaps. Would it be unreasonable to expect suppliers to provide copies of their accounts, and allow the customer's auditors to check on the supplier's financial stability and probity? Well, maybe not. Would it be reasonable to use knowledge of a supplier's financial difficulties to force through lower prices? Maybe, maybe not.

Business isn't exactly a coffee morning, but there are ethical and practical issues at stake. Knowing where to draw the line might not be so easy.

Sometimes the simplest way to control a distribution channel is to buy out the channel members. Buying out members across a given level (for example, a wholesaler buying out other wholesalers in order to build a national network) is called **horizontal integration**; buying out members above or below in the distribution chain (for example a retailer buying out a wholesaler) is **vertical integration**. An example of extreme vertical integration is the major oil companies, which extract crude oil, refine it, ship it and ultimately sell it retail through petrol stations. At the extremes, this type of integration may attract the attention of government monopoly regulation agencies, since the integration may cause a restriction of competition.

Producers need to ensure that the distributors of their products are of the right type. The image of a retailer can damage (or enhance) the image of the products sold (and vice versa). Producers need not necessarily sell through the most prestigious retailer, and in fact this would be counter-productive for many cheap, everyday items. Likewise a prestigious product should not be sold through a down-market retail outlet.

In the long run, establishing good relationships between channel members will improve overall profitability for all members. As the relationship between members of the distribution channel becomes closer, power and conflict still remain important, but they are expressed in other ways, and the negotiations for their resolution change in nature (Gadde 2004).

EFFICIENT CONSUMER RESPONSE

Efficient consumer response (ECR) seeks to integrate the activities of manufacturers and retailers using computer technology; the expected result is a more responsive stocking system for the retailer, which in turn benefits the manufacturer. Some of the features of ECR are as follows:

- *Continuous replenishment* under which the supplier plans production using data generated by the retailer.

- *Cross-docking* attempts to co-ordinate the arrival of suppliers' and retailers' trucks at the distribution centres so that goods move from one truck to the other without going into stock. Although transport efficiency falls because a supermarket truck collecting (say) greengrocery might have to wait for several suppliers' trucks to arrive, the overall speed of delivery of products improves, which can be crucial when dealing with fresh foods.

- *Roll-cage sequencing* allows storage of products by category at the warehouse; although this adds to the labour time at the warehouse, it greatly reduces labour time at the retail store.

The main problem with ECR is that it relies on complete co-operation between supplier and retailer. In any channel of distribution where the power base is unequal, this is less likely to happen; despite the overall savings for the channel as a whole, self-interest on the part of channel members may lead to less than perfect co-operation.

Case study 8
Eddie Stobart

The Eddie Stobart logistics company is probably the best-known transport organisation in the UK. Its giant articulated lorries (950 of them) are seen all over the country, and on the Continent, their distinctive livery making them stand out among all the others on the road.

The Stobart family started an agricultural business in the 1950s, but by the 1970s the trucking side of the business was taking over. In 1976, Edward Stobart took over trucking (his brothers taking the other parts of the business) and the company established a new depot in Carlisle in 1980. At that time, Carlisle was a hub for UK road transport (as indeed it is today), being near the Scottish border and conveniently located near the port of Liverpool and the Lancashire conurbation centred on Manchester. Eddie Stobart adopted a logistics approach very early on – whatever the delivery needs of the customer, Eddie Stobart would work out a way to achieve them. For example, Crown Packaging required a 99% reliable just-in-time delivery system for its manufacturing plant. Eddie Stobart exceeds this target, by having over 50 44-ton Drawbar trucks and half a million square feet of warehouse space devoted just to this one client. Eddie Stobart now manage Crown's processes allowing Crown to concentrate on core manufacturing and marketing activities while leaving the entire logistics process to Eddie Stobart.

Of course, the company still needs to show a profit, and Stobart have become experts in finding return loads (goods which can be carried back by the trucks after delivery). This means that Eddie Stobart trucks are rarely empty – and since the company provides a service 24 hours a day, 7 days a week, the trucks are rarely idle either.

The company expects a great deal from its employees, but it gives a great deal in return. The co-ordinating factor in the company is always customer needs – the trucks are smart, modern and clean, and the drivers wear uniforms and are required to be courteous not only to customers but also to other road users. All of Eddie Stobart's 2000 employees are thoroughly trained in customer care:

the company even runs its own driver training school where the emphasis is on good customer practice. Eddie Stobart himself has been fascinated by lorries since his childhood, and his passion for the haulage business communicates throughout the firm – each lorry has a name (a female name), the first four in the fleet having been named after female celebrities of the 1970s (Dolly Parton and Suzi Quattro being two of them). History does not record what these ladies thought of being accorded this honour. Partly because of the individual character of each truck, and partly because of the distinctive corporate livery, Eddie Stobart has acquired a fan club of 'Eddie spotters' who note down the names of every Stobart truck they see. Several websites are devoted to Eddie spotters.

Because Eddie Stobart lorries have become so well known, the company now sells Eddie Stobart souvenirs such as scale model trucks, toys, mementoes, and even clothing. Coupled with the company's sponsorship of motor racing, these activities serve to enhance the corporate image and make the brand even more recognisable.

When Sara Lee, the American food company, entered the UK market they chose Eddie Stobart as their logistics manager. Their reasons went beyond the simple need to move product from factory to retailer – they recognised that Eddie Stobart is a company which exhibits strong ethical principles, and consequently is a company which keeps its promises. In 2004, Sara Lee contracted Eddie Stobart to carry out all their logistics operations for all the brands they sell in the UK.

Eddie's brother William now heads the company, but the basic principles continue. As a logistics operation, Eddie Stobart is at the forefront of innovation – but few haulage companies could have inspired the public recognition that Eddie Stobart has. After all, how many hauliers have their own fan club?

Questions

1 How does having a fan club benefit Eddie Stobart?

2 What advantages are there for Sara Lee in giving all their logistics operations to one contractor?

3 What is the significance of finding return loads?

4 What have Eddie Stobart gained from having a customer orientation?

5 How does Eddie Stobart's customer orientation manifest itself?

SUMMARY

This chapter has been about getting the goods to the consumer in the most efficient and effective way possible.

Here are the key points from this chapter:

- Distribution forms part of the product because it has benefits attached to it.
- The faster the transport, the more expensive in upfront costs, but the greater the savings in terms of wastage and in capital tied up.
- Transport methods must consider the needs of the end user of the product.
- Cutting out the middleman is likely to increase costs in the long run, not decrease them.

■ Retailing includes every transaction in which the purchase is to be used by the buyer personally or for family use.

■ Retailing is not necessarily confined to high street shops.

CHAPTER QUESTIONS

1 Under what circumstances might airfreight be cheaper than surface transport?

2 How might wholesalers improve the strength of their position with retailers?

3 Why might a wholesaler be prepared to accept a restricted-territory sales agreement?

4 When should a manufacturer consider dealing direct with retailers?

5 When should a manufacturer consider dealing direct with the public?

Further reading

Marketing Concepts and Strategies, 3rd edn, by S. Dibb, L. Simkin, W. Pride and O.C. Ferrell (London, Houghton Mifflin, 1998). This text has some very detailed chapters on distribution, using UK and European examples.

Marketing Channels: A Management View, 4th edn, by Bert Rosenbloom (New York, Dryden, 1991). A readable text, with a practically orientated view of how to deal with distribution issues.

European Logistics by James Cooper, Michael Browne and Melvyn Peters (Oxford, Blackwell, 1991) gives a good readable overview of logistics problems.

References

Argo, Jennifer J., Dahl, Darren W. and Morales, Andrea C.: 'Consumer contamination: how consumers react to products touched by others', *Journal of Marketing*, **70** (2) (2006), pp. 81–94.

Bitner, Mary Jo: 'Servicescapes: the impact of physical surroundings on customers and employees', *Journal of Marketing* (April 1992), pp. 57–71.

Coyle, J., Bardi, E. and Langley C.: *The Management of Business Logistics* (St Paul, MN, West, 1988).

Dibb, S., Simkin, L., Pride, W. and Ferrell, O.C.: *Marketing: Concepts and Strategies* (London, Houghton Mifflin, 1998).

Evans, Martin: 'Domesday marketing', *Journal of Marketing Management*, **10** (5) (1994), pp. 409–31.

Gadde, Lars-Erik: 'Activity co-ordination and resource combining in distribution networks: implications for relationship involvement and the relationship atmosphere', *Journal of Marketing Management*, **20** (1) (2004), 157–84.

Marx, W.: 'The co-marketing revolution', *Industry Week* (2 October 1995), pp. 77–9.

Michman, R.D. and Sibley, S.D.: *Marketing Channels and Strategies*, 2nd edn (Worthington, OH, Publishing Horizons Inc., 1980).

Verhoef, Peter C.: 'Understanding the effect of customer relationship management efforts on customer retention and customer share development', *Journal of Marketing*, **67** (4) (October 2003), pp. 30–45.

Voluntary Service Overseas

VSO is a voluntary organisation which sends skilled volunteers overseas to help with projects in the Third World. The volunteers are usually people with significant experience in industry or education, who are prepared to work for up to two years in another country. Volunteers are paid at local rates. Often this is well below their previous salaries, but the typical volunteer is someone who has had a successful career, and now wants to put something back.

Volunteers find the whole process very rewarding – but the professionals still need to be recruited, and there are many needs that volunteers have. VSO, like most charities, has a relatively small budget for marketing, so the organisation has to get the most from its funding by careful targeting. Professional needs are very diverse – some go for the experience of living abroad, some get a warm glow of satisfaction, some go for the professional challenge, but clearly none of them do it for the money!

Obviously VSO needs cash donations as well as volunteers: the volunteers still need to be sent overseas, and even at Third World rates they still need to be paid.

Vicky Starnes, Head of Marketing

Watch the video clip, then try to answer the following questions. The answers are on the companion website.

Questions

1 Which communications tools are most appropriate for VSO?

2 What is the role of public relations in VSO's work?

3 How might VSO use database marketing?

9

Marketing communications and promotional tools

Objectives

After reading this chapter you should be able to:

■ explain how marketing communications operate;

■ plan a promotional campaign;

■ explain how the elements of the promotional mix fit together to create a total package;

■ select suitable promotional tools for achieving a given objective;

■ understand what PR will do for you and what it will not do;

■ explain the main pitfalls of defensive PR;

■ plan a media event;

■ understand the problems facing a public relations executive or agent;

■ formulate a suitable PR policy for a given set of circumstances;

■ plan an advertising campaign;

■ formulate a brief for an advertising agency;

■ explain the main criteria for writing advertising copy;

■ understand what personal selling is intended to achieve for the firm;

■ outline the main features of sales management;

■ explain the role of word-of-mouth communication;

■ explain how sponsorship helps in building a positive corporate image.

INTRODUCTION

This chapter is about communicating the organisation's messages to the public. The tools of communication (advertising, personal selling, PR and sales promotions) are the most visible aspects of marketing, and for some people represent the whole of marketing.

Communication requires the active participation of both the sender and the receiver, so the messages not only have to contain the information the organisation wishes to convey, but also must be sufficiently interesting to the consumers (or the organisation's other publics) for them to pay attention to it.

MARKETING COMMUNICATIONS THEORY

Communication is one of the most human of activities. The exchange of thoughts that characterises communication is carried out by conversation (still the most popular form of entertainment in the world), by the written word (letters, books, magazines and newspapers) and by pictures (cartoons, television and film).

Communication has been defined as a transactional process between two or more parties whereby meaning is exchanged through the intentional use of symbols (Engel *et al.* 1994). The key elements here are that the communication is intentional (a deliberate effort is made to bring about a response), it is a transaction (the participants are all involved in the process), and it is symbolic (words, pictures, music and other sensory stimulants are used to convey thoughts). Since human beings are not telepathic, all communication needs the original concepts to be translated into symbols that convey the required meaning.

This means that the individual or firm issuing the communication must first reduce the concepts to a set of symbols, which can be passed on to the recipient of the message; the recipient must decode the symbols to get the original message. Thus the participants in the process must share a common view of what the symbols involved actually mean. In fact, the parties must share a common field of experience. This is illustrated in Figure 9.1.

The sender's field of experience and the receiver's field of experience must overlap, at least to the extent of having a common language. In fact the overlap is likely to be much more complex and subtle in most marketing communications; **advertisements** typically use references from popular culture such as TV shows, from proverbs and common sayings, and will often make puns or use half-statements, which the audience is able to complete because it is aware of the cultural referents involved. This is why foreign TV adverts often seem unintentionally humorous, or even incomprehensible.

Figure 9.1 Model of the communication process

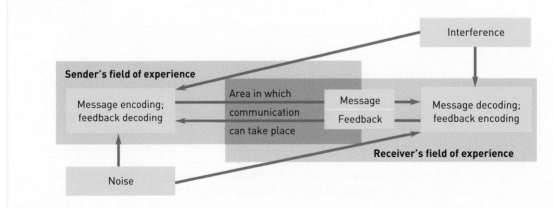

Noise is the surrounding distraction present during the communications process, and varies from children playing during the commercial break, through to arresting headlines in a magazine. **Interference** is deliberate attempts to distract the audience's attention with intelligent communications. For example, a car driver may be distracted away from a radio ad by another car cutting in (noise) or by seeing an interesting billboard (interference). For most marketing purposes the difference is academic.

The above model is essentially a one-step model of communication. This is rather over-simplified; communications do not necessarily occur in a single step in this way. Katz and Lazarsfield (1955) postulated a two-step model in which the messages are filtered through opinion leaders, and in most cases the message reaches the receiver via several routes. Sending the same message by more than one route is called **redundancy**, and is a good way of ensuring that the message gets through. Figure 9.2 shows this diagrammatically.

In the diagram, the sender sends almost identical messages via different routes. The effect of noise and interference is to distort the message, and the opinion leader will moderate the message, but by using three different routes the meaning of the message is more likely to get through. This is the rationale behind the integration of marketing communications.

Figure 9.2   Redundancy in communication

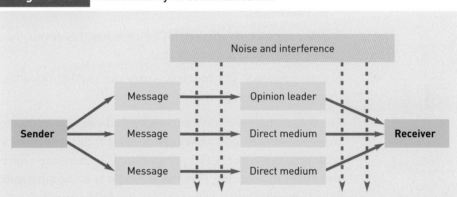

Critical thinking

When messages are sent by different routes, the medium must surely affect the message. After all, a news story written for a tabloid newspaper comes across very differently from the same story printed in a respectable broadsheet. And that's a comparison between two newspapers! How different the story would be if it were to be broadcast on TV or read over the radio!

Yet we're being asked to believe that an advertisement can be designed which will convey the same message, even though it is sent through several different media. How is that going to be accomplished?

An alternative view of communication is that it is concerned with the co-creation of meaning (Mantovani 1996). In this view, communication is not something which one person does to another; the communication is subject to interpretation by the recipient, and may even be ignored. Communication might be better thought of as involving an initiator, an apprehender and appreciation: acceptance of a common meaning arises from the apprehender's choice, not from the initiator's intention (Varey 2002).

DEVELOPING COMMUNICATIONS

Developing effective marketing communications follows a six-stage process, as follows:

1 *Identify the target audience.* In other words, decide who the message should get to.

2 *Determine the response sought.* What would the marketer like members of the audience to do after they get the message?

3 *Choose the message.* Write the copy, or produce an appropriate image.

4 *Choose the channel.* Decide which newspaper, TV station or radio station the audience uses.

5 *Select the source's attributes.* Decide what it is about the product or company that needs to be communicated.

6 *Collect feedback.* For example, carry out market research to find out how successful the message was.

Communication is always expensive: full-page advertisements in Sunday colour supplements can cost upwards of £11 000 per insertion; a 30-second TV ad at peak time can cost £30 000 per station. It is therefore worthwhile spending time and effort in ensuring that the message is comprehensible by the target audience. Communications often follow the **AIDA** approach:

Attention

Interest

Desire

Action

This implies that marketers must first get the customer's *attention*. Clearly, if the receiver is not 'switched on' the message will not get through. Second, the marketer must make the message *interesting*, or the receiver will not pay attention to it. This should, if the message is good, lead to a *desire* for the product on the part of the receiver, who will then take *action*. Although this is a simplistic model in some ways, it is a useful guide to promotional planning; however, it is very difficult to get all four of these elements into one communication. For this reason, marketers usually use a mixture of approaches for different elements called the **promotional mix**.

THE PROMOTIONAL MIX

The basic promotional mix consists of advertising, **sales promotion**, **personal selling** and **Public relations (PR)**. When the concept of the promotional mix was first developed, these were the only elements available to marketers, but in the past 40 years more promotional methods have appeared which do not easily fit within these four categories. For example, a logo on a T-shirt might be considered as advertising or as public relations. For the purposes of this book, however, the original four components are still considered to be the main tools available to marketers.

The important word here is 'mix'. The promotional mix is like a recipe, in which the ingredients must be added at the right times and in the right quantities for the promotion to be effective. Figure 9.3 shows how the mix operates. Messages from the company about its products and itself are transmitted via the elements of the promotional mix to the consumers, employees, pressure groups and other publics. Because each of these groups is receiving the messages from more than one transmitter, the elements of the mix also feed into each other so that the messages do not conflict.

The elements of the promotional mix are not interchangeable, any more than ingredients in a recipe are interchangeable; a task that calls for personal selling cannot be carried out by advertising, nor can public relations tasks be carried

Figure 9.3 The promotional mix

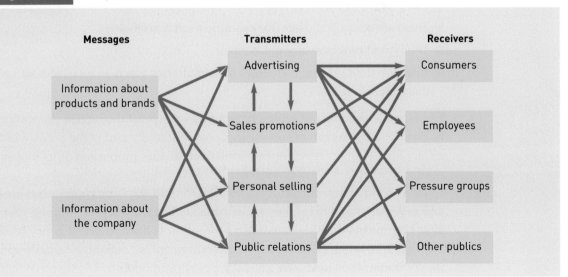

out by using sales promotions. Promotion is all about getting the message across to the customer (and the consumer) in the most effective way, and the choice of method will depend on the message, the receiver and the desired effect.

MANAGING ADVERTISING

Advertising is defined as 'a paid message inserted in a medium'. This definition can be broken down as follows:

- *Paid*: news about a company or its products is not necessarily advertising; sometimes a medium (television, radio, newspaper or magazine) will carry a message about a company in the form of a news item, but this is not advertising unless the space is paid for.
- *Message*: there must be some kind of communication intention in an advertisement, however obscure.
- *In a medium*: the message must appear in a newspaper, magazine, billboard or broadcast medium. Leaflets through doors, company names printed on T-shirts, and telephone selling are not necessarily advertising (but they are promotion).

Most advertising works below the conscious level. People are often familiar with a brand name, and even know a lot about the product, without being able to remember where they saw the product advertised. Advertising is a *non-personal* communication, in that it has to speak to a large number of people, so the message has to be clear for all the target audience to understand. Research by Farris and Buzzell (1979) indicated that the proportion of promotional spending devoted to advertising is higher under the following conditions:

- The product is standardised, rather than produced to order.
- There are many end users (for example most households).
- The typical purchase amount is small.
- Sales are made through channel intermediaries (such as retail shops) rather than direct to users.

For example, a company selling detergents will spend the largest proportion of its promotional budget on advertising, probably on TV and in the press, whereas a company selling cars will spend a relatively higher proportion of its money on salespeople's salaries and commission.

TV and video remote controls allow viewers to 'zap' the commercial breaks, and newspaper and magazine readers quickly become adept at flipping past the ads. This means that the consumer's attention is hard to get. It is not usually possible to cover all of AIDA in one advertisement, so marketers usually spread the communication load over several types of promotion.

For this reason, there are many different categories of ad campaign. Here are some examples:

- **Teaser campaigns**. Here the advertiser runs an initial advertisement that is meaningless in itself. Once the advertisement has run for a few weeks, the advertiser runs a second ad which explains the first one. The first ad is intended to attract attention by being mysterious. An example is the campaign run by modu, the mobile phone brand, in January 2008. A video was placed on YouTube showing people going about their normal day's activities, making calls, driving, preparing for work in the morning, and so forth without any explanation of what modu is or does. The video clip was engaging and entertaining, but the product was not featured – just the brand name at the end of the clip. Eventually the actual nature of the product was revealed, during February of that year.

- **Lifestyle campaigns**. These associate the product with a desirable lifestyle. Many perfume ads have taken this approach, showing women leading interesting or exciting lives. Lifestyle campaigns are mainly about positioning the product in the consumer's mind, and linking it to an aspirational group (see Chapter 3).

- **Rational campaigns** appeal to the consumer's cognition. These advertisements are heavy on facts, and seek to persuade by rational argument. Often an authoritative figure (a doctor, dentist or scientist) appears in the ad in order to lend greater weight to the arguments. Typically this style is used for medicated shampoos, acne creams and over-the-counter medicines.

Advertising is mainly about getting the consumer's attention and arousing interest (the A and I of AIDA). To stimulate desire and action, marketers often link a special offer (sales promotion) to the advertisement.

Advertising is always culturally based. This means that an advertisement shown in one country, or aimed at a particular audience, is unlikely to work for consumers in other countries, or for a different audience. Research into standardisation of advertising shows that relatively few firms use an entirely standardised approach (Harris 1996). Of 38 multinational companies surveyed, 26 said that they used standard advertisements, but only 4 of these were completely standardised; the others varied from limited standardisation (perhaps only a corporate logo in common), through limited standardisation of the key executional elements, to standard execution with some modifications. Even though the sample of firms is relatively small, it appears likely that the majority of multinationals would adapt their approaches to fit the markets they are targeting.

Advertising can often be over-used because firms place greater faith in it than is perhaps justified. There is an underlying assumption that a bigger advertising spend will inevitably lead to a greater sales volume. Table 9.1 contains a checklist for making decisions about advertising.

Table 9.1	Advertising decision-making checklist

Question	Explanation
Does the product possess unique, important features?	Homogeneous products such as salt, petrol and cigarettes require considerably more advertising effort than differentiated products such as cars or holiday resorts. The product must not only be different, but the consumers must believe that those differences are important.
Are hidden qualities important to buyers?	If the product can be judged by looking at it or trying it out, advertising has less of a role to play than if there are features that are not apparent to the naked eye. For instance, the Pentium computer chip has been successfully advertised because it would not be immediately apparent to a computer purchaser that the machine has one.
Is the general demand trend for the product favourable?	If the product category is in decline, advertising will be less effective than if the category is generally increasing its sales.
Is the market potential for the product adequate?	Advertising will work only when there are enough actual or potential users of the product in the market. This is because advertising is a mass medium; much of the spend is wasted on advertising to people who will not be interested anyway.
Is the competitive environment favourable?	A small firm would have great difficulty competing with a large firm in terms of getting the message through. Advertising will not be sufficient when competing against a company with a large market share and correspondingly large budget.
Are general economic conditions favourable for marketing the product?	It is much easier to promote in times of rising prosperity, particularly for durable goods such as videos, cars, computers and household appliances. Such products are difficult to advertise successfully during a recession.
Is the organisation able and willing to spend the money required to launch an advertising campaign?	As a rule of thumb, if the organisation seeks to achieve a 20% market share, it must be willing to spend at least 20% of the total advertising spend of the industry on capturing that market. In other words, if the industry as a whole spends £5 million per annum on advertising, the company must be prepared to commit at least £1 million to the campaign.
Does the firm possess sufficient marketing expertise to market the product?	The company will need to co-ordinate all its activities, not just expect the advertisements to produce business. Not all firms possess this capability.

Source: Adapted from Patti 1977.

Of course, the checklist in Table 9.1 should also include a monitoring and review procedure to ensure that the advertising has achieved its objectives. Advertising can be used for the following purposes:

■ *To help the salesforce to open sales.* For example, an advertisement may contain a reply coupon for a brochure, which the salesperson can follow up.

- *To stimulate demand for the product category.* This is used by institutions, or firms that have a large market share: for example, the UK Meat and Livestock Commission advertises British meat on behalf of farmers and butchers.

- *To promote specific brands.* This accounts for most advertising activity.

- *To counteract competitors' promotional activities.* Often used to counteract a possible loss in market share due to a new competitor entering the market.

- *To suggest new ways to use the product.* Sherry importers Harvey's of Bristol ran a series of advertisements showing sherry served with various mixers in an effort to attract a younger group of consumers and reposition sherry as a pub drink.

- *To remind consumers about the product.* For example, advertisements for traditional Christmas foods are run during December.

- *To reinforce consumers' good feelings about the product.* For example, in the United Kingdom Tetley Tea is advertised using down-to-earth cartoon characters representing 'typical' Yorkshire people who have heart-warming personalities.

- *To support the value of the company's shares.* There is evidence that advertising expenditure helps reduce the risk of a fall in share values (McAlister *et al.* 2007).

Advertising can also be used to improve awareness of the company itself. This type of advertising is called **institutional advertising** and is commonly carried out by very large firms such as BP or Ford. It is almost a **public relations** activity, but the media space is paid for. Most advertising is **product advertising**, which means the products are the main part of the advertisement.

Since advertising is a paid-for medium, there will be a budgetary constraint on the management as well as a creative constraint. The advertising manager must therefore carry out the planning functions shown in Table 9.2.

Following on from the planning stage, the advertisements themselves will need to be produced. Some firms do this themselves, but most large firms will use specialist advertising agencies. Ad agencies are paid via discounts from the media, so provided the advertising budget is big enough to interest an agency, their services cost the advertiser nothing. Typical agency discount is 15%.

Producing advertisements

Advertisements contain three key elements: the brand itself, the pictorial element and the text. The pictorial element is superior for capturing attention, regardless of the size of the ad or the picture. The text element captures attention proportional to its size, and the brand element transfers attention to the other elements (Pieters and Wedel 2004).

When writing advertising **copy** the primary rule is to keep it short and simple. This is because people will not read a lengthy advertisement. Equally, the headline of the advertisement is important because people frequently read only the headline, quickly skipping on as they realise it is an advertisement. Declining literacy skills also play a role – many people are actually unable to read and understand a long and complicated message.

| Table 9.2 | Advertising planning functions |

Planning function	Explanation
Setting the budget	This can be done in four ways. First, the objective and task approach involves setting *objectives*, and setting aside an appropriate amount of money to achieve the objectives. This method is difficult to apply because it is difficult to assess how much will be needed to achieve the objective. Second, the *percentage of sales* approach sets the budget as a percentage of sales. This is based on the false idea that sales create advertising, and usually results in less being spent on advertising when sales fall, thus reducing sales further. Third, the *competition matching approach* means that the company spends the same as the competition: this means that the firm is allowing its budgets to be set by its enemies. Fourth, there is the *arbitrary* approach whereby a senior executive (usually a finance director) simply says how much can be allowed within the firm's overall budgets. This does not take account of how the firm is to achieve the objectives.
Identifying the target	Deciding to whom the ad is to be directed. It is better to approach a small segment of the market than try to use a 'scattergun' approach on everybody (see Chapter 4).
Media planning	This is about deciding where the ads are going to appear. There are two main decision areas: the **reach** (number of potential consumers the ad reaches) and the **frequency** (number of times each consumer sees the ad) of coverage. The decision is frequently made on the basis of cost per thousand readers/viewers, but this does not take into account the impact of the ad or the degree to which people are able to skip past it.
Defining the objectives	Deciding what the ads are supposed to achieve. It is essential here to give the advertising agency a clear brief: 'We want to raise awareness of the product to 50% of the adult population' is a measurable objective. 'We want to increase sales as much as possible' is not measurable, so there is no way of knowing whether it has been achieved.
Creating the advertising platform	Deciding the basic issues and selling points that the advertising must convey. This clarifies the advertising agency briefing, or at least clarifies the thinking on producing the advertising materials.

For example, Figures 9.4 and 9.5 show two fictitious advertisements for a surfboard. The first is written factually, the second is written as an advertisement. The first ad clearly contains more information, and is really much more use to the consumer, but the second ad is much more likely to be read and acted upon because it has a more lively **execution format**. What the **copywriter** wants the consumers to do is go to the surfboard retailer and look at the SurfKing (this could be linked with a sales promotion). There is no need to tell the readers everything in one advertisement. A surprising number of advertisements are written in the first style because the advertisers are trying to communicate everything about the product to the consumer without having first ensured that people will read the advertisement.

Artwork should be eye-catching and relevant to the purpose. It is usually a good idea to include a picture of the product where this is possible, since it aids recognition when the consumer sees the product on the supermarket shelf. Much artwork is available off-the-shelf for smaller businesses, either from computer clipart folders or from books of non-copyright artwork.

Figure 9.4   Factual advertisement for a surfboard

SurfKing Surfboards are hand-made from the finest materials at our factory in Edinburgh.

They are used by some of the world's top surfers, and use the latest technology to ensure the maximum surfing pleasure.

They are available from all leading surf shops, or can be ordered direct from our mail office.

Please allow 14 days for delivery.

Figure 9.5   Simpler advertisement for a surfboard

Memory is stimulated by emotion-arousing advertisements, but it appears that women are more affected by this factor than are men (Baird *et al.* 2007). The reasons for this are obscure. Creating annoying or irritating copy, or using several variants of a slogan, also helps to fix an advertisement in people's memories, as well as helping in matching the slogan to the brand (Rosengren and Dahlen 2006).

Assessing advertising effectiveness

Four elements appear to be important in the effectiveness of advertising:

- awareness,
- liking,
- interest, and
- enjoyment.

There is a high correlation between brand loyalty and **brand awareness** (Stapel 1990): likeability appears to be the single best predictor of sales effectiveness since likeability scales predict 97% of sales successes (Biel 1989), interest clearly relates to likeability (Stapel 1991) and enjoyment appears to be a good indicator in advertising pre-tests (Brown 1991). People's responses to advertising can be positive or negative: recent research shows that people who complain about advertising fall into four groups, as follows (Volkov *et al.* 2006):

1 *Advertising aficionados*. These people believe that, in general, advertising is a good thing, paints a fair picture, and is a good source of information.

2 *Consumer activist*. These people are on a mission to protect other people, and will complain to the manufacturer or through the press.

3 *Advertising moral guardians*. These people believe advertising is creating a materialist society, and that it appeals to people's baser instincts.

4 *Advertising seeker*. This type of person watches a lot of TV advertising and enjoys it as entertainment.

Clearly, people will complain about advertising which offends them: in the UK, such complaints are regulated by the Advertising Standards Authority (see Chapter 12).

It is worthwhile making some efforts to find out whether the advertising has been effective in achieving the objectives laid down. This is much easier if clear objectives were set in the first place, of course, and if the advertising agency was given a clear brief.

Advertising effectiveness can be assessed by market research, by returned coupons and (sometimes) by increased sales. The last method is somewhat risky, however, since there may be many other factors that could have increased the sales of the product. Table 9.3 shows some common techniques for evaluating advertising effectiveness.

Table 9.3	Advertising effectiveness
Technique	**Description and explanation**
Pre-tests	These are evaluations of the advertising before it is released. Pre-tests are sometimes carried out using focus groups (see Chapter 5).
Coupon returns or enquiries	The advertiser counts up the number of enquiries received during each phase of an advertising campaign. This allows the marketing management to judge which advertisements are working best, provided the coupons have an identifying code on them.
Post-campaign tests (post-tests)	The particular testing method used will depend largely on the objectives of the campaign. Communications objectives (product awareness, attitude change, brand awareness) might be determined through surveys; sales objectives might be measured according to changes in sales that can be attributed to the campaign. This is difficult to do because of other factors (changes in economic conditions, for example) that might distort the findings.
Recognition tests and recall tests	In recognition tests, consumers are shown the advertisement and asked if they recognise it. They are then asked how much of it they actually recall. In an **unaided recall** test the consumer is asked which advertisements he or she remembers seeing recently; in an **aided recall** test the consumer is shown a group of advertisements (without being told which is the one the researcher is interested in) and is asked which ones he or she has seen recently.

SALES PROMOTION

Sales promotions are short-term activities designed to generate a temporary increase in sales of the products.

Sales promotion has many guises, from money-off promotions to free travel opportunities. The purpose of sales promotion is to create a temporary increase in sales by bringing purchasing decisions forward and adding some immediacy to the decision-making process. Sales promotions have four characteristics, as follows (D'Astous and Landreville 2003):

1 *Attractiveness*. This is the degree to which the customer perceives the promotion as being desirable.

2 *Fit to product category*. A promotion which has no relationship with the product is less likely to appeal to customers.

3 *Reception delay*. If the promotional gift or discount will not arrive for some time, it is less attractive.

4 *Value*. High-value promotions work better than low-value ones, but it is the value as perceived by the customer which is important.

These characteristics interact with each other, so that an unattractive offer may still work if it is a good fit with the product category (for example).

Table 9.4 shows some of the techniques of sales promotion, and when they should be used to greatest effect.

| Table 9.4 | Sales promotion techniques |

Sales promotion technique	When to use to best effect
Free 'taster' samples in supermarkets	When a new product has been launched on the market. This technique works by allowing the consumer to experience the product first-hand, and also places the consumer under a small obligation to buy the product. The technique is effective, but expensive.
Money-off vouchers in press advertisements	Has the advantage that the company can check the effectiveness of the advertising by checking which vouchers came from which publications. It tends to lead to short-term brand switching: when the offer ends, consumers frequently revert to their usual brand.
Two-for-the-price-of-one	May encourage short-term brand switching. Appeals to the price-sensitive consumer, who will switch to the next cheap offer next time. Can be useful for rewarding and encouraging existing customers.
Piggy-backing with another product: e.g. putting a free jar of coffee whitener onto a jar of instant coffee	Good for encouraging purchasers of the coffee to try the whitener. Can be very successful in building brand penetration, since the consumer's loyalty is to the coffee, not to the whitener. Will not usually encourage brand switching between the 'free sample' brand and its competitors. Can also use vouchers on the backs of labels of other products (see co-marketing in Chapter 8).
Instant-lottery or scratchcards	Commonly used in petrol stations. The intention is to develop a habit among motorists of stopping at the particular petrol station. In the United Kingdom, for legal reasons, these promotions cannot require a purchase to be made, or be linked to spending a specific amount, but few people would have the courage to ask for a card without buying anything.
Free gift with each purchase	Often used for children's cereals. Can be good for encouraging brand switching, and is more likely to lead to permanent adoption of the brand because consumers do not usually switch brands when buying for children. This is because the children are not price-sensitive and will want their favourite brand.

Sales promotion will often be useful for low-value items, and is most effective when used as part of an integrated promotion campaign. This is because advertising and PR build sales long term, whereas sales promotion and personal selling tend to be better for making quick increases in sales. The combination of the two leads to the **ratchet effect**: sales get a quick boost from sales promotions, then build gradually over the life of an ad campaign (Moran 1978).

Care needs to be taken with sales promotions. First, a sales promotion that is repeated too often can become part of the consumer's expectations: for example, UK fast-food restaurant Pizzaland's promotional offer of a second pizza for a penny was so widely used that some consumers would not go to Pizzaland unless they had a voucher for the penny pizza. Eventually, Pizzaland was taken over by a rival firm and now no longer exists.

Second, brand switching as a result of a sales promotion is usually temporary, so it is unlikely that long-term business will be built by a short-term sales promotion.

Third, the promotion will benefit consumers who would have bought the product anyway, so a proportion of the spend will have been effectively wasted (though this is true of most promotional tools). Good targeting can help overcome this, but care should be taken that existing customers do not feel that they have been unfairly dealt with because they did not receive the promotional offer.

Fourth, discounting on price can seriously damage brand values because the product becomes perceived as being cut-price. Since price is widely used as a signal for quality, the potential for damage is obvious.

Sales promotions can be carried out from manufacturer to intermediary (*trade promotions*), from retailer to consumer (*retailer promotions*) or direct from the manufacturer to the consumer (*manufacturer promotions*).

Trade promotions can be used for the following purposes:

- *To increase stock levels.* The more stock the intermediary holds, the more commitment there will be to selling the stock and the less space there is for competitors' stock. (See push strategies in Chapter 10.)

- *To gain more or better shelf space.* The more eye-catching the position of the product in the retail shop, the more likely it is to sell.

- *To launch a new product.* New products always carry an element of risk for retailers as well as manufacturers (see Chapter 6). This means that the manufacturer may need to give the retailer an extra incentive to stock the product at all.

- *To even out fluctuating sales.* Seasonal offers may be used to encourage retailers to stock the products during slack periods. For example, the toy industry sells 80% of its production over the Christmas period, so it is common for firms to offer extra incentives to retailers to stock up during the rest of the year.

- *To counter the competition.* Aggressive sales promotion can sometimes force a competitor off the retailer's shelves, or at least cause the retailer to drive a harder bargain with a competitor.

Retailer promotions are used for the following purposes:

- *To increase store traffic.* Almost any kind of sales promotion will increase the number of people who come into the shop, but retailers would commonly have special events or seasonal sales.

- *To increase frequency and amount of purchase.* This is probably the commonest use of sales promotions: examples are two-for-one offers, buy-one-get-discount-off-another-product, and so forth.

- *To increase store loyalty.* Loyalty cards are the main example of this (although these have other uses – see Chapter 12). Using the loyalty card enables the customer to build up points, which can be redeemed against products.

- *To increase own-brand sales.* Most large retailers have their own brands, which often have larger profit margins than the equivalent national brands. Own-brands sometimes suffer from a perception of lower quality, and therefore increased sales promotion effort may need to be made. In fact, own brands help to increase sales of manufacturers' brands, but since heavy own-brand consumers contribute less to the retailer's overall profits (because they spend less overall, being bargain hunters) retailers might do better to encourage sales of manufacturers' brands as a way of encouraging bigger-spending customers (Ailawadi and Bari 2004).

■ *To even out busy periods.* Seasonal sales are the obvious examples, but some retailers also promote at busy times in order to ensure a larger share of the market.

Manufacturer promotions are carried out for the following reasons:

■ *To encourage trial.* When launching a new product the manufacturer may send out free samples to households, or may give away samples with an existing product. (See Chapter 10 for pull strategies.)

■ *To expand usage.* Sales promotion can be used to encourage re-invention of the product for other uses (see Chapter 6).

■ To attract new customers.

■ *Trade up.* Sales promotions can encourage customers to buy the larger pack or more expensive version of the product.

■ *Load up.* Encouraging customers to stock up on a product (perhaps in order to collect coupons) effectively blocks out the competition for a period.

■ *To generate a mailing list for direct marketing purposes* (for example by running an on-pack competition).

■ *To enhance brand values* by (for example) running some types of **self-liquidating offers**. For example, a promotion offering a discounted wristwatch that carries the brand logo might encourage sales of the product as well as ensuring that the brand remains in the forefront of the consumer's attention.

Often, the gains made from sales promotions are only temporary, but in many cases this is acceptable since a temporary shift in demand is all that is required to meet the firm's immediate need. Also, much sales promotion activity is carried out with the intention of spoiling a competitor's campaigns: using sales promotion to respond to a competitive threat, particularly by offering a price incentive, can be very fast and effective.

MANAGING PERSONAL SELLING

Selling is probably the most powerful marketing tool the firm has. A salesperson sitting in front of a prospect, discussing the customer's needs and explaining directly how the product will benefit him or her, is more likely to get the business than any advertising, PR or sales promotion technique available.

Unfortunately, selling is also the most expensive promotional tool for the firm: on average, a sales representative on the road will cost a firm around £60 000 p.a. and will probably call on only 1600 prospects or so in that time, at best. Selling is therefore used only for high-order-value or highly technical products that need a lengthy decision-making procedure.

Some retail shop assistants are trained in selling techniques, in particular in shops where the customer needs advice, such as electrical goods outlets or shoe shops. In these cases the retailer may spend considerable time and effort in training salespeople both in the technicalities of the product range and in selling techniques. Selling is learned – there is no such thing as a 'born' salesperson, although (as is true of any skill) some people have a greater aptitude for selling than do others.

Salespeople fall into four categories:

- **order takers**, who collect orders for goods from customers who have already decided to buy;
- **order getters**, who find solutions for new and existing customers and persuade them to buy;
- **missionaries**, who seek out new customers and prepare them to buy; and
- support staff such as technical salespeople who demonstrate technical products and persuade users to adopt them.

What the firm expects of its salespeople is that they will close business by persuading customers to buy the firm's products rather than a competitor's products. The firm wants its salespeople to be able to explain the benefits of the products in terms of the customer's needs, then ask for the order – in some industries, this results in a better than 50% success rate, which is of course vastly greater than the best advertising responses.

Salespeople have a bad reputation, largely undeserved, for being pushy and manipulative. In practice successful salespeople know that they are as much there to help the customer as to help the firm achieve its sales objectives. It is a common saying among salespeople that it is easier to get another company than it is to get new customers, so salespeople find it pays to look after the customer's interests.

Good salespeople begin by finding out the customer's needs, and go on to decide which of the company's products will best meet those needs. The next stage is to give an explanation of the product's benefits to the customer, connecting these to the customer's needs. Finally the salesperson closes the deal by asking for the order. The process is the same as that conducted by marketers

generally, except that the salesperson is dealing on a one-to-one basis rather than with a mass market. In this sense, selling can be seen as micro-marketing.

This means that the customer can 'pick the brains' of the salesperson, who presumably has superior knowledge of the products that are available. This can cut a lot of the effort out of the search for the most suitable product, and the salesperson can also help people through the decision-making barrier.

Experienced salespeople often say that the hardest part of the job is to get a decision, not necessarily to get a sale.

The salesperson therefore combines knowledge of the product (obtained beforehand) with knowledge of the customer's needs (obtained during the presentation) and knowledge of sales techniques (which are aids to decision-making) to help the customer arrive at a decision.

MANAGING THE SALESFORCE

Possibly the most expensive marketing tool the company has, the salesforce is in some ways the hardest to control. This is because it is composed of independently minded people who each have their own ideas on how the job should be done, and who are working away from the office and out of sight of the sales managers.

Sales managers are responsible for recruitment, training, motivation, controlling and evaluating salesforce activities, and managing sales territories.

Recruitment

Recruitment is complicated by the fact that there is no generally applicable set of personality traits that go to make up the ideal salesperson. This is because the sales task varies greatly from one firm to another, and the sales manager will need to draw up a specific set of desirable traits for the task in hand. This will involve analysing the company's successful salespeople, and also the less successful ones, to find out what the differences are between them.

Some companies take the view that almost anybody can be trained to sell, and therefore the selection procedures are somewhat limited, or even non-existent; other companies are extremely selective and subject potential recruits to a rigorous selection procedure. Sources of potential recruits are advertising, employment agencies, recommendations from existing sales staff, colleges and universities, and internal appointments from other departments.

Training

Training can be long or short, depending on the product and the market. Table 9.5 illustrates the dimensions of the problem. The role the salesperson is required to take on will also affect the length of training: *missionary salespeople* will take longer to train than order takers, and *closers* will take longer than *telephone canvassers*.

Typically, training falls into two sections: *classroom training*, in which the recruits are taught about the company and the products and may be given some grounding in sales techniques; and *field training*, which is an ongoing training

Table 9.5	Factors relating to length of training of sales staff
Factors indicating long training	**Factors indicating short training**
Complex, technical products	Simple products
Industrial markets with professional buyers	Household, consumer markets
High order values (from the customer's viewpoint)	Low order values
High recruitment costs	Low recruitment costs
Inexperienced recruits – for example, recruited direct from university	Experienced recruits from the same industry

programme carried out in front of real customers in the field. Field training is often the province of the sales managers, but classroom training can be carried out by other company personnel (in some cases, in larger firms, there will be specialists who do nothing else but train salespeople).

People tend to learn best by performing the task, so most sales training programmes involve substantial field training, either by sending out rookies (trainees) with experienced salespeople, or by the 'in-at-the-deep-end' approach of sending rookies out on their own fairly early in their careers. The latter method is indicated if there are plenty of possible customers for the product; the view is that a few mistakes (lost sales) will not matter. In industrial selling, though, it is often the case that there are fewer possible customers and therefore the loss of even one or two could be serious. In these circumstances it would be better to give rookies a long period of working alongside more experienced salespeople.

Sales team learning is impacted by their perceptions of the organisation's readiness to change. Salespeople working for an organisation which has demonstrated the ability to adapt to new conditions are more willing to spend time learning new techniques and new products than they would be in organisations which rarely move with the times (Ranganjaran *et al.* 2004).

Ultimately, of course, salespeople will lose more sales than they get. In most industries, fewer than half the presentations given result in a sale; a typical proportion would be one in three.

Payment

Payment for salespeople traditionally has a commission element, but it is perfectly feasible to use a *straight salary* method, or a *commission-only* method. Although it is commonly supposed that a commission-only salesperson will be highly motivated to work hard, since otherwise he or she will not earn any money, this is not necessarily the case. Salespeople who are paid solely by commission will sometimes decide that they have earned enough for this month, and will give themselves a holiday; the company has very little moral power to compel them to work, since there is no basic salary being paid. Conversely, a salesperson who is paid a salary only may feel obligated to work in order to justify the salary.

Herzberg (1966) said that the payment method must be seen to be fair if demotivation is to be avoided; the payment method is not in itself a good motivator. Salespeople are out on the road for most of their working lives and do not see what other salespeople are doing – whether they are competent at the job, whether they are getting some kind of unfair advantage, even whether they are working at all. In these circumstances a commission system does at least reassure the salesperson that extra effort brings extra rewards. The chart in Table 9.6 shows the trade-offs between commission-only and salary-only; of course, most firms have a mixture of salary and commission.

Salespeople tend to judge whether their pay is fair or not by looking at factors other than the actual money (Ramaswamy and Singh 2003). They tend to look at such factors as the fairness of their supervision, trust between themselves and the sales manager, and interactional fairness (negotiation and explanation). This is perhaps not surprising: the implication is that people only become concerned about their salary levels if they feel they are being unfairly dealt with or are unhappy in the job.

Table 9.6 Trade-offs in salespeople's pay packages

Mainly salary	Mainly commission
Where order values are high	Where order values are low
Where the sales cycle is long	Where the sales cycle is short
Where staff turnover is low	Where staff turnover is high
Where sales staff are carefully selected against narrow criteria	Where selection criteria for staff are broad
For new staff, or staff who have to develop new territories	For situations where aggressive selling is indicated (e.g. selling unsought goods)
Where sales territories are seriously unequal in terms of sales potential	Where sales territories are substantially the same

Motivation

Motivation, perhaps surprisingly, tends to come from sources other than payment. The classic view of motivation was proposed by Abraham Maslow (1954). Maslow's Hierarchy of Need theory postulates that people will fulfil the needs at the lower end of a pyramid (survival needs and security needs) before they move on to addressing needs at the upper end (such as belonging needs, esteem needs and self-actualisation needs). Thus, once a salesperson has assured his or her basic survival needs, these cease to be motivators; the individual will then be moving on to esteem needs or belonging needs. For this reason sales managers usually have a battery of motivational devices for salespeople to aim for.

For rookies (new salespeople), the award of a company tie might address the need to belong; for more senior salespeople, membership of a Millionaire's Club (salespeople who have sold more than a million pounds' worth of product) might address esteem needs. Many sales managers offer prizes for salespeople's spouses or partners. This can be a powerful incentive since salespeople often work unusual hours, and thus have disrupted home lives; the spouse or partner is sometimes neglected in favour of the job, so a prize aimed at them can help assuage the salesperson's natural feelings of guilt.

Sales territory management

Sales territory management involves ensuring that the salesforce have a reasonably equal chance of making sales. Clearly a home-improvement salesperson in a major city will have an easier task than one in a rural area, simply because of the shorter distances between **prospects**; such a salesperson would spend more time in presentations and less time driving. On the other hand, the city salesperson would probably face more competition and might also have to cover poorer homes who would be less likely to spend much money on improvements.

Territories can be divided *geographically* or by *industry*; IBM divides territories by industry, for example, so that salespeople get to know the problems and needs of the specific industry for which they have responsibility. IBM salespeople might be given responsibility for banks, or insurance companies, or local government departments. This sometimes means that salespeople have greater distances to travel in order to present IBM products, but are more able to make sensible recommendations and give useful advice. Geographical territories are more common, since they minimise travel time and maximise selling time.

It is virtually impossible to create exactly equal territories. Thus it is important to discuss decisions with salespeople in order to ensure that people feel they are being treated fairly. For example, some salespeople may be quite happy to accept a rural territory because they like to live and work in the country, even if it means earning less.

MANAGING PR

PR or public relations is about creating favourable images of the company or organisation in the minds of consumers. Public relations officers and marketers often have differing viewpoints: PR people tend to see their role as being about image-building with everybody who has anything at all to do with the firm, whereas marketers are concerned mainly with customers and consumers. There is therefore a lack of fit between the information-processing requirements of marketers and PR people (Cornelissen and Harris 2004).

Public relations is defined as 'the planned and sustained effort to establish and maintain goodwill and mutual understanding between an organisation and its publics: customers, employees, shareholders, trade bodies, suppliers, Government officials, and society in general' (Institute of Public Relations 1984). The PR managers have the task of co-ordinating all the activities that make up the public face of the organisation, and will have some or all of the following activities to handle:

- Organising press conferences.
- Staff training workshops.
- Events such as annual dinners.
- Handling incoming criticisms or complaints.
- Grooming senior management for the press or for TV appearances.
- Internal marketing; setting the organisation's culture towards a customer orientation.

The basic routes by which PR operates are word-of-mouth, press and TV news stories, and personal recommendation. The aim is to put the firm and its products into people's minds and conversations in a positive way. PR is not advertising: advertising can be both informative and persuasive, but PR is used for conveying information only.

Here are some examples of good PR activities:

- A press release saying that a company has developed a way of recycling garbage from landfills to produce plastics.
- The company sponsors a major charitable or sporting event (e.g. the London Marathon or a famine-relief project).
- An announcement that one of the firm's senior executives has been seconded to a major government job-creation programme.
- Body Shop requires all their franchise operations to run projects to benefit their local communities. This gives a positive image of the company to the community, and also gives the staff pride in working for a caring firm. Such initiatives are not always exportable, however: McDonald's ran into difficulties in Norway when they tried to establish a Ronald McDonald house, with strong resistance from political parties, academics and others (Bronn 2006).

■ McDonald's counters the negative publicity from environmental pressure groups by running litter patrols outside the restaurants.

These examples have in common that they are newsworthy and interesting, that they put the companies concerned in a good light, and that they encourage people to talk about the companies in a positive way.

Public relations and staff

PR is largely concerned with creating favourable impressions in people's minds. It is rarely, if ever, connected with directly bringing in business, and in this respect it differs from the other tools in the promotional mix. Although most of the time and for most activities PR will be the responsibility of a press agent or PR officer, PR is the responsibility of everybody who comes into contact with people outside the organisation. This will include the 'front-liners', the people whose day-to-day work brings them into contact with outsiders. For example:

■ receptionists;

■ telephonists;

■ truck drivers;

■ warehouse staff;

■ serving staff in the canteen.

This is apart from the marketing staff, such as salespeople, who come into contact with outsiders. In a sense, everybody in the organisation must take some responsibility for PR since everybody in the organisation goes home after work (and discusses their company with their friends).

In this context a bad approach to PR (but one that is all too common) is to hire somebody with a nice smile and a friendly voice to sit by the telephone to handle complaints and smooth over any problems that arise. This is a *fire-fighting* or **reactive** approach.

A good PR approach is to make all the staff feel positive about the company. This is done by ensuring that everybody knows what the organisation is doing, what the policies are and what the company's overall aims are, in simple language. Most people would like to think they are working for a good, responsible, successful organisation; it is part of the job of public relations to ensure that this is communicated to staff. This is sometimes done by using a slogan or company motto to sum up the company's main aim. Some examples are given in Table 9.7.

Internal PR uses staff newsletters, staff training programmes and staff social events to convey a positive image. More recently, intranets (internal computer-based communications systems) have increased in importance. Intranet-enabled PR can include e-mailing staff about corporate developments, chatrooms and blogs to encourage discussion of issues of interest, and the capacity for direct

Table 9.7	Examples of company slogans
Example	**Explanation**
We're Number Two, So We Try Harder (Avis)	This communicates to staff that the company is among the biggest, but that their efforts to 'try harder' are recognised and appreciated. It also conveys a valuable image to the customers. This slogan has become so well-known that Avis have now reduced it to 'We try harder'.
Créateur des Automobiles (Renault)	The literal translation of this French phrase, Creator of Automobiles, may not mean much but the French phrase conveys an image of care and artistry – the cars are created, not manufactured.
Putting the Community First (Barnet Council)	Like many local government organisations, Barnet wants to reassure residents that they come first in its thinking. This slogan emphasises the community and implies that there is neighbourliness and solidarity within Barnet.

contact with senior management. Such systems can be abused, but in most cases they are a force for good in helping to develop the corporate culture.

Because most of the front-liners are working away from the company's head-quarters, the PR process has to be handled by persuasion, not through diktat. It would be impossible for the PR staff to be everywhere at once, following people around to ensure that they say and do the 'right' things.

PR has a role in conciliation and internal arbitration, although much of this will be handled by human resources departments. Because internal conflict can lead to bad feeling towards the organization, part of the PR role is to provide a clear lead in terms of corporate culture.

Public relations and the press

Usually, PR communicates through the news media. Newspapers and magazines earn their money mainly through paid advertising, but they attract readers by having stimulating articles about topics of interest to the readership.

Press releases

PR often involves creating a news story or event that brings the product or company to the public attention. A news story is more likely to be read than an advertisement, and is also more likely to be believed. A press release differs from advertising in that the message is not paid for directly; the newspaper or magazine prints the story as news, and of course is able to slant the story any way it wishes to. PR people are often ex-journalists who have some contacts with the news media, and who know how to create a story that will be printed in the way the company wants it to be done. Newspaper editors are wary of thinly disguised advertisements and will only print items that are really newsworthy.

Good press releases can be much more effective than advertising for the following reasons:

- The press coverage is free, so there is better use of the promotional budget.
- The message carries greater credibility because it is in the editorial part of the paper.
- The message is more likely to be read, because while readers tend to skip past the advertisements, their purpose in buying the paper is to read the news stories.

Table 9.8 shows the criteria under which the press stories must be produced if they are to be published.

The news media will, of course, reserve the right to alter stories, add to them, comment on them or otherwise change them around to suit their own purposes. For example, a press agent's great little story on the launch of Britain's most powerful sports car may become part of an article on dangerous driving. There is really very little the firm can do about this.

For this reason, a large part of the PR manager's job lies in cultivating good relationships with the media. Sometimes this will involve business entertaining, but more often it will involve making the journalists' lives as easy as possible. A well-written press release will often be inserted in the paper exactly as it stands, because the editorial staff are too busy to waste time re-writing something that is already perfectly acceptable.

The journals and newspapers gain as well. Normally editors have to pay for editorial, either paying freelance writers to produce articles, or paying the salaries of journalists to come up with interesting stories. A good press release can go in with little or no editing, and no legwork on the part of journalists, so it fills space with minimal cost to the paper.

Media events

Often companies will lay on a **media event**, a launch ceremony for a new product or to announce some change in company policy. Usually this will involve

Table 9.8 Criteria for successful press releases

Criterion	Example
Stories must be newsworthy, i.e. of interest to the reader.	Articles about your new lower prices are not newsworthy; articles about opening a new factory creating 200 jobs are.
Stories must not be merely thinly disguised advertisements.	A story saying your new car is the best on the market at only £7999 will not go in. A story saying your new car won the East African Safari Rally probably would.
Stories must fit the editorial style of the magazine or paper they are being sent to.	An article sent to the *Financial Times* about your sponsored fishing competition will not be printed; an article about the company's takeover of a competitor will.

inviting journalists from the appropriate media, providing a free lunch with plenty of free drinks, and inviting questions about the new development in a formal press conference. This kind of event has only a limited success, however, unless the groundwork for it has been very thoroughly laid.

Journalists tend to be suspicious of media events, sometimes feeling that the organisers are trying to buy them off with a buffet and a glass of wine. This means they may not respond positively to the message the PR people are trying to convey, and may write a critical article rather than the positive one that was hoped for.

To minimise the chance of this happening, media events should follow these basic rules:

- Do not call a media event or press conference unless you are announcing something that the press will find interesting.
- Check that there are no negative connotations in what you are announcing.
- Ensure that you have some of the company's senior executives there to talk to the press, not just the PR people.
- Only invite journalists with whom you feel you have a good working relationship.
- Do not be too lavish with the refreshments.
- Ensure that your senior executives, in fact anybody who is going to speak to the press, has had some training in doing this. This is particularly important for TV.
- Be prepared to answer all questions truthfully. Journalists are trained to spot lies and evasions.

Journalists much prefer to be able to talk directly to genuine corporate executives rather than being allowed only to talk to the PR department; however, care should be exercised in ensuring that the executives spoken to are able to handle this type of questioning. It is also a good idea to have a press office that can handle queries from journalists promptly, honestly and enthusiastically and can arrange interviews with senior personnel if necessary.

PR and other publics

PR involves dealing with the company's other **publics**, apart from the consumers. These are typically the following groups:

- Shareholders, for whom the company will produce end-of-year reports, special privileges and so forth.
- Government departments, with whom the company will liaise about planned legislation or other government activities.
- The workforce.
- External pressure groups such as environmentalists or lobbyists.

Pressure groups can cause problems for companies by producing adverse publicity, by picketing company plants, or by encouraging boycotting of company products. This can usually be dealt with most effectively by counter-publicity.

Sometimes adverse publicity from pressure groups is dealt with by advertising. For example, McDonald's was attacked by environmental groups for indirectly encouraging the destruction of rainforests for the purpose of producing cheap beef. McDonald's responded with a series of full-page press adverts proving that beef for their hamburgers comes only from sources in the countries where it is eaten, and is not imported from the Third World.

Usually a journalist who is offered a story from a pressure group will respond by trying to get the other side of the story from the firm. This is partly for legal reasons, since newspapers can be sued for libel if they print stories that turn out to be untrue, but it is also because most journalists want to ensure the accuracy and fairness of their stories. This means that a firm's press office, a PR manager or even a senior executive may be asked for comment with little or no prior warning. It is therefore advisable to be as prepared as possible beforehand, and to answer as fully as possible in the event of being asked questions. However, it is better to delay comment than to say something that will make matters worse.

In these circumstances, it is better to use a phrase such as 'I'm sorry, I'll have to look into that and get back to you later' than to use the standard 'No comment'. The former phrase at least gives the impression that you are trying to help, whereas 'No comment' gives the impression that you are trying to hide something.

Defensive PR

Defensive PR is about responding to attacks from outside the firm and counteracting them as they arise. The attacks might come from pressure groups, from investigative reporters, or from members of parliament. The safest way to handle this type of attack is to begin by trying to understand the enemy, and to this end the following questions should be asked:

- Are they justified in their criticism?
- What facts do they have at their disposal?
- Who are they trying to influence?
- How are they trying to do it?

If the pressure group is justified in its criticisms, it may be necessary to help them to effect the changes in the organisation in order to quell the criticism. Otherwise the problem will simply continue. Good PR people will always respond in some way, however; as anyone who watches investigative reporters on TV will know, the company managers and directors who flee with a hasty 'No comment' always look guilty, whereas the ones who are prepared to be interviewed always appear honest (until the reporter produces the irrefutable evidence, of course).

Another aspect of defensive PR is crisis management. Some industries (for example airlines) are more prone to crises than others, but any company can be subject to bad publicity of one sort or another. A good approach to handling crises is to be prepared beforehand by establishing a crisis team who are able to speak authoritatively to the media in the event of a problem arising. The crisis team should meet regularly and should consider hypothetical cases and their responses to them. They should also ensure that they are immediately available in the event of a crisis occurring.

Proactive PR

Proactive PR means setting out deliberately to influence opinion, without waiting for an attack from outside. Here the manager will decide on the following:

- whom to influence;
- what to influence them about;
- how to influence them;
- how to marshal the arguments carefully to maximise the impact.

Overall, it is probably better to be proactive rather than defensive (or reactive) because that way the PR office is in control of the process and is better-prepared. If the firm is planning on dumping toxic waste in a beauty spot, in other words, it is better to contact Greenpeace beforehand and get its opinion rather than suffer the inevitable protests afterwards and take a chance on being able to patch up any problems.

What PR will do

Good PR will achieve the following outcomes for the firm:

- help build a positive image;
- counter bad publicity;
- improve employee motivation;
- improve the effectiveness of both advertising and the salesforce.

On the other hand, here are some of the things that PR will *not* do for the firm:

- directly increase sales;
- cover up something adverse to the company;
- replace other promotional activities.

Ultimately, PR works best as part of a planned and integrated programme of promotional activities which includes advertising, sales promotion and personal selling. It works worst when used only occasionally, and in isolation.

Word-of-mouth

Word-of-mouth is probably the most powerful communication medium in existence, and can be used by marketers to good effect. The reasons for the power of word-of-mouth are as follows:

- It is interactive, involving a discussion between the parties. This forces the recipient to think about the communication. The problem for marketers is that the interaction takes place between parties who are not usually under the control of the firm.
- It allows for feedback and confirmation of the messages.
- The source, being a disinterested friend or acquaintance, carries a lot more credibility than any marketer-generated communications.

People often discuss products and services; they like to talk about their own recent purchases, to advise people considering a purchase, to show friends and family their latest acquisitions, and even to discuss controversial or interesting marketing communications. The problem for marketers is that people will talk about products and companies whether the firm likes it or not, and there is very little that firms can do to control the process. Word-of-mouth communications can therefore be positive or negative, and it often appears that bad news travels twice as fast as good news, so that much word-of-mouth is negative. Interestingly, some word of mouth is more effective before the initiator of it has experienced the product: there is evidence that word of mouth is at its most active before a movie is released, rather than afterwards (Yong 2006). The richness of the message and the degree of implied or explicit advocacy of the product are key themes in the success of positive word-of-mouth (Mazzarol et al. 2007).

Table 9.9 shows some of the ways marketers can increase positive word-of-mouth. Part of the problem for the marketer lies in identifying the opinion leaders in a given market. Journalists, influential individuals and organisations in industry, and some prominent TV pundits are obviously easy to identify, but among the general public it usually takes careful research to identify the people who are likely to be opinion leaders regarding a particular product. The main characteristics of influentials are shown in Table 9.10.

Much word-of-mouth communication is, unfortunately, negative. Some authorities state that dissatisfied customers tell three times as many people about the product than do satisfied customers; if true, this means that preventing negative word-of-mouth is actually a more pressing problem for marketers than is generating positive word-of-mouth. Complaint-handling is therefore a key issue (see Chapter 3).

Sponsorship

Sponsorship of the arts or of sporting events is an increasingly popular way of generating positive feelings about firms. Sponsorship has been defined as 'An investment, in cash or kind, in an activity in return for access to the exploitable commercial potential associated with this activity' (Meenaghan 1991).

Table 9.9 Ways to encourage positive word-of-mouth

Method	Explanation and examples
Press releases	A press release with a good, newsworthy story will usually stimulate discussion, particularly if it is linked to another promotion. For example, a press release announcing a sports competition for school squash players will generate word-of-mouth among squash players.
Bring-a-friend schemes	In these schemes an existing customer is invited to recruit a friend in exchange for a small reward. In some cases, the reward is given to the friend rather than to the introducer – some people feel uncomfortable about accepting a reward for 'selling' to a friend. For example, a health club might have special 'bring a friend' days when the friend is allowed to use all the facilities free for a day. This gives the member a chance to show off his or her club, and encourages the friend to join.
Awards and certificates	Trophies and certificates are sometimes displayed, and often talked about. For example, Laphroaig Whisky distillery has a Friends of Laphroaig club, in which the members (regular drinkers of the whisky) are given a square foot of land on the island of Islay, and a certificate of ownership. The proud owners of this little piece of Scotland frequently mention it to their friends, especially when offering them a glass of the whisky itself. The distillers also occasionally invite the Friends of Laphroaig to nominate a friend to receive a free miniature of the whisky, on the grounds that the 'Friend' could be sure of a 'dram' when calling on the 'friend'.
T-shirts	Promotional clothing often excites comment from friends: designer labels, names of bands, names of tourist destinations and names of concert venues all provoke comment from friends and acquaintances.
Viral marketing	Some websites include games, jokes or interesting images which visitors are invited to 'e-mail to a friend'. In most cases, the web address would only be sent on to those friends the original visitor thinks might be interested in the product category. Note: this is entirely different from the unsolicited e-mails called spam which are sent out indiscriminately.

Table 9.10 Characteristics of influentials

Characteristic	Description of influential
Demographics	Wide differences according to product category. For fashions and film-going young women dominate. For self-medication, women with children are most influential. Generally, demography shows low correlation and is not a good predictor.
Social activity	Influencers and opinion leaders are usually gregarious.
General attitudes	Generally innovative and positive towards new products.
Personality and lifestyle	Low correlation of personality with opinion leadership. Lifestyle tends to be more fashion conscious, more socially active, more independent.
Product related	Influencers are more interested in the specific product area than are others. They are active searchers and information gatherers, especially from the mass media.

Sponsorship in the United Kingdom has grown from £4 million in 1970 (Buckley 1980) to £35 million by 1980 (Mintel 1990) and £400 million by 1993 (Mintel 1993). Much of this increase in expenditure came about because tobacco firms are severely restricted in what they are allowed to advertise, and where they are allowed to advertise it: thus sponsorship of Formula One racing and of horse racing and cricket matches by tobacco firms became commonplace. This source of sponsorship has now ceased, because tobacco firms are no longer allowed to sponsor events: in some cases this has forced events to cut back or even disappear altogether.

Companies sponsor for a variety of different reasons, as Table 9.11 shows (Zafer Erdogan and Kitchen 1998).

Table 9.11 Reasons for sponsorship

Objectives	% Agreement	Rank
Press coverage/exposure/opportunity	84.6	1
TV coverage/exposure/opportunity	78.5	2
Promote brand awareness	78.4	3
Promote corporate image	77.0	4
Radio coverage/exposure/opportunity	72.3	5
Increase sales	63.1	6
Enhance community relations	55.4	7
Entertain clients	43.1	8
Benefit employees	36.9	9
Match competition	30.8	10
Fad/fashion	26.2	11

Sponsorship attempts to link beliefs about the sponsoring organisation or brand and connect them to an event or organisation that is highly valued by target consumers (Zafer Erdogan and Kitchen 1998). The success of a sports team has a significant effect on fans' purchase of sponsors' products (Lings and Owen 2007) so it is worthwhile spending some time choosing the correct team to back – it is also worthwhile being loyal to a team, as audiences become increasingly aware of the sponsor's brand the longer the sponsorship continues (Mason and Cochetel 2006; Lacey *et al.* 2007). Sponsoring rival teams is a mistake: although it might seem as if the company is hedging its bets, supporters of each team resent support of the rivals, thus cancelling out any goodwill engendered by support for their own team (Davies *et al.* 2006).

Sponsorship is not adequate as a stand-alone policy. Although firms can run perfectly adequate PR campaigns without advertising, sponsorship will not work effectively unless the sponsoring firm is prepared and able to publicise the link. Some researchers estimate that two to three times the cost of sponsorship needs to be spent on advertising if the exercise is to be effective (Heffler 1994). In most cases it is necessary to spell out the reasons for the firm's sponsorship of the event in order to make the link clear to the audience; merely saying 'Official snack of the Triathlon' is insufficient. Since the audience is usually interested in anything about the event, it is quite possible to go into a brief explanation of the reasoning behind the sponsorship: for example, to say 'Our snack gives energy – and that's what every triathlete needs more than anything. That's why we sponsor the Triathlon.'

The evidence is that consumers do feel at least some gratitude towards the sponsors of their favourite events; whether this is gratitude *per se* or whether it is affective linking is hard to say, and the answer to that question may not be of much practical importance anyway (Crimmins and Horn 1996). There are certainly spin-offs for the internal PR of the firm; most employees like to feel that they are working for a caring organisation, and sponsorship money also (on occasion) leads to free tickets or price reductions for staff of the sponsoring organisation.

Sponsorship appears to work best when there is some existing link between the sponsoring company and the event itself. In other words, a company that manufactures fishing equipment would be more successful sponsoring a fishing competition than it would in sponsoring a painting competition. More subtly, a bank would be better off sponsoring a middle-class, 'respectable' arts event such as an opera rather than an open-air rock concert. The following criteria apply when considering sponsorship (Heffler 1994):

- The sponsorship must be economically viable; it should be cost-effective, in other words.
- The event or organisation being sponsored should be consistent with the brand image and overall marketing communications plans.
- It should offer a strong possibility of reaching the desired target audience.

- Care should be taken if the event has been sponsored before; the audience may confuse the sponsors, and you may be benefiting the earlier sponsor.

Occasionally a competitor will try to divert the audience's attention to themselves by implying that they are sponsoring the event: this is called ambushing (Bayless 1988). For example, during the 2006 World Cup it was common for firms to use World Cup events in their advertising or sales promotions without actually sponsoring anything to do with the event itself.

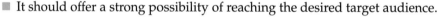

Critical thinking

If it's so easy to ambush an event, why would anybody pay to be a sponsor? After all, ambushing is easy – all the firm has to do is put 'Olympic-Size Offers!' on its publicity to cash in on the Olympic Games, or 'Marathon Guarantees!' to ride piggyback on the London Marathon.

On the other hand, maybe supporters and fans of these events can see through that kind of ploy – and react accordingly. Being exposed as a bit of a liar is hardly good for the corporate image.

Sponsorship is likely to grow in importance in the foreseeable future. More credible than advertising, it is often cheaper and has important effects on both brand and corporate image; given the restrictions being imposed on advertising, sponsorship has much to offer.

INTEGRATING THE PROMOTIONAL MIX

Communication does not necessarily create all its impact at once. A series of communications will move the recipient up a 'ladder' of effects, as shown in Figure 9.6. At the bottom of the ladder are those consumers who are completely unaware of the product in question; at the top of the ladder are those who actually purchase the product.

Given the differing nature of the consumer's involvement at each stage of the hierarchy, it is clear that no single communication method will work at every stage. Equally, not every consumer will be at the same stage at the same time; therefore it follows that several different communications approaches will need to run at once if the communications package is to work effectively.

■ In the early stages of a product launch, moving consumers from *brand ignorance* to *brand awareness* will be largely the province of advertising. At first, the marketer needs to get the consumers' attention and prepare them for the more detailed information which is to follow. A teaser campaign is almost entirely concerned with creating awareness.

■ Having made the target audience aware of the product, the next stage is to build *knowledge*. Again, mass advertising will play a major role, but if the product is complex it may be necessary to use **mailshots** or other more personal communications. This is because the emphasis is on providing information about the product: what it is, what it does, how it works and even that it works at all. In some cases an element of prior knowledge can be assumed: for example, most people would already know that fluoride is a good thing to have in toothpaste, not quite so many would know that it helps prevent tooth decay, and very few would know how it works.

■ *Liking* for the product might come from trying it (perhaps through a sales promotion), or from reading positive news stories about it (PR), or from persuasive advertising. Liking is an attitude towards a product, and therefore has elements of affect, cognition and conation (see Chapter 3).

■ *Preference* for the product implies comparison with other brands, so is very much concerned with positioning. An important point to note is that preference will come about only if the product matches up to (or exceeds) the claims made for it in the earlier advertising; if the claims made were inaccurate, unrealistic or simply misunderstood the consumer will be disappointed and will not buy the product again. Also, preference implies that the consumer will need to have sufficient knowledge of the pros and cons of other brands; salespeople will play a role in this part of the process if the product is a high-value one, since they will often be able to point out the drawbacks of competing brands.

- **Conviction** may come about only after several trials of the product (if it is a fast-moving consumer good) or after a lengthy discussion with a salesperson if the product is a high-value or high-involvement item. **Adoption** is the final stage of the process, when the consumer builds the product into his or her daily life.

There is likely to be some 'slippage' because it is not possible to expose all the target audience to the communication at the same time. Also, some consumers will already know more than others about the product category. Marketers will need to overlap the promotional effort to give maximum coverage.

One of the problems with the hierarchy of communications effects is that it implies that the process is invariably linear. This is not necessarily the case: an individual can become aware of a product and form an instant liking for it, without having detailed knowledge of the product. Equally, it is perfectly possible for a consumer to buy a product on impulse and form an opinion about it afterwards.

Having said that, the hierarchy of effects model is helpful in planning communications campaigns, since different communications methods and styles can be used according to the consumer's level on the hierarchy. For example, when a new product is introduced (or a product is introduced into a new market), few of the target audience will know anything about it.

Figure 9.6　The hierarchy of communications effects

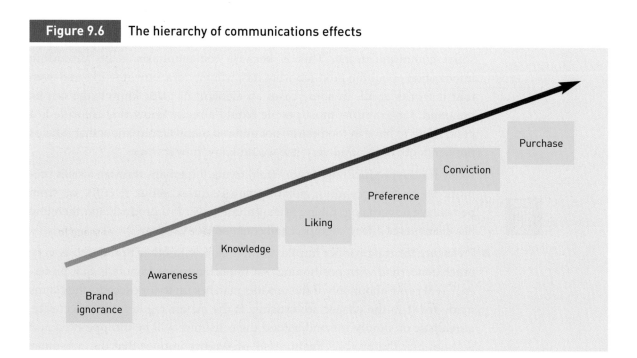

Case study 9
Sponsoring Milton Keynes

Milton Keynes is a new town, famous for its modernistic, concrete buildings and often considered (as are many new towns) to be a somewhat soulless place. In fact, the criticism is unfair – it's a lively town, spacious and people-friendly, a town where one can walk late at night in relative safety and where traffic and people are kept well separated. As a machine for living in, Milton Keynes has a lot to offer.

Of course, keeping the traffic under control and the people safe is expensive. Like most local authorities in the UK, Milton Keynes Council is often short of cash for providing basic services, and like most citizens in the UK Milton Keynes residents do not like paying any more taxes than they have to. So the council allow businesses to sponsor street furniture.

Milton Keynes has 125 roundabouts, 80% of which are sponsored by firms at a cost of between £2000 and £4000 per annum. Roundabouts carry advertising from the company, and of course work better than billboards because drivers have to slow down to negotiate the roundabout, and will see the signs. The more prominent the roundabout, the higher the sponsorship fee, and of course the greater the impact on the drivers and their passengers.

Sponsoring companies include national firms such as B&Q, Amway and Seimens, but the majority are local firms such as the Jaipur Restaurant, Steven Eagell Toyota and Kimbell's Solicitors. These local firms sponsor roundabouts near their businesses, as a reminder of their presence or as a promotion to passers by.

Most people drive the same routes fairly regularly, to work or school or the shops, so the sponsorship messages have a cumulative effect. Sponsoring a roundabout also has the advantage of being less obviously promotional than an advertisement – a more subtle approach than putting up a billboard. It also carries connotations of caring for the community. At an average of around £3000 per roundabout, Milton Keynes Council (and hence the taxpayers) gain around a quarter of a million pounds a year in revenue – a useful boost to the council's income.

Of course, the council owns a lot more than just the roundabouts. In 1999, as part of the publicity for the English Hockey Association's pre-Olympic event, the council allowed the Association to put banners on the lampposts in the town centre. This was such a success that the council are now selling the space to interested companies as ambient advertising space, at a charge of between £1000 and £1500 per banner. Given the number of lampposts in Milton Keynes, this could represent a very large contribution to council finances – but it's early days yet. Another scheme involving lampposts is being piloted – illuminated panels on the posts themselves. Currently, there are only a few of these in Central Milton Keynes, advertising local businesses, but in conjunction with Mediasign Marketing Ltd Milton Keynes Council is looking to expand the scheme further. Mediasign Marketing are themselves a local firm, based in Stourbridge.

Having come this far, the sponsorship team at Milton Keynes Council really began to build on the possibilities. Strategically sited street maps, free-standing signs and bus shelters all carry advertising, and even the boundary signs which welcome visitors to Milton Keynes can be sponsored. Having a sign saying, 'Welcome to Milton Keynes, home of "thecentre.mk"' conveys an important message to people arriving in the town: a one-year contract will set a company back £3000, but the impact is worth it.

Of course, Milton Keynes is not the only town offering these possibilities for sponsorship and advertising, but they have certainly been proactive in doing so. The result? Over £440 000 a year in extra revenue for the council, and a boost to local businesses which would be hard to beat.

Questions

1 What benefits are there in sponsoring a roundabout?

2 What other sponsorship or advertising opportunities might be available?

3 Why would advertising on a lamppost be more effective than a billboard?

4 What is the role of ambient advertising in Milton Keynes Council's strategy?

5 What might be the drawbacks of advertising on a bus shelter in Milton Keynes?

SUMMARY

This chapter has been about the ways companies communicate with their publics. In it, we have looked at the main promotional tools that marketers have at their disposal, and at the strengths and weaknesses of each of those tools.

Here are the key points from this chapter:

■ Communications work best when there is feedback.

■ It is essential for the sender of the message to have a common field of experience with the receiver.

■ The AIDA model can rarely be achieved with one form of communication.

■ The promotional mix is a recipe; the ingredients are not interchangeable.

■ Publicity and PR are probably the most cost-effective promotional tools you have available.

■ The media are interested only in newsworthy items, not in thinly disguised advertisements. PR works best when used as part of an integrated programme of activities.

■ PR requires a long-term commitment to cultivating the media.

■ It is advisable to invest in training anybody who may have to deal with the press, and even more so with TV.

■ PR will only help publicise your good points; it will not give you what you have not got.

■ Advertising is not the only way to increase sales, and may not even be the best way.

■ Advertising needs to be planned and targeted to the right segment in order to avoid wasting money and effort on people who will not buy the product.

■ People will not read long-winded advertisements.

■ Artwork is more memorable than copy.

■ Selling is about meeting the customer's needs with a suitable product from the range.

■ Selling is learned, not somehow magically inborn.

■ Sponsorship tends to have strong positive effects on both brand and corporate images.

CHAPTER QUESTIONS

1 How can sales promotions help a company's production planning process?

2 What are the main advantages of PR over advertising?

3 'The aim of marketing must be to make selling superfluous.' Discuss.

4 Which part of the AIDA model does personal selling best achieve?

5 What is the purpose of sponsorship?

Further reading

Marketing Communications: An Integrated Approach **by P.R. Smith** (London, Kogan Page, 1998) gives an excellent account of marketing communications in a practically orientated way.

Business-to-Business Marketing Communications **by Norman Hart** (London, Kogan Page, 1998) is very much a practical guide to marketing communications in the business-to-business environment.

Marketing Through Effective Communication **by Don Booth** (Tudor Business Publishing, 1992), Chapter 9. Some excellent advice for salespeople, covering appearance, approach and planning aspects. See also Chapter 11 on negotiation.

Marketing Communications **by Jim Blythe** (Harlow, Financial Times Prentice Hall, 2000) offers a more in-depth look at marketing communications theory and practice than is possible in this chapter.

How I Raised Myself from Failure to Success in Selling **by Frank Bettger** (London, Cedar Press, 1990; 1st edn, World's Work 1947). Anecdotes of a highly successful American salesman. This book is out of print at present, but if you can find a copy in a library or second-hand bookshop it makes riveting bedtime reading. A real classic!

References

Ailawadi, Kusum L. and Harlam, Bari: 'An empirical analysis of the determinants of retail margins: the role of store brand share', *Journal of Marketing*, **68** (1) (January 2004), pp. 147–55.

Baird, Thomas R., Wahlers, Russel G. and Cooper, Crystal K.: 'Non-recognition of print advertising: emotional arousal and gender effects', *Journal of Marketing Communications*, **13** (1) (2007), pp. 39–57.

Bayless, A.: 'Ambush marketing is becoming a popular event at Olympic Games', *Wall Street Journal* (8 February 1988).

Biel, A.: 'Love the advertisement, buy the product?', *ADMAP* (October 1989).

Bronn, Peggy Simcic: 'Building corporate brands through community involvement: is it exportable? The case of the Ronald McDonald House in Norway', *Journal of Marketing Communication*, **12** (4) (2006), pp. 309–20.

Brown, G.: 'Modelling advertising awareness', *ADMAP* (April 1991).

Buckley, D.: 'Who pays the piper?', *Practice Review* (Spring 1980).

Cornelissen, Joep P. and Harris, Phil: 'Interdependencies between marketing and public relations disciplines as correlates of communication organization', *Journal of Marketing*, **20** (1) (February 2004), pp. 237–65.

Crimmins, J. and Horn, M.: 'Sponsorship: from management ego trip to marketing success', *Journal of Advertising Research*, **36** (4) (July/August 1996), pp. 11–21.

D'Astous, Alain and Landreville, Valerie: 'An experimental investigation of factors affecting consumers' perceptions of sales promotions', *European Journal of Marketing*, **37** (11) (2003), pp. 1746–61.

Davies, Fiona, Veloutsou, Cleopatra and Costa, Andrew: 'Investigating the influences of a joint sponsorship of rival teams on supporter attitudes and brand preferences', *Journal of Marketing Communications*, **12** (1) (2006), pp. 31–48.

Engel, James F., Warshaw, Martin R. and Kinnear, Thomas C.: *Promotional Strategy* (Chicago, Irwin, 1994).

Farris, P.W. and Buzzell, R.D.: 'Why advertising and promotional costs vary: some cross-sectional analyses', *Journal of Marketing* (Fall, 1979).

Harris, Greg: 'International advertising: developmental and implementational issues', *Journal of Marketing Management*, **12** (1996), pp. 551–60.

Heffler, Mava: 'Making sure sponsorship meets all the parameters', *Brandweek* (May 1994), p. 16.

Herzberg, F.: *Work and Nature of Man* (London, William Collins, 1966).

Institute of Public Relations: *Public Relations Practice: Its Roles and Parameters* (London, The Institute of Public Relations, 1984).

Katz, E. and Lazarsfield, P.: *Personal Influence: The Part Played by People in the Flow of Mass Communications* (New York, Free Press, 1955).

Lacey, Russel, Sneath, Julie Z., Finney, Zachary R. and Close, Angeline G.: 'The impact of repeat attendance on event sponsorship effects', *Journal of Marketing Communications*, **13** (4) (2007), pp. 243–55.

Lings, Ian N. and Owen, Kate M.: 'Buying a sponsor's brand: the role of affective commitment to the sponsored team', *Journal of Marketing Management*, **23** (5/6) (2007), pp. 483–96.

McAlister, Leigh, Srinavasan, Raji and Kim, Minching: 'Advertising, research and development, and systematic risk of the firm', *Journal of Marketing*, **71** (1) (2007), pp. 35–45.

Mantovani, G.: *New Communication Environments: From Everyday to Virtual* (London, Taylor & Francis, 1996).

Maslow, Abraham: *Motivation and Personality* (New York, Harper and Row, 1954).

Mason, Roger B. and Cochetel, Fabrice: 'Residual brand awareness following the termination of a long-term event sponsorship and the appointment of a new sponsor', *Journal of Marketing Communications*, **12** (2) (2006), pp. 125–44.

Mazzarol, Tim, Sweeney, Gillian C. and Soutar, Geoffrey N.: 'Conceptualising word-of-mouth activities, triggers and conditions: an exploratory study', *European Journal of Marketing*, **41** (11/12) (2007), pp. 1475–94.

Meenaghan, J.A.: 'The role of sponsorship in the marketing communication mix', *International Journal of Advertising*, **10** (1) (1991), pp. 35–47.

Mintel: *Special Report on Sponsorship* (London, Mintel, 1990).

Mintel: *Special Report on Sponsorship* (London, Mintel, 1993).

Moran, W.T.: 'Insights from pricing research' in E.B. Bailey (ed.), *Pricing Practices and Strategies* (New York, The Conference Board, 1978), pp. 7 and 13.

Patti, Charles H.: 'Evaluating the role of advertising', *Journal of Advertising* (Fall, 1977), pp. 32–3.

Pieters, Rik and Wedel, Michel: 'Attention capture and transfer in advertising: brand, pictorial and text-size effects', *Journal of Marketing*, **68** (2) (April 2004), pp 36–50.

Ramaswamy, Sridhar N. and Singh, Jagdip: 'Antecedents and consequences of merit pay fairness for industrial salespeople', *Journal of Marketing*, **67** (4) (October 2003), pp. 46–66.

Ranganjaran, Deva, Chonko, Lawrence B., Jones, Eli and Roberts, James A.: 'Organisational variables, sales force perceptions of readiness for change, learning and performance among boundary-spanning teams: a conceptual framework and propositions for research', *Industrial Marketing Management*, **33** (4) (2004) pp. 289–305.

Rosengren, Sara and Dahlen, Micael: 'Brand-slogan matching in a cluttered environment', *Journal of Marketing Communication*, **12** (4) (2006), pp 263–79.

Stapel, J.: 'Monitoring advertising performance', *ADMAP* (July/August 1990).

Stapel, J.: 'Like the advertisement but does it interest me?', *ADMAP* (April 1991).

Varey, Richard: *Marketing Communications: A Critical Introduction* (London, Routledge, 2002).

Volkov, Michael, Harker, Michael and Harker, Debra: 'People who complain about advertising: the aficionados, guardians, activists and seekers', *Journal of Marketing Management*, **22** (3/4) (2006), pp. 379–405.

Yong, Liu: 'Word of mouth for movies: its dynamics and impact on box-office revenue', *Journal of Marketing*, **70** (3) (2006), pp. 74–9.

Zafer Erdogan, B. and Kitchen, P.J.: 'The interaction between advertising and sponsorship: uneasy alliance or strategic symbiosis?', *Proceedings of the 3rd Annual Conference of the Global Institute for Corporate and Marketing Communications*, Strathclyde Graduate Business School, 1998.

Indian tourism

Marketing an entire country is not easy – there are too many factors to take into account. In the case of India, the Tourist Authority is dealing with an extremely diverse nation. India has everything – from beaches to ancient monuments, deserts to the highest mountains in the world, internationally famous cuisine to adventure trips in the jungle. The potential customers are also diverse: student backpackers on gap years, middle-aged tourists on world cruises, adventure seekers and sports enthusiasts, amateur historians, wildlife enthusiasts and beach-lovers all come to India. In recent years, as the Indian economy has taken off, more than 400,000 internal tourists travel to resorts and sites of interest in India every year.

Promoting this diversity led to the 2008 'Incredible India' campaign, which involved TV advertising on international cable channels such as CNN. This was coupled with poster advertising at major airports to appeal directly to regular travellers. The aim is to move Indian tourism upmarket: currently, the majority of tourists visiting India do so on a tight budget, since it is one of the world's cheapest destinations. India is a very big country, well able to absorb and cater for much larger numbers of tourists: the difficulty lies in attracting wealthier tourists.

Sujata Thakur, Regional Director, Incredible India

Watch the video clip, then try to answer the following questions. The answers are on the companion website.

Questions

1 How would you measure the results of the Incredible India campaign?

2 What targets are the Tourist Authority setting – and how realistic are they?

3 How should the Tourist Authority plan for attracting a more upmarket group of tourists?

10

Marketing planning, implementation and control

Objectives

After reading this chapter you should be able to:

■ analyse the firm's current situation and develop a forward strategic plan;

■ explain the difference between strategy and tactics;

■ explain the main issues surrounding budgeting;

■ describe the basic approaches to budgeting;

■ set up systems for the monitoring and control of your plans;

■ develop strategic approaches to integrating a firm's marketing activities.

INTRODUCTION

This chapter is about integrating and co-ordinating the firm's marketing efforts, producing marketing plans, and ensuring that the plans are carried out in a cost-effective manner. In most cases, marketing planning takes place in the context of overall corporate strategy, which may or may not be market-orientated: in any event, marketers have to decide where the organisation's resources need to be directed in order to ensure customer satisfaction and maximise opportunities for exchange.

THE MARKETING PLANNING PROCESS

The basic process of planning is as shown in Figure 10.1. Strategic decisions concern the overall direction of the organisation. **Strategy** is about where we want to be; decisions on **tactics** are about how we are going to get there.

Figure 10.1   The marketing planning process

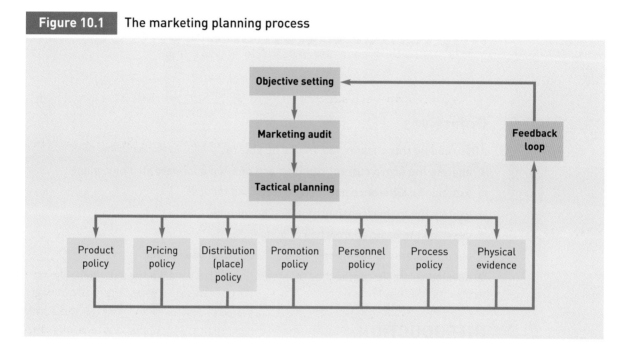

Strategic decisions tend to be difficult to reverse; they usually involve a rejection of other strategic options; and they generally involve strong personal commitment on the part of the decision maker. Tactical decisions are relatively easy to change, involve less commitment, and can often run alongside other options. A comparison of strategic and tactical decisions is given in Table 10.1.

Strategy must be integrated across the whole range of marketing activities, it must be formulated in the light of good analysis of the environment, and it must

Table 10.1   Comparison of strategic and tactical decisions

Strategic decisions	Tactical decisions
Concern overall direction	Concern methods of achievement
Difficult to reverse	Relatively easy to change
Involve rejection of alternatives	Allow combination of alternatives

include a feedback system so that the strategy can be adapted in the light of environmental changes. Strategy is influenced by organisational objectives and resources, competitor activities, the structure of the market itself and the firm's willingness to make changes and take risks.

From an overall strategic perspective marketers need to decide on the following issues, and formulate strategies for coping with them:

- Which market should the firm be in?
- What strengths and weaknesses is the firm bringing to the marketplace?
- Where does the firm intend to be in 5 to 30 years' time?
- What will the firm's competitors do in response to the market?
- Does the firm have sufficient resources to achieve the objectives decided upon?

The first stage in the planning process is to determine where the firm is now; this can be determined by carrying out a marketing audit.

THE MARKETING AUDIT

In marketing, strategic planning revolves around issues such as launching new products, changing brand names, deciding which segments to target and designing new promotional campaigns. The **marketing audit** is a review of the firm's current objectives, strategies, organisation, performance and activities, and its primary purpose is to pick out the firm's strengths and weaknesses so that managers can improve on them in future. It evaluates how effectively the organisation is performing its marketing tasks within the context of the seven Ps – products, price, place, promotion, people, processes and physical evidence (Band 1984).

The marketing audit is a snapshot of what is actually happening now in the firm. It should therefore be carried out on a fairly regular basis – within the limits of the amount of money that can be spared for the task, and the amount of time that can be spared from doing the marketing tasks at hand.

Table 10.2 shows an overview of the scope of the marketing audit. Such an audit encompasses the SWOT and STEP analyses introduced in Chapter 2, but goes into considerably more detail. Once the exercise has been carried out, managers will have a very clear idea of what needs to be changed to meet the firm's objectives.

| Table 10.2 | The marketing audit |

Main areas	Subsections	Issues to be addressed
Marketing environment audit *Macro-environment*	Economic–demographic	Inflation, materials supply and shortages, unemployment, credit availability, forecast trends in population structure.
	Technological	Changes in product and process technology, generic substitutes to replace products.
	Political–legal	Proposed laws, national and local government actions.
	Cultural	Attitude changes in the population as a whole, changes in lifestyles and values.
	Ecological	Cost and availability of natural resources, public concerns about pollution and conservation.
Task environment	Markets	Market size, growth, geographical distribution, profits; changes in market segment sizes and opportunities.
	Customers	Attitudes towards the company and competitors, decision-making processes, evolving needs and wants.
	Competitors	Objectives and strategies of competitors, identifying competitors, trends in future competition.
	Distribution and dealers	Main trade channels, efficiency levels of trade channels.
	Suppliers	Availability of key resources, trends in patterns of selling.
	Facilitators and marketing firms	Cost and availability of transport, finance and warehousing; effectiveness of advertising (and other) agencies.
	Publics	Opportunity areas, effectiveness of PR activities.
Marketing strategy audit	Business mission	Clear focus, attainability.
	Marketing objectives and goals	Corporate and marketing objectives clearly stated, appropriateness of marketing objectives.
	Strategy	Core marketing strategy, budgeting of resources, allocation of resources.
Marketing organisation audit	Formal structure	Seniority of marketing management, structure of responsibilities.
	Functional efficiency	Communications systems, product management systems, training of personnel.
	Interface efficiency	Connections between marketing and other business functions.
Marketing systems audit	Marketing information system	Accuracy and sufficiency of information, generation and use of market research.
	Marketing planning system	Effectiveness, forecasting, setting of targets.
	Marketing control system	Control procedures, periodic analysis of profitability and costs.
	New product development system	Gathering and screening of ideas, business analysis, pre-launch product and market testing.

Main areas	Subsections	Issues to be addressed
Marketing productivity audit	Profitability analysis	Profitability of each product, market, territory and distribution channel. Entry and exit of segments.
	Cost-effectiveness analysis	Costs and benefits of marketing activities.
Marketing function audits	Products	Product portfolio; what to keep, what to drop, what to add, what to improve.
	Price	Pricing objectives, policies and strategies. Customer attitudes. Price promotions.
	Distribution	Adequacy of market coverage. Effectiveness of channel members. Switching channels.
	Advertising, sales promotion, PR	Suitability of objectives. Effectiveness of execution format. Method of determining the budget. Media selection. Staffing levels and abilities.
	Salesforce	Adequate size to achieve objectives. Territory organisation. Remuneration methods and levels. Morale. Setting quotas and targets.

Source: Adapted from Kotler, P., 2003, *Marketing Management, 11th edn*, © 2003. Reprinted by permission of Pearson Education Inc., Upper Saddle River, N.J.

CORPORATE OBJECTIVES

Corporate objectives are the strategic statements of where the company wants to be. The objectives might be as follows:

- *Financial*: market share, sales, profit, return on investment, etc.
- *Philosophical*: perhaps a mission statement expressing the core values of the organisation.
- *Qualitative*: service levels, innovation, etc.

Corporate objectives often involve trade-offs, since all firms have limited resources and can concentrate on only one area at a time. In some cases the trade-offs involve diametrically opposed objectives. Weinberg (1969) proposed a set of eight trade-offs in setting objectives, as follows:

1 Short-term profit *v* long-term growth.
2 Profit margin *v* market positioning.
3 Direct sales effort *v* **market development**.
4 Penetrating existing markets *v* developing new ones.
5 Profit *v* non-profit goals.
6 Growth *v* stability.
7 Change *v* stability.
8 Low-risk *v* high-risk environments.

Table 10.3	Strategic alternatives
Strategic objective	**Explanation**
Backward integration	Taking control of suppliers, either by purchase or by merger.
Forward integration	Taking control of customers (in industrial or commercial markets).
Horizontal integration	Taking control of competitors.
Concentric diversification	Developing new products that fit well with the existing product range, but delivering them to new markets.
Conglomerate diversification	Developing new products that are unrelated to the firm's existing technology. This is a high-risk strategy: see Chapter 6.
Horizontal diversification	Introducing new products (unrelated to the present range) into existing markets. For example, Virgin markets everything from records to life insurance to the same target group of consumers.

Setting the overall corporate objectives may indicate strategic sub-objectives; Table 10.3 contains some examples of strategic objectives.

As a general rule, most firms want to grow. Growth increases the firm's security in the market it increases the power and influence of managers (not to mention their salaries) and it reduces costs. There are four main advantages to growth, as shown in Table 10.4.

Table 10.4	Advantages of growth
Advantage	**Explanation**
Protection against competition	If the firm becomes the largest in the industry, competitors find it harder to enter the market. Growing firms are able to apply more resources to the market, and take away market share from their competitors thus reducing the competitors' ability to compete effectively.
Improved economics of scale	Greater size means greater efficiency in the purchase of raw materials, use of employee skills and use of corporate resources. This eventually results in higher profit margins, and consequently a greater ability to survive if business worsens.
Better control of distribution networks	Growing firms are attractive to distributors and suppliers because they will provide more business in the future. This gives the firm a negotiating advantage.
More opportunities for career advancement	Managers and staff have better opportunities for promotion when working for a growing firm. This means greater motivation, which in turn means improved working practices.

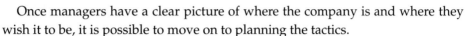

Growth in growing markets is likely to happen in any case, even without any formal strategic attempts to encourage it: the key to success here lies in measuring whether the company is growing faster than the market, slower than the market, or at the same pace as the market. Often firms which express their growth objectives in financial terms fail to notice that they are growing more slowly than the market, and are thus (in effect) losing ground to competitors. Expressing growth targets in terms of market share will avoid this pitfall, although obviously a reliable measure of the overall size of the market needs to be available.

Once managers have a clear picture of where the company is and where they wish it to be, it is possible to move on to planning the tactics.

INTERNATIONALISATION STRATEGY

Although governments encourage firms to internationalise (and in particular to export), this is not in itself enough reason to seek markets overseas. Table 10.5 shows some of the other reasons firms have for becoming international.

Table 10.5 Rationale for international marketing

Reason	Explanation
Small or saturated domestic markets	If the firm cannot expand any further in its domestic market, further growth can occur only by internationalising. In fact, most firms would go international long before the domestic market is saturated, if only because it would be easier to enter the overseas markets than to extract the last possible sale from the domestic market. Notably, the USA trades relatively little of its production; the home market is large enough that most firms do not need to consider exporting.
Economies of scale	For many industries, notably the electronics industry and the chemical industry, the cost of initiating a new product is so huge that it needs to be spread across a very large production run. Automation of production lines is making this more of an issue for more and more firms; recouping the capital cost of automation almost forces the firm into world markets.
International production	The capacity to source components and assemble finished products on a global scale means that the firm can take advantage of the most competitive prices worldwide. Shipping costs are relatively low compared with the savings made.
Customer relationships	Manufacturers who supply multinational firms must themselves be able to deliver worldwide and price in any currency in order to supply assembly plants in different countries.
Market diversification	The broader the range of markets served, the less likely that the firm will suffer if one market fails. For example, recessions do not happen in all countries at the same time; a truly multinational company will be able to make up losses in one market with gains in another.
International competitiveness	No firm is immune from competitors coming in from outside. If a firm is to remain viable in the long run, it may be forced to meet foreign competition on their own ground before having to meet them in the domestic market.

A further reason for internationalising is that the product life cycle will vary from one country to another. What is a mature product in one country may be at the introduction stage in another, so that the firm gains all the advantages of introducing new products to the market without the costs of research and development that would result from developing new products for the domestic market.

When dealing with foreign markets marketers will meet barriers that would not be present in domestic markets. In addition, of course, marketers will sometimes find advantages that would not be present in the domestic market. Table 10.6 shows how internationalisation affects the 7-Ps. The basic problem for companies who seek to internationalise is that nothing can be taken for granted in a foreign country. This places a heavy premium on forward planning.

Overall, a firm's internationalisation strategy decisions will depend on the following factors:

- The size of the firm in its domestic market.
- The firm's strengths compared with overseas competitors.
- Management experience of dealing in other countries.
- The firm's objectives for long-term growth.

Table 10.6 Internationalisation and the 7-P framework

Element of the marketing mix	Effect in international markets
Product	Different cultural, climatic, technical or economic issues will affect product design. Modification of product policy ranges from the obvious issue of electricity supply to more subtle cultural differences (e.g. Americans prefer top-loading washing machines; Europeans prefer front-loaders).
Place	Distribution systems vary internationally. Germans have a much higher propensity to buy by mail order than do Italians; there are relatively few hypermarkets in Italy compared with Spain.
Promotion	Clearly, promotion issues are deeply affected by cultural differences. This is why advertisements shown on foreign TV stations often seem humorous.
Price	Pricing is usually done in the currency of the target country. This leads to problems with exchange-rate fluctuations, which can be overcome by buying or selling currency on the futures markets; most banks can arrange this.
People	Employing foreign sales staff, for example, can lead to problems in motivation and control.
Processes	In Brazil it is normal for patrons of bars and restaurants to pay the cashier for meals or drinks, receive a receipt, then order the items from the waiters. In Spain it is normal to pay for drinks only when leaving a bar. Processes do not necessarily cross national boundaries.
Physical evidence	For many years American banks have given free gifts to new depositors; merely handing over a cheque book and a deposit book would not be sufficient for a US customer.

Table 10.7 International market entry strategies

Strategy	Explanation
Keep product and promotion the same worldwide	The advantage of this is that it minimises entry costs. Coca-Cola often uses this approach, using basically the same advertising worldwide but translating any voiceovers into the local language. The major drawback of the approach is that it takes no account of local customs and attitudes, and tends to lead to a 'lowest common denominator' advertisement which can be understood by everybody and offends nobody.
Adapt promotion only	The product remains the same, but the promotion is adapted to local cultural norms. This is a fairly common approach, since it enables the marketing communications to reach the consumers more effectively while at the same time avoiding a redesign of the product itself.
Adapt product only	This is less common, but has been done by some detergent manufacturers to allow for differences in local water supplies and washing machines. Likewise, the supposedly 'global' Ford Focus is substantially modified for different markets in order to meet local emission standards and road-safety laws.
Adapt both product and promotion	Sometimes it is necessary to adapt both the product and the promotion, as in the case of Cheer washing-powder, a Procter & Gamble product marketed in Japan. Cheer was reformulated to allow for the extra fabric softeners the Japanese use, and the promotion emphasised that the powder worked well in cold water (since most Japanese wash clothes in cold water).
Invent new products	If the existing products cannot meet the conditions in the new market, a new product must be invented. For example, the clockwork radio was invented for use in countries where there is no mains power supply and batteries are difficult to obtain.

Having chosen a target country, the marketer is in a position to decide which are the market entry tactics appropriate to the case. There are five basic strategies for entering foreign markets, as shown in Table 10.7.

Once the approach to the promotion and product development strategies has been decided, the firm needs to choose an entry strategy. The **stages of development** model suggests that firms seeking to internationalise go through a series of stages.

- *Exporting* implies the smallest commitment to the foreign market. Here the manufacturer sells the firm's products to a foreign importer, who then handles the marketing of the product. The advantage of this approach is that it involves the least cost; the disadvantage is that the exporting firm has little or no control over the way the product is marketed or used in the foreign market. This could lead to problems later on as the firm's reputation may be adversely affected. **Export agents** bring together buyers and sellers and are paid on commission; **export houses** buy goods for export to foreign countries. Sometimes foreign buyers will deal direct with companies, and some major stores (for example Sears of the USA) maintain buying offices in foreign capitals.

- *Establishing a sales office* in the foreign market might be a next stage. This implies a greater financial commitment, but also gives more control. **Joint**

ventures involve collaborating with a same-nationality firm that is already in the target market, or with a foreign firm in its own country. A joint venture could involve a **piggy-backing** arrangement, under which one firm agrees to market the other firm's product alongside its own. This works best if the firms have complementary, non-competing products. For example, a cosmetics firm may agree to carry a perfumer's products. **Licensing** agreements allow a foreign manufacturer to use the firm's patents: for example, Pilkington licenses foreign glass manufacturers to use the float-glass technique. This is useful when the product itself is difficult to export owing to fragility or perishability, but it relies on the firm having good patents or other protection for its intellectual property. **Franchising** is similar; the franchisee agrees to run the business by a specific format. McDonald's hamburger restaurants are an example.

■ *Overseas distribution* would involve establishing a warehousing and distribution network in the foreign country. This gives strong control over the marketing of the product, but still relies on importing from the home country.

■ *Overseas manufacture* includes warehousing and distribution, but allows the firm to shorten the lines of supply and to adapt the product more easily for the overseas market. In some cases the manufacturing costs are lower in the foreign market, so there will be further economies made.

■ Finally, the firm might become a true **multinational marketer**. The true multinational firm manufactures and markets in those countries that offer the best advantages. Although such a company may have originated in a particular country, it may well employ far more foreigners than it does its own nationals, and will think in global terms rather than national terms.

Broadly speaking a firm can decide on a **globalisation** strategy, by which the company's products and attitudes are basically standardised throughout the world (examples are Coca-Cola and IBM), or a **customisation** strategy, where the company adapts its thinking and its marketing to each fresh market (examples are Sony and Nestlé). As global barriers to trade break down, more and more companies will be taking an international view of their marketing opportunities, and will be seeking to do business across national borders and cultural differences.

An alternative view of internationalisation strategy is the **eclectic theory** proposed by Dunning (1993). Broadly, this theory supposes that the firm will look at its specific advantages over other firms both at home and overseas, and will plan its market entry strategies accordingly without necessarily going through a series of stages. For example, a firm with a strength in franchising is likely to use franchising as a market entry method into overseas markets, rather than begin by exporting, then setting up a salesforce, and so forth. The eclectic paradigm also has implications for production, since a true multinational will produce in whichever country offers the best advantages: Ford, for example, produces all the engines for its European cars in Wales, exporting them for assembly into car bodies in Germany, and perhaps re-importing them back into the United Kingdom. Since transport costs are relatively low compared with the final price of the car, Ford deems it worthwhile to centralise production of the various components. In addition the company can take advantage of government incentives to locate in high-unemployment areas, and can also use transfer pricing to minimise its tax liabilities.

Whether firms adopt the 'born global' approach of Dunning or the incremental approach does not appear to be dependent on the characteristics of the firms themselves. Most characteristics of 'born global' firms are shared with those taking an incremental approach, the difference between them depending on the attitudes of the managers rather than the nature of the firm (Chetty and Campbell-Hunt 2004).

TACTICAL PLANNING

Because marketers are usually looking for a competitive edge, they will usually try to offer their customers something that is unavailable elsewhere. In this respect, marketing differs from the other main business disciplines. If the legal directors were swapped over from one competing firm to another, they would have no trouble in carrying on with their jobs; the law remains the same for firms in the same industry. If the finance directors or the production managers were exchanged they would simply carry on working, because each industry operates with its own financial structure and production techniques. If the marketers were swapped, though, they would probably be completely lost for the first few weeks, because each should be addressing a different segment of the market, dealing with different distributors, different clients, different overall philosophies and different promotional campaigns.

For example, cosmetics are traditionally sold in pharmacies and department stores. Yet Avon Cosmetics has become one of the world's largest cosmetics companies by breaking the rules, and selling the cosmetics door-to-door, training millions of women worldwide in sales techniques and then sending them out to sell to family, friends, neighbours, work colleagues and strangers. Even though the original door-to-door approach has been modified because of safety issues, the maverick approach still pays off.

There are three generic strategies (Porter 1980):

■ **cost leadership**, which is about keeping costs low enough to be able to maintain high profits even when competition is strong. There can only be one cost leader in the market, because only one firm can be the cheapest provider;

■ **differentiation**, which means distinguishing the firm and its products from all competitors; and

■ **focus**, which is about concentrating on specific segments of the market.

Porter also identifies a fourth strategy, which is a strategy for failure: he says that a firm which tries to combine the above strategies will fail, because it is impossible to be the lowest cost provider while offering a range of products, or while concentrating on a small part of the market, due to the lack of economies of scale.

Competitive tactics will depend largely on the company's current product portfolio, and on the activities of competitors. The Boston Group matrix (see Chapter 6) will help in making strategic decisions about which products to keep and which to discard, but the tactical problem still remains of approaching the appropriate markets.

Critical thinking

If Porter was right, and there are only three strategies available, how do low-cost airlines figure in the equation? They all try to compete by being the cheapest, yet at the same time they differentiate by flying different routes. It could even be argued that, by flying into and out of obscure regional airports, they are operating on a focus basis.

Maybe they aren't as low-cost as they pretend to be – after all, such airlines should be looking for economies of scale, yet they do not own the largest, most economical aircraft.

The tactical possibilities in a marketing campaign are huge in number. Most of the tactics of marketing involve creativity on the part of practitioners, so it is virtually impossible to lay down any hard and fast rules about approaching different marketing problems. However, the following might prove to be useful guidelines:

- Try to do something that the competition has not thought of yet.
- Always consult everybody who is involved in the day-to-day application of the plans. Salespeople in particular do not like to be told what to do by somebody back at Head Office.
- Do not expect instant results from anything you do – but monitor the results anyway.
- Ensure that the messages you give the consumers, the middlemen, the suppliers and all your other publics are consistent.
- Be prepared for a response from your competitors – try to anticipate what it might be when you are formulating your plans.
- Communications tools cannot be used to achieve marketing objectives; they can only achieve communications objectives. Marketing objectives may well follow on from this, but this is not a good way to judge a communications medium.

Cost-effectiveness will always be an issue in promotional campaigns, and it is for this reason that there has been a growth in direct marketing worldwide (see Chapter 12). The accurate targeting of market segments made possible by computer technology has enabled marketers to refine the approach, and hence increase the response rate. Marketers now talk in terms of response rates from promotions, not in terms of contact numbers.

When considering tactical options it is useful to remember that marketers talk about mixes: the marketing mix, the promotional mix and so forth. This implies that each area of marketing impinges on every other area, and that decisions about (say) advertising tactics cannot be taken independently of decisions about pricing.

Having determined the details of what is to be done, the programme can be implemented. Sometimes the marketing managers will meet with resistance from colleagues from other disciplines (see Chapter 1), and sometimes the plan will need to be revised in the light of experience and later events. There will therefore need to be a degree of flexibility in the plan.

ORGANISATIONAL ALTERNATIVES

In general there are five broad ways to organise marketing tasks, as shown in Table 10.8.

An extension of the matrix organisation structure is the **organismic structure**. Unlike the traditional **mechanistic** or **bureaucratic** pyramid, there is no clear 'boss'. Each individual contributes expertise (and effort) towards achieving the **corporate objectives**. The leader for each task is determined by the project being tackled at the time. This type of structure is typical of small consultancy firms

Table 10.8 Organisational alternatives

Alternative	Description
Functional organisation	Each marketing activity has a specialist in charge of it. This structure would have an advertising manager, a **product development** manager, a market research manager and so forth.
Product organisation	Each manager is responsible for all the marketing decisions concerning a particular product. The firm may also employ specialists to advise and assist, but each product manager would have overall responsibility.
Regional organisation	This approach is usually used in international markets, but can also be used elsewhere. The regional managers are each responsible for all the marketing activities within their own geographical region.
Segmental organisation	Here each manager is responsible for a given market segment. For example, a glass manufacturer might have one manager in charge of marketing to the automotive industry, another for marketing to the building trade, another marketing to the bottling industry, and so forth. Each manager would thus be able to develop specialist knowledge of the customers' needs.
Matrix	Here there is joint decision-making between the specialist market researchers, sales managers, etc. and the product managers. No one manager is in overall control, and decisions are made by balancing each person's role and demands. This method is surprisingly effective in decision-making, since it pools the available expertise.

who may be dealing with a wide range of disparate tasks, but can be found in larger organisations or departments of larger organisations. The main advantage of the organismic structure is that it is extremely flexible, which makes it a more appropriate structure for dealing with changing environments. On the other hand, there is some evidence that organismic structures may not be effective in relationship marketing, because of the difficulties inherent in maintaining relationships when people change roles frequently (Desmond 2004).

In smaller firms there may be no specific marketing department, and of course in some firms marketing is not very high on the agenda because the firm has little control over the variables of the marketing mix. Such firms may have a marketing department, but it may be concerned only with running the occasional advertisement and organising trade fairs.

PROMOTIONAL STRATEGIES

Formulating a promotional strategy is concerned with deciding overall aims and objectives. The aims of the promotion strategy can be selected from the following:

- *Category need* is the aim of persuading consumers that the product will meet a need. This can be difficult when the product is first introduced, particularly if it is a novel product.

- *Brand awareness* is the process of fixing the brand and its characteristics in the consumer's mind. The brand must be made to stand out from the competition, and must be positioned accordingly.

- *Brand attitude* leads on from brand awareness. Here the marketer is trying to build a favourable attitude in the consumer's mind; merely being familiar with the brand is only part of the story. (See Chapter 3 for an overview of attitude.)

- *Brand purchase intention* is a positive conation on the part of the consumer. Here the marketer is suggesting that the consumer should 'get some today!'

- *Purchase facilitation* is the part of promotion geared to ensuring that the product is readily available, and the consumer knows where to go to get it.

The above five aims have been presented in sequence, but there is not always a necessity for a promotion strategy to follow exactly along this order. Sometimes the earlier stages will already have been covered by other earlier marketers. For example, when Radion washing-powder was launched in the United Kingdom the promotion strategy omitted the first stage and went straight to brand awareness. This was achieved by using Day-Glo billboard advertisements with the brand name in 1 metre high letters. Having established the brand name, the company could then go on to develop positive brand attitudes, but there was little need to tell the consumers where to buy the product, since they would naturally expect to buy washing powder in a supermarket.

Regarding distribution channels, marketers need to decide whether to adopt a push strategy or a pull strategy, or rather to decide what the balance will be between the two.

Push strategies

Push strategies involve promoting the product only to the next link down the distribution channel: this means selling hard to the wholesalers, and letting the wholesalers in their turn sell hard to the retailers, who then push the product out to the consumers. This method has the advantage of being cheap and relatively straightforward, and could be justified on the grounds that each member of the distribution chain is most familiar with the ways of marketing to the next member down the chain. On the other hand, it really cannot be said to be consumer-orientated.

Pull strategies

Pull strategies involve focusing effort on the consumer, on the basis that an increase in consumer demand for the product will pull it through the distribution chain.

A push strategy emphasises personal selling and advertising aimed at the members of the distribution channel. A pull strategy is aimed at the final consumers and emphasises consumer advertising and strong merchandising. Most launch strategies would involve elements of both push and pull. For example, retailers tend to be positive about TV advertising and will stock a product if they know there is to be a TV campaign aimed at consumers. The retailers believe that the campaign will stimulate demand for the product, thus generating sales; it is equally possible that the act of displaying the product prominently is what generates the sales, however.

If the distribution channels are properly managed and are co-operating well (see Chapter 8), a pull strategy is indicated; in other words, greater effort can be devoted to stimulating consumer demand, since the other channel members are likely to co-operate anyway. If the channel is uncoordinated or is dominated by the wholesalers or retailers, a push strategy is more likely to work, since the channel members will need to be convinced to carry the product line. Again, there will always be elements of both push and pull in any promotional strategy, because channel members and consumers both need to move up the hierarchy of communications effects.

From a tactical viewpoint, the promotional mix should be carefully monitored so as to ensure that the right things happen at the right times.

TACTICAL APPROACHES

In the real world, marketers will adopt a combination strategy for setting budgets, using several of the methods outlined in Table 10.9. Even an objective and task approach might begin by looking at what the competition is spending (comparative parity approach), if only to determine what the likely spend would have to be to overcome clutter. Likewise, a marketer may be part-way through a campaign and be told by the finance department that no more money is available (or perhaps be told that more than anticipated is available) and will switch to an all-you-can-afford policy.

Setting the right objectives is an essential part of any planning. Without objectives, the organisation as a whole has no clear direction to follow: objectives are what hold organisation members together in achieving success. It is important to distinguish between aims and objectives. An aim is a general statement about

Table 10.9 Advertising planning functions

Planning function	Explanation
Setting the budget	This can be done in four ways. First, the objective and task approach involves setting *objectives*, and setting aside an appropriate amount of money to achieve the objectives. This method is difficult to apply because it is difficult to assess how much will be needed to achieve the objective. Second, the *percentage of sales* approach sets the budget as a percentage of sales. This is based on the false idea that sales create advertising, and usually results in less being spent on advertising when sales fall, thus reducing sales further. Third, *the competition matching approach* means that the company spends the same as the competition: this means that the firm is allowing its budgets to be set by its enemies. Fourth, there is the *arbitrary* approach whereby a senior executive (usually a finance director) simply says how much can be allowed within the firm's overall budgets. This does not take account of how the firm is to achieve the objectives.
Identifying the target	Deciding to whom the ad is to be directed. It is better to approach a small segment of the market than try to use a 'scattergun' approach on everybody (see Chapter 4).
Media planning	This is about deciding where the ads are going to appear. There are two main decision areas: the reach (number of potential consumers the ad reaches) and the frequency (number of times each consumer sees the ad) of coverage. The decision is frequently made on the basis of cost per thousand readers/viewers, but this does not take into account the impact of the ad or the degree to which people are able to skip past it.
Defining the objectives	Deciding what the ads are supposed to achieve. It is essential here to give the advertising agency a clear brief: 'We want to raise awareness of the product to 50% of the adult population' is a measurable objective. 'We want to increase sales as much as possible' is not measurable, so there is no way of knowing whether it has been achieved.
Creating the advertising platform	Deciding the basic issues and selling points that the advertising must convey. This clarifies the advertising agency briefing, or at least clarifies the thinking on producing the advertising materials.

the type of things we want to do as an organisation, for example 'we aim to be the best in our field'. This is not an objective, because there is no way of measuring whether we have achieved it – if only for the reason that we have not specified a timescale. An objective, on the other hand, is a statement of something which we can measure, for example 'We intend to be the largest supplier in our industry within five years.'

Objectives need to be SMART, in other words:

- *Specific*. The objective needs to be stated precisely, with a clear boundary. Vague statements such as 'being the best' are fine as aims, but since they are likely to be defined differently by different people they are open to misinterpretation.

- *Measurable*. Planners need to have some way of knowing whether the objective has been reached, and if the objective has been missed they need to be able to say by how wide a margin. Many objectives will be expressed numerically (for example, 'we want this campaign to increase brand recognition to 40% of the population') which is helpful in deciding how far the campaign met, or exceeded, expectations.

- *Achievable*. If the objective is unrealistic, staff will not 'buy into' it and will not try to achieve it. This is especially important when setting objectives for sales people, since they can easily decide not to do more than the minimum needed to maintain their standard of living.

- *Realistic*. Planners need to take account of the marketing environment, particularly competitive responses. For the same reasons that an objective must be achievable, planners need to ensure that what they are proposing is realistic within the constraints of the business environment.

- *Time-bound*. Without a timescale, there is no way of measuring whether an objective has been missed. Rather like making a decision to lose weight or give up smoking, unless we say by what date we will do these things the resolution is meaningless. Obviously if the objective is achieved the timescale is irrelevant, but business objectives should always include a timetable.

DECIDING THE TYPE OF CAMPAIGN

Whether this stage comes before or after the budget-setting will depend on whether the marketer is adopting an objective-and-task policy or not. In most cases, though, planning the campaign in detail will come after the budget is known and agreed upon; few companies give the marketing department a blank cheque for promotional spending. Campaigns can be carried out to achieve many objectives; a new product launch was used in the example given earlier, but in most cases the products will be in the maturity phase of the product life cycle (see Chapter 6).

■ Image-building campaigns are designed to convey a particular status for the product, and to emphasise ways in which it will complement the user's lifestyle. For example, Volvo promotes the reliability and engineering of the car rather than its appearance, thus appealing to motorists who prefer a solid, reliable vehicle.

■ **Product differentiation** campaigns aim to show how the product is better than the competitors' products by emphasising its differences. In most cases this will take the form of the **unique selling proposition** or **USP** for short. The USP is the one feature of the product that most stands out as different from the competition, and is usually a feature that conveys unique benefits to the consumer. Mature products often differ only very slightly from each other in terms of performance, so a USP can sometimes be identified in terms of the packaging or distribution. Of course, the USP will only be effective if it means something to the consumer – otherwise it will not affect the buying decision.

■ Positioning strategies are concerned with the way consumers perceive the product compared with their perceptions of the competition. For example, a retailer may claim 'lower prices than other shops' or a restaurant may want to appear more up-market than its rivals.

■ **Direct response** campaigns seek an immediate response from the consumer in terms of purchase, or request for a brochure, or a visit to the shop. For example, a retailer might run a newspaper campaign that includes a money-off coupon. The aim of the campaign is to encourage consumers to visit the shop to redeem the coupon, and the retailer can easily judge the effectiveness of the campaign by the number of coupons redeemed.

PUTTING IT ALL TOGETHER

To make the best use of the promotional effort it is worth spending time planning how it will all fit together. The recipe will need to be adapted according to what the product is and how the company wants to promote it.

The elements marketers need to consider are:

■ size of budget;

■ size of individual order value;

■ number of potential buyers;

■ geodemographical spread of potential buyers;

■ category of product (convenience, unsought, shopping, etc.);

■ what it is the firm is trying to achieve.

It is impossible to achieve everything all at once, so marketers plan the campaign as an integrated package. For example, Table 10.10 shows a product launch strategy designed to maximise penetration of a new food product.

Table 10.10 Example of a promotional calendar

Month	Activity
May	Press release to the trade press; retailers.
June	Sales campaign to persuade retailers to stock the product. Aim is to get 50% of retailers stocking the product, so the salesforce tells them a big ad spend is forthcoming. Run teaser campaign.
July/August	Denouement of teaser campaign. Promotion staff appear in major retail outlets offering free samples. Press releases to cookery writers, possibly reports on daytime TV if product is newsworthy enough.
September/October	Once 50% retailer penetration has occurred, start TV campaign. Brief ad agency to obtain maximum awareness.
January/February	Begin new campaign to *inform*. Possibly use money-off sales promotion, linked promotions, etc. Review progress so far using market research. Possibly some press releases, if the product is innovative enough, to the business/cookery press.

Carrying out this kind of planning needs the co-operation of all the members of the marketing team. It is no use having the PR people doing one thing, and the salesforce doing something else that negates their efforts. If the campaign is to be effective it is important that all the team members are involved in the discussions so that unrealistic demands are not made of the team members.

Although this section has used promotional campaigns as an example, the same principles apply to other marketing mix elements. New product development needs to have objectives in place, as does developing a new distribution network.

MONITORING AND EVALUATING MARKETING PERFORMANCE

Once the plan has been implemented managers need to make sure it works in practice. Feedback is essential for monitoring performance, and (in an ideal world) no marketing activity would be undertaken without having a monitoring and evaluation system in place beforehand.

There are two basic groups of approaches for performance analysis:

- **sales analysis**, which looks at the income generated by the firm's activities; and
- **marketing cost analysis**, which looks at the costs of generating the income.

Table 10.11 illustrates some sales analysis measures.

Table 10.11 Methods of sales analysis

Analysis method	Explanation
Comparison with forecast sales	The firm compares the actual sales achieved against what was forecast for the period.
Comparison with competitor's sales	Provided the information is available, the firm can estimate the extent to which marketing activities have made inroads into the competitor's business. The problem here is proving that the difference has been caused by the high quality of the firm's marketing activities, rather than by the ineptness of the competitor.
Comparison with industry sales	Examination of the firm's performance in terms of market share. This is commonly used in industries where a relatively small number of firms control the market: for example, the car industry.
Cash volume sales analysis	Comparison of sales in terms of cash generated. This has the advantage that currency is common to both sales and costs; it has the disadvantage that price rises may cause the company to think it has done better than it has.
Unit sales analysis	Comparison of sales in terms of the number of units sold, or sometimes the number of sales transactions. This is a useful measure of salesforce activities, but should not be taken in isolation; sometimes the figures can be distorted by increased sales of cheaper models.
Sales by geographic unit	Sales are broken down regionally so that the firm can tell whether one or two regions are accounting for most of the sales, and whether some less-productive regions are not worth what they cost to service.
Sales by product group or brand	This is particularly important for judging the product portfolio (see the BCG matrix in Chapter 6). This serves two purposes: it is possible to identify products that should be dropped from the range, and it is also possible to identify products that are moving into the decline phase of the product life cycle and should therefore be revived.
Sales by type of customer	Can reveal, for example, that most effort is being expended on a group of customers who make relatively few purchases. May reveal that the firm's customers tend to be ageing, and may therefore be a declining group in years to come.

Considerable amounts of information will be needed if the firm is to make effective use of sales analysis to monitor activities. This may involve the firm in substantial market research expenditure, since market research is the cornerstone of monitoring and evaluation (see Chapter 5).

Evaluating customers is a particularly important exercise in a relationship marketing scenario. Estimating customer equity (the value of the customers) can be complex: it is a combination of deciding on the profitability of the customer (i.e. a comparison between cost of serving the customer and revenue which will result), lifetime value of the customer (how long the relationship is likely to last, coupled with frequency and quantity of purchase), and likely loyalty of the customer (if the customer is likely to defect to a competitor the customer's value will be low). Once calculated, however, customer equity can be used to focus marketing efforts on the most valuable customers (Rust *et al.* 2004).

The other part of the picture is to examine the cost of achieving the objectives which have been specified. *Marketing cost analysis* is a set of techniques for breaking down the costs of the firm's activities and associating them with specific marketing objectives. Costs can be broken down (broadly) into:

- **direct costs** such as salespersons' salaries which can be directly attributable to a given activity;
- **traceable common costs** such as costs of advertising that can be traced back to specific products; and
- **non-traceable common costs** such as the cost of PR or corporate advertising that cannot be allocated to any particular product range or brand.

The main problem with marketing cost analysis lies in organising the firm's accounting systems in such a way as to permit analysis. For example, payroll records may not be easily broken down by job function: it may be difficult to sort out which of the administration staff spend most of their time on marketing-related tasks, or even to find out what the pay bill is for the salesforce. Likewise, defining which jobs constitute marketing jobs and which do not also presents problems. Clearly the cost of servicing customers in remote areas is a marketing cost – so should transportation costs be taken into account as well as the salesforce mileage costs? Also, if a given product is not performing well, should we be looking at the costs of production?

For the dyed-in-the-wool customer-orientated firm these answers are obvious, since all the activities of the firm are regarded as marketing activities. In other firms, not all managers agree with the basic premises on which marketing is based. At the very least, many people find it difficult to translate the theory into practice and to gear the organisation's activities towards a consumer orientation, as seen in Chapter 1.

FEEDBACK SYSTEMS

When a discrepancy appears between the expected performance and the actual performance, the marketing manager will need to take action. This will usually take the following sequence:

1 *Determine the reason for the discrepancy.* Was the original plan reasonable? Have the firm's competitors seized the initiative in some way, so that the situation has changed? Is someone at fault?

2 *Feed these findings back to the staff concerned.* This can be in the form of a meeting to discuss the situation, or in the form of memos and reports.

3 *Develop a plan for correcting the situation*. This will probably involve the co-operation of all the staff concerned.

Feedback should be both frequent and concise, and any criticisms should be constructive; managers should never (for example) go to a sales meeting and offer only criticisms since this sends the salesforce out with negative feelings about themselves and the company.

Marketing strategy and planning is much like any other planning exercise: it relies on good information, a clear idea of where the organisation is going, and regular examination of both outcomes and methods to ensure that the plan is still on target.

Case study 10
Microemissive Displays

The communications revolution has made tremendous changes in the way we talk to each other and entertain ourselves. It has relied almost entirely on the development of miniature electronic devices – silicon chips being the most obvious one – and on the use of miniature display screens, which are rapidly replacing cathode-ray tubes as the main means of displaying visual information.

So far, however, even the smallest screens have been too big to mount easily on a headset, providing a head-mounted display. This could provide a personal TV set, a miniature screen for a portable computer, or an improvement on normal spectacles – not to mention the military possibilities. MED's screens are comparable in size to the pupil of the eye, and use extremely low levels of power – useful for devices which are battery-powered such as cameras and portable computers.

At the sharp end of this development is the Edinburgh-based company, Microemissive Displays (MED), founded in 1999 by Dr Ian Underwood of the University of Edinburgh and Dr Jeff Wright of Napier University. As scientists, they recognised the need to bring in business acumen if the new venture was to be a success, and they did this by raising three rounds of venture capital between 2000 and 2004, at which point the company launched on the Alternative Investment Market in London (a scaled-down stock market for smaller firms).

In 2006, the company appointed Paul van Eynde to the Board of Directors as sales and marketing director. Paul came to the company from Vativ Technologies Inc., another innovative small firm in a high-tech field. MED is unusual in having a marketing person on the Board – relatively few firms do this. Sales are handled by agents in the UK, Hong Kong, Singapore and Taiwan: other regions are covered directly from MED's head office in Edinburgh. Manufacture of product is carried out in Dresden, Germany: the company obtained a generous grant (£2.7 million) from the State of Saxony in exchange for setting up the plant in this economically depressed area.

The problem at present is that the sales are not exactly flooding in. Despite having a superb product, with a wide range of applications, the company only turned over £65 000 in 2007, making a loss of over £6 million. Naturally, a start-up of this type will make large losses at first – after all, the product is so innovative that, at present, there are few applications since the rest of the devices which will use the displays have not yet been developed. Once a major manufacturer decides to develop a personal TV, MED will be ready to leap in with the display units. Meanwhile, the company is faced with a major marketing planning problem.

Questions

1 How might Paul van Eynde plan for stimulating the market?
2 What problems does MED have in terms of sales forecasting?
3 What problems might arise from using agents?
4 Why is MED apparently focusing on the Far East?
5 What type of strategic position is MED adopting?

SUMMARY

This chapter has been about the ways in which marketers assemble the elements of marketing into a coherent whole.

Planning is not necessarily a tidy process; there will be many iterations of the plan, and much discussion. The difficulties of foretelling the future, and of anticipating competitor response, will always militate against a perfect planning scheme, yet the evidence is that companies that plan effectively tend to be more successful than those that do not: if we don't know where we are going, then any road will do to take us there.

Here are the key points from the chapter:

- Marketing is harder than not marketing, but it works better.
- The marketing audit will tell us where we are now; we need to know this to plan our route to where we want to be.
- Objectives are the route map to where we are going as a company, and the need to be specific, measurable, achievable, realistic and time-bound.
- When considering tactics, be creative. Success in marketing lies in doing something the competitors are not doing.
- Feedback is essential if the plan is to remain on course.
- Plans need to be sufficiently flexible to allow for the unexpected.

CHAPTER QUESTIONS

1 What is the difference between strategy and tactics?
2 Who should be consulted when setting objectives?
3 Describe three main methods of sales analysis.
4 What is the purpose of integrating marketing tactics?
5 What organisational structures might a multinational computer manufacturer (e.g. IBM) use?
6 Compare Dunning's eclectic theory of internationalisation with the stages of development approach.

Further reading

Michael Porter's Competitive Advantage (New York, The Free Press, 1985) is a somewhat elderly, but very readable, text on competition and competitive strategy.

Marketing Management, Analysis, Planning and Control, **10th edn, by Philip Kotler** (Upper Saddle River, NJ, Prentice Hall, 1999). The original American marketing guru, Kotler still provides a strong framework for management decision-making.

Marketing Plans **by Malcolm McDonald** (Oxford, Heinemann, 1989) gives a practically orientated approach to planning.

Exploring Corporate Strategy **by Gerry Johnson and Kevan Scholes**, 5th edn (Harlow, Prentice Hall Europe, 1999) gives a readable overview of corporate planning.

References

Band, William A.: 'A marketing audit provides an opportunity for improvement', *Sales and Marketing Management in Canada* (March 1984), pp. 24–6.

Chetty, C. and Campbell-Hunt, Colin: 'A strategic approach to internationalization: a traditional vs. a "born-global" approach', *Journal of International Marketing*, **12** (1) (2004), pp. 57–81.

Desmond, John: 'An evaluation of organizational control strategies for relationship marketing', *Journal of Marketing*, **20** (1) (February 2004), pp. 209–37.

Dunning, John H.: *The Globalisation of Business* (London, Routledge, 1993).

Kotler, Philip: *Marketing Management*, 11th edn (Pearson Education Inc., Upper Saddle River, NJ, 2003).

Porter, M.E.: *Competitive Strategy: Techniques for Analysing Industries and Competitors* (New York, Free Press, 1980).

Rust, Roland T., Lemon, Katherine N. and Zeithaml, Valeria A.: 'Return on marketing: using customer equity to focus marketing strength', *Journal of Marketing*, **68** (1) (January 2004), pp. 109–17.

Weinberg, R.: 'Developing marketing strategies for short term profits and long term growth', paper presented at the Advanced Management Research Inc. Seminar, New York (1969).

IKEA

IKEA is a huge, and hugely successful, furniture retailer. The stores are huge, and are incredibly popular: some stores in the UK attract more visitors than any tourist attraction or theme park in the country. The company's innovative designs are built around low prices – IKEA say they design the price tag first.

Scandinavian design is world famous, and the furniture is designed to be easy to transport and assemble. The store image

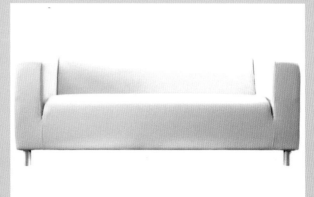

is much the same throughout the world, but of course the cultures of the host countries are very different, and like most service industries the company's staff are at the heart of the shopping experience for customers. Transferring the culture across borders and maintaining a level of consistency between stores is in part a matter of transferring Swedish culture across borders. The company's founder, Ingvar Kamprad, is still in evidence in the company even though he is now officially retired. His ideas about how people can and should work together are very much in evidence. The company believes that people want to share the IKEA culture, in which staff are referred to as co-workers and are empowered to provide solutions for customers who have problems.

IKEA is almost surprised by its own success. Suddenly becoming a world citizen, rather than just a Swedish furniture shop, is something the company is still coming to terms with.

Josephine Rydberg-Dumont, President, IKEA Sweden

Watch the video clip, then try to answer the following questions. The answers are on the companion website.

Questions

1 What is the importance of staff empowerment for IKEA?

2 What problems might arise from running a global service company for consumers?

3 How does IKEA add value to the basic physical product?

11 Services marketing

Objectives

After reading this chapter you should be able to:

- explain the role of people, process and physical evidence in service provision;
- describe how empowerment of employees can enhance service provison and improve complaint handling;
- explain the role of risk on consumer decision-making about services;
- describe ways of improving customer loyalty in services;
- appreciate the importance of services in the economy;
- show how to motivate employees in service industries;
- describe the consumer decision process as it applies to service products.

INTRODUCTION

In recent years services markets have reached greater prominence in industrialised countries. In part this is due to increased automation, which has meant that physical products are cheaper and easier to produce with fewer employees, and in part it is due to the fact that there is a limit to how many physical products an individual might want to own. Service industries employ a far higher proportion of the workforce than does manufacturing, and services markets account for a far higher proportion of GDP than manufacturing.

SERVICES *v* PHYSICAL PRODUCTS

For many marketers, the difference between services marketing and the marketing of physical goods is negligible. This is for the following reasons:

- The marketer's definition of a product as being a bundle of benefits. An individual seeking to be cheered up may achieve this by going to a good movie (a service) or by buying a new shirt (a physical product). The benefit is basically the same.

- Difficulties of definition. Most physical goods contain a service aspect, and most services contain a physical product. In other words, most products lie somewhere along a continuum between purely service and purely physical products.

- Consumer orientation means that we should be looking at what the consumer thinks, needs and wants, not at defining our product in terms of its characteristics.

Having said that, there are clearly products where the service element is the major part of the cost of the product: for example, a restaurant meal. Here the cost of the raw materials (the ingredients of the food served) is only a tiny part of the overall cost of the meal. A gourmet dinner costing a week's wages may have been made from ingredients costing a tenth of the final bill; the diner is paying for the skill of the chef, the time and efforts of the waiters, and the pleasure of dining in luxurious surroundings (not to mention not having to do the washing-up). The main differences between service products and physical goods are shown in Table 11.1.

Successful brands in service industries have the following characteristics (DeChernatony and Cottam 2006):

- the companies concerned have a holistic, consistent and integrated approach to branding;

- they focus on excellent customer service;

- they have an ethos which challenges the norm, in other words they do things differently from competitors;

- they are responsive to change;

- they have a high level of brand literacy, in other words they understand how branding works;

- there is synergy between the brand and the corporate culture.

Brand strength in service industries is linked to four factors: first, investment in marketing communications; second, contributing to the wider community; third, improving internal communication; and fourth, improving service quality (Gray 2006). These factors affect staff working in the industries as much as they affect consumers and other stakeholders.

Table 11.1	Factors distinguishing services from physical products
Factor	**Explanation and examples**
Services are intangible	An insurance policy is more than the paper it is written on; the key benefit (peace of mind) cannot be touched.
Production and consumption often occur at virtually the same time	A stage play is acted out at the same time as the consumer enjoys the performance.
Services are perishable	An airline seat is extremely perishable; once the aeroplane takes off, the seat cannot be sold. Services cannot be produced in advance and stockpiled.
Services cannot be tried out before buying	It is not usually possible to try out a haircut before agreeing to have it done, nor will most restaurants allow customers to eat the meal before deciding whether to order it.
Services are variable, even from the same supplier	Sometimes the chef has a bad day, or the waiter is in a bad mood; on the other hand, sometimes the hairdresser has a flash of inspiration that transforms the client's appearance.

SERVICES AND CONSUMER BEHAVIOUR

From the consumer's viewpoint, the risk attached to buying a service will inevitably be higher than is the risk of buying a physical product. Physical products are easily returned if they fail to satisfy; it is impossible to return a poor haircut, and unless the standard is very poor, it may even be difficult to avoid paying for it. Even a minor defect in a personal stereo can justify returning the item; an uncomfortable tram ride with a rude conductor will not result in a refund of the fare.

The result of this is that consumers are likely to spend more time on information-gathering, and will rely more heavily on word-of-mouth recommendations than they would when buying a physical product. For professional services, the consumer is likely to examine the credentials and experience of the service provider. For example, a consumer looking for a doctor may want to know what experience and qualifications the doctor has to treat a particular complaint; few car buyers would be interested in the qualifications and experience of Ford's chief design engineer.

Service purchasing follows a slightly different sequence from purchase of a physical good, as shown in Figure 11.1. For a physical product, the experience of using the product (and consequently its evaluation) mainly occurs after purchase, in some cases over a period of years after purchase. For a service product,

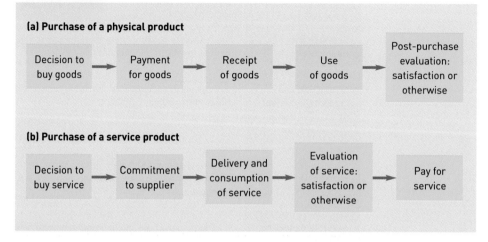

Figure 11.1 Service purchasing sequence compared with physical product purchasing sequence

(a) Purchase of a physical product

Decision to buy goods → Payment for goods → Receipt of goods → Use of goods → Post-purchase evaluation: satisfaction or otherwise

(b) Purchase of a service product

Decision to buy service → Commitment to supplier → Delivery and consumption of service → Evaluation of service: satisfaction or otherwise → Pay for service

the consumption experience happens immediately, as does virtually all of the evaluation – one decides whether a meal was enjoyable while enjoying it, and one either enjoys a flight or one does not. Some post-purchase evaluation may happen through discussion or second thoughts for products such as hairstyles, but in the main services are evaluated immediately. Equally, some services are paid for in advance (transport, for example) but most are paid for after evaluation. This creates a risk for the supplier.

Most of the risk attached to buying a physical product is limited to the purchase price (though no doubt there will be exceptions to this general rule). Services carry additional risks.

■ *Consequential losses* arise when a service goes wrong and causes a loss to the customer. For example, a poorly handled legal case could result in the loss of thousands of pounds, or even loss of liberty in a criminal case. Service providers usually are careful to explain the risks beforehand, use disclaimers in contracts, and carry professional liability insurance. Consumers can sue for consequential losses.

■ *Purchase price risk* is the possible loss of the purchase price when the consumer buys a service that does not work. The usual consumer response is to refuse to pay for the service, so it is advisable for the supplier to check during the service process that everything is satisfactory. This is why waiters will check that the food is satisfactory during a meal out, and why service stations call customers when they find something serious is wrong with the car. Checking during the service provision not only makes it easier to correct problems early, it also makes it harder for customers to claim that the service went wrong in order to avoid paying.

■ *Misunderstanding* is common in service provision because of inability to try out services (trialability). Particularly in professional services the provider may feel that the customer would not understand the finer details of what is being done, and may therefore not bother to explain properly. This can easily result in post-purchase dissonance and refusal to pay.

Because consumers are buying a promise, they are more likely to use indirect measures of quality such as price. Diners tend to assume that more expensive restaurants will provide better food and/or service; that expensive hairdressers will provide better hairdos; and that expensive lawyers are more likely to win cases. Long-established firms tend to be trusted more than new firms, the assumption being that they must be good to have survived (Desai *et al.* 2008).

Having made a purchasing decision, the consumer is more likely to become *involved* with the service provider. Consumers therefore tend to have favourite restaurants, hairdressers and family solicitors with whom the relationship might continue for a lifetime. Customers are reluctant to switch bank accounts, even when problems have become apparent; even though customers will readily change brands of canned tuna in order to save a few pence, they will still buy the tuna from the same supermarket as usual. This is because the customer knows where everything is kept in the supermarket, understands the store's policy on returned goods, knows which credit cards are acceptable, and perhaps even knows some of the staff on the tills.

Obviously things can go wrong, and people will complain. Complaints about physical products are usually resolved fairly easily: a simple replacement of the faulty product will usually be sufficient, but it is always better to go a step further and provide some further recompense if possible. Services often require a more complex and extended complaint handling procedure.

Services fall into the following categories, for the purpose of correcting complaints:

- Services where it is appropriate to offer a repeat service or a voucher. Examples are dry cleaners, domestic appliance repairers and takeaway food outlets.
- Services where giving the money back will usually be sufficient. Examples are retail shops, cinemas and theatres and video rental companies.
- Services where consequential losses may have to be compensated for. Examples are medical services, solicitors and hairdressers.

The above categories are not necessarily comprehensive or exclusive; sometimes it may be necessary to give back the consumer's money and also make some other redress.

People who complain have the following expectations of service employees (Gruber *et al.* 2006):

1 Positive non-verbal signals.

2 Sufficient product and process knowledge to handle the complaint.

3 Sufficient authority to resolve the issue (see the section on empowerment below).

4 That the employee should try hard to resolve the problem.

5 For the employee to take the complaint seriously.

PROVIDING SERVICES

In services markets there is more emphasis on Booms and Bitner's additional three Ps: people, process and physical evidence (see Chapter 1) (Booms and Bitner 1981). Because most services involve direct contact between the producer and the consumer, the attitude and behaviour of the *people* involved are an integral part of the product: a hairdresser's personality affects trade in a way that the personality of a production-line worker does not.

Since the consumer is usually present during all or part of the *process* of providing the service, process becomes as important as outcomes in a service market. United Airlines' streamlined check-in procedures at airports give the company a distinct edge over its competition, and makes the airline more pleasurable to fly with.

Physical evidence gives the consumer something to refer to and to show other people if necessary. Since service products are usually intangible, the consumer of (say) an insurance policy will need some written evidence of its existence in order to feel confident in the product. Physical evidence may not be as important as people: a study of Irish theme pubs showed that patrons and employees are at least as important as the rather expensive and contrived décor of the pub (Munoz *et al.* 2006).

In many ways services can be marketed in similar ways to physical products. In most cases there is no clear demarcation between physical products and services, so the techniques for marketing them will not differ greatly. However, the additional three Ps do require some changes in the way the firm operates, as the following sections show.

People

Employees can be categorised into four groups in terms of their contact with customers (Judd 1987).

1 **Contactors**. These people have frequent and regular contact with customers. Usually they are directly involved with marketing, as salespeople, telesales operators and customer service people. They may need to be trained in customer relations because they are dealing with customers on a day-to-day basis, and they should be recruited on the basis of their social skills as well as on their business skills. They should also be the kind of people who enjoy dealing with customers – not always an easy task – and they should be genuinely interested in customers, not just trained to smile at everyone. Research

shows that smiling has little or no effect on customers, probably because they believe the smiles to be false (Hennig-Thurau *et al.* 2006).

2 **Modifiers**. These people have no direct marketing role, but they deal with customers regularly. They are receptionists, truck drivers, switchboard operators, and (sometimes) warehouse personnel or progress chasers. Modifiers need good social skills, and training and monitoring of performance regarding their customer contacts: they should be given a clear view of the organisation's marketing strategy, and be aware of their own role within it.

3 **Influencers**. These people deal with some elements of the marketing mix, but have little or no contact with customers. In a service firm, influencers are in a distinct minority, whereas in a physical product company they may well represent the majority of staff. An example of an influencer in a service company might be a solicitor's clerk, who rarely meets clients but whose effectiveness at the task will affect the service level the customer receives. Many back-room staff in financial services also fall into this category.

4 **Isolateds**. Isolateds have no customer contact and very little to do with conventional marketing functions. Again, these people are rare in service industries, although in large financial services companies there may well be a number of people (such as canteen staff, cleaners, and so forth) who fall into this category. Although they need to be alerted to the idea that their efforts are important in supporting the other staff, they do not need any specific training for dealing with customers. In essence, their role is to create the right conditions under which the customer-focused staff can do their jobs.

Figure 11.2 displays this graphically.

Of course, everyone goes home at the end of the day and talks to family and friends about the firm, and as such everyone in the firm bears some

Figure 11.2 **Employees and customers**

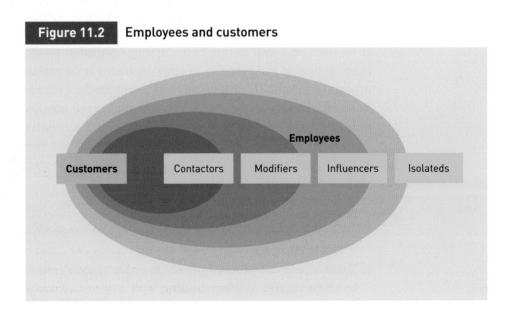

responsibility for the corporate image and for marketing (see Chapter 9). Creating shared values and especially creating a feeling of corporate justice (that one is working for a fair-minded company) affects how employees deal with customers: the brand image of the firm also affects employees' desire to work for the company (Knox and Freeman 2006). This in turn affects customers' perception of the organisation (Maxham and Netemeyer 2003).

Critical thinking

So if we're all marketers now, where does that leave the marketing department? Are they out of work all of a sudden? The rest of the organisation don't expect the marketers to sweep the floor, make the product and do the accounts – so surely marketers can't expect everybody else to do the marketers' work for them.

Or maybe that's what marketers are for. To create the right conditions for people to say good things about the company – and thus improve the interface between the company and its customers.

In practice, no matter how hard companies try to deliver the perfect service, the natural variability of employee performance will mean that there will always be some occasions on which the service falls below standard. This means that firms need to concentrate on recovering from service mistakes when they do occur (Rasmusson 1997). The first step in this is to empower front-line employees.

Empowerment means giving employees the authority to sort out problems without having to refer to management. This implies making employees responsible for their own actions, and more importantly makes them responsible for controlling the service delivery. The purpose of empowering employees is to ensure that problems are dealt with as they arise, without the customer (who is already irritated) having to wait for a decision from senior management. Because service provision is carried out largely by people who are dealing with customers on a one-to-one basis, managers cannot be expected to supervise every aspect of the process, so empowerment is important if the system is to operate smoothly. This differs from physical product manufacture: the efforts of a factory worker can be checked by examining the tangible output (a physical product), but because production and consumption of services take place at the same time, it is often not possible to check outputs and therefore the onus must be on the staff member to act professionally, and on the employer to provide the staff member with the authority to do so.

The objectives of staff empowerment are:

■ To make the organisation more responsive to problems, and deal with them faster.

■ To remove levels of management in order to save costs. Managers can spend less time on fire-fighting (dealing with day-to-day problems) and more time on supporting and coaching staff (providing the right conditions for staff to work effectively).

■ To create employee networks. If employees work more closely together and develop social links, this will encourage collaboration, teamwork and horizontal communication. This tends to improve employee motivation.

In most cases, staff prefer to be empowered since otherwise they can feel like unimportant functionaries in a large corporate machine. Being part of a small, empowered team is a strong motivator because it makes the workplace more manageable, putting everything on a human scale. Empowerment is not always a good thing, however, especially if it is poorly-managed. The following problems can arise:

■ Some people are risk-averse, and would prefer not to accept the responsibility that empowerment implies. Sometimes managers can give extra support to these staff, and may be able to offer additional motivation.

■ A culture of blame can develop in which staff are blamed for wrong decisions. If staff make mistakes, this should be seen as a learning experience, not an occasion for punishment: the occasional wrong decision is much better than a situation where staff are afraid to make any decisions at all.

■ Empowerment should not be taken back as soon as any important or interesting decisions have to be made. This is extremely demotivating for staff.

■ Employees can become afraid of making wrong decisions, because the boundaries are not clear. Clear guidelines need to be given, but without having too many rigid rules: it is impossible to anticipate every possible situation, so fixed regulations are counter-productive.

■ Communication can sometimes be poor within the group. Whether the communication fails between management and employees, or between employees, failure to communicate means that customer problems can be dealt with in wildly different ways, leading to further customer dissatisfaction.

Murphy (2001) warns that empowerment can become a negative factor for some employees, who feel that management is abdicating responsibility and expecting employees to carry out extra tasks for which they are not being paid. Employees who become alienated (for whatever reason) may act in ways which are detrimental to the firm or to customer relations. For example, an alienated employee might neglect a customer who is regarded as a nuisance, or be over-generous to a favourite customer. Figure 11.3 shows some of the trade-offs in staff empowerment.

Successful empowerment of staff can be achieved by following these policies:

■ Empowerment needs to be kept in mind when selecting, training, motivating and coaching employees.

■ Employees need to be given clear guidelines without being straitjacketed by rules which cannot, in any case, be designed to cover every eventuality.

Figure 11.3 Trade-offs in staff empowerment

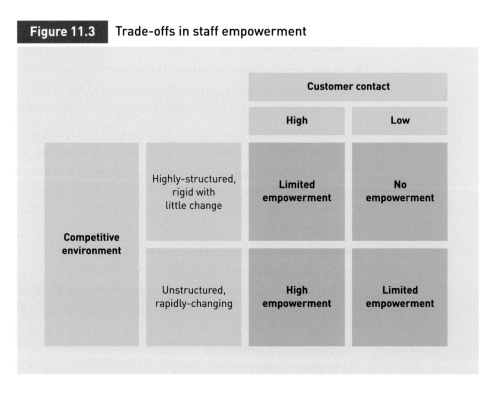

- A team approach needs to be cultivated, since support of other team members offers reassurance. Often, an empowered employee will need to ask for a second opinion on a course of action – this is likely to be much more easily available from a colleague than from management.

- Employees should be rewarded appropriately for the extra responsibility empowerment brings.

- There should not be a culture of blame. Mistakes are an opportunity to learn.

- Power is not being devolved from management to employees – rather, employees are being asked to use their initiative.

Team building is an important management role, whether in service industries or not. Effort on the part of employees is driven by their personal needs, not the needs of the organisation – the need for personal development, the need to belong to a group, the need for promotion, and so forth (Cummings 1981). Successful teams should be allowed to develop shared objectives, preferably agreed within the group rather than imposed by management. Belbin (1981) suggests that teams should be allowed to perform the following tasks between them:

- create useful ideas;

- analyse problems effectively;

- get things done;

- communicate effectively;

- have leadership qualities;

- evaluate problems and options logically;.

- handle technical aspects of the job;

- control their work;

- report back effectively either verbally or in writing.

Handy (1989) further suggested that leaders (managers) should be able to shape and share a vision which gives point to the work of others. This may be a difficult ideal to live up to.

Because people are an expensive part of any business, and even more so in the case of services, in recent years many service companies have tried to reduce the input of people, particularly for routine tasks which can be handled by computer, for example booking hotel rooms. There is evidence that, although personal service in hotels is still important for assessment of satisfaction, self-service technology for many hotel services may actually help customers in establishing relationships with hotels (Beatson *et al.* 2006).

In international service markets, cultural differences are often more apparent because of the 'people' element. For example, in fast food outlets the quality of the food affects buying intentions in Australia, China, Germany, Morocco and the United States, but not in the Netherlands and Sweden, where the surroundings are more important (Harris 1996).

Process

A process is a series of actions taken in order to convert inputs to something of greater value (Finlay 2000). In services, the process by which the product is developed and delivered should always add greater value, otherwise it is neither efficient nor effective. For example, a chef might take flour, eggs, apples, butter and so forth and create an apple pie, thus adding to the value of the ingredients. A master chef could take the same ingredients and create a work of art: a bad chef might take the same ingredients, which are already valuable, and end up with an inedible mess.

Every process combines the following basic resources:

- *Basic assets.* These include plant and equipment, cash in hand, work in progress, building, fixtures and fittings and so forth (the tangible assets of the firm). Intangible assets include goodwill (which is an accountancy term for most intangible assets), and the reputation of the company and its brands.

- *Explicit knowledge.* This is knowledge which can be recorded, either in writing or otherwise. It includes intellectual property such as patents, market research information, customer databases, and so forth.

- *Tacit knowledge.* This is knowledge which employees have in their heads, rather than written down. In service industries, this would include specific training (such as being a qualified hairdresser or chef) and of course experience built up over a number of years. In some cases, this tacit knowledge makes a key employee difficult to replace: a lawyer specialising in Lithuanian business law, for example, might be virtually irreplaceable.

- *Procedure*. This is the mechanism by which all the other resources are brought together to create a value proposition for customers.

In services markets, customers can sometimes be seen as co-producers of the product. For example, a bar relies on having the right type of customer to create an appealing ambience, and a theatre relies on having an audience to respond to the show. Without the other customers, the experience can seem bleak and uninteresting. At the extreme, a nightclub is an example of a service where the main product is the other customers – people go to nightclubs largely to meet members of the opposite sex. The same is true of dating services.

Service processes fall into three categories:

1 *Before-sales service processes*. These would include helpful staff, ready access to information and ensuring the availability of people to carry out the service.

2 *During-sales processes*. The actual provision of the service.

3 *After-sales processes*. Courtesy calls, prompt attention to complaints and careful record-keeping for future encounters are useful processes.

Because all these processes involve human interaction, they all provide opportunities to improve customer loyalty. There is a trade-off here between service level and cost: the level of service needs to be fixed at a point which provides value for money for the target audience, some of whom may be happy to pay more for a first-class service, while others might not be prepared to pay much at all and are happy with a basic service. Some firms (such as low-cost airlines) have created competitive advantage by reducing the service level to an absolute minimum, but being extremely cheap; other firms have built their success on luxurious service (for example the Orient Express). The important point for the firm is to set the right level of service for the desired audience – too high, and the costs will price the service out of reach of the target audience, too low and people will simply go elsewhere.

Some service processes are complex (for example airlines). Several hundred different tasks need to be undertaken and dozens of separate service processes need to be co-ordinated before the aircraft even takes off – quite apart from the services which are needed once the flight leaves. First, a travel agent needs to sell the ticket to ensure that the passenger is on the right aircraft at the right time, and leaves from the right airport. Second, the aircraft needs to be correctly serviced and fuelled by ground crews. Third, food and drink for the passengers needs to be prepared and delivered to the aircraft by yet another service company. Fourth, airports at either end of the journey need to be prepared to handle the aircraft on departure and arrival, and several air traffic control and advice agencies in different countries need to become involved. Fifth, passenger entertainment services such as in-flight movies, music and games need to be provided, and sixth, many service companies at the airports need to become involved in the process. In fact, almost every type of company from Hollywood film studios to airport bookstalls becomes involved in the process one way or another.

On the other hand, a flight is not a divergent service. The experience is much the same for all passengers, except for the differences between first class, business class and economy: the meals are the same, the flight attendants treat everyone the same, and of course the start point and finish point of the flight is the same for everyone. Even the safety announcements are identical.

Hairdressing is a service which displays exactly the opposite characteristics. In most salons, only one or two people will deal with the client, and few (if any) other companies are involved. The process is therefore not complex. On the other hand, it is highly divergent – each person should leave the salon with a different hairstyle, produced to suit the individual's physical features and personal tastes. This variability of outcome does mean that things go wrong more often in hairdressing salons than they do on aircraft, of course.

The divergence and complexity of a service process can be adjusted to establish a competitive position, with the following consequences:

- Reducing divergence will reduce costs, improve productivity and make distribution easier. Fast-food restaurants offer limited menus of standardised food at low cost, for example.
- Increased divergence will offer more possibilities for customisation, greater flexibility and (usually) premium pricing. High divergency is what distinguishes *à la carte* restaurants, hairdressers and bespoke tailors.
- Reduced complexity means offering the core benefits of the product and not much else.
- Increased complexity increases customer choice by widening the range of products and the range of features on offer.

Process often becomes the main differentiator between services. Often the core product is the same from several suppliers – for example, air travel – but the process may be more or less straightforward, more or less efficient, and more or less variable.

Physical evidence

Because services are often largely intangible, people often have little lasting evidence that the service ever took place; perhaps more importantly, there is very little evidence on which to base judgements about the quality of the service prior to actually committing to purchasing it. In some cases, physical evidence might be needed to demonstrate to others that the service has happened – a certificate from a training course, an insurance policy document, or a medical certificate might all be needed for this purpose. Sometimes physical evidence acts as a reminder of the service: souvenirs from a holiday, a menu from a restaurant, a travel kit from an airline, or even a simple business card might bring back happy memories or provide the means for repeating the experience.

As a way of assessing the likely quality of a service beforehand, aspects such as the décor of a bank, the menu in the window of a restaurant, or the cleanliness of a supermarket all help. In some cases the service will have a substantial physical component anyway – restaurant meals fall into this category, and to an extent hairdressing does as well. In both cases the physical element will not last long, but it is at least possible to observe other customers enjoying the physical aspects and thus be able to judge the probable quality of the service.

There are four generic ways to add value through physical evidence, as follows:

1 *Create physical evidence which increases loyalty.* Loyalty cards and frequent-flyer cards are typical of this, as are 'collectables' such as vouchers or ornaments. Some airline loyalty schemes include baggage tags which let the baggage handlers know they are dealing with an important suitcase; this probably has more effect on the customer than on the baggage handlers, of course.

2 *Use physical evidence which enhances the brand image.* Insurance companies convey a solid, respectable image by producing smart, glossy policy documents: low-cost airlines convey their thrifty image by requiring passengers to print off their own tickets on ordinary paper, or by having no tickets at all.

3 *Use physical evidence which has an intrinsic value of its own.* This is common in the financial services sector: insurance companies give away carriage clocks, pen sets, DVD players and so forth to new customers. Obviously very few people would take out an insurance policy just to be given a clock, but the clock does serve as a useful reminder of the policy's existence.

4 *Create physical evidence which leads to further sales.* This could include reminder cards sent out when the next service is due (many garages do this), a desk calendar or wall calendar (often supplied by take-away food suppliers), or notepads and pens (hotels supply these). Such reminders are helpful to consumers, but also may generate new sales because the service provider's telephone number is convenient to hand when the need arises.

Physical evidence will not substitute for a poor service, of course. The core of a service will always be the intangibles, but it is important to remember that almost all products have both tangible and intangible elements: the intangibles are often as important as the tangibles.

Service quality

Under this regime, service quality can be defined as the ability of the organisation to meet or exceed customer expectations. The relationship marketer therefore needs to monitor the quality of the firm's output against two criteria: the customer's expectations and the firm's actual output. Parasuraman *et al.* (1985) developed a model of service quality which is reproduced in Figure 11.4.

The model shows various gaps in the understanding of service quality. These are as follows:

Figure 11.4 Service quality model

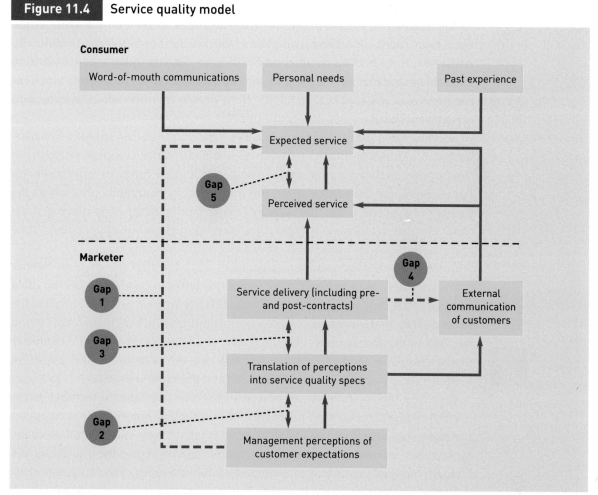

Source: Reprinted with permission from Parasuraman *et al.*, 1985

- Gap 1: difference between actual customer expectations and management perceptions of customer expectations.
- Gap 2: difference between management perceptions of customer expectations
  and service quality specifications.
- Gap 3: difference between service quality specifications and the service actually delivered.
- Gap 4: difference between service delivery and what is communicated about
  the service to customers.
- Gap 5: difference between customer expectations and perceptions of what is
  actually received. This gap is influenced by the other four.

In order to close these gaps, marketers need to adopt a range of quality control
procedures.

Benchmarking is the process of comparing everything the company does with
the same activities carried out by competitors, and seeking to match the best of

the competitors in each activity. For example, a manufacturer might decide which competitor is best at engineering, and seek to match that while at the same time matching another competitor which is best at delivery reliability. By doing this, firms end up as 'the best of the best'. **Service-quality benchmarking** takes this a step further: the comparison is made with both competitors and non-competitors. Christopher *et al.* (1991) have drawn up a five-stage approach to service benchmarking, as shown in Table 11.2.

Defining the competitive arena is not as simple as it at first appears. For marketers, the question has to be who does the customer compare us with? A cinema-goer may well compare the service with other forms of entertainment. For example, are the sales staff on the confectionery counter as pleasant as the bar staff at the pub? Is the film on offer as entertaining as the band playing at the club? The real assessment of the service level takes place not against other firms in the same business, but against other services the customer buys.

In terms of physical products, customers who find that the vacuum-cleaner company is reluctant to honour the guarantee will compare this with the cable company that sent somebody round immediately to fix a problem, or with the car company that lent them a car to get around in while their own was being repaired under the warranty. Having had a good service from the TV company or car company tends to reduce the risk for the consumer, and therefore increases the chances of a repeat purchase from the same company.

Regarding the key components of customer service, this again is too often left to executive judgement without reference to the customers. For example, a computer purchaser may regard on-site maintenance as being far more important than online assistance. A car owner whose car is in for servicing may regard the availability of a lift to the train station as being more important than the speed of servicing of the car.

Following on from establishing the key components, it is essential to establish the relative importance. This is simply because it is almost impossible, in a world with limited resources, to provide every customer with everything he or she wants. The firm therefore needs to concentrate on providing the most important aspects first.

Table 11.2 **Five stages for service benchmarking**

Step 1	Define the competitive arena: that is, with whom are we compared by customers and with whom do we want to be compared?
Step 2	Identify the key components of customer service as seen by customers themselves.
Step 3	Establish the relative importance of those service components to customers.
Step 4	Identify customer position on the key service components relative to competition.
Step 5	Analyse the data to see if service performance matches customers' service needs.

Source: Christopher *et al.,* 1991

Having found out where we want to be, we now need to find out where we are by establishing our position on service provision as compared with the competition. Again, we need to be careful who we are defining as competition, and also be aware of the possibilities of comparing ourselves with firms who are not direct competition, but who have something to teach us about service levels. This process is part of the marketing audit discussed in Chapter 10.

This leaves the firm in a position to compare its service provision with the service priorities of its customers.

LOYALTY IN SERVICES

Many service industries engender strong customer loyalty, in particular personal services such as hairdressing and beauty therapy, food and beverage services such as pubs and restaurants, and some technical services such as car maintenance and building. Banks generate a spurious loyalty: people only remain loyal because switching banks is time-consuming and risky, and also people often suppose that a long-term relationship with a bank will lead to special treatment in case they need an unexpected overdraft or loan.

Critical thinking

If a customer remains loyal, do we really need to know the reason why? If they stay loyal because they love us, that's great of course, but if they stay loyal because it's too much hassle to switch to someone else, does it really matter?

We don't need to love our banks, surely. Provided they look after the money and don't charge too much, what else do we want? Of course, if another bank made it easy to switch, that might be different!

Other services do not engender loyalty in themselves. Taxis and buses are examples: although people often use the same taxi firm when ordering a cab from home, they are unlikely to do so when arriving at a railway station or airport. It would be extremely rare for someone to use the same taxi driver on a regular basis, except in rural areas where there are few choices.

Generating loyalty carries distinct benefits for any organisation. There are six main benefits, as follows:

1 *Increased purchases* (Reichheld and Sasser 1990). Customers tend to increase their purchases when dealing with a firm with which they have a relationship. Naturally, people are prepared to spend money with firms they know and trust.

2 *Lower cost.* Attracting new customers is almost always more expensive than retaining existing ones, although there are exceptions to this general rule.

3 *Lifetime value of a customer increases.* Lifetime value is a key concept in relationship marketing: the value of a customer is measured by how much he or she will spend in a lifetime, rather than in a single transaction.

4 *Sustainable competitive advantage.* The intangible aspects of a service are often difficult to copy: a particular hairstylist or chef may be unique. By definition, loyal customers are difficult for competitors to lure away (Roberts *et al.* 2003).

5 *Word-of-mouth.* Because services are intangible and often difficult to judge in advance, word-of-mouth plays a much stronger role than is the case for physical products. People rely heavily on the recommendations of friends when choosing a restaurant, a hairdresser or a builder, and loyal customers are more likely to make those recommendations. Decisions about life insurance are based first on previous experience, second on personal recommendation (Devlin 2007). Published performance and cost are of much less importance.

6 *Employee satisfaction.* Staff often prefer to work for a firm with a loyal customer base, since they have to deal directly with the customers. Dealing with strangers is stressful, whereas dealing with familiar customers is more likely to involve being praised. Regular complaints will demoralise staff very rapidly.

Lowering the rate of customer churn will cause a substantial rise in overall profits (Reichheld and Sasser 1990). Part of the process involves ensuring that complaints are handled properly, since the variability of services can lead to a higher rate of complaint and a more difficult process of resolution.

Customer loyalty in service industries appears to be related positively to technical service quality, functional service quality and customer education (Bell and Eisingerich 2007). This means that the loyalty function is not only related to quality of service, but also to customer characteristics: interestingly, the same authors found that customer expertise, i.e. skill and knowledge of the market, was not negatively related to loyalty as had been expected. The assumption was that expert customers would be more likely to shop around for the best deals, but this turned out not to be the case. Price is generally not an issue – regular brand 'switchers' turn out to be more price-sensitive than loyal 'stayers' (Leong and Qing 2006).

Loyalty is easily lost, however. For example, airlines frequently overbook aircraft by as much as 10% in order to ensure full use of the aircraft: no-shows and last-minute cancellations usually take care of the surplus, and economy passengers can be upgraded into business class (or even first class) in the event that economy class is overbooked. Sometimes business or first class are overbooked, or the aircraft is completely full, in which case some passengers might be downgraded or refused boarding. In those circumstances, airlines which downgrade passengers or are unable to carry them almost always lose the customer: upgrading, on the other hand, only creates marginally greater loyalty (Wangenheim and Bayon 2007).

Case study 11
Vidal Sassoon

Vidal Sassoon was born into a poor Jewish family in London's Whitechapel in 1928. His family were so poor he was placed in an orphanage for part of his childhood, and at 14 he left school and was apprenticed to a local barber, to learn a trade and help support his family. In order to get work in the more fashionable West End, he deliberately lost his Cockney accent by going to the theatre and imitating the 'posh' accents of the actors.

Despite this unpromising start, Sassoon made an impact in the 'swinging Sixties' by teaming up with fashion designer Mary Quant. He developed a new hairdressing technique – precision cutting – which, together with blowdrying (rather than using curlers and a stand dryer) gave his clients a unique look.

Sassoon's other major contribution to modern hairdressing was his view that the stylist is the expert, and should decide the customer's hairstyle. Pre-Sassoon, hairdressers had meekly done clients' hair exactly as the client wanted it – but Sassoon changed all that, creating styles which would suit the client's face and hair type, and working with the natural characteristics of the hair rather than trying to force it into a style for which it was not suited.

Sassoon's fame spread, and he became the hairdresser of choice for the artists, aristocrats, film stars and celebrities of the 1960s. His salon on Bond Street became so busy that clients often had to queue outside – Sassoon once revealed in an interview that the Duchess of Bedford had to sit on the stairs because there was no room in the salon. Sassoon began to spend more and more time training other stylists in his techniques, and eventually opened a training school to which hairdressers from throughout the UK came. The Vidal Sassoon Academy is still highly-respected to this day, with a base in Los Angeles as well as in London.

Spin-offs from the Sassoon empire include hair care products, both for home use and for professionals, and a chain of franchised salons throughout the world. Sassoon dragged himself up out of poverty the hard way – but he is a much tougher character than the stereotype view of hairdressers would have us believe. As a Jew living in the East End, he fought the Fascists on the streets, and in 1948 he fought in Israel's War of Independence – hardly someone who would be intimidated by the rich and famous.

Sassoon is now a multi-millionaire, living in California: at the age of eighty, he sports a permanent tan and still takes an interest in his business empire, as well as the Vidal Sassoon International Center for the Study of Anti-Semitism, which he founded in 1982. His salons are worldwide, but more importantly his techniques are used worldwide. His style and creativity have made him a household name, have revolutionised hairdressing, and (almost as a by-product) made him a multi-millionaire.

Questions

1 How does Sassoon's view that the hairdresser should decide the style fit with the marketing concept?
2 Why would Sassoon train other hairdressers, thus apparently providing them with his only competitive edge?
3 Why is hairdressing such big business?
4 What is the strength of the Sassoon brand?
5 Why would Sassoon have wanted to lose his East End accent?

Services are the major part of most economies in the industrialised world. Service provision relies on all elements of the marketing mix, but people, process and physical evidence become more important in service marketing than in physical product marketing.

Companies in service industries therefore rely heavily on staff, most (though not all) of whom are in the front line of dealing with customers on a day-to-day basis. Therefore, motivating and looking after staff becomes of even greater importance than would be the case in physical product marketing.

The key points from this chapter are as follows:

- All products have some element of service and some element of physical product.
- From the consumer's viewpoint, buying a service is riskier than buying a physical product.
- Front-line employees should be empowered to deal with problems as they arise.
- Employees need to feel that they are working for a good company.
- Loyalty is more common in services as a way of reducing risk.
- Word-of-mouth is important in services, again to reduce risk.
- Physical evidence can be used to create more business.
- Process can be complex or simple, divergent or standard: each of these has implications for marketing.

CHAPTER QUESTIONS

1 How might complaint handling be improved in the airline business?
2 What problems might arise from reducing staff levels in the hotel trade?
3 What are the implications of divergency and complexity in the fast-food business?
4 How does staff empowerment help in recruitment?
5 What mechanisms account for complaint behaviour in services?

Further Reading

Principles of Services Marketing by **Adrian Palmer** (Maidenhead, McGraw-Hill, 2005) is a well-established, readable and comprehensive textbook. Now in its fourth edition, this book has become established as the leading text in the field.

Services Marketing by **Valerie Zeithaml and Mary Jo Bitner** (New York, McGraw-Hill, 2003) is an American text with a good pedigree. Zeithaml and Bitner almost invented services marketing between them, so the text is certainly definitive, but of course uses American examples and contexts which are not always familiar to non-Americans.

References

Beatson, Amanda, Coote, Leonard V. and Rudd, John M.: 'Determining consumer satisfaction and commitment through self-service technology and personal service usage', *Journal of Marketing Management*, **22** (7/8) (2006), pp. 853–82.

Belbin, R.M.: *Management Teams: Why They Succeed or Fail* (London, Heinemann, 1981).

Bell, Simon and Eisingerich, Andreas B.: 'The paradox of customer education, customer expertise and loyalty in the financial services industry', *European Journal of Marketing*, **41** (5/6) (2007), pp. 466–86.

Booms, B.H. and Bitner, M.J.: 'Marketing strategies and organisation structures for service firms', in *Marketing of Services*, J. Donnelly and W.R. George, eds (Chicago, IL, American Marketing Association, 1981).

Christopher, M., Ballantyne, D. and Payne, A.: *Relationship Marketing* (Oxford, Butterworth-Heinemann, 1991).

Cummings, T.G.: 'Designing effective work groups', in *Handbook of Organisational Design*, P.C. Nystrom and W.H. Starbuck, eds (Oxford, Oxford University Press, 1981).

DeChernatony, Leslie and Cottam, Susan: 'Internal brand factors driving successful financial services brands', *European Journal of Marketing*, **40** (5/6) (2006), pp. 611–33.

Desai, Preyas S., Kalra, Ajay and Murthi, B.P.S.: 'When old is gold: the role of business longevity in risky situations', *Journal of Marketing*, **72** (1) (2008), pp. 95–107.

Devlin, James F.: 'Complex services and choice criteria: an example from the life assurance market', *Journal of Marketing Management*, **23** (7/8) (2007), pp. 631–50.

Finlay, P.: *Strategic Management: An Introduction to Business and Corporate Strategy* (Harlow, Financial Times Prentice Hall, 2000).

Gray, Brandan J.: 'Benchmarking services branding practices', *Journal of Marketing Management*, **22** (7/8) (2006), pp. 717–58.

Gruber, Thorstein, Szmigin, Isabelle and Voss, Roediger: 'The desired qualities of customer contact employees in complaint-handling encounters', *Journal of Marketing Management*, **22** (5/6) (2006), pp. 619–42.

Handy, C.: *The Age of Unreason* (London, Hutchinson, 1989).

Harris, Greg: 'International advertising: developmental and implementational issues', *Journal of Marketing Management*, **12** (1996), pp. 551–60.

Hennig-Thurau, Thorsten, Groth, Markus, Paul, Michael and Gremler, Dwayne D.: 'Are all smiles created equal? How emotional contingence and emotional labour affect service relationships', *Journal of Marketing*, **70** (3) (2006), pp. 58–73.

Judd, V.C.: 'Differentiate with the fifth P', *Industrial Marketing Management*, **16** (1987), pp. 241–7.

Knox, Simon and Freeman, Cheryl: 'Measuring and managing employer brand image in the service industry', *Journal of Marketing Management*, **22** (7/8) (2006), pp. 695–716.

Leong, Yow Peng and Qing, Wang: 'Impact of relationship marketing tactics (RMTs) on switchers and stayers in a competitive service industry', *Journal of Marketing Management*, **22** (1/2) (2006), pp. 25–59.

Maxham III, James G. and Netemeyer, Richard G.: 'Firms reap what they sow: the effect of shared values and perceived organisational justice on customers' evaluation of complaint handling', *Journal of Marketing*, **67** (1) (January 2003), pp. 46–62.

Munoz, Caroline L., Wood, Natalie T. and Solomon, Michael R.: 'Real or blarney? A cross-cultural investigation of the perceived authenticity of Irish pubs', *Journal of Consumer Behaviour*, **5** (3) (2006), pp. 222–34.

Murphy, J.A.: *The Lifebelt: The Definitive Guide to Managing Customer Retention* (Chichester, John Wiley, 2001).

Parasuraman, A., Zeithaml, V.A. and Berry, L.L.: 'A conceptual model of service quality and its implications for future research', *Journal of Marketing*, **49** (Fall 1985).

Rasmusson, E.: 'Winning back angry customers', *Sales and Marketing Management* (October 1997), p. 131.

Reichheld, F.F. and Sasser, W.E. Jr: 'Zero defections, quality comes to services', *Harvard Business Review*, Sept–Oct (1990), pp. 105–11.

Roberts, K., Varki, S. and Brodie, R.: 'Measuring the quality of relationships in consumer services: an empirical study', *European Journal of Marketing*, **37** (1/2) (2003), pp. 169–96.

Wangenheim, Florian and Bayon, Tomas: 'Behavioural consequences of overbooking service capacity', *Journal of Marketing*, **71** (4) (2007), pp. 36–47.

Land Rover

Land Rover originally started up just after the Second World War, producing utility vehicles for farmers and others who needed off-road capacity. The cars were built mainly from aluminium, because it was widely available at the time, rather than steel which was in short supply. The vehicles were a huge success, and became iconic. The company, originally part of the Rover Cars group, has continued in business even though Rover has now disappeared.

The original utility vehicle has been considerably updated. Modern Land Rovers are luxury four-by-fours, owned by the wealthy rather than the working farmer. Land Rover is now positioned as a premium brand: the TV advertising, using the strapline 'Go Beyond', shows how the car can be used in cities as well as off-road in harsh conditions.

Environmentalism represents something of a threat to the four-by-four market: gas-guzzling four-wheel drives, many of which are only used to go to the cash point or deliver children to school, are coming under fire from many critics. Land Rover meet these criticisms by contributing to carbon offset schemes, and by reducing the company's carbon footprint.

Phil Popham, Global Managing Director

Watch the video clip, then try to answer the following questions. The answers are on the companion website.

Questions

1 How might Land Rover respond to the criticisms of environmentalists?

2 How might Land Rover establish a relationship with its end consumers?

3 What threats are apparent from globalisation for Land Rover?

12

Sustainable marketing

Objectives

After reading this chapter you should be able to:

- explain the role of quality in building long-term relationships;
- describe how relationship marketing builds long-term profitability;
- formulate strategies for developing customer loyalty;
- establish quality procedures within organisations;
- describe the basis for societal marketing;
- develop strategies for assessing responsibility towards stakeholders;
- establish ethical guidelines;
- take an ethical approach to marketing strategy decisions.

INTRODUCTION

During the first years of the twenty-first century, marketing thinking has been undergoing some radical changes. Much marketing thinking in the past has concentrated on the single transaction between producer and customer, on the assumption that customers who like the product will continue to buy, and that no one else has any right to an input into the exchange. This approach, while laudable, ignores the fact that some customers are more valuable than others, that some customers can become very loyal indeed, and that marketers should also take into consideration the needs and attitudes of other **stakeholders** in society at large.

At the same time, new communications media (the Internet, cellular telephones, short message systems (texting) and so forth) have made previous marketing communications strategies almost obsolete. Falling birthrates and increased competition through globalisation have meant that consumers are fewer and more firms are chasing them; at the same time, rapidly rising prosperity levels mean that the rewards for firms which get it right are much greater than ever before.

This chapter is about creating long-term relationships with customers – selling 'products that don't come back to customers that do' (Baker 1991). It is about ensuring that the marketing-orientated firm is sustainable in the long run, both in terms of use of finite resources and also in terms of ethical behaviour towards society at large. Finally, it is about the successful exploitation of new technology in a rapidly changing world.

RELATIONSHIP *v* TRADITIONAL MARKETING

Traditional marketing is concerned with the exchanges between organisations and their customers. The emphasis has always been on producing products that will satisfy customer needs, and the focus has tended to be on the single transaction. This has led to an over-emphasis on acquiring new customers, at the expense of ensuring that the firm keeps its old ones. Most of the marketing transactions in a traditional firm are undertaken anonymously, and the customer is reduced from being an individual person, with needs and wants and problems, to being a member of a market segment.

Relationship marketing, on the other hand, looks at the customer as an individual and tries to establish a relationship. Relationship marketing is concerned with the lifetime value of the customer. For example, over the course of a lifetime's motoring, a motorist might own 30 or more cars. This represents a total expenditure of perhaps hundreds of thousands of pounds on cars, yet car manufacturers and dealers rarely keep in touch with their customers in any organised way. The focus is on the single transaction, that of buying one (and only one) car at a time. A relationship marketing approach would seek to look at the customer in terms of his or her total value to the company over (potentially) 30 or 40 years.

This orientation values the loyal customer ahead of the one-off big deal, and gives the firm more chance of maintaining its customer base in the long run. Figure 12.1 illustrates how the concepts of customer service, quality and marketing come together to establish a relationship marketing orientation.

The key to relationship marketing is understanding that customers are buying a bundle of benefits, some of which include such factors as product reliability and a pleasant service from the company they are dealing with. Increasingly, customers expect suppliers to value their custom; during the nineteenth century, every shopper would expect the shopkeepers to know them by name, to be respectful and polite, to anticipate their needs, and to arrange delivery or otherwise show that they regarded the customer as important to the firm. As firms have grown bigger, this level of personal attention has largely disappeared. Economic forces have removed the old systems from grocery shops, so that customers are now expected to find the goods themselves, carry them to the checkout, pay for them and carry them home, sometimes without exchanging any conversation with the store staff.

This increasingly impersonal and functional view of marketing is now being questioned, and relationship marketing seeks to address this issue by encourag-

| Figure 12.1 | Relationship marketing, quality and service |

Source: Christopher *et al.*, 1991

ing firms to treat customers as individuals, with individual needs and aspirations. This goes beyond the 'have a nice day' approach of the fast-food restaurant, replacing it with a genuine interest and concern for the customer.

Critical thinking

This idea of being looked after on a personal basis looks really good on paper. Having the shop assistants smile at us, having somebody thinking about our every need, having them wish us to come back soon: it's like having an extra mother, but better!

Do we really want all this attention, though? Wouldn't it be better if everything just worked properly first time, without all the soft soap? Or maybe we expect things to work as well! We're just getting spoiled rotten!

In fact, business relationships do not divide entirely into **transactional** or relationship marketing – relationships develop, and can range from a single exchange through to a fully developed co-operative system. Table 12.1 shows the comparison between traditional, or transaction, marketing and relationship marketing.

Table 12.1	Transaction *v* relationship marketing
Transaction marketing	**Relationship marketing**
Focus on single sale	Focus on customer retention
Orientation on product features	Orientation on product benefits
Short time-scale	Long time-scale
Little emphasis on customer service	High emphasis on customer service
Limited customer commitment	High customer commitment
Moderate customer contact	High customer contact
Quality is the concern of the production department	Quality is the concern of all

Source: Christopher *et al.*, 1991

Although many firms have adopted the relationship approach, most firms still keep to the traditional view. This tends to lead to the following bad practices:

- Reactive approach to customer complaints.
- Failure to recognise the needs of long-term customers.
- Greater expenditure on promotion than is necessary, owing to the emphasis on acquiring new customers.
- Inner conflict within departments as production people expect marketers to sell the goods, and marketers expect production people to handle quality issues.

As customer expectations rise, and more particularly as customers become longer lived, there is likely to be an increasing emphasis on establishing relationships. This is because the value to the firm of the customer's continued custom is greater, and the customer knows this and expects better treatment in return.

Relationship marketing has been most apparent in business-to-business markets, possibly because business needs do not change much over a period of time, whereas consumer needs change as people grow older, pass through different life stages, and become wealthier or poorer. The view has been expressed that products are not bundles of benefits, but are instead relational processes (Tuli *et al.* 2007). There is some logic behind this, at least in business-to-business markets: each benefit is a step in strengthening the relationship.

Some fallacies of relationship marketing and the concept of customer retention have been discovered by recent research, as follows (East *et al.* 2006):

- The evidence is that in many consumer markets long-term customers are no more valuable than short-term ones. The key factor is the relative costs of acquisition and retention – if acquisition is cheap and retention expensive, long-term customers will be less profitable.
- It is often difficult to influence long-tenure customers.
- Customer satisfaction does not lead to retention, but it does lead to increased acquisition through word of mouth.

Roemer (2006) has outlined a model for assessing the impact of dependence on customer lifetime value. This model also offers some insight into the power split between customer and supplier in business-to-business markets: the model is shown in Figure 12.2.

The figure shows that, if each company has high dependence on the other, dependence is symmetrical and the relationship should last: if, on the other hand, either party has the upper hand the relationship becomes asymmetrical and is less likely to last.

One of the key concepts in relationship marketing is that of customer intimacy. This means getting close enough to the customer to be able to understand his or her needs almost before he or she does – being able to think like the customer is a key skill in establishing and maintaining the relationship. Research shows that there is a strong positive relationship between marketing orientation and customer intimacy (Tuominen *et al.* 2004). This means that companies which adopt a marketing orientation will usually try to get as close as possible to their customers.

Relationship marketing, when the concept first appeared, was compared to a courtship (Levitt 1986). At the beginning, both parties are keen to present the

| Figure 12.2 | Dependence between suppliers and customers in business-to-business markets |

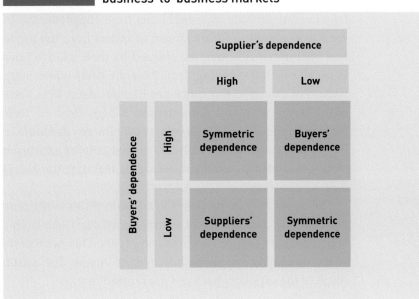

best possible aspects of themselves; as the relationship progresses, they seek to know more about each other and adapt to fit each others' needs, until finally they become very close, sharing confidential information, and regarding each other as allies in fighting the competitive battle. This is equivalent to a couple meeting, dating for a while, and finally marrying. For example, IBM and Microsoft worked extremely closely together during the 1980s and 1990s. Although each company was a separate entity, each recognised that it could not succeed without the other. Although they have eventually gone their separate ways, and Microsoft now works with many computer manufacturers (as IBM does with software houses), the relationship created a massive increase in home computing worldwide.

Adaptation tends to be one-sided, however. Suppliers are much more likely to adapt their business approach than are suppliers, for the following reasons (Brennan *et al.* 2003):

- *Relative power.* Buyers are usually in a position of power, especially in business-to-business markets, since they can always spend their money elsewhere.

- *Buyer support.* Buying companies will often help suppliers to make the necessary changes. For example, a motor manufacturer might supply design services to a component supplier in order to ensure that the components are produced to the right specification.

- *Managerial preference for a more or less relational exchange.* Suppliers typically want to get close to their customers in order to ensure a continuation of orders. The pressure is not as great for buyers to get close to suppliers (although there are advantages to doing so, and some buying firms actively seek long-term relationships).

Figure 12.3 shows the forces which combine to create pressure on companies to adapt. In the figure, the supplying firm is pressured by managerial preference, by a need to exclude its competitors from supplying the buying firm, and by a need to guarantee a future stream of orders from the buying firm. The supplier and the buyer might both be affected by their relative power – although power is usually with the buying firm, there are cases where suppliers have the upper hand. For example, the American hair-products firm Redken will only supply hairdressers who can demonstrate a high level of technical competence – Redken's products and reputation make them a desirable company to buy from, but Redken protect their brand by only supplying salons with whom they have a close relationship, even extending to training the hairstylists in the use of Redken products.

The buyer may be prepared to adapt in order to simplify the buying process. For example, Fiat reduced the number of suppliers from over 500 to less than 100 in order to reduce its purchasing costs. This necessitated closer supervision of the remaining suppliers, however, to ensure that quality did not suffer as a result of the suppliers having a guaranteed market.

Figure 12.3 Pressures to adapt in developing relationships

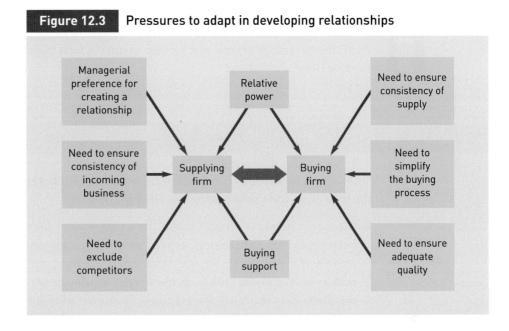

In some cases the relationship goes beyond a simple one-to-one arrangement. Relationships may extend to whole groups, or networks, and the companies involved may need to balance a whole set of relationships rather than just one. Key network management has three basic elements (Ojasalo 2004):

1 *Identify a key network.* Choosing which is most important of the many networks a firm is involved in is the starting-point for network management.

2 *Develop a strategy for managing actors within the key network.* Each separate member of the network has separate needs, and will respond to different management tactics.

3 *Develop and apply operational level networks for managing actors.* Putting the strategies into effect means developing separate tactics for each strategy and each member of the network.

Creating value through closer relationships also means bringing weaker relationships into the portfolio (Johnson and Selnes 2004). Companies need to be aware that customers with whom they have a weak relationship should be encouraged, and efforts need to be made to strengthen the relationships. For example, firms offering products with low economies of scale (such as personal services or professional services such as accountancy and law) need to build closer relationships in order to create value – they are unlikely to be able to increase value by reducing prices, because there is little room for manoeuvre in the cost structure and relatively little to be gained by an increase in business. A lawyer who is already fully booked can increase value for clients by improving the closeness of the relationship, and can raise his or her fees accordingly. Cutting prices for clients would add value for the client, but the lawyer would make less money because there is only a certain amount of working time available, and hiring more help would not make the situation much better. A good relationship is a better predictor of buying behaviour than is service quality (Roberts *et al.* 2003) but it is service quality which builds the relationship in the first place.

PEOPLE WITH WHOM BUSINESS IS DONE

Transaction marketers focus on the customer. Relationship marketers broaden the view to include other players in other markets.

- Customer markets remain much the same, except there is an emphasis on keeping existing customers as well as gaining new ones. For example, the growth of the use of loyalty cards in supermarkets worldwide is now moving into a second phase in which the loyalty cards are accepted at some other retailers, thus trapping the customer's money within the system (Mitchell 1996). Some retailers have gone even further, and have membership fees (the UK's MVC video and music store being one example). Customers who pay the initial fee can buy goods at a discount, in effect a two-part pricing system. The evidence is that such schemes ensure loyalty at least until the initial investment is recouped (Dick 1995).

- **Referral markets** are those people who might be expected to recommend the company to others. These could be existing customers, but could also be professional recommenders. For example, a holiday tour operator clearly needs to look after the holidaymaker; but tour operators also need to look after the travel agents, because these are the people who are in the best position to recommend the holidays to customers. In service industries this is common; in physical product manufacturing industries it is less so. Manufacturers are less likely to spend time and effort on establishing a good relationship with their retailers.

- **Supplier markets** are those people who provide raw materials and components for the company. A view has grown up that these suppliers are part of the team, and the traditional somewhat adversarial relationship is being replaced by the logistics paradigm of co-operation towards a common goal (see Chapter 8). Previously the emphasis has been on getting the lowest possible price from the suppliers, but the emphasis has now shifted towards other goals such as reliability of delivery, zero-fault quality control procedures, and co-operation in design and production.

- **Employee markets** refer to the need to recruit and train appropriately talented and motivated staff. Despite high unemployment rates in some areas, there is still an acute shortage of enthusiastic and skilled people to work in industry. Even when suitable employees have been found, firms need to ensure that they are market-orientated and understand the company's aims and objectives.

■ **Influence markets** comprise those individuals who might have influence on the firm's activities. They include government departments, financial institutions, pressure groups and so forth. Although the traditional marketers address these influence groups through PR activities, relationship marketing goes further than this. While PR concentrates on building a favourable image of the company by providing information, relationship marketing examines ways of meeting the needs of those institutions and individuals and helping them achieve their own aims (see Chapter 9).

■ *Internal marketing* is concerned with ensuring that everybody inside the firm is not only aware of the company's policies, but is also enthusiastic and supportive of them. This means more than simply informing staff of the policies; staff must feel that their own needs are being met, beyond the salary cheque at the end of the month. A prime example of this is Body Shop, which requires staff to participate in local community ventures. It is difficult to find Body Shop staff who are unenthusiastic about working for the company. All of them know what the aims of the firm are; all of them feel motivated and keen to participate in those aims. Strangely, Body Shop founder Anita Roddick was fond of saying that she does not believe in marketing – yet she was consummately good at doing it.

Internal marketing is not generally a separate activity, carried out in isolation. It is built into quality programmes, customer service programmes, and ad hoc activities throughout the normal working lives of the staff.

DEVELOPING A RELATIONSHIP MARKETING APPROACH

Quality

Quality is the relationship between what customers expect and what they get. If a customer's expectations of a product are disappointed, his or her perception will be that the product is poor quality. If, on the other hand, the product exceeds expectations, the perception will be that the product is high quality.

Much of this is bound up in what customers perceive as value for money. The aim of the relationship marketer is not simply to satisfy the customer, or even to please the customer, but to delight the customer.

It follows from this that quality is not an absolute. It is only relevant to what the customer feels; what is good quality to one person may not be to another, simply because both are beginning with different expectations. For this reason, service support is critical to relationship marketing because it is during the pre-sale and after-sale support that the customers are approached as individuals. It is at this time that the customer's perception of quality can be addressed, either

by ensuring that the expectations of the product are realistic (pre-sale) or by correcting any faults or errors after-sale.

In former years, quality has been seen as very much the province of the production department. This has led to the *product concept*, which holds that the company need only produce the best-quality product on the market and the customers will flock in. In fact this is not true – even Rolls-Royce have gone through bankruptcy by following this precept. Under a relationship marketing ethos, quality becomes the integrating concept between production orientation and marketing orientation.

Total quality management

The basis of the **total quality management** (TQM) approach is to ensure that the firm does the right things at every stage of the production process in the expectation that this will result in a high-quality outcome at the end. The problem with this approach is that it does not take account of the customer's expectations and perceptions, but instead relies on the management's preconceptions of what constitutes good manufacturing practice. There is also some difficulty in judging the level at which the quality of the product should be pitched. Probably the main contribution that TQM has made is in reducing defects (the zero-defects target), which will, by reducing wastage, reduce costs.

Managing the relationship

Ultimately, the purpose of the relationship marketing philosophy is to ensure that customers come back, and keep coming back. As was discussed earlier, a loyal customer of a car manufacturer might easily spend £100 000 on cars over a lifetime of motoring, yet most manufacturers do not take the trouble to contact the customer periodically to check that everything is OK with the car. Developing loyalty is an ongoing process: early on in the relationship, loyalty is a function of perceived value, but as the relationship progresses affective (emotional) factors become more important (Johnson *et al.* 2006).

Here are some examples of managing the relationship to generate loyalty.

Supermarket loyalty cards

These loyalty cards are in use throughout the world as supermarkets try to reward customers who use the store regularly. Previously, many shoppers would buy from whichever supermarket they happened to be passing, but the loyalty schemes have encouraged people to shop at the same supermarket every time, and establish a shopping pattern. The next stage of the procedure is to use the EPOS (electronic point-of-sale) equipment to track the customer's spending patterns and thus be in a position to advise shoppers about their individual needs. For example, it is theoretically possible with current technology to be able to advise a shopper that he or she has forgotten the tomato ketchup. (The EPOS system knows how often this customer buys ketchup, and knows what brand and size the customer favours.) Whether this is seen as a wonderful service for the customer or as an unwarranted invasion of privacy has been the subject of considerable debate (Evans 1994). In practice, legislation has been passed in the UK that makes it harder for supermarkets to use information in this way, since it would involve divulging personal information to junior store staff.

Critical thinking

OK, stores don't do it, but wouldn't it be marvelous? Just think if the store knew you so well, they could tell exactly when you were going to run out of sugar, and make sure to remind you next time you're in the store! Maybe we could get to the point where you just telephone the store and tell them you're coming, and they have everything ready for you when you arrive! What a time-saver!

Hands up anybody who finds that scary ...

Customer care

The UK's Nationwide Building Society has a commitment to customer care. It has declared that it will not follow the lead of other building societies and become a bank, since this would mean paying dividends to shareholders rather than offering benefits to customers. The intention is to retain the existing customers as customers rather than encouraging them to become shareholders in a new institution.

Frequent flyer programmes

Frequent flyer programmes on airlines offer the regular users of the airlines the opportunity to have free flights or major discounts on travel. The frequent flyer programmes are usually extended to partner airlines: United Airlines of the United States has formed the Star Alliance with Thai Air, Lufthansa, Aloha Airlines in Hawaii, British Midland in the UK, and a large number of other airlines throughout the world. Frequent flyer points can be earned by travelling with any of these airlines, and can be exchanged with any of them. Thus a regular transatlantic flyer can use the points to travel with British Midland to Frankfurt, for example. Frequent flyer members receive newsletters and some special treatment on the aeroplanes themselves – this encourages loyalty.

Museum or theatre season tickets

The museum uses the names and addresses of its season ticket holders to promote forthcoming attractions. By mailing people who are already known to be interested in the museum's activities, the management ensures a much higher response rate than would be the case if a 'scattergun' approach were adopted. Mailings to already interested parties are not expensive, even compared with placing advertisements in local newspapers. An example is the Sydney

Symphony Orchestra's Friends of the SSO scheme: members are entitled to attend selected rehearsals, buy tickets at a discount and be invited to special events.

Direct marketing

This is a rapidly growing area in marketing, as computer technology is becoming more refined. The growth in **databases** (computer-based files on customers) has allowed firms to keep ever more accurate information about their customers' buying habits. The capacity for exchanging databases between firms gives a potential for building very detailed profiles of each individual in the country.

In practice, this is still some way off, but in the meantime the detailed information available enables companies, and in particular database brokers, to develop extremely accurate segmentation of markets. Because most of the relevant information about the customers concerned is on file, mailing-list brokers are able to offer very specific mailings to companies. Ultimately, this will mean that customers will no longer receive junk mail – they will instead only be sent information that is of direct, immediate interest. Theoretically it should be possible to approach customers with a purchase suggestion almost at the point when they are considering the purchase. Database marketing was a major growth area in the 1990s and will probably continue to grow in the early part of this century: because the database allows the firm to retain and access large amounts of information about its customers, database marketing has become strongly associated with relationship marketing. In the nineteenth century each shopkeeper knew his regular customers personally; for a modern supermarket to do this a computer is required.

An important point to bear in mind about relationship marketing is that many of the techniques used to generate loyalty are expensive and require considerable commitment; overall, the result for the firm is a steadier and more secure market, but relationship marketing is not necessarily a cheap option. There is evidence that satisfaction leads to loyalty which in turn leads to profitability, but the relationship is non-linear (Helgesen 2006). Firms may need to be cautious before deciding to try to retain every customer.

Firms also need to remember that, whatever happens, some customers will leave: acquisition is therefore still important, yet less than half of all companies have a formal customer acquisition plan (Ang and Buttle 2006). Having a budget specifically for customer acquisition appears to be the key to success.

INTERNET MARKETING

Nobody owns the Internet; it is a communications medium spread across thousands (even millions) of computers worldwide, which operates independently of the telephone companies that supply its cable connections, of the governments in whose countries it resides, and even of the computer owners in whose machines data are stored. The Internet therefore operates under its own rules; there is little or no international law to govern its use (or abuse). This means that consumers have the power to communicate bad experiences with companies very quickly – most major companies' websites are shadowed by anonymous counter-culture sites known as McNitemares, after the McSpotlight site which shadows McDonald's and which carries derogatory stories about McDonald's products and restaurants. Few companies are adequately prepared for this type of attack (Conway *et al.* 2007) and there is, in fact, a battle for supremacy going on between consumers and suppliers, with no clear winner in sight yet (Denegri-Knott 2006).

This type of website plays a major role in PR and newsgathering. Environmental pressure groups, charitable organisations, self-help groups and others have all used websites to raise the profile of their causes, and some have had remarkable successes as a result. All in all, the consumer has most of the real power on the Internet. Online virtual communities, established through chatrooms and forums, replace some sources of information such as salespeople and mailings, but have yet to replace the main sources of information such as advertisements and brochures (Jepsen 2006). Communication via such forums, and via e-mail, is known as word of mouse.

Internet marketing has the characteristics outlined in Table 12.2.

Table 12.2 Characteristics of the Internet as a marketing tool

Characteristic	Explanation
Communication style	The style is interactive, and is either synchronous (happens immediately) or asynchronous (there are significant time delays between message and response).
Social presence	The feeling that the communications are taking place at a personal level. Internet communications have relatively high social presence if they are synchronous, particularly as the recipient is usually within his or her home environment when the communication takes place.
Consumer control of contact	Because the consumers are able to control the time and place at which they access the information, they are more willing to participate in the process of getting information from a machine. Most websites are interactive so that customers can control the information-gathering (and buying) process.
Consumer control of content	If the consumers can control the content of the message to some extent, the communication becomes truly interactive. For example, a consumer accessing a website can use a hyperlink to move to another page, or can skip past information. An e-mail address allows customers to ask specific questions and thus tailor the communications.

Website design

Below is a checklist for establishing a successful website:

■ The objectives for establishing the site must be clear from the outset.

■ The site itself should be informative rather than persuasive, since it is a sought communication.

■ Graphics should be kept as simple as possible; they take a long time to download, and many users are too impatient to wait, and in many cases do not have sufficient bandwidth or sufficient computer power to download large files quickly.

■ The impact of the communication should not depend entirely on the graphics; particularly in Europe, where local telephone calls are paid for, the graphics can be expensive to download if the user is on a dial-up connection. This is not a problem in the United States or Australia.

■ The site must be integrated with other communications; cross-marketing will encourage subscribers to visit the site.

■ The site should be set up to gather information from those who visit it.

■ The site should encourage interactivity by the use of offers, competitions, sales promotions and other incentives: people prefer interactive communications, in general (Vlasic and Kesic 2007).

■ Hyperlinks need to be fast, so that users can access the information they really need quickly.

The Internet can be a useful tool for increasing customer intimacy. Because of the social presence effect, customers feel more comfortable in divulging information, and feel closer to the website owner. There are five dimensions of service quality on the Internet (Jayawardene 2004):

1 *Access*. The website should be easy to access, quick to download and simple to understand.

2 *Website interface*. This should be informative, easy to navigate and engaging for the individual.

3 *Trust*. Establishing trust is particularly important, since ordering goods over the Internet involves divulging credit card details. Although security is constantly being tightened, fraudsters are also becoming more adept at breaching security.

4 *Attention*. Websites should attract attention, and should also show that attention has been paid to customer needs.

5 *Credibility*. Exaggerated claims, small print and unverifiable statements are likely to detract from the overall credibility of the site.

Security is a key issue in adoption of Internet purchasing by consumers. Many people are put off buying online because of the perceived risk, and this can be even more apparent in the international context. The effects are strongest if the website is located in a country where the rule of law is weak, but also people from countries with a strong national identity give a great deal of weight to cultural similarities between the website and their own culture (Steenkamp and Geyskens 2006). The same research showed that people from individualistic cultures such as the UK and United States give greater weight to privacy, security and customisation options than do people from collectivist cultures. In general, people tend to prefer websites which are linked to their local culture (Singh *et al.* 2006).

People enjoy sensory stimuli from online retailers as much as they do from bricks-and-mortar retailers (Parsons and Conroy 2006). This means that good graphics, perhaps with an element of humour attached, will go down well with online consumers. People become frustrated and leave the website early if information is inaccurate, poorly-presented, insufficient or of doubtful credibility (Grant *et al.* 2007). Using an avatar (a cartoon character which guides the individual through the site) leads to higher satisfaction with the retailer, a more positive attitude towards the product, and greater purchase intention (Holzwarth *et al.* 2006). This is probably due to the perception of friendliness avatars engender, leading to increased pleasure and arousal (Wang *et al.* 2007).

In an analysis of the factors influencing the extent to which people visit a given website, Wolk and Theysohn (2007) discovered the following:

- The number of visitors to a site is influenced by the quality of the offering, the level of interactivity, the accessibility and the relevance of the site to the individual.

- The number of page views (i.e. the length of time the individual stays on the site) is influenced by credibility, interactivity, personalisation and navigation issues.

- Credibility, branding and visibility also influence traffic levels.

- Accessibility, in itself, is not enough to ensure success since it reduces the number of page views per visitor, despite attracting more visitors. In other words, the number of hits on a page is not the main criterion for measuring success.

Future developments

Current thinking is that the effect of increased use of the Internet for marketing purposes has led to a new environment for marketing. The speed of information flow within firms, especially those operating globally, has offered greater possibilities for real-time negotiations between firms. The rapid growth in virtual shopping (accessing catalogues on the Internet) means that consumers can buy goods anywhere in the world and have them shipped – or, in the case of computer software, simply downloaded – which means that global competition has reached unprecedented levels, particularly among small firms which have, until now, been unable to access global markets. Virtual shoppers are able to access high-quality pictures of products, holiday destinations and even pictures of restaurant food before committing to a purchase. A recent development is the use of bots, which can be programmed to search the Internet on behalf of an individual and find products which might be of interest. A correctly programmed bot acts exactly like the individual, knowing what the person likes or dislikes, and developments in the pipeline will enable the bot to negotiate prices on behalf of the individual.

Online consumers can be seen as co-creators of brand value (Christodoulides *et al.* 2006). The brand value of an online retailer has five dimensions:

1 *Emotional connection*. Because the buying situation is usually taking place within the customer's home environment, there is an emotional element involved, and the brand should reflect this.

2 *Online experience*. This is a quality of both the retailer and the consumer – a consumer with very little online experience might have entirely different feelings about a website than would a more experienced online shopper.

3 *Responsive service nature*. If the service is poor or unresponsive, the brand will suffer.

4 *Trust*. Online consumers need to feel trusted as well as need to feel that the website is trustworthy.

5 *Fulfilment*. The delivery of the order, or the successful outcome of the sale, is a strong indicator of brand quality.

It is of course important to remember that Internet users are still individuals: currently, segmenting the market is difficult because the Internet and its users have gone through so much change in recent years: fifteen years ago, only real computer enthusiasts and a few scientists used the Internet, ten years ago its users were limited to the educated and wealthy, now the Internet is used by everyone. A suggested segmentation was proposed in 2007: the researchers categorised Internet users as risk-averse doubters, open-minded online shoppers, and reserved information seekers. The doubters would be unlikely to have much to do with the Internet and could be called laggards, the online shoppers are clearly heavy Internet users, and the information seekers use the Internet to find out about products, but then buy from traditional bricks-and-mortar retailers (Barnes *et al.* 2007).

Permission marketing

Permission marketing is the process by which consumers give a company permission to e-mail information about new products and special offers. A core principle of permission marketing is the shift in power from the marketer to the consumer (Kent and Brandal 2003; Cross 2003). Dufrene *et al.* (2005) suggest that a key benefit of permission marketing (PM) for consumers is that they can be in control over what they receive.

Webcasting is the automatic delivery of items of interest direct to the individual's PC, and is one form of permission marketing. Webcasting involves the subscriber in stating in advance what type of information he or she is interested in, and having this automatically delivered by the webcaster, thus avoiding the time and effort spent in searching the Internet using a search engine. This type of permission marketing became extremely popular in the early part of the century, but recently there have been signs of a fall in interest on the part of consumers.

Consumer fatigue (the fall in interest caused by over-use of communications) has been growing with regard to permission-based e-mails (Eccles 2006; Nussey 2004). This may be because communication is still one-way with the 'power' resting with the marketer: permission marketing is simply a gate that consumers can choose to open or not, but once the gate is opened consumers suffer the same intrusiveness that they used to experience from spam (Smith and Wood, 2004).

The average consumer received six marketing e-mails a day in 2004 (Duffy 2006) and this figure continues to grow: 63% of UK consumers now delete e-mail advertising without reading it, while 56% believe they receive too many e-mail marketing messages, therefore making it harder for marketers to 'cut through bloated inboxes' (Brookes 2005). Several writers also cite the frequency of mailings as a major concern for consumers (Quiris 2003; Nussey 2004).

Self-selection of messages is dependent on level of involvement, and since the Internet represents sought communication, the messages should be informative rather than persuasive. The Internet is not merely a simulation of the real world, it is an alternative to it in which consumers can have the illusion of being present in a computer-mediated environment (Hoffman 1996). Consumers have a role in creating the communications themselves; bulletin boards attract users, and the success of the board attracts more users and adds credibility to the site. This means that more consumers will see the marketer's messages.

Using the Internet for research

Bulletin boards of newsgroups allow marketers to monitor the success of word-of-mouth campaigns, and also can be directly useful in market research; Internet users' comments are often useful in assessing consumer attitudes. However, research shows that using the Internet for market research purposes is risky: although a large number of people respond to surveys, the proportion of respondents is less than 4% of the population. There is evidence that the remaining 96% differ from these respondents in some important ways (Grandcolas *et al.* 2003). The reasons for this may be as follows:

■ Some people are better at using the Internet.

■ Respondents may be faster typists, and therefore need to dedicate less time to answering surveys.

■ Respondents may have more time, for example be retired or unemployed people who can spend time on surveys, rather than people who use the Internet for work purposes and have deadlines to meet.

■ Respondents may have unmetered Internet access. People with broadband provision or who do not pay for the Internet connection by the minute (i.e. are using a dial-up connection with unlimited time) may be more prepared to stay online to complete a questionnaire.

These differences may or may not be crucial, depending on what is being researched. Checking whether respondents differ from non-respondents is, of course, difficult simply because non-respondents (by definition) withhold the information.

Other research possibilities inherent in the Internet include virtual focus groups and rapid concept testing of new products.

Increased consumer control of the communication channels may even result in consumers being able to invite tenders for supplying major purchases such as cars and home improvements, and (given the flexibility and speed of response of the Web) some firms will find this extremely advantageous. Although many of these consumers will be shopping for the lowest price, it should be possible to follow up these leads with further information as well as a quotation. Internet reverse-auction sites have become popular: consumers bid for goods, and manufacturers are approached regarding their willingness to supply at the prices offered.

Although much of the interest in the Internet has focused on business-to-consumer marketing, the medium has proved most useful in the business-to-business context. Full participation in e-marketing management of supply chains requires firms to integrate their internal and external supply-chain activities and share strategic information with the other members of the supply chain (Eng 2004). This is most easily accomplished by the use of the Internet, allowing other members of the supply chain to access confidential parts of the company's website by using a password. Using technology to mediate the relationship between supplier and purchaser has been shown to have a significant positive effect on buyers' future intention to buy – in other words, buyers like to buy from suppliers who have an effective website (McDonald and Smith 2004). This may be because the website offers possibilities for fast after-sales service, particularly in the computer software industry, where online troubleshooting is used to correct errors in the software. This is often the main use that software companies have for their websites (Moen *et al.* 2003).

Integrating the company's database with its Internet activities can be used to provide one-to-one customer relationship management (O'Leary *et al.* 2004). For example, returning visitors to the website can be greeted by name, their details can be kept on the database so that there is no need to re-enter (for example) address and credit card details, and the customer's preferences can be noted. This is achieved by the use of cookies (small programs downloaded onto the customer's computer). Ultimately, a profile of the customer's likes and dislikes can be built up, allowing the supplying company to target special offers and promotions much more accurately.

A further use of the Internet is to use internal networks within the firm to replace or supplement internal communications such as staff newsletters. This can have a stronger effect than paper versions, because it is rather harder to ignore; the staff member is generally more likely to read an e-mail than to open a staff newsletter, and the e-mail version is also quicker and cheaper to produce and distribute. In most organisations paper memos and newsletters have virtually disappeared (although so many people make hard copies of their e-mails that the paperless office is still some way off).

MARKETING ETHICS

Ethics are the principles that define right and wrong. Ethical thinking divides into the **teleological** (basically that acts should be defined as ethical or otherwise according to the outcome of the acts) and **deontological** (that acts can be defined as ethical or unethical regardless of outcome). The teleological approach implies that the end justifies the means, but is concerned with the greatest good of the greatest number; the deontological approach is best illustrated by Kant's Categorical Imperative, which states that each act should be based on reasons that everyone could act on, and that actions must be based on reasons that the decision-maker would accept for others to use.

In most cases marketers do not become enmeshed in the deeper recesses of philosophy, but instead rely on the moral rules which are part of the corporate culture. Research shows that most business people have separate sets of morals for work and for home (Fraedrich 1988). For example, much of the jargon of marketing is warfare-based (counterattacks, offensive product launches, etc.) and of course 'all's fair in love and war'; soldiers may kill or maim the enemy, but would not do so in civilian life. Having said that, while the moral code of a company may not be the same as the moral code of its employees and managers, there will be less dissonance among the staff if the firm conforms reasonably closely to a code of ethics.

- *Products* should be honestly made and described; commercial pressures may tempt companies to use cheaper raw materials or to use new additives to make the product perform differently. The ethical issue arises when customers are not informed of such changes.

- *Promotions* can involve deceptive or misleading advertising, manipulative sales methods, and even bribery in selling situations. While a certain amount of advertising 'puff' is acceptable and even expected, it is clearly not acceptable to tell outright lies or even to use misleading phrases: for example, in the United Kingdom the Sainsbury supermarket chain banned sales of Perrier water because it felt that the labelling falsely implied that the water was naturally gaseous, whereas in fact the bubbles are added during the bottling process. For some marketers (Perrier included) the label is perfectly clear, and is acceptable; for others this is not the case. Likewise, salespeople often face ethical conflicts: perhaps a salesperson is faced with correcting a customer's mistaken belief about a product, and thus losing the business, or allowing the customer to continue with the false belief right up to the point of taking delivery of the goods. Once a salesperson has deceived a customer it becomes increasingly difficult to tell the truth later, and eventually the customer will discover the truth anyway. At that point the business will be lost, probably for ever.

■ *Pricing* raises ethical issues in the areas of price fixing, predatory pricing (pricing below the cost of production in order to bankrupt competitors) and not revealing the full cost of purchase. For example, some high street chains of opticians fail to mention that the prices displayed are for spectacle frames only – the lenses are extra.

■ *Distribution ethics* involve abuse of power in channel management (see Chapter 8), and failure to pay for goods within the specified credit terms. Some stores (for example Toys 'R' Us) operate no-quibble sale-or-return contracts which mean that manufacturers have to accept damaged goods back, even when there is no fault in the manufacture: this has been seen as unethical by some smaller manufacturers, who have little negotiating power and few choices of outlet for their products.

Establishing a code of ethics within an organisation should not be left to chance. It is better to have a code of practice, and monitor the code in practice, so that employees and others know exactly what the firm is doing about its ethical responsibilities. As with any other question of marketing, the decision as to what the code should contain can be made by reference to the firm's customers and consumers: what would these people regard as ethical behaviour?

The recent phenomenon of the ethical consumer has caused many firms to rethink their policies. Valor (2007) has identified three key factors in ethical consumption: should (ethical obligation), want (conflicting identities), and can (personal action to change). The concept of 'should' is based on individual conscience, of a moral sense of what is the right thing to do. 'Want' is based on the conflict between acting in an unethical but desirable way (in this case buying clothes which have been made by low-paid workers) and doing the right thing. 'Can' is based on what the consumer actually has the power to do in order to change things – in some cases, there may be no ethical choices available. Personality variables which may have an effect are extroversion, agreeableness and conscientiousness, all of which have a positive impact on the tendency to act ethically (Fraj and Martinez 2006).

Ultimately, of course, people working within the firm have to be able to live with their consciences; establishing a code of ethical conduct will help them do so.

GLOBALISATION

Globalisation is a business philosophy under which firms regard the entire planet as their marketplace and source of supply. The truly global firm identifies competitors, suppliers, customers, employees, threats and opportunities throughout the world regardless of national boundaries.

For some individuals, globalisation represents a threat; American Presidential hopeful Pat Buchanan fought an unsuccessful campaign in 1996 based on protectionism. His campaign, which proposed that the United States close its borders to immigrants for five years, withdraw from all World Trade initiatives and impose high **tariffs** on imports of goods from low-wage economies, found favour with voters who felt that their livelihoods were threatened by free trade. In fact, two factors militate against the **protectionist** approach: first, global businesses are so powerful that anyone standing in their way is likely to be the loser, and second the advantages of international trade are too great (in the long run) to be set aside in favour of a short-term advantage.

The main drivers for globalisation are as follows:

- Increasing economies of scale and scope for firms in the market.
- Convergence of consumer tastes and preferences.
- Rapidly improving communications, in terms of both telecommunications and transport systems.
- Increased political acceptance of global trading.
- The continuing growth of large firms, coupled with limits imposed by national monopoly regulators on domestic growth.

Firms going global move through three stages:

- ethnocentrism;
- polycentrism; and
- geocentrism.

These stages are shown in Table 12.3.

Obviously it is not always possible to take a completely global view. Even firms such as McDonald's have to adapt their product somewhat for local markets. For example, in India McDonald's burgers are made from mutton, since the cow is sacred to Hindus; in Japan the company offers teriyaki burgers; in Russia the main beverage offered is tea rather than coffee.

In fact, although there is a concentration of interest on business-to-consumer markets, the bulk of global marketing is conducted within the business-to-business area. The practical, economic considerations of industrial buyers are likely to be the same whatever their cultural backgrounds: a Japanese steel buyer will source from whichever country offers the best deal, as would a steel buyer in New York or Buenos Aires. Buyers may be affected by the nationality of the

Table 12.3	Stages in globalisation

Stage	Explanation
Ethnocentrism	Home-country orientation. The foreign market is seen as secondary, perhaps as a place to dispose of excess production. The assumption is that the foreign market is basically the same as the domestic market, so marketing strategies are hardly adapted at all for the overseas market.
Polycentrism	A polycentric firm only identifies the differences in each market. The firm treats each market as being unique, with its own marketing strategies; the products are modified to suit the local market, and tactical issues such as price and promotion are decided locally.
Geocentrism	The firm sees the world as a single market and seeks to identify market segments within that market. This results in developing uniform policies for approaching the segments which have been identified, so that promotions and products are similar across the globe.

supplying firm, because countries acquire reputations which affect the reputations of their companies. If both the supplier and the purchaser are global, a further problem arises. Because there are several decision-makers involved in industrial buying, and they may be scattered across several countries, each buyer is subject to a separate set of cultural influences. This situation requires considerable negotiation and adaptation of both the product and the business methods to achieve agreement.

Globalisation is important for all firms, even those who are not themselves planning to expand into the international arena; those firms will still be affected directly or indirectly by foreign competition and by the growing strength of domestic competitors who have themselves expanded overseas.

Anti-globalisation movements have sprung up worldwide – in fact, anti-globalisation movements are themselves examples of globalisation. During 2001 major riots occurred at global summit conferences in Genoa and Seattle, with some loss of life and considerable property damage. Those who are opposed to the increasing globalisation of business cite the power of the global companies, which are not accountable to anyone except their shareholders, and in many cases are able to transcend national governments. Global companies do have greater power than national governments in terms of controlling international exchange rates, and can switch production between countries in order to take advantage of tax breaks and other incentives. Some small countries' economies are controlled almost entirely by major corporations: for example, the 'banana republics' of Central America have almost no other products but fruit, which they supply exclusively to a handful of American fruit importers. Governments of such countries cannot afford to offend their only customers, so the fruit companies are able to exert almost total power.

Another objection to globalisation is the erosion of cultural values. Major firms are often accused of forcing cultural changes on the population: this is called McDonaldisation, a reference to the well-known McDonald's practice of standardising the product worldwide. For example, there has been an overall growth in tobacco smoking worldwide in recent years as the tobacco companies have targeted Third World countries, in effect exporting the vices of the industrial world.

A final criticism is that global companies do not have any allegiance to individual countries, and therefore have no compunction about causing environmental damage or economic disruption in supplier countries. For example, farmers in Africa are encouraged to grow cash crops to supply global corporations, while neglecting to grow sufficient crops to feed the local population.

Anti-globalisation campaigns are likely to be a feature of twenty-first century business for some time to come, but they are unlikely to have much impact on the way firms do business. In the last analysis, consumers indicate their support (or lack of support) for companies by the way they spend their money. If people in, say, France decide that they would rather have a quick snack at McDonald's than take their traditional two-hour lunch break, they will do so – and in practice McDonald's has many home-grown imitators in France, including Quick and Buffalo Grill.

MARKETING STRATEGY REVISITED

In previous chapters, strategy has been discussed in terms of knowing where the firm is now, and knowing where it is going. Tactical decisions have been illustrated, describing methods of achieving the destination.

In the broader contexts examined in this chapter, marketing strategy needs also to take account of the long-term sustainability of the company. Although it has been a general rule in the past that companies cannot stand still, there may in future be pressures requiring a company to mark time, so that 'reaching a destination' becomes 'remaining where we are'. Analysis therefore needs to go beyond the SWOT and STEP analyses described in Chapters 2 and 10, and include further analysis to take account of societal marketing (see Chapter 1). Tactically, marketers must take account of ethical thinking; the route to achieving the company's objectives needs to be an ethical one if the objective is to be reached.

Strategies for dealing with issues of societal marketing are as follows:

- **Reaction strategy** means ignoring a problem unless somebody complains. When the problem becomes known, the business managers usually deny responsibility, resolve the problem and clear up any consequential losses, and carry on as usual.

- **Defence strategy** seeks to wriggle out of any problems. The firm might lobby politicians to avoid adverse legislation, or change the way the business is run to avoid complying with regulations. For example, some shipping companies respond to safety regulations by registering the vessels in countries that have few regulations, such as Liberia and Panama.

■ **Accommodation strategy** involves accepting responsibility for the firm's actions and accommodating the views of the stakeholders. A business might take action if it feels that a pressure group or government legislation is about to force an issue.

■ **Proactive strategy** involves regularly examining the company's activities in the light of ethical and societal responsibilities, and repairing any failings or shortcomings without waiting for outside groups to notice the problem. This strategy requires the greatest effort (and cost) to the firm, but also ensures the maximum return in terms of maintaining a caring reputation.

THE TWENTY-FIRST CENTURY MARKETPLACE

According to Schultz and Schultz (1998) marketing has gone through two distinct phases since 1950, and is about to enter a third. In the 1950s and 1960s markets were dominated by manufacturers, who used market research to find out what consumers wanted and used intensive promotional campaigns to control markets or at least have the strongest influence in them. During the 1970s and 1980s retailers began to dominate, because they were closest to the market. They have been able to determine which products are offered to consumers and which are not. The third phase, brought about by the increasing use of IT by consumers, is consumer domination of the marketplace.

In the decade since Shultz and Shultz published their prophetic view of marketing, much of what they predicted has happened. The Internet has become almost universal in the wealthy countries of Europe and the Americas, and even in less-favoured countries the advent of Internet cafés means that a large proportion of the world's population are able to carry out information searches and shop online. This represents a dramatic shift of power towards consumers.

As consumers become more powerful in the relationship, the role of marketing is shifting from a strategic function to a tactical one. The model of marketing as a patriarchal function has been breaking down for some time now, in the face of unpredictable consumer responses, fragmentation of societies and increasing individualism. Consumers are impatient with the concept of the powerful, all-knowing marketers providing them with what the research says is best for them. This means that market research findings no longer act as truly effective predictors in many cases, and marketers are therefore left to respond as effectively as they can to consumer demands as expressed through interactive media.

Of course, the traditional manufacturer domination will continue in some markets, and the retailer domination of major store chains will also continue, but the increasing ability of consumers to make their purchases almost anywhere in the world and to access information from almost anywhere will increase the pressure on marketers to integrate their activities to maximise effectiveness and efficiency. This set of circumstances will lead to a change in the way marketing operates.

Firms go through four levels of marketing integration, as shown in Table 12.4. Evidence for this change manifests itself mainly on the Internet, where reverse-auction sites are springing up almost daily; sites such as adabra.com allow consumers to bid for manufactured products. Once the bids are in, the manufacturers are invited to supply products at the heavily discounted prices that the consumers have said they are prepared to pay. This type of consumer power is likely to become more prevalent as the decade unfolds.

Overall, marketing in the twenty-first century presents many new challenges. Shrinking markets, green issues, runaway advances in communications technology, and rapidly changing public attitudes towards consumption and communication predicate major changes not only in marketing techniques but also in corporate strategy. The role of marketing is still, at the end of the day, to meet customers' needs in the most effective, efficient and sustainable way possible for as long as it is possible to do so. Marketers will need to re-examine their models of marketing strategy many times; in an era where change is the only constant, marketing cannot afford to stand still. Ultimately, the firms who take the greatest care of their customers' interests are the ones most likely to maintain their competitive edge in a cut-throat world.

Table 12.4 Stages of integration of marketing communications

Stage	Explanation
Level 1: **Tactical co-ordination**	The 1980s and 1990s saw a massive increase in the available tools for communicating with consumers; Level 1 response is to create 'one sight, one sound' by consolidating communications planning. Often this leads to the formation of teams of specialists from different areas of expertise to increase synergy and cross-fertilisation of ideas.
Level 2: **Redefining the scope of marketing**	Rather than viewing marketing as a series of outbound activities, the firm begins to consider all the points at which the consumer and the brand are in contact. One of the most important results of Level 2 thinking has been the inclusion of employees both as targets for marketing communications and as communicators in their own right. Internal marketing thus becomes one of the driving forces of Level 2 thinking.
Level 3: **Application of IT**	IT is both driving the changes in marketing, and providing the solutions. The key ingredient in Level 3 thinking is the use of databases to capture individual transactions. This enables the firm to move away from marketing to the average customer at the middle of a segment, and to market to groups of individuals instead.
Level 4: **Strategic and financial integration**	Two issues are paramount: the ability to measure the return on customer investment, and the ability to use marketing to drive organisational and strategic directions. Rather than measuring (for example) extra sales resulting from an advertising campaign, the firm would now measure the returns from a specific group of customers against the costs associated with all the marketing efforts directed at that group. Under this approach, financial directors would have sufficient information to be able to compare investment in communicating with a particular group of customers with, for example, investing in new manufacturing facilities.

Case study 12
Call centres

Call centres have become the communications phenomenon of the decade. The huge increase in the ownership of mobile telephones, plus the desire for rapid (indeed instant) communication with companies, has generated a corresponding increase in the number of firms using a dedicated call centre, staffed by dozens of operators ready to answer queries from customers. At the same time, rising costs of putting salespeople on the road have forced companies down the road of using outbound call centres to telephone prospective customers with offers.

Many companies see the call centre as being the front line for relationship marketing. Having an actual human being to talk to about new purchases, problems, or simply for advice is far more powerful (and human) than relying on letters and e-mails. Outbound call centres can follow up on purchases, can offer upgrades and sales of peripherals, and can follow up on referrals by satisfied customers.

Of course, call centres do have a downside. For one thing, they are often disliked by members of the public – the Telephone Preference Service, which arranges for people to be removed from calling lists, has been a runaway success: in a Parliamentary reply in July 2006, the Secretary of State for Trade and Industry reported that 12.7 million numbers were registered with TPS. This amounts to more than half the private telephones in the UK – although it is difficult to be specific, as the TPS confidentiality systems mean that there is no way to check whether consumers have registered the same number more than once.

Call centres also suffer from high staff turnover. The job itself is stressful, even when only dealing with inbound calls: customers can be abusive, or may ask difficult questions, or may simply be stupid. Call centre staff still need to approach each new call with a positive attitude. Outbound call centre staff face even greater stress: many people find the calls irritating, and even when they are happy in principle with being called at home, the call may come at an inconvenient time, leading to a sharp response from the customer. Staff in Indian call centres have reported racist abuse, sexual harassment and general rudeness from callers as being the main reasons for leaving the job altogether. 'I wanted to cry, but I had to take the next call' one female call centre worker said.

A survey by the Citizen's Advice Bureau, published in February 2008, reported that utilities such as British Gas and British Telecom had the worst track record for dealing with customers through their call centres: 77% of respondents to the survey said they had been unable to resolve their problem in only one call, and almost one third reported being kept on the telephone for more than half an hour. A separate survey by Ipsos Mori makes equally depressing reading – 27% of those who contacted a utility company were dissatisfied with the outcome, and 89% of people who had contacted a landline telephone provider were either dissatisfied or very dissatisfied with the outcome.

Not every call centre is the same. First Direct, the UK telephone bank, uses call centres in Yorkshire and Scotland: staff are not pressured to finish calls quickly, customers are generally polite and pleasant, and there are very few outgoing sales calls to be made. Staff are well-trained and have good prospects for promotion – a feature lacking in many call centres, where opportunities are few. They are also allowed to terminate calls which become abusive – a privilege not accorded to all call centre staff.

Ultimately, call centres are here to stay. Love them or hate them, they exist to make communication between companies and consumers more effective and efficient: communication is the main building block of developing relationships, so call centres are likely to be in the forefront of relationship marketing for years to come.

Questions

1 Why might people be resentful of call centres?

2 Given that 12 million telephone numbers are registered with TPS, why do firms continue to use outgoing calls?

3 How might a call centre owner reduce staff turnover?

4 Why do callers become abusive with the only person who can help them?

5 How might call centres help in establishing good relationships?

SUMMARY

In this chapter we have looked at current issues in marketing: the ways in which companies try to establish long-term relationships with their customers, ethical issues and Internet marketing.

Here are the key points from this chapter:

■ Relationship marketing suggests that manufacturers should try to develop the same closeness to the customer that service industries have.

■ Traditional marketing is concerned with single transactions; relationship marketing is concerned with long-term business.

■ It is cheaper to keep existing customers than find new ones.

■ Quality is the relationship between expectations and results.

■ Benchmarking may make a firm the best of the best, but it is likely in the long run to stifle innovation.

■ Companies that fail to establish a good relationship with their customers will lose out to firms that do.

■ Responsible ethical approaches are likely to be directly beneficial to the firm in the long run; unethical approaches may be beneficial in the short run, but affect survival prospects long-term.

■ The Internet is not without its problems, but Internet marketing is likely to continue to grow in future.

CHAPTER QUESTIONS

1 Describe the two main schools of thought on ethics.

2 How would you go about establishing a code of ethics?

3 Why might transaction marketing be less effective than relationship marketing in the long run for, say, a car manufacturer?

4 What reasons might a firm have for consulting environmentalists about strategy?

5 What are the key issues in establishing a website?

Further reading

Good Business: Your World Needs You by **Steve Hilton and Giles Gibbons** (London, Texere Publishing, 2002) offers a view of how ethically run businesses can actually be more profitable than those run on purely self-centred lines. It is a cheerfully optimistic book, positive about the capitalist system, and offers plentiful advice on how to make it even better.

E-Marketing, 3rd edn, by **Judy Strauss, Adel el-Ansary and Raymond Frost** (Englewood Cliffs, NJ, Prentice-Hall, 2002) is structured like an introductory marketing text, but covers all the topics from an e-marketing perspective. It is thus currently the most comprehensive available book on Internet marketing. Obviously it is likely to date quickly – new editions will replace this one fairly regularly!

Customer Relationship Management by **Francis Buttle** (Oxford, Butterworth-Heinemann, 2003). This book looks at customer relationship management as the core activity of the business, and gives a comprehensive overview of what information technology will (and will not) do in helping to manage customer relations, retention and development.

An alternative view is provided in *Why CRM Doesn't Work: How to Win by Letting Customers Manage the Relationship* by **Frederick Newell** (London, Kogan Page, 2003). Newell argues that trying to manage the relationship fails because the customer is not empowered – letting the customers manage the relationship is actually more successful.

References

Ang, Lawrence and Buttle, Francis: 'Managing for successful customer acquisition: an exploration', *Journal of Marketing Management*, **22** (3/4) (2006), pp. 295–317.

Baker, M.J.: *Marketing: An Introductory Text*, 5th edn (Basingstoke, Macmillan 1991).

Barnes, Stuart, Bauer, Hans H., Neumann, Marcus M. and Huber, Frank: 'Segmenting cyberspace: a customer typology for the Internet', *European Journal of Marketing*, **41** (1/2) (2007), pp. 71–93.

Brennan, Ross D., Turnbull, Peter W. and Wilson, David T.: 'Dyadic adaptation in business-to-business markets', *European Journal of Marketing*, **37** (11) (2003), pp. 1636–8.

Brookes, G.: 'Online: overcrowded inbox', *Marketing*, 13 July 2005.

Christodoulides, George, DeChernatony, Leslie, Furrier, Olivier, Shiu, Eric and Abimbola, Temi: 'Conceptualising and measuring the equity of online brands', *Journal of Marketing Management*, **22** (7/8) (2006), pp. 799–825.

Christopher, M., Ballantyne, D. and Payne, A.: *Relationship Marketing* (Oxford, Butterworth-Heinemann, 1991).

Conway, Tony, Ward, Mike, Lewis, Gerard and Bernhardt, Anke: 'Internet crisis potential: the importance of a strategic approach to marketing communication', *Journal of Marketing Communication*, **13** (3) (2007), pp. 213–28.

Cross, R.: 'Permission marketing', *Admap*, **440** (June 2003), pp. 30–3.

Denegri-Knott, Janice: 'Consumers behaving badly: deviation or innovation? Power struggles on the Web', *Journal of Consumer Behaviour*, **5** (1) (2006), pp. 82–94.

Dick, A.S.: 'Using membership fees to increase customer loyalty', *Journal of Product and Brand Management*, **4** (5) (1995), pp. 65–8.

Duffy, P.: 'How to grow and enhance your customer email database', *Brand Republic*, 3 February 2006.

Dufrene, D., Engelland, B., Lehman, C. and Pearson, R.: 'Changes in consumer attitudes resulting from participation in a permission e-mail campaign', *Journal of Current Issues and Research in Advertising*, **27**, (1) (2005), pp. 65–77

East, Robert, Hammond, Kathy and Gendall, Philip: 'Fact and fallacy in retention marketing', *Journal of Markeing Management*, **22** (2006), pp. 5–23.

Eccles, M.: 'Email marketing growing, along with consumers fatigue', *Brand Republic*, 20 January 2006.

Eng, Teck-Yong: 'The role of e-marketplaces in supply chain management', *Industrial Marketing Management*, **33** (2) (February 2004), pp. 97–105.

Evans, M.J.: 'Domesday marketing?', *Journal of Marketing Management*, **10** (5) (1994).

Fraedrich, John: 'Philosophy type interaction in the ethical decision making process of retailers', PhD Dissertation (Texas, A&M University, 1988).

Fraj, Elena and Martinez, Eva: 'Influence of personality on ecological consumer behavior', *Journal of Consumer Behaviour*, **5** (3) (2006), pp. 167–181.

Grandcolas, Ursula, Rettie, Ruth and Marusenko, Kira: 'Web survey bias: sample or mode effect?', *Journal of Marketing Management*, **19** (2003), pp. 501–61.

Grant, Robert, Clarke, Rodney J. and Kyriazis, Elias: 'A review of factors affecting online consumer search behavior from an information value perspective', *Journal of Marketing Management*, **23** (5/6) (2007), pp. 519–33.

Helgesen, Oyvind: 'Are loyal customers profitable? Customer satisfaction, customer (action) loyalty, and customer profitability at the individual level', *Journal of Marketing Management*, **22** (3/4) (2006), pp. 245–66.

Hoffman, D. and Novak, T.: 'A new marketing paradigm for electronic commerce', *The Information Society*, **13** (1) (1996).

Holzwarth, Martin, Janiszewski, Chris and Neumann, Marcus M.: 'The influence of avatars on online consumer shopping behavior', *Journal of Marketing*, **70** (4) (2006), pp. 19–36.

Jayawardene, Chanaka: 'Management of service quality in Internet banking: the development of an instrument', *Journal of Marketing*, **20** (1) (February 2004), pp. 185–207.

Jepsen, Anna Lund: 'Information search in virtual communities: is it replacing use of off-line communication?' *Journal of Marketing Communications*, **12** (4) (2006), pp. 247–61.

Johnson, Michael D. and Selnes, Fred: 'Customer portfolio management: towards a dynamic theory of exchange relationships', *Journal of Marketing*, **68** (2) (April 2004), pp. 1–16.

Johnson, Michael D., Herrman, Andreas and Huber, Frank: 'The evaluation of loyalty intentions', *Journal of Marketing*, **70** (2) (2006), pp. 122–32.

Kent, R. and Brandal, H.: 'Improving email response in a permission marketing context', *International Journal of Market Research*, **45** (4) (2003), pp. 489–503.

Levitt, T.: *The Marketing Imagination* (New York, Free Press, 1986).

McDonald, Jason B. and Smith, Kirk: 'The effects of technology-mediated communication on industrial buyer behaviour', *Industrial Marketing Management*, **33** (2) (2004), pp. 107–16.

Mitchell, A.: 'How will the loyalty card evolve now?', *Marketing Week* (30 August 1996), pp. 20–1.

Moen, Oysten, Endresen, Iver and Gavlen, Morten: 'Executive insights: use of the Internet in international marketing: a case study of small computer firms', *Journal of International Marketing*, **11** (4) (2003), pp. 129–49.

Nussey, B.: 'The quiet email revolution', *iUniverse* (Inc, New York, 2004).

O'Leary, Chris, Rao, Saly and Perry, Chad: 'Improving customer relationship management through database/Internet marketing: a theory-building action research project', *European Journal of Marketing*, **38** (3/4) (2004), pp. 338–54.

Ojasalo, Jukka: 'Key network management', *Industrial Marketing Management*, **33** (3) (2004), pp. 195–205.

Parsons, Andrew and Conroy, Denise: 'Sensory stimuli and e-tailers', *Journal of Consumer Behaviour*, **5** (1) (2006), pp. 69–81.

Quiris: *How Email Practices Can Win or Lose Long-term Business: A View from the Inbox* (2003).

Roberts, Keith, Varki, Sajeev and Brodie, Rod: 'Measuring the quality of relationships in consumer services: an empirical study', *European Journal of Marketing*, **37** (1) (2003), pp. 169–96.

Roemer, Ellen: 'The impact of dependence on the assessment of customer lifetime values in buyer–seller relationships', *Journal of Marketing Management*, **22** (2006), pp. 89–109.

Schultz, D.E. and Schultz, H.E.: 'Transitioning marketing communications into the twenty-first century', *Journal of Marketing Communications*, **4** (1) (1998), pp. 9–26.

Singh, Nitish, Rassott, Georg, Zhao, Hongzhin and Bouftor, Paul D.: 'A cross-cultural analysis of German, Chinese and Indian consumers' perception of website adaptation', *Journal of Consumer Behaviour*, **5** (1) (2006), pp. 56–68.

Smith, J. and Wood, C. 'Opt-in is just a start', *Direct*, **16** (4) (2004), p. 39.

Steenkamp, Jan-Benedict E.M. and Geyskens, Inge: 'How country characteristics affect the perceived value of websites', *Journal of Marketing*, **70** (3) (2006), pp. 136–50.

Tuli, Kapil R., Kohli, Ajay K. and Bharadwaj, Sundar G.: 'Rethinking customer solutions: from product bundles to relational processes', *Journal of Marketing*, **71** (3) (2007), pp. 1–17.

Tuominen, Matti, Rajalo, Arto and Möller, Kristian: 'Market-driving versus market-driven: divergent roles of market orientation in business relationships', *Industrial Marketing Management*, **33** (3) (2004), pp. 207–17.

Valor, Carmen: 'The influence of information about labour abuses on consumer choice of clothes: a grounded theory approach', *Journal of Marketing Management*, **23** (7/8) (2007), pp. 675–95.

Vlasic, Goran and Kesic, Tanja: 'Analysis of consumers' attitudes towards interactivity and relationship personalization as contemporary developments in interactive marketing communications', *Journal of Marketing Communications*, **13** (2) (2007), pp. 109–29.

Wang, Liz C., Wagner, Judy A. and Wakefield, Kirk: 'Can a retail website be social?', *Journal of Marketing*, **71** (3) (2007), pp. 143–57.

Wolk, Agnieszka and Theysohn, Sven: 'Factors influencing website traffic in the paid content market', *Journal of Marketing Management*, **23** (7/8) (2007), pp. 769–96.

Glossary

Accommodation strategy Consulting with stakeholders to determine a strategy which will be acceptable to all parties.

Accumulation Collecting small production batches from one or more manufacturers into amounts large enough to be worth shipping.

Actual state The current position of the individual in terms of well-being and possessions.

Adoption Building a given brand or product into one's regular daily life.

Advertisement A paid insertion of a message in a medium.

Affect What is felt about a product; liking, dislike, fear, etc.

Affective states Conditions of the emotional or physical well-being of the individual that cause interrupts.

Agent An individual or firm who arranges sales of goods and services without actually taking possession of them.

AIDA Acronym for Attention, Interest, Desire and Action – the four stages of response to communications.

Aided recall The degree to which an individual can recognise an advertisement when it is shown to him/her.

Allocation (bulk breaking) Breaking down large shipments into smaller amounts.

Analogy A projective technique in which the respondent is invited to identify himself/herself with a non-human object.

Assorting Gathering together groups of related goods under one roof in order to sell them to specialist retailers.

Assortment depletion The consumption of the whole or most of an item in the consumer's stock of possessions.

Assortment extension The act of adding to an existing stock of possessions.

Auxiliary characteristics Those features and benefits that are secondary to the primary characteristics; the less essential aspects that differentiate the product from its close substitutes.

Backward integration Taking control of suppliers.

Balance of payments The difference between the value of exports and the value of imports.

Barter The exchange of goods for other goods without the exchange of money.

Behavioural segmentation Grouping potential customers according to their activities, attitudes and lifestyles.

Brand architecture The process of structuring brands in order to transfer brand equity from product levels to corporate levels.

Brand awareness The degree to which the consumer has knowledge of a given brand.

Brand extension Marketing new products under an old brand name.

Brand manager The person with responsibility for decisions concerning a specific brand.

Brand switching The act of buying a different brand from the one usually purchased.

Break-down forecasting Predicting sales by calculating the firm's share of the overall market.

Build-up forecasting Predicting sales by calculating the firm's share of each segment and adding these together.

Buy-back A form of countertrading in which capital equipment is sold in exchange for a future stream of the goods that the equipment will produce.

Buyer The individual who carries out the mechanical processes of purchasing.

Cash-and-carry wholesalers Stockists whose retailer customers visit the warehouse, pay for goods on the spot, and remove them in their own transport.

Cash Cow A product with a large share of a low-growth market.

Catalogue showrooms High street retailers who display goods only by means of a catalogue.

Channel conflict Differences of direction between channel members.

Channel co-operation The process of co-ordinating the activities of channel members to achieve agreed objectives.

Channel of distribution The routes and intermediaries through which a product passes from producer to end user.

Channel power The means by which one channel member is able to exert his/her will over another channel member.

Clinical focus group A heterogeneous group of respondents brought together under clinical conditions to discuss an issue.

Cognition What is thought about a product; beliefs and opinions.

Co-marketing The marketing of one brand alongside another.

Comparative advantage The natural advantage one country has over another in terms of production or resources.

Compatibility The degree to which the new product fits in with the customer's existing purchases and lifestyle.

Competitor-based pricing Using competitors' prices as a starting-point for price-setting.

Complexity The degree to which the product is difficult to learn to use.

Compositioning Grouping products under a single brand name with a single position in the consumer's perceptual map.

Conation Planned behaviour regarding a product or event.

Concentric diversification Developing new products for new markets, but with production synergies with the present range.

Concessionaires Retailers who rent space in department stores and use their own staff to sell goods to consumers.

Confidence The degree to which the individual feels sure that the attitude is the correct one.

Conglomerate diversification The introduction of new products unrelated to the firm's existing technology.

Consideration set The group of products which the individual is aware would adequately meet his or her needs.

Consumer products Goods and services purchased for the personal consumption of an individual or his/her family.

Contactors Those individuals within an organisation whose work brings them into direct contact with stakeholders.

Convenience products Cheap, frequently purchased items which do not require much thought or planning.

Convenience store Small retailer located in a residential area offering household items and food.

Conviction The belief that a given product will meet one's needs better than any other.

Copy The words used in advertisements.

Copywriter Individual who supplies the words for advertisements.

Core benefits The benefits that would apply to all consumers of the product category. For example, all cars provide the core benefit of personal transportation.

Corporate objectives The ultimate goals that the corporate management hope to achieve.

Cost leadership The maintenance of a competitive edge by means of keeping costs low.

Cost-plus pricing Basing the price calculation on the firm's production costs, plus a predetermined allowance for profit.

Countertrading Exporting into a market on condition that goods of equal value will be imported from the same market.

Culture A set of shared beliefs and behaviours common to a society.

Customary pricing A price applied to a product or for a minimum amount of a product and fixed for a number of years.

Customer research Information gathering regarding the customer's needs and wants.

Customer survey Forecasting sales by asking customers how much of the product they expect to buy.

Customisation Adapting the firm's products to meet local market conditions.

Customs union A treaty between nations under which the member states agree to common external tariffs in most goods.

Cut-off The maximum or minimum acceptable values for product attributes.

Cycle analysis Examining earlier sales figures to see whether there is evidence of a recurring pattern over a period of years.

Data Facts gathered in the course of research.

Database marketing The use of computers to profile and contact customers and potential customers.

Decider The individual who has the power to make the final purchasing decision.

Decision support systems Computer-based information-gathering and interpreting systems used to inform marketing decisions.

Defence strategy Changing the way the business is run in order to avoid outside pressures.

Delphi technique Forecasting by asking each interested party to make their own estimate, then circulating the estimates to the other members of the group for comment and revision.

Demand A want which can be paid for.

Demand pricing Prices based on the customers' demand for the product.

Demographic segmentation Grouping potential customers according to their position in the structure of the population.

Demographics The study of population structure.

Deontology The belief that actions can be deemed ethical or unethical independently of outcomes.

Department store A large city-centre store offering a wide range of household goods, clothing, cosmetics and food.

Depth interview An interview with an individual, using probing questions to arrive at the individual's innermost feelings.

Derived demand The state of affairs where the demand for a component derives from the demand for the finished product.

Description The process of industrial buying whereby the buyer describes the required product and asks suppliers to provide tenders for its supply.

Desired state The position the individual would like to be in, in terms of well-being and possessions.

Differentiated marketing Concentrating effort on a segment or segments by offering a product which the target customers would see as superior.

Differentiation Distinguishing the firm and its products from all competitors.

Direct costs Expenses attributable solely to a particular product.

Direct response Promotions that include a coupon or telephone number for the customer to contact the manufacturer or service provider without going through intermediaries.

Discount sheds Large out-of-town stores offering consumer durables or hardware.

Discounter A retailer offering a very limited range of goods at low prices.

Distribution research Studies of distribution methods and systems with a view to improving distribution in the future.

Distribution strategy The planning process concerned with selecting the most effective outlet for goods and services.

Distributor survey Forecasting sales by asking the firm's distributors to estimate how much of the product they expect to sell.

Divestment The act of disposal of a used-up or worn out product or its packaging.

Dodo A product with a low share of a shrinking market.

Dog A product with a low share of a low-growth market.

Drive The state of unease that derives from the gap between the desired and actual states.

Drop shippers Individuals or firms who take orders from retailers and buy the goods from manufacturers, shipping the goods without taking physical possession of them.

Early adopters People who adopt a new product after the innovators have already adopted it.

Early majority Consumers who adopt a product once it has been thoroughly tried and tested, but before more than half the population have adopted the product.

Eclectic theory The view that firms choose their internationalisation strategy according to their own strengths and weaknesses.

Economic choice The decisions forced on customers and producers by the scarcity of resources.

Economies of scale Savings made as production and marketing activity increase; the reduction in unit costs brought about by more efficient large-scale production.

Editing The act of removing spoiled or aberrant data, prior to analysis.

Elastic demand A state of affairs where the amount of the product that will be purchased is strongly affected by its price.

Employee markets Those individuals who provide time and expertise to the firm in exchange for salaries or wages.

Empowerment Authorising employees to make decisions regarding customer service reparation without recourse to managers.

Environmental stimulus A factor in the search or purchase environment that causes an interrupt.

Equitable performance The level of product performance which the individual would regard as reasonable, given the cost of the search in terms of time and effort and financial cost of the product.

Ethnocentrism The belief that one's own culture is 'right' and that other cultures are pale imitations.

Exchange rates The prices at which foreign currency is exchanged for national currency.

Exclusive dealing Agreements that prevent a channel member from dealing with a competing channel member.

Execution format The overall style of an advertisement.

Executive judgement Forecasting sales by asking senior management to estimate the potential business.

Expected performance The level of product performance the consumer expects, given the pre-purchase information collected.

Experiencing focus group A homogeneous group of respondents brought together to give the researcher experience of talking to a group from the population of interest.

Experiment A controlled event in which a subject is given a stimulus and his/her reactions are noted.

Export agents Firms that arrange the export of goods without taking possession of the goods themselves.

Export houses Firms that buy goods for resale abroad.

Exporting Manufacturing in the home country and selling the goods abroad.

External environment Those cultural, social, economic, legal and competitive factors that are outside the organisation.

External search Information obtained from sources other than the individual's personal experience and memories.

Extremity The strength of attitude towards a product.

Family branding Grouping products under a single brand.

Fluctuating demand This is common in industrial markets, whereby a small reduction in consumer demand for a product will lead to de-stocking, thus causing a big reduction in demand for components.

Focus The degree to which the firm is concentrating on a specific segment or segments of the market.

Focus group A group of respondents brought together to discuss an issue in the presence of a moderator, who records the group's deliberations.

Forward integration Taking control of customers.

Franchising Allowing a foreign firm to operate a business concept (including intellectual property) in exchange for royalties and other fees.

Frequency The number of times a given individual will see a given advertisement.

Full-service merchant wholesalers Merchant wholesalers who also offer marketing services to retailers.

Functional organisation Organising the marketing responsibilities according to the function of the staff concerned.

Gatekeeper An individual who controls the flow of information to a decision-maker.

General-merchandise wholesalers Stockists of a broad range of goods to sell to retailers.

Geographic segmentation Dividing potential customers into groups according to their location, either nationally or in smaller areas, for example areas of a city.

Globalisation Marketing a standardised product worldwide.

Hedonic needs The pleasurable or aesthetic aspects of product ownership or service use.

Heuristic A simple 'if ... then' decision-making rule.

Horizontal diversification Introducing new products (unrelated to the current range) to existing markets.

Horizontal integration The act of merging with, or buying out, competitors at the same level in the distribution channel.

Hypermarket A large out-of-town store offering a very wide range of consumer goods.

Ideal performance The level of product performance that the consumer would regard as meeting or exceeding all criteria.

Importing Bringing goods into the home country from a foreign country.

Industrial products Goods or services purchased by a business for use in the course of running the business.

Inelastic demand A state of affairs where the amount of the product that will be purchased is relatively unaffected by its price.

Influence markets Individuals and organisations in the marketing environment who have influence over the firm's activities.

Influencer An individual who has influence, but not power, in a buying decision.

Influencers Those individuals within an organisation who have no contact with customers but who do have a marketing role.

Information Data that have been interpreted and explained.

Informational influence The need to seek information from a reference group.

Innovators The first people to adopt a new product.

Inspection The act of examining a variable product to ensure that it meets particular criteria.

Institutional advertising Advertising in which the company or institution is promoted rather than a specific product.

Interference Purposeful noise that interrupts communications.

Internal environment Those cultural, social and economic factors that are contained within the organisation itself.

Internal PR Public relations exercises aimed at the workforce and other stakeholders within the organisation.

Internal publics Those groups within the firm to whom the firm needs to communicate its objectives and policies.

Internal search Information retrieved from the individual's memories and experience.

Interpreting The act of extracting meaning from data in order to create information.

Interrupt An event or piece of information that temporarily suspends the information search.

Interviewer bias Errors in results caused by deliberate or accidental acts of the interviewer.

Isolateds Those individuals within an organisation who have no contact with customers and have no marketing role.

Joint demand The state of affairs where the demand for one product is affected by the demand for another product.

Joint ventures A collaboration between two firms in the same or complementary industries to carry out a specific task with a view to mutual profit.

Laggards The last people to adopt a new product.

Late majority People who only adopt a product when approximately half the customers in the market have already done so.

Law of primacy The rule that states that later information is interpreted in the light of earlier experience, thus implying that early experience is more important than later experience.

Licensing Allowing a foreign firm to utilise the intellectual property of the owner in exchange for a royalty.

Lifestyle campaign A series of advertisements showing a product being used as part of a desirable lifestyle.

Limited-line wholesalers Stockists of a small range of goods for specialist retailers to buy.

Limited-service wholesalers Dealers who buy in bulk and arrange delivery to retailers without actually taking physical possession of the goods.

Line family branding Grouping related products under a single brand name.

Loading The level of demand for a service at different times of the day, week, month or year.

Logistics The process of strategically managing the movement and storage of materials, parts and finished goods from suppliers, through the firm, and on to consumers.

Loyalty card A plastic card entitling the bearer to discounts on purchases at a particular store.

Macro-environment Those environmental factors that are common to all firms and that can be influenced, but not controlled.

Mailshots Postal communications intended to obtain business or appointments for selling interviews.

Margin The amount of profit calculated as a percentage of the selling price.

Market development Increasing sales of current products in new markets.

Market research Studies of consumer needs, wants, behaviour and personalities in order to inform marketing decisions.

Marketing The management process which identifies, anticipates and supplies customer requirements efficiently and profitably.

Marketing audit A systematic assessment of the organisation's current marketing activities in order to inform the planning process.

Marketing cost analysis Examination of the costs of getting business in.

Marketing environment research Information gathering about the organisation's environment in terms of political, socio-cultural, economic and technological threats and opportunities.

Marketing information systems Ongoing information-gathering systems and record-keeping systems used to inform marketing decisions.

Marketing mix The seven areas of activity with which marketers are most concerned; price, product, place, promotion, people, process and physical evidence.

Marketing orientation The approach that puts the customer at the centre of everything the firm does.

Marketing research All forms of information-gathering used to inform marketing decisions.

Markets Groups of customers or consumers with similar needs and wants.

Mark-up The amount of profit calculated as a proportion of the bought-in price.

Mark-up pricing Adding a fixed percentage to the bought-in-price of a product.

Matrix A table in which data are arranged in two or more dimensions.

Mechanistic (bureaucratic) organisation An organisation in which leadership is chosen according to qualifications and experience, regardless of the current tasks facing the organisation.

Media event A meeting held to announce corporate news, to which journalists are invited.

Meet-the-competition strategy Setting prices close to those of the nearest competitors.

Merchant wholesalers Buyers of goods to sell to retailers, often using a salesforce.

Micro-environment Environmental factors that are close to the firm and to an extent controllable by the firm.

Missionaries Salespeople who seek to promote the company and its products to new prospects.

Modifiers Those individuals within the organisation who have regular contact with stakeholders but have no direct marketing role.

Monopolistic competition A condition where one supplier has a significant market share obtained by differentiating its product from those of its competitors.

Monopoly A condition where one firm produces a product that has no close substitutes.

Motivation The predisposition that arouses and directs behaviour towards certain goals.

Multinational marketing Operating production, promotion, pricing and distribution in the most beneficial countries regardless of national boundaries.

Multivariable segmentation Grouping potential customers according to several segmentation bases.

Need A perceived lack of something, e.g. food when hungry.

Negotiation The act of discussing with a supplier what would be the best way of approaching a new-purchase task.

Network A diagrammatic representation of the relationships between concepts.

New product development (NPD) The process of developing new products from idea stage through to launch on the market.

Niche marketer A retailer offering a depth of range of a single product line.

Niche marketing Concentrating effort on a very small market segment.

Noise Non-purposeful interference with communications.

Non-store retailing Any sales to consumers which do not take place in a shop.

Non-traceable common costs Expenses incurred across a range of products that cannot be allocated to any specific product.

Normative compliance The pressure exerted by reference groups to behave in the same way as the rest of the group.

Observability The degree to which the product can be seen by others.

Odd–even pricing The practice of ending prices with an odd number of cents, pence, etc., in order to give the impression of a lower price.

Oligopoly A condition where the market is controlled by a small group of suppliers.

Omnibus studies Surveys carried out on behalf of several researchers at once.

Optimal stimulation level The level of gap between desired and actual states at which the individual feels stimulated, but not yet uncomfortable.

Order getters Salespeople who provide solutions for new and existing customers from among the available product portfolio.

Order takers Salespeople who record and process purchase orders from people who had already decided to purchase.

Organismic organisation An organisation where the leadership devolves to the individual with the most appropriate expertise for the task facing the organisation.

Outshopping Buying goods from retailers outside the area where one lives.

Panels Permanent or semi-permanent groups of respondents who are prepared to comment on a wide range of issues.

Penetration pricing Pricing a new product low in order to maximise market penetration before competitors can enter the market.

Per capita income Average earnings per head of population.

Perception The analytic and synthetic process of developing a world view.

Perceptual mapping The process of positioning products, events and experiences in relation to one another.

Perfect competition A condition where the market contains a large number of suppliers, no one of which can significantly influence price or supply.

Persistence The stability of an attitude over time.

Personal selling A person-to-person communication intended to meet a customer's needs at a profit.

Physical distribution Moving products from producer to consumer.

Piggy-backing Exporting or promoting one product alongside another complementary product, often from a different firm.

Piloting The act of testing a questionnaire or other research tool on a small group of respondents in order to detect errors in its design.

Planned impulse Buying behaviour in which a planned course of action is changed as the result of a new stimulus.

Positioning The grouping of similar product types together in the consumer's perceptual map.

Postal surveys Questionnaires sent and returned through the mail.

Post-purchase consonance The state of affairs where the product's characteristics and benefits match up to or exceed the purchaser's expectations.

Post-purchase dissonance The state of affairs where the product's characteristics and benefits do not meet the purchaser's expectations in one or more respects.

Post-purchase evaluation The examination of the purchased product to determine whether it meets, exceeds or fails to meet pre-purchase expectations.

Post-tests Testing of the effectiveness of advertising materials after they have been shown to the general public.

Predatory pricing Pricing products so far below those of competitors that the competitors will be bankrupted.

Premium The amount a customer is prepared to pay above the price of a standardised product in order to obtain a product which more closely fits his or her needs.

Prestige pricing Applying a high price to a product to indicate its high quality.

Pre-tests Testing of advertising materials before they are shown to the general public.

Price elasticity of demand The extent to which the demand for a product is affected by its price.

Price leaders Firms whose market share and share of the capacity in the industry are great enough for them to be able to set the prices in the market.

Primary characteristics The main aspects of a product which provide the core benefits to the consumer.

Primary research Research carried out first-hand; original, previously unpublished work.

Private responses Complaints made about the product or supplier to friends or others.

Proactive management A management approach that seeks to anticipate problems and act before they arise.

Proactive PR Public relations exercises undertaken as a result of internal planning within the organisation.

Proactive strategy Seeking out stakeholders and changing their viewpoints in advance of action.

Problem Child A product with a low share of a high-growth market.

Product A bundle of benefits.

Product advertising Advertising in which a product category is promoted rather than an individual brand.

Product development Improving the present products or adding new products to current markets.

Product differentiation The features and benefits of a product that distinguish it from its near substitutes.

Product life cycle (PLC) The stages a product goes through from launch to obsolescence.

Product manager The person with responsibility for a particular product type.

Product orientation The paradigm that suggests that the 'perfect' product will suit all consumers.

Product research Studies of customer and consumer responses to product offerings with a view to adapting future offerings.

Production orientation The paradigm that suggests that efficiency in the production process is the main way for a firm to succeed.

Product-line pricing Applying differential pricing policies to products that are co-dependent in terms of demand.

Projective technique A research method which invites respondents to project their own views onto a third party, or a cartoon character, in order to avoid embarrassment.

Promotion research Organised information-gathering regarding the effectiveness of promotional activities or potential audience responses to proposed promotional activities.

Promotional mix The combination of PR, advertising, personal selling and sales promotion leading to purposeful marketing communications.

Prospects Individuals who are prepared to talk to a salesperson about their needs.

Protectionism The tendency of a government to exclude foreign competition.

Psychographic segmentation Grouping potential customers according to their personality traits.

Psychological pricing Applying prices that appeal to the customer's emotions and subconscious thought processes.

Psychological proximity The degree to which two or more nations share cultural attributes.

Public relations (PR) Activities intended to convey an organisation's messages to its publics.

Publics Those groups and individuals which have a direct or indirect impact on an organisation's activities.

Pure impulse Buying behaviour undertaken without prior rational thought.

Qualitative research Gathering of non-numerical data.

Quality The relationship between what is expected and what is received.

Quantitative research Gathering of numerical data.

Quota sample A group of respondents having the same mix of relevant characteristics as the sample frame.

Rack jobbers Retailers who rent shelf space in retail shops and stock the shelves themselves.

Random factor analysis Examining the abnormal figures within the analysis of sales trends to attribute causation.

Random sample A group of respondents taken from a sample frame, each member of which has an equal chance of being included in the random sample.

Ratchet effect The phenomenon whereby an increase in sales resulting from a sales promotion tends to remain after the promotion ends.

Rational campaign An advertisement or series of advertisements using facts and figures in an authoritative way to appeal to the consumer's cognition.

Reach The number of people who are exposed to an advertisement.

Reaction strategy Waiting until outside pressures force change.

Reactive management An approach that involves responding to outside and inside influences as they arise.

Reactive PR (defensive PR) Public relations exercises undertaken as a response to outside pressures.

Redundancy Sending the same message via different routes to overcome the distorting effects of interference and noise.

Reference group A formal or informal group from which the individual seeks cues regarding appropriate behaviour.

Referral markets Those individuals or firms who do not themselves buy from the firm, but who can influence others to do so.

Regional organisation Giving responsibility for all marketing tasks to the regional management.

Re-invention The process of finding new uses for old products.

Relationship marketing A business approach that concentrates on the long-term relationship between the firm and its stakeholders rather than on single transactions.

Relative advantage The degree to which a new product is better than the product the customer is currently using.

Reminder impulse Buying behaviour undertaken when the individual is reminded of something.

Resistance The level of difficulty experienced in changing an attitude.

Respondents Individuals who participate in research studies.

Retailer An individual or firm who buys goods or services and sells them on to consumers.

Role The group of behaviours expected of the occupant of a given position.

Sales analysis Examination of the sources of income the company has.

Sales manager The manager responsible for controlling, recruiting, training and motivating the salesforce.

Sales orientation The view that customers will not ordinarily buy enough of a product without an aggressive selling and advertising campaign.

Sales promotion A temporary offer used to increase immediate sales.

Sales research Information gathering about the selling process in order to improve training and motivation of the salesforce.

Sales territory The geographical or industrial area allocated to an individual salesperson.

Salesforce survey Forecasting sales by asking members of the salesforce to estimate how much of the product they expect to be able to sell.

Salesperson The person responsible for finding solutions for customers' needs on an individual basis, within the constraints of what the firm has to offer.

Sample A representative sub-group of respondents taken from the population as a whole.

Sampling The act of testing a small part of a bulk supply to judge whether the whole meets particular criteria.

Sampling bias Errors in results caused by studying an unrepresentative group of respondents.

Sampling frame The population of potential respondents from which a sample will be taken.

Seasonal analysis Examining earlier sales figures to see whether there is evidence of a recurring pattern over a period spanning less than a year.

Secondary research Published research; second-hand information, already published and available.

Second-market discounting Offering products at a lower price in a second market than is charged in the main market.

Segmental organisation Giving responsibility for marketing tasks to individuals who deal with specific segments of the market.

Segmentation The process of categorising consumers into groups with similar needs.

Self-liquidating offers Sales promotions in which the consumer makes a purchase of an associated product, the price of which more than covers the cost of the promotion.

Service-quality benchmarking Adopting best practice in terms of customer service from both competitors and non-competitors.

Shelf price The retail selling price.

Shopping products Goods or services that are purchased infrequently and therefore require an extended decision-making process.

Signals Attributes of the product or its peripheral aspects that indirectly indicate its quality.

Single-variable segmentation Grouping potential customers according to one segmentation base.

Skimming Applying high prices on the launch of a novel product and steadily reducing them as the product penetrates the market.

Societal marketing The paradigm that suggests that the firm's activities must be carried out in a sustainable way if customers' needs are to be met in the longer term.

Sorting out A wholesaler function of grading or classifying variable goods for resale.

Speciality line wholesalers Stockists of a limited range of goods specific to an industry.

Speciality products Goods or services that are available only from a limited range of outlets.

Stages of development theory The view that companies go through stages of internationalisation from simple exporting through to global manufacture and marketing.

Stakeholders Those who have a direct or indirect interest in the organisation's activities.

Standby airfreight Cargo that will be loaded onto the next available aircraft with room for it.

Star A product with a large share of a fast-growing market.

Strategy The overall direction in which the organisation is heading.

Stratified sample A group of respondents whose individual characteristics fall within specified strata of the overall sampling frame.

Structured interviews The administering of a questionnaire-type survey in a face-to-face situation.

Suggestion impulse Buying behaviour undertaken when the individual receives a new stimulus.

Supermarket A large high street store offering food and household items.

Supplier markets Those individuals and firms who provide goods and services to the firm.

Symbol A universally agreed sign that stands for the concept being communicated.

Tabulating The arrangement of data in tables.

Tactics The methods by which an organisation achieves its strategic objectives.

Tamper resistance Creating packages that cannot be surreptitiously opened and resealed.

Targeting Selecting the segments that would be most effective in meeting the firm's overall aims.

Tariffs Customs duties.

Taxonomy The arrangement and naming of data.

Teaser campaign An advertisement shown in two parts, each part some weeks or months apart, in which the hook line is in the second advertisement.

Teleconferencing Focus groups conducted over the telephone.

Telemarketing Canvassing for business by telephone.

Teleology The belief that actions should be judged ethically by their outcomes.

Telephone surveys Administering a questionnaire over the telephone.

Test marketing Offering a new product within a small geographical area in order to obtain data for estimating sales for the market as a whole.

Third-party responses Complaints made to the supplier through a third party, such as a lawyer or consumer protection agency.

Time-series analysis Estimating future sales by looking at a series of sales figures from an earlier time.

Total quality management The practice of ensuring that each step in the production process meets the quality criteria, with the intention of ensuring that the finished product also meets those criteria.

Traceability The degree to which a shipment can be located within the distribution network.

Traceable common costs Expenses that are incurred across a range of products, but that can be allocated to specific products.

Transaction marketing A business approach that concentrates on transactions between a firm and its customers.

Trend analysis Predicting future sales by examining tendencies in past sales figures and projecting forwards.

Trialability The degree to which the product can be tested before purchase.

Tying contracts Agreements that insist on a channel member buying additional products to the main one being bought.

Unaided recall The degree to which an individual can remember an advertisement without being prompted.

Undercut-the-competition strategy Setting prices consistently below those of the nearest competitors.

Undifferentiated marketing Marketing to the entire population, on the assumption that everybody is a possible customer for the product, and therefore the market is not segmented.

Unsought products Products that the consumer would recognise a need for, but would not ordinarily seek out.

Usage rate The quantity of the product that an industrial customer will use in a given period.

User The individual who will actually use the product (usually considered in an industrial buying situation only).

USP (unique selling proposition) The feature or benefit of a product that no other product has.

Utilitarian needs Needs that derive from the practical aspects of ownership of a product or use of a service.

Valence The direction of feeling about a product; positive or negative.

Value-expressive influence The pressure to experience psychological association with a group by conforming to its norms, values or behaviours, even if membership is not sought.

Variety store A retailer offering a limited range of related goods.

Vertical integration The act of merging with, or buying out, suppliers and customers in order to control the channel of distribution.

Video-conferencing Focus groups conducted over a video link.

Voice responses Complaints made direct to the supplier.

Want A specific satisfier for a need, e.g. a steak.

War Horse A product with a large share of a shrinking market.

Wealth concentration The degree to which the wealth of a country is concentrated in the hands of the richest citizens.

Wholesaler A distribution intermediary who buys goods with the intention of selling them on to retailers.

Index

Note: Terms appearing in **bold** can be found in the Glossary.